PHILOPOEMEN

PHILOPOEMEN

R. M. ERRINGTON

OXFORD
AT THE CLARENDON PRESS
1969

Oxford University Press, Ely House, London W. 1

GLASGOW NEW YORK TORONTO MELBOURNE WELLINGTON
CAPE TOWN SALISBURY IBADAN NAIROBI LUSAKA ADDIS ABABA
BOMBAY CALCUTTA MADRAS KARACHI LAHORE DACCA
KUALA LUMPUR SINGAPORE HONG KONG TOKYO

PRINTED IN GREAT BRITAIN

FOR
CATHERINE

PREFACE

POLYBIUS and Plutarch both gave biographies of Philopoemen to their contemporaries, but their example has not been widely followed in modern times. Only A. Neumeyer's 1879 dissertation and W. Hoffmann's article in the *Real-Encyclopädie* have devoted more than a few lines to Philopoemen *suo iure*. The present book is an attempt to remedy this deficiency. Biography is a dangerous genre for the historian to write, for it can induce a narrow outlook and a temptation to psychological speculation. I hope to have avoided these pitfalls by making this a political biography, which means that in practice it has become almost a political history of the Achaean League during the years of Philopoemen's predominance. For if a political biography is to be meaningful its subject must be seen in the broad political context in which he worked. Philopoemen's friends and opponents, their policies and attitudes, are therefore also treated as fully as the fragmentary source material allows.

The original form of this book was a Durham University doctoral thesis. Since its acceptance in February 1966 it has been extensively revised, and I have tried to take account of the most important publications which appeared before the spring of 1967. Unfortunately, the second volume of F. W. Walbank's *Commentary on Polybius* and J. A. O. Larsen's *Greek Federal States* became available too late for me to be able to take them into consideration.

My debts to my predecessors in the general field are substantial. I hope obligations on points of detail are everywhere acknowledged in the footnotes. But I must express a more general indebtedness to the work of four modern scholars: to Maurice Holleaux's extensive work on Rome and the east; to André Aymard's works on the Achaean League; to F. W. Walbank's many works on Polybius; to E. Badian's *Foreign Clientelae* and many associated articles—my greatest debt, both in concept and substance, which will be apparent on almost every page of the later chapters of my book.

viii PREFACE

Obligations of a more personal kind must now be recorded. I was fortunate to have as supervisor Professor E. Badian, to whom my personal obligation for his constant interest and stimulating enthusiasm is as inexpressibly great as my more formal obligation to his publications. Without his freely conferred *beneficia* the merits of the present book would be few indeed. Professor F. W. Walbank, who has shown interest in my project from the beginning, and who, with Mr. P. J. Rhodes, examined the thesis, made many helpful criticisms. The proof reading has been shared by my generous colleagues Dr. E. M. Smallwood, Professor A. E. Astin, and Mr. J. B. Salmon, whose care has produced many improvements. I am also most grateful to Professor K. M. T. Atkinson for her encouragement and support, and to the Queen's University of Belfast for two grants which enabled me to visit the Peloponnese. Finally I must record my thanks to the staff of the Clarendon Press for their careful efficiency, and to the Press itself for honouring me by publishing my book.

R. M. E.

Belfast
June 1968

CONTENTS

FIGURES

ABBREVIATIONS

PERIODICALS are cited according to the system of *L'Année philologique*. Some short abbreviations for standard works are listed below: other abbreviated titles may be easily identified by consulting the bibliography under the author's name.

CAH	*Cambridge Ancient History.*
Ditt. *Syll.*	W. Dittenberger, *Sylloge Inscriptionum Graecarum*³, 4 vols., Leipzig, 1915–24.
Ditt. *OGIS*	W. Dittenberger, *Orientis Graecae Inscriptiones Selectae*, 2 vols., Leipzig, 1903–5.
FGH	F. Jacoby, *Die Fragmente der griechischen Historiker*, Berlin–Leiden, 1923– .
GGMS	B. Niese, *Geschichte der griechischen und makedonischen Staaten seit der Schlacht bei Chaeronea*, 3 vols., Gotha, 1893–1903.
IG	*Inscriptiones Graecae.*
Inscr. Cret.	*Inscriptiones Creticae*, ed. M. Guarducci, 4 vols., Roma, 1935–50.
MRR	T. R. S. Broughton, *The Magistrates of the Roman Republic*, 2 vols. and suppl., New York, 1951–60.
RE	Pauly–Wissowa–Kroll, *Real-Encyclopädie der classischen Altertumswissenschaft.*
SEG	*Supplementum Epigraphicum Graecum.*

THE PELOPONNESE
Early 2nd Century B.C.

0   20   40 Miles

I

INTRODUCTION

THE century after the death of Alexander the Great saw the gradual weakening of Macedonian control over Greece. This relaxation allowed the development of two new powers in central and southern Greece, the Aetolian and Achaean Leagues. By the time of the accession of Philip V to the Macedonian throne in 221, these Leagues had developed into controlling influences in their respective areas.[1] The Aetolians had first become prominent as a result of their successful resistance against Antipater in the Lamian War. They maintained their independence by changing their alliances to suit the prevailing conditions of the subsequent years, and enhanced their prestige by taking control of Delphi around 300. They exploited this prestige and the weakness of the central government of Macedon, which resulted from the death of Lysimachus in 281, to expand their territories. As a result, by 245 they controlled, whether by incorporation in their League or by less direct methods, all central Greece outside Attica, an area stretching from the Malian Gulf to Acarnania.[2]

In the Peloponnese Macedonian weakness after the death of Lysimachus allowed the reconstitution of the Achaean League, which had been dissolved on the orders of Alexander the Great after 324. The cities which first collaborated in the reconstruction of the League were four of the original cities: Patrae, Dyme, Pharae, and Tritaea. The first federal magistrates assumed their offices in May 281. In 277/6 Aegium, the chief city of the original League, joined the new union, and was quickly followed by Bura and Cerynea—also members of the original League—after Margus of Cerynea had brought pressure to bear on the tyrants who ruled these cities with Macedonian support. The remaining

---

[1] On this general background, cf. Niese, *GGMS* ii; Beloch, *GG* iv. 1 and iv. 2; *CAH* vi and vii; Cary, *History of the Greek World*; Will, *Histoire politique du monde hellénistique* i.

[2] In addition to the general works cited in n. 1, cf. Flacelière, *Les Aitoliens à Delphes*, *passim*.

four of the original Achaean cities, Leontion, Aegira, Pellene, and Olenus, soon followed suit, again probably urged by Margus. In 253/2 the administration of the League was overhauled and the cumbersome annual triarchy—two *strategoi* and one *grammateus*—was replaced by a single annual *strategos*. Margus was the first man to occupy this new position and had probably led the agitation for the change. It made possible a more active and precise policy, for up to this time the League had made little impact on Peloponnesian politics, except that its success in existing served to emphasize the current weakness of Macedonian control. Nevertheless, tyrants who may have enjoyed Macedonian support still held Corinth, Sicyon, and Argos.[1]

A change was suddenly brought about in 250/49, when Aratus of Sicyon overthrew Nicocles, the tyrant of Sicyon, and enrolled his city in the League. Extra-ethnic expansion of this kind had occurred in the first League, and the bargain was not so one-sided as our sources, based on Aratus' *Memoirs*, maintain.[2] Margus, who may have been *strategos*,[3] must have supported Aratus' claim to unite Sicyon with the League; and if credit is to be given, he should have at least as much as Aratus, who dominates the tradition, for his foresight in persuading the Achaeans to accept the neighbouring non-Achaean city, and thus in initiating the period of expansion which eventually made Achaea synonymous with the Peloponnese. Little is now heard of Achaea until eight years later when Aratus, now *strategos* of the League for the second time, led a successful attack on the Macedonian garrison of Corinth in 243/2. With Corinth came Megara, Troezen, and Epidaurus.[4] After these accessions Aratus confirmed

---

[1] On the early years, see Pol. ii. 41–3. 1 with Walbank, *Comm.* i, ad loc. On the chronology, cf. Appendix 2 C.

[2] Cf. Larsen, *Robinson Studies*, pp. 807 ff.; *Rep. Gov.*, p. 27; p. 75.

[3] This depends on an ambiguous statement of Polybius (ii. 43. 3): Aratus' liberation of Sicyon was τετάρτῳ δ' ὕστερον ἔτει τοῦ προειρημένου στρατηγοῦντος. Paton (Loeb) translates, 'Four years later during Margus' term of office'. Walbank, *Comm.* i, ad loc., gives 'four years after his term of office'. Paton's version seems easier (*a*) to explain the word order; (*b*) on grounds of general probability: Margus had clearly been *strategos* before (ii. 41. 14), perhaps many times (cf. ii. 10. 5). If Polybius meant, as Walbank takes it, the first *strategia* after the reorganization, it should have been made clearer. But this is not decisive: both explanations remain possible.

[4] Pol. ii. 43. 3; Plut. *Aratus*, 5–9 (Sicyon). Pol. ii. 43. 4; Plut. *Aratus*, 16.2–24. 1 (Corinth). Pol. ii. 43. 5; Plut. *Aratus*, 24. 3; Paus. ii. 8. 5, cf. vii. 7. 2 (Megara, Troezen, Epidaurus).

his open hostility to Macedon by causing the League to assign honorary hegemony to Ptolemy Euergetes. In return Aratus received an annuity of six talents, which the Egyptian government no doubt viewed as a cheap method of maintaining an anti-Macedonian influence in the Peloponnese.[1] This series of events must have made it clear that under the leadership of Margus and Aratus the League had passed beyond the point of being another ephemeral attempt of weak states to unite against a common danger, and had become a solid community of interests.

Achaean expansion made it almost inevitable that Achaea would eventually come into more or less violent conflict with Megalopolis. Megalopolis had been founded after the battle of Leuctra as a symbol of Arcadian nationalism and independence of Sparta. In the period of more than a century since then, hostility to Sparta and a strong particularist feeling had been maintained intact, despite the dismemberment of the Arcadian League. During the third century Megalopolis, along with so many other Peloponnesian cities, was ruled by tyrants. The current tyrant, Lydiadas, had already had experience of Aratus' abilities when sometime before 243 he had co-operated with Achaean troops led by Aratus in a battle fought near Mantinea against Agis IV of Sparta.[2] Lydiadas' period of power at Megalopolis coincided with Aratus' increasing influence in the League. But there seemed to be no urgency to decide how the relationship of the two neighbouring states should be regulated: the threat to Megalopolis from Achaean expansion was not immediately urgent enough to make a decision pressing. On the other hand Aratus seemed determined to pursue policies directly opposite to Lydiadas' view of Megalopolitan interests, both in form of government and in foreign policy. The expulsion of tyrants had been the League's policy from the beginning, and cannot have attracted Lydiadas. In 242 Megalopolis' vital interests in foreign policy were opposed by Achaea when the League allied itself with Sparta against Aetolia. Although this alliance was quickly broken off when Aratus suspected that the influence of Agis' domestic policies was being extended to Achaea,[3] there was

---

[1] Plut. *Aratus*, 24. 4; 41. 3; *Cleomenes*, 19. 4; Paus. ii. 8. 5. Cf. Walbank, *Aratos*, pp. 45–9.

[2] Paus. viii. 10. 5–9; cf. Beloch, *GG* iv. 2. 521; 609; Walbank, *Aratos*, p. 36, n. 1; Schoch, *RE* xiii. 2. 2202, 'Lydiadas'.

[3] Plut. *Aratus*, 31. 1; *Agis*, 15; cf. Walbank, *Aratos*, p. 53.

clearly no possibility of co-operation between Aratus and Lydiadas, whose traditional and immediate Megalopolitan opposition to Sparta could not be compromised, and who maintained friendly relations with Aetolia.[1] Aratus' rupture with Agis was followed in 239 by the death of Antigonus Gonatas and the accession of Demetrius II to the Macedonian throne, whereupon a re-alignment of forces took place in Greece. To exploit the weakness of the new Macedonian king Achaea and Aetolia formed an alliance.[2] In itself this alliance did not bring any closer a Megalopolitan *rapprochement* with Achaea. But since Elis was closely allied to Aetolia and hostile to Sparta, the Achaean alliance with Aetolia, following closely upon Aratus' break with Agis, tended to bring the whole Achaean/Aetolian alliance into opposition to Sparta, and hence into sympathy with Megalopolis' traditional *raison d'être*.

The close similarity of the Spartan policies of Achaea and of Megalopolis was emphasized by the pressure which Lydiadas was beginning to feel from Achaean expansion into Arcadia. Probably before 235, the League under Aratus and Dioetas had expanded to include large parts of the Arcadian hinterland of Megalopolis.[3] Lydiadas was thus in continually increasing danger of being sandwiched between a hostile and expansionist Achaea to the north, and a traditionally hostile Sparta to the south, where Cleomenes III had just come to power. Prospects could not have seemed much less favourable for his preserving Megalopolis' independence. These developments must have made it clear to Lydiadas that he would soon be faced with a critical decision: if he anticipated the course of events and resigned his tyranny at Megalopolis, he could apply to join the League. His

---

[1] After his accession Lydiadas gave Alipheira to Elis, which was closely allied to Aetolia (Pol. iv. 77. 10; cf. Walbank, *JHS* 1936).

[2] Pol. ii. 44. 1; Plut. *Aratus*, 33. 1.

[3] Polyaenus (ii. 36) records the accession of Heraea under Dioetas, who is otherwise unknown. It is probably best placed at this time of Achaean expansion into Arcadia. The *strategos*-list (cf. Walbank, *Aratos*, pp. 167 ff.) allows 238/7 or 236/5 as the most probable years. If the accession of Heraea was a result of an attack on Sparta (as Walbank, *Aratos*, p. 58) it is best to place it in 236/5. With Heraea went Cleitor and Thelphusa (Beloch, *GG* iv. 1. 632). Alea may also have been taken with Heraea: in 227 Cleomenes took Heraea and Alea (Plut. *Cleomenes*, 7. 3) and they may have gone together in 236: but in any case, Alea was Achaean before 227. Cleonae was added to Achaea probably in 235—a Nemean year (Plut. *Aratus*, 28. 3). Perhaps at this time Cynaetha and Stymphalus were annexed (cf. Niccolini, *La Conf. Ach.*, pp. 28–9).

action would diminish Megalopolis' national sovereignty, but it would effectively remove the threat from Achaea. He could also reasonably expect aid against Sparta. If he did not take this course he would inevitably be compelled to face mounting hostility from both Sparta and Achaea. He therefore chose to meet the major current threat, and to secure safety for himself and for Megalopolis. Accordingly, in 235/4 he enrolled Megalopolis in the Achaean League, and was immediately rewarded by being elected to the federal *strategia* for 234/3.[1] The Megalopolitans became Achaean citizens, and as a result a much wider sphere for political activity was opened to the ambitious among them. There can have been few who disapproved of the long-term considerations which had influenced Lydiadas' decision.

The Achaean League which Lydiadas joined is described by Polybius as an incomparable institution: 'One could not find a political system and principle so favourable to equality and freedom of speech, in a word so genuinely democratic, as that of the Achaean League.'[2] Elsewhere he describes the League, as it existed in the second century, as 'a growth of power and political union in the highest degree remarkable ... for in my own time not only have the Achaeans formed an allied and friendly community, but they have the same laws, weights, measures, and coinage, as well as the same magistrates, councillors, and courts; and the whole Peloponnese only falls short of being a single *polis* in the fact of its inhabitants' not being enclosed by one wall. In every other respect, both as regards the federation and the separate towns, conditions are very nearly identical.'[3]

Clear evidence supports the technical aspects of Polybius' description. Extant coins support his statement about the coinage; we have no reason to doubt that the weights and measures matched the uniformity of the coinage.[4] While federal laws certainly applied to all participants in the League, individual cities might also possess their own laws.[5] Consonant with this arrangement federal dicasts are known who dealt with federal offences without superseding the local application of local systems of justice in the individual cities.[6]

[1] Pol. ii. 44. 5; Plut. *Aratus*, 30. 2; cf. Walbank, *Aratos*, pp. 62–3.
[2] Pol. ii. 38. 6; cf. Walbank, *Comm.* i. 221.   [3] Pol. ii. 37. 8–11.
[4] Cf. Head, *Hist. Num.*, pp. 417–18; Walbank, *Comm.* i. 218–19.
[5] Cf. Aymard, *Assemblées*, p. 167, n. 5.   [6] Cf. Walbank, *Comm.* i. 220.

The federal magistrates, elected annually, consisted of the *strategos* and the hipparch, who were supported by the secretary (an important official only before 254/3), the admiral and the *hypostrategos*, who was some kind of deputy *strategos*. The *strategos* and ten *damiourgoi*, who represented on some unknown principle the individual Achaean cities, seem to have formed a board which probably acted as the standing government.[1] Additionally the *boule* met four times a year (until 188 always at Aegium). Until about 200 these four regular meetings of the *boule*, called *synodoi*, were also attended by the *ecclesia*—the large popular assembly which might be attended by all citizens over 30 years of age. After about 200, however, the *ecclesia* met only irregularly (at meetings probably called *syncletoi*) to discuss matters of exceptional importance, and the *synodos* became a meeting of the *boule* only.[2]

It is in this connection that we must consider Polybius' description of the Achaean constitution as democratic. If Larsen's convincing explanation of the composition of the *synodos* can be accepted, it reveals in operation in Polybius' time a form of representative government. But more than this: it was *de facto* a timocratic representative government, since the members of the *synodos* appear to have been unpaid.[3] Admittedly the *ecclesia*

---

[1] Cf. Walbank, *Comm.* i. 219.

[2] Discussions of the Achaean assemblies are notoriously obscure. This explanation, which seems to satisfy all the phenomena, is Larsen's, *Rep. Gov.*, pp. 75–105. The chief earlier discussion is Aymard's *Assemblées*, which gives a full bibliography of the problems.

[3] Cf. Aymard, *Assemblées*, pp. 331 ff. The only evidence for this is Polybius' report (xxii. 7. 3 ff.) of a *synodos* in 187 at which the Achaeans refused to accept 120 talents offered by Eumenes, the interest from which was to be used to pay the members of the *synodos*. This has reasonably been taken to imply that the *synodos* was not paid. Lehmann, *Glaubwürdigkeit*, pp. 380 ff., argues that the matter at issue was simply whether or not the Achaeans should allow themselves to become indebted to Eumenes, and that no inference can be drawn regarding the regular system of pay. He quotes the case of Rhodes, which, though rich, accepted money from Eumenes and incurred Polybius' disfavour (Pol. xxxi. 31. 1 ff.), but non-Achaean examples are irrelevant. Lehmann lays too much stress on the speech of Apollonidas of Sicyon which persuaded the Achaeans to reject Eumenes' offer so as not to incur obligations to Eumenes. Perhaps more deserving of attention, from the present point of view—because not pleading a case—is Polybius' own introduction of the issue: ἐξαπεστάλκει δὲ ⟨καὶ⟩ ὁ βασιλεὺς Εὐμένης πρεσβευτάς, ἐπαγγελλόμενος ἑκατὸν καὶ εἴκοσι τάλαντα δώσειν τοῖς Ἀχαιοῖς, ἐφ᾽ ᾧ, δανειζομένων τούτων, ἐκ τῶν τόκων μισθοδοτεῖσθαι τὴν βουλὴν τῶν Ἀχαιῶν ἐπὶ ταῖς κοιναῖς συνόδοις (xxii. 7. 3). The prima facie implication here is clearly that Eumenes' offer was an innovation, and that up to this time there had been no pay for the *synodos*.

still met to consider extraordinary matters; but the regular autumn *synodos* elected the magistrates who governed the state—for whom again there was certainly no payment—and took routine administrative decisions. The effect of this *de facto* restriction of the government to the moneyed classes was important, for it meant that to be successful a politician had to be rich. Philopoemen, for instance, had his chief income from his estate;[1] and no doubt income from landed property was the usual source of wealth for the traditionally agricultural Arcadians. Aratus may have been rather different: his source of wealth is not certain, but his father Cleinias was one of the Sicyonian aristocracy.[2] Sicyon, as well as Corinth, was conveniently situated for trade, and trading may have been an additional source of wealth. Sicyon was also a centre of artistic production, and Aratus was wealthy enough—from whatever source—to collect paintings and to share his enthusiasm with Ptolemy Euergetes.[3]

The effective dominance of the rich propertied classes meant that politicians valued family connections. Aratus' own son was active (and grossly inefficient) during Aratus' own later career.[4] Another Aratus was an Achaean ambassador to Rome and Egypt in 179;[5] and Aratus' descendants still lived at Sicyon and Pellene in Plutarch's time.[6] Another influential family was Lycortas'. He himself was the son of Thearidas, a leading Megalopolitan in the 220s; he was a political associate, and perhaps a relation by marriage, of Philopoemen; Polybius, his son, took his place without difficulty in Achaean politics; another Thearidas, who may be another son of Lycortas, also participated in Achaean politics in the second century.[7] Other families can also be traced into the second generation of influence. In 179 a Lydiadas was appointed ambassador to Rome: clearly he was a representative of the family of the ex-tyrant of Megalopolis.[8] Diophanes of Megalopolis was the son of Diaeus;[9] another Diaeus, also from Megalopolis, was Achaean *strategos* in 150/49 and was a prominent leader in the Achaean War.[10] It is difficult to believe

---

[1] Plut. *Phil.* 4. 1–3.   [2] Plut. *Aratus*, 2. 1; cf. 4. 1.
[3] Plut. *Aratus*, 12. 5–13. 4.   [4] Cf. Niese, *RE* ii. 1. 390–1, 'Aratos' (3).
[5] Pol. xxiv. 6. 3; 8. 8.   [6] Plut. *Aratus*, 54. 3.
[7] Cf. *stemma* in Ditt. *Syll.* 626; Stähelin, *RE* xiii. 2. 2386, 'Lycortas'; *RE* x. A. 1382, 'Thearidas' (1); Ziegler, *RE* xxi. 2. 1445, 'Polybios'.
[8] Pol. xxiv. 8. 8.   [9] Paus. viii. 30. 5; 51. 1.
[10] Cf. Lehmann, *Glaubwürdigkeit*, pp. 322 ff.; Niese, *GGMS* iii. 339 ff.

that there was not some relationship: at its closest, Diaeus may have been Diophanes' son.[1] These large rich families—as is plain from the tradition—could clearly develop an influence in their own districts, and from there in Achaean affairs, which totally outweighed their numerical importance. This was the Achaean aristocracy, descended from the traditional land-holding aristocracy of the constituent cities of the League. As a result Achaean politics was in practice the politics of aristocratic families which could afford to serve the state at their own expense.[2]

Why then does Polybius claim Achaea for a democracy when it is clear that in practice it was far from democratic in the sense in which fifth- and fourth-century Athens was democratic? It is not, in fact, necessary to assume that Polybius meant to be deliberately misleading. It seems rather that the answer must lie in the Hellenistic conditions in which the Achaean League operated, in which a state which could maintain some form of self-government might be regarded, by virtue of that very fact, as in some sense democratic. The word seems to have become much looser in meaning as a result of the long dominance of the Hellenistic great powers over the smaller states. In this sense— perhaps coloured to some degree by Polybius' patriotism—his assessment can be allowed to have some meaning.[3] But from the point of view of the policies of the League, these were formulated and executed in almost every case by the aristocratic, rich, and influential individuals (or groups of individuals) who managed at any one time to secure the approval of their peers at the electoral *synodos*.[4]

Until 230/29 Aratus and Lydiadas alternated in holding the federal *strategia*. After a few years friction occurred between these two outstanding personalities of the League, which was certainly increased by Lydiadas' emphasizing as League policy his natural Megalopolitan fear of Sparta. Aratus may have been unwilling to recognize the seriousness of the new threat from resurgent

[1] So Niese, *GGMS* iii. 339, n. 4; cautiously accepted by Lehmann, *Glaubwürdigkeit*, p. 319; p. 323.

[2] Lehmann, *Glaubwürdigkeit*, p. 382, points out that even in the classical Athenian democracy aristocrats tended to dominate politics. But this occurred within a complicated system of state pay for many offices, and (more important) the *boule*—which prima facie evidence suggests did not exist in Achaea.

[3] Cf. Walbank, *Comm.* i. 221–2 (and bibliography).

[4] Lehmann's examination of the nature of the League (*Glaubwürdigkeit*, pp. 377 ff.) does not succeed in disproving this *de facto* state of affairs.

Sparta and probably attributed Lydiadas' fears to Megalopolitan tradition rather than to political reality. But personal jealousy was certainly another factor which exacerbated the hostility between the two men. Margus, who had probably acted as a mediating influence up to now, died in 229, and the jealousy of Aratus and Lydiadas was no longer restrained.[1] Aratus could see his personal supremacy threatened by the newcomer whom he had supported, and in 230/29 he provoked a crisis.

Lydiadas was *strategos*, and in his official capacity he opened negotiations with Aristomachus, the current tyrant of Argos, with a view to taking Argos into the League. When Aristomachus formally applied for membership with Lydiadas' support, his application was successfully opposed by Aratus. Plutarch faithfully retails Aratus' propagandist accusation against Lydiadas, of poaching patronage. This was clearly an issue on which Aratus was prepared to fight. Far more was at stake than simply Argive membership: Margus' death had thrown open the whole issue of political predominance within the League. Aratus clearly saw himself as Margus' successor as senior statesman—although it is probably the fault of his self-centred *Memoirs* that we have so little information about Margus' earlier activities. In the present circumstances, a success for Lydiadas over Aristomachus' application might seem to Aratus to represent a potent challenge for the succession to Margus' unofficial position of predominance: the whole basis of his own present and future dominance within the League seemed to be threatened. He therefore suggested that Lydiadas was in some way acting illegitimately in supporting Aristomachus' application. In fact, in Lydiadas' *strategia*, it is difficult to see why Aratus objected to Lydiadas' negotiations for new members of the League. It was Lydiadas' duty, and if Aratus persisted, a clash was clearly inevitable, with legitimacy on the side of Lydiadas. Aratus, of course, was able to gloss over this detail in his *Memoirs*, and to lay the blame firmly on Lydiadas' φιλοτιμία.[2] Aratus' influence proved to be overwhelming, despite his fears, and Lydiadas was badly defeated. This defeat effectively

---

[1] Pol. ii. 10. 5 (death of Margus). Plut. *Aratus*, 30. 3: φιλοτιμούμενος δὲ εὐθὺς ὑπερβαλεῖν δόξῃ τὸν Ἄρατον. Aratus, Plutarch's source for this, clearly had the sole intention of developing his own point of view: Plutarch presents the faults as all Lydiadas'. Cf. Plut. *Aratus*, 35. 3, for further evidence of Aratus' interpretation of Lydiadas' φιλοτιμία.

[2] Plut. *Aratus*, 35. 1–3; Pol. ii. 44. 6.

ended Lydiadas' political career. He had failed to appreciate that he was a comparative newcomer to an Achaea which Aratus had had a substantial influence in creating. He had accordingly underestimated Aratus' personal following in Achaea and the personal bitterness which his own ambitions had engendered. The crisis was engineered by Aratus, and his victory secured his personal predominance. When he was himself *strategos* in 229/8 Aristomachus was quietly enrolled in the League under Aratus' patronage. During the years of Lydiadas' activity Mantinea and possibly Orchomenus had joined the League.[1] But after the accession of Argos, when other Peloponnesian tyrants saw the friendly reception which had ultimately been offered to Aristomachus, many more cities entered the League. Aratus was consolidating his own position, and he supported Aristomachus' successful bid for the *strategia* of 228/7.[2]

Yet signs of serious trouble for Achaea were already apparent. Before 229 Mantinea had been lost to the Aetolians, and in 229 it was taken from them by the militant Cleomenes. Although it was recovered by Aratus in 227, it was almost immediately lost again in the succession of disasters of 226/5.[3] Caphyae was taken in 228 by Aratus, but its accession marked the end of Achaea's independent expansion. For the future, accessions were to be *de facto* subject to the permission or acquiescence of the dominant power, whether Macedon or Rome. In 226 and 225, under the

[1] Mantinea: Aetolian in 229 (Pol. ii. 46. 2); Achaean before this (Pol. ii. 57. 1). Orchomenus: probably Achaean at this time. In 223, after Antigonus' capture of the town from Cleomenes, οὐκ ἀποκατέστησε τοῖς Ἀχαιοῖς (Pol. iv. 6. 5).This implies that Orchomenus had been Achaean before 223; but in 229 it was Aetolian (Pol. ii. 46. 2), so that *c*. 234/3, the time of Achaean expansion into Arcadia, seems the necessary date. Dittenberger, *Syll.* 490, attributed the accession terms of Orchomenus to 234/3. On the other hand Foucart, the original publisher of the inscription (*RA* 1896), followed by Niese, *GGMS* iii. 35, n. 3, preferred to take it with Liv. xxxii. 5. 4 (199 B.C.), where Livy describes how Philip evacuated Orchomenus and gave it to Achaea. This may be correct, notwithstanding Polybius' use of ἀποκαθ-ίστημι in iv. 6. 5. Cf. Pol. xxx. 9. 8, where the word means only 'hand over' (although this is the only example of this usage cited by Mauersberger, *Polybios-Lexikon*, s.v.).

[2] Pol. ii. 44. 6 (Hermione and Phlius). Plut. *Aratus*, 34. 5 (Aegina and 'most of Arcadia': in this phrase may be included at least Pheneus and Lasion, for in 225 they were among towns taken by Cleomenes (Pol. ii. 52. 2; Plut. *Cleomenes*, 14. In this latter passage MSS. read Λάγγωνι, which is otherwise unknown. Manso suggested Λασιῶνι, which is accepted with reservations by Walbank, *Aratos*, p. 81); 229 seems the most likely time for them to have joined Achaea). Plut. *Aratus*, 35. 3 (*strategia* of Aristomachus).

[3] Pol. ii. 46. 2 (Aetolian, taken by Cleomenes); Pol. ii. 57. 2 (recovered in 227); Pol. ii. 58. 4; Plut. *Aratus*, 39. 1 (loss in 226/5).

strategoi Hyperbatus and Timoxenus, Achaea lost many of her recent acquisitions to Cleomenes and became the object of violent attacks. The loss of Heraea and Alea was rapidly followed by that of Mantinea, Caphyae, Pellene, Argos, Phlius, Cleonae, Epidaurus, Hermione, Troezen, Corinth, Pheneus, Lasion, and Megara.[1] One result of this situation, which rapidly appeared desperate, was that Megalopolis, although itself remaining for the moment intact, was physically cut off from the rest of Achaea. Since the federal authorities were currently fully occupied in dealing with Cleomenes in northern Achaea, Megalopolis could expect to be left to fend for itself. And this expectation can only have seemed more justified when Lydiadas died in battle at Ladoceia in 227.

In the circumstances it is not altogether surprising that Aratus, quite early in the series of disasters—in 227 after Ladoceia— used two Megalopolitans, Nicophanes and Cercidas, to make an exploratory approach to the new Macedonian king, Antigonus Doson, in an attempt to negotiate Macedonian aid for the League against Cleomenes. This was, for Aratus, a direct change of policy from the violent hostility to Macedonian domination which had brought him to influence in Achaea. But the situation had changed immeasurably: he was now faced with a straight choice between suffering rapid and ignominious defeat at the hands of Cleomenes and accepting the tutelage of Doson. In the circumstances the latter seemed by far the lesser evil. In the case of the Megalopolitans, hostility to Sparta and support for Macedon had been the traditional policy of their period of independence. Megalopolitans would therefore seem to be the most satisfactory negotiators. But Antigonus demanded the Acrocorinth as the price of his intervention—a demand which Aratus could not grant in 227 for both personal and public reasons of prestige. The negotiations therefore hung fire until Corinth revolted from Achaea in summer 225 and was captured by Cleomenes. The stumbling-block of Achaean prestige, which had hindered the preliminary negotiations, was now shattered. By this time Achaea was so hard pressed by Cleomenes that the autumn

[1] Plut. *Cleomenes*, 4. 4 (accession of Caphyae); 7. 3 (loss of Heraea and Alea); Pol. ii. 52. 2 (Caphyae, Pellene, Pheneus, Argos, Phlius, Cleonae, Epidaurus, Hermione, Troezen, Corinth); 58. 4 (Mantinea); cf. Plut. *Aratus*, 39. Plut. *Cleomenes*, 14. 2 (Lasion); Pol. xx. 6. 8 (Megara). On these events cf. Walbank, *Aratos*, pp. 89 ff.

synodos of the League voted to accept Antigonus' demand for Corinth in return for military aid.[1]

Antigonus accordingly appeared in the Megarid early in 224. With the support of Timoxenus, the Achaean *strategos* of 225/4, and of Aratus, who was again *strategos* in 224/3, he quickly dislodged Cleomenes from his strong points of Corinth and Argos, and by the end of 224 Cleomenes was confined to the south of Argos. During 223 Antigonus advanced into Arcadia, took Tegea, Orchomenus, Mantinea, Thelphusa, and Heraea from Cleomenes, and confined him still further within the traditional boundaries of Laconia. Spartan pressure on Megalopolis and southern Arcadia was thus successfully relieved, but at the expense of Achaean independence of action.[2]

[1] Pol. ii. 47. 5–51. 1 (preliminary negotiations); 52. 3–4 (loss of Corinth and final agreement with Antigonus). On the date of the first negotiations (227/6), cf. Walbank, *Philip*, pp. 13–14; Porter, *Plutarch's Aratus*, p. lxxii.

[2] Pol. ii. 52. 5 ff.; Plut. *Cleomenes*, 20; *Aratus*, 43 (Antigonus in the Peloponnese). On the chronology, cf. Walbank, *Comm.* i. 254–5. Pol. ii. 54. 5–14; Plut. *Aratus*, 45; *Cleomenes*, 23 (events of 223).

II

YOUTH

I

DURING these years of unremitting Megalopolitan hostility to Sparta Philopoemen reached maturity and gained his early political and military experience. He was born in 252 into an aristocratic Megalopolitan family.[1] His father Craugis was one of the most distinguished citizens of Megalopolis, and Philopoemen was accordingly born to inherit his wealth and influence. Unfortunately Craugis died before his son was old enough to have political ambitions, and Philopoemen was brought up by Cleander, a Mantinean exile living in Megalopolis.[2] His education was furthered by his association with Ecdemus and Megalophanes: Ecdemus had helped Aratus to capture Sicyon, and the pair had been responsible for assassinating Lydiadas' predecessor as tyrant of Megalopolis, Aristodemus 'the Good'.[3] They had therefore a reputation for being freedom-fighters—a fact which acquires some prominence in the biographical tradition, and for which a philosophical motivation has often been adduced. Their training of Philopoemen, however, seems to have been practical rather than philosophical. According to Polybius, the results of their training were that Philopoemen 'soon came to excel all his contemporaries in endurance and courage both in hunting and in war'.[4]

Philopoemen cannot have been uninfluenced by the experiences of his early years. He had seen Lydiadas lay down his tyranny in favour of participation in the larger political unit, and must have realized that this did not imply betraying the local and sectional interests which could, in the circumstances, be better

[1] On the date of Philopoemen's birth, see Appendix 2 A (ii).
[2] Pol. x. 22. 1; Plut. *Phil.* 1. 1–2; Paus. viii. 49. 1–2.
[3] Pol. x. 22. 2; Plut. *Phil.* 1. 2–3; Paus. viii. 49. 2. The correct form of the names seems impossible to discover: cf. Capelle, *RE* xx. 1, 'Megalophanes' (accepted here); Beloch, *GG* iv. 1. 614; Ziegler, *RhM* 1934, 211 f.
[4] Pol. x. 22. 4.

defended by participation in the Achaean League. These considerations were not necessarily invalidated by Achaea's inability to provide Megalopolis with complete security against Cleomenes. Plutarch clearly refers to the continuous warfare of these years when he says that Philopoemen 'accustomed himself to march first on the outward march and last on the return'.[1] He probably took part in all the serious fighting of 227, and may well have been present when Lydiadas was killed at Ladoceia.[2] But his comparative youth must have prevented him from taking any active part in Megalopolitan politics at this time, and he can have had little to do with the Achaean appeal to Macedon. However, as a soldier he must have appreciated the need for military reinforcement for Megalopolis against Cleomenes—which was not forthcoming from Achaea alone—and therefore have supported the negotiations. There was, after all, no loss of prestige for the Megalopolitans in an appeal to Macedon. But although Philopoemen can have played little part in the political activity of these years, he must have taken an important part in the defence of Megalopolis until 223, when the pressure on the city was relieved by Antigonus' penetration into Arcadia. For by that time he was recognized as an important military figure by the Megalopolitans, although he had apparently not yet made his mark in federal military matters.

Philopoemen's first major recorded activity was in 223. During the summer Cleomenes had made an unsuccessful attack on Megalopolis, apart from which Antigonus had contained him.[3] In the autumn the Macedonian troops were allowed to return home instead of spending the winter uselessly in billets in the Peloponnese. They left while the roads to the north were still easily passable.[4] This involved the gamble that Cleomenes would not use the remainder of the fine weather to attack Achaea; but it seemed justified, since Cleomenes must have appeared chastened as a result of his reverses during the summer. Cleomenes, however, took a different view of the situation. Antigonus seemed to him to be making him the gift of an opportunity for a successful

---

[1] Plut. *Phil.* 4. 1.

[2] At Sellasia Philopoemen was a cavalryman (Plut. *Phil.* 6), which suggests that he had been in the habit of serving with cavalry. Cavalry certainly fought under Lydiadas at Ladoceia (Plut. *Aratus*, 37) and Philopoemen may have been among them.

[3] Pol. ii. 55. 5.   [4] Pol. ii. 54. 14.

surprise attack on Megalopolis. He made his preparations quickly, and in a night attack on the inadequately defended city —it was too large for its population in normal times, and must have suffered substantial losses in the years of fighting—he gained possession. In the course of the fighting some 1,000 Megalopolitans were killed or taken prisoner. The remainder, including women and children, were led by Philopoemen to the safety of friendly Messene. Messene was not, in fact, a member of the Achaean League, nor yet of the symmachy which Antigonus had created in 224 to fight against Cleomenes.[1] But the common hostility to Sparta, traditional in both cities, was sufficient to make Messene a safe retreat for the refugees.[2]

Three accounts are extant of events subsequent to the capture of the city, all biased to some extent. Plutarch in his *Cleomenes*[3] relies largely on Phylarchus, whose bias was in favour of Cleomenes. In his *Philopoemen*[4] his source must again be Phylarchus, but here the material is selected with Philopoemen's part to the fore, and it therefore seems to present a glorification of Philopoemen's achievement. For this reason it appears to be somewhat biased against Cleomenes. The third account is Polybius' in his *Histories*,[5] taken from Aratus' *Memoirs* or Megalopolitan tradition, to which he has added a polemical discussion of Phylarchus' account—which he does not altogether succeed in refuting.

[1] Pol. ii. 54. 4–5; Plut. *Aratus*, 45; cf. Freeman, *History of Federal Government*, pp. 382–3; Beloch, *GG* iv. 1. 712–13; Walbank, *Philip*, pp. 15–16 (and bibliography); *Comm.* i. 256. It is surprising that the large amount of detailed study of the working of the symmachy has obscured to scholars the primary truth, so clearly (but emotionally) observed by Freeman, that the symmachy was simply a façade to disguise the regularization of Macedonian domination. Its structure, less oppressive —and less effective—than that of the Leagues of Philip II and Alexander, and of Demetrius Poliorcetes, reflects not Doson's greater sympathy with the Greeks, but simply his less overwhelming power. Nevertheless in Achaea Doson was *hegemon* of the Achaean League (Plut. *Aratus*, 38. 6) and the beneficiary of a law which enjoined the Achaeans to summon an assembly whenever the *hegemon* wished (Pol. v. 1. 6–7).

[2] Pol. ii. 55; 61–3; Plut. *Phil.* 5; *Cleomenes*, 23–5. Pausanias, iv. 29. 7, says that Messene was a member of the League at this time; but he seems to be inferring this from the friendly reception of the Megalopolitans. As late as 221 an alliance with the Aetolians was still officially in operation (Pol. iv. 3. 9), and in 220 the Messenians had to appeal to the League as friends, but not members, for help (Pol. iv. 7. 2–5). That they were not members of Doson's symmachy seems clear from Pol. iv. 5. 8—although again friendly relations are implied. Cf. Walbank, *Philip*, p. 24; *Comm.* i. 453, against Fine, *AJPh* 1940, 156–7.

[3] *Cleomenes*, 23–5.   [4] *Phil.* 5.
[5] Pol. ii. 55; 61–3.

To these accounts Pausanias adds little of value.[1] As the longest and most detailed account is that in Plutarch's *Cleomenes*, it will be most convenient to use that as a basis for discussing Polybius' variations and criticisms.

Of those who were captured in the attack on Megalopolis, Plutarch names Lysandridas and Thearidas, 'men of the greatest reputation and influence in Megalopolis'. They were brought before Cleomenes, and Lysandridas immediately began negotiations to secure the safety of the city, in the course of which he suggested that the Megalopolitans would be willing to join Cleomenes if he guaranteed the safety of their homes. As a result, Cleomenes sent both Lysandridas and Thearidas to Messene to present his conditions to the Megalopolitans who had escaped: that Megalopolis would be spared if its union with Achaea was abandoned and support for Sparta promised. Philopoemen's influence was decisive in persuading the Megalopolitans not to abandon Achaea, and he drove out Lysandridas and Thearidas from Messene as traitors. Cleomenes then did his best to wreck and loot the abandoned city before leaving for Sparta.[2] Polybius' account ignores these negotiations altogether, because it suited Aratus, his source, and Polybius himself to paint as black a picture as possible of the destruction—Aratus to justify his application for Macedonian aid and Polybius for patriotic Megalopolitan reasons. He goes on to explain Cleomenes' violence: 'I believe him to have acted so, because the Megalopolitans and the Stymphalians were the only peoples from among whom in the varied circumstances of his career he could never procure himself a single partisan to share his projects or a single traitor.'[3] This motivation does not account for the facts. It had been one of the main aims of Spartan policy towards Arcadia from the time of the foundation of Megalopolis to destroy the city. Cleomenes' violence needs no personalized motivation.

How can the authenticity of the mission of Lysandridas and Thearidas be judged when Polybius says that Cleomenes could never procure himself a partisan from Megalopolis? Plutarch, in chapter 5 of his *Philopoemen*, mentions the mission and

---

[1] Paus. ii. 9. 2; iv. 29. 7–8; viii. 49. 4. Pausanias seems to have as his source the same material as Plutarch, but indulges in some melodramatization: Plutarch's νυκτὸς ἐξαίφνης (*Phil.* 5. 1) turns into παράσπονδα ἐκ τοῦ φανεροῦ (ii. 9. 2), and εἷλεν . . . ἐν σπονδαῖς (iv. 29. 7). Cf. Appendix 1, pp. 238 ff.

[2] Plut. *Cleomenes*, 24. 2–25. 1.   [3] Pol. ii. 55. 8.

Philopoemen's part in rejecting it, but he does not mention Lysandridas and Thearidas by name. But since Plutarch was writing biography, he probably omitted the names in the *Philopoemen* as irrelevant. Polybius, however, does not have the same excuse for omitting the names. In his polemic against Phylarchus he mentions the episode, but gives no names, and although he suggests that Phylarchus whitewashed Cleomenes, it is not this which he specifically objects to so much as his omission of 'praise and honourable mention of conduct noteworthy for its excellence'. Polybius' polemic clearly reveals his patriotic bias, and his failure in this place to deny explicitly the existence of the negotiations seems conclusive for their being historical.[1]

Why did Polybius attempt to conceal the existence of these negotiations—of which he certainly knew Phylarchus' version—and the names of the collaborators? He was certainly influenced by the desire of his chief source (Aratus) to paint as black a picture of Cleomenes as possible; and his own patriotic desire to praise the noteworthy conduct of Megalopolitans made him naturally sympathetic to Aratus' view. However, a more personal motive can perhaps be found. The name Thearidas is known to have been the name of Lycortas' father, Polybius' paternal grandfather.[2] Although there is no chronological difficulty in the way of accepting the identification of the present Thearidas with Lycortas' father, it is perhaps safer not to insist on the precise relationship. However, it is difficult to believe that the comparatively rare name Thearidas should have been borne by two important and influential Megalopolitan contemporaries who were not related. If this identification of a member of Lycortas' family is acceptable, Polybius' failure to mention the negotiators by name becomes intelligible: the episode was clearly discreditable to his family, and his father Lycortas and Polybius himself—both confirmed federalists—must have preferred to forget it. The clash of Thearidas with the family friend, Philopoemen, could not be easily or consistently explained in the family history, but he could eliminate it from his own work by omitting it and attacking Phylarchus' credit.[3]

---

[1] Pol.ii.61.4–6: τὸν ἔπαινον καὶ τὴν ἐπ' ἀγαθῷ μνήμην τῶν ἀξιολόγων προαιρέσεων (6).

[2] Ditt. *Syll.* 626, and *stemma* of Polybius suggested there; cf. Stähelin, *RE* x. A. 1382, 'Thearidas' (1); Africa, *Phylarchus*, pp. 32–3.

[3] The suggestion of Hiller von Gaertringen (*ad* Ditt. *Syll.* 626) that Lycortas married a daughter of Philopoemen, which made Philopoemen Polybius' maternal

We can therefore accept as historical the negotiations between Cleomenes and the Megalopolitan refugees led by Philopoemen, conducted through the medium of Lysandridas and Thearidas. The conversations, however, which Plutarch records—presumably from Phylarchus, if he did not make them up himself—cannot be historical.[1] Nevertheless, the considerations which they represent seem reasonable. The only reason why Cleomenes should begin negotiations at all was the hope of immediate political advantage: he would gain nothing in the long term by destroying Megalopolis. Philopoemen's competent rescue of the greater part of the civilian population had even made the financial prospects from the sack of the city meagre. If the Megalopolitans could be persuaded to renounce their friendship with Achaea, Megalopolis would become a Spartan forward post against the inevitable resumption of Macedonian and Achaean aggression the following year. The empty shell of the city was strategically valueless, since it was far too large for Cleomenes to hold with the forces at his disposal. Even the goods and chattels of the devastated city could not be expected to yield much, as Polybius points out. It was therefore a reasonable policy to undertake negotiations with the refugees: no Macedonian reinforcements could be expected, and he could deal adequately with whatever forces Achaea could muster.

While Lysandridas and Thearidas may have been willing to sacrifice long-term Achaean interests for their particularist desire to preserve their city intact—far more valuable, admittedly, to the Megalopolitans than to Cleomenes—Philopoemen was wholly unwilling to compromise, although some of his fellow refugees had to be persuaded of the value of his stubbornness.[2] For both personal and traditional reasons he viewed with distaste a capitulation to Sparta, although this cannot have been

grandfather, cannot be proved since Polybius himself does not mention it. But since another Philopoemen appears among Lycortas' posterity, it seems likely that Philopoemen had some relationship with Lycortas. Also suggesting this is the choice of Polybius to carry Philopoemen's ashes in his funeral procession (Plut. *Phil.* 21. 3). Polybius also spoke with the urgency of personal commitment in Philopoemen's defence in 146 (Plut. *Phil.* 21. 5–6; Pol. xxxix. 3. 3–10; cf. chapter XI, pp. 222–3). Ziegler, *RE* xxi. 2. 1445, 'Polybios', denies relationship and explains the continuation of Philopoemen's name in the *stemma* of Lycortas' family as being out of respect for Philopoemen's glory.

[1] Plut. *Cleomenes*, 24.
[2] Plut. *Phil.* 5. 2.

his only reason for treating the negotiations with contempt and sacrificing the city. He must have realized, as an experienced soldier, that since the appearance of Antigonus in the Peloponnese, Macedonian power had become the key factor in the situation. Antigonus' present impotence was only temporary; and any advantage which was gained by a Megalopolitan agreement with Cleomenes would last just as long as Antigonus was without troops. Both for traditional and for immediate reasons, therefore, Antigonus' presence in Achaea and his involvement in the war with Cleomenes forbade any consideration of short-term gains, which would inevitably prejudice the city's long-term welfare. Polybius might rant about the loyalty of the Megalopolitans to the League, the praiseworthy sacrifice of their 'land, tombs, temples, homes, and possessions rather than break faith with their allies'. But he must have realized, had he not allowed his patriotic rhetoric to govern his thinking, that the decision which involved these things could be supported by a cool assessment of present political reality and of the expected development of events in the near future.[1]

Cleomenes had no alternative but to make the best of his disappointment. The empty city was useless to him. In order that his expedition might not end wholly without result, he sacked it and removed all valuables to Sparta. A sum of about 300 talents, Polybius estimates, was the total result. Phylarchus, in an attempt to make the affair a triumph for Cleomenes, exaggerated the figure to 6,000.[2] But despite the unsatisfactory result of his attack on Megalopolis, Cleomenes had not yet finished taking advantage of Antigonus' temporary incapacity. In spring 222, before the Macedonian troops had returned to the Peloponnese, he entered the territory of Argos where Antigonus was wintering with a small force. Antigonus did not dare, in the circumstances, to march out against Cleomenes, and the Argives had to watch their countryside being devastated while their protector was helpless to prevent it. In this case Polybius is compelled to express his admiration at the coolness of Cleomenes' calculation, and sets his claim to expertise against the popular view of 'those who think this was a rash and hazardous act'.[3]

[1] Pol. ii. 61. 9–10.
[2] Pol. ii. 62. On the whole episode, cf. Beloch, *GG* iv. 1. 715; Walbank, *Aratos*, pp. 107–8; Africa, *Phylarchus*, pp. 32–5.   [3] Pol. ii. 64.

In July of the same year, 222, Cleomenes was brought to battle with the forces of Antigonus' symmachy near Sellasia. A detailed account of the battle would be out of place here;[1] but the part played by Philopoemen, which first brought him to general notice outside his strictly Megalopolitan activities, must be examined. In Antigonus' army were the Achaean ἐπίλεκτοι, an élite corps of 3,000 infantry and 300 cavalry, and 1,000 Megalopolitans led by Cercidas and armed in Macedonian fashion.[2] The number of Achaeans is small—only the ἐπίλεκτοι—but this was probably arranged by Antigonus: the Achaeans would have to feed the army. The independent group of Megalopolitans and their Macedonian equipment can best be explained by the personal nature of Megalopolis' grievance against Cleomenes, now aggravated by the sack of the city. Megalopolis' longstanding friendship with Macedon, coupled with Antigonus' recent failure to prevent the sack of the city, is sufficient to explain the Macedonian provision of equipment for the destitute Megalopolitans. Cercidas himself had been one of the original envoys from Megalopolis to Antigonus in 227; and this established personal connection may have again been used to secure the equipment for the troops.[3] It is known that Philopoemen participated in the battle as a cavalryman, and since there is no mention in any source of a separate contingent of Megalopolitan cavalry, he must have served in the cavalry division of the federal Achaean ἐπίλεκτοι.[4]

The whole of the allied cavalry was placed in the centre of Antigonus' line, in the comparatively flat valley of the Oenus, between the two hills Euas and Olympus. To their left on Olympus was the Macedonian phalanx with 5,000 mercenaries under Antigonus, facing that of Cleomenes who was fortified higher up the slope. On the right of the allied line were the Achaeans and Megalopolitans, facing Euas on which the other Spartan king Eucleidas commanded some 5,000 men. In the

---

[1] Pol. ii. 65–9; Plut. *Cleomenes*, 28; *Phil.* 6. On the site, cf. Pritchett, *Studies in Ancient Greek Topography* i. 59–70, criticizing convincingly the standard account in Kromayer, *Antike Schlachtfelder* i. 199–277. On Polybius' account and the date of the battle, cf. Walbank, *Comm.* i. 272 ff.

[2] Pol. ii. 65. 3.

[3] So Walbank, *Comm.* i. 274–5.

[4] Plut. *Phil.* 6. The Achaean ἐπίλεκτοι seem to have been a standing force of picked infantry and cavalry, perhaps composed of upper-class young men (so Feyel, *Polybe et l'histoire de Béotie*, pp. 203–4). Cf. Walbank, *Comm.* i. 274. References in Mauersberger, *Polybios-Lexikon*, s.v. ἐπίλεκτος.

valley between right and left were 1,000–2,000 Spartan mercenaries shielding the Spartan cavalry. Hidden overnight in the tributary valley between the allied right and Euas were Illyrians and Acarnanians.[1] Antigonus' plan was to attack Euas with these surprise troops, and, outflanking the Spartan left, to take them at a disadvantage, while the Macedonian phalanx prevented Cleomenes' leaving Olympus to aid Eucleidas. The Macedonian centre was probably to be held back until both wings were engaged.[2]

The battle began at dawn with the Acarnanians' attack on Euas. The Spartan light-armed mercenaries from the centre were at once dispatched to take them in the rear, in the space between them and the allied centre. This move was clearly dangerous for the Acarnanians, but was perhaps not altogether unforeseen by Antigonus. In any case he did not yet give the sign for his centre to join battle, as he wanted to give the outflanking Illyrians on the right of the ambush time to engage and to commit the Spartan mercenaries on the less favourable ground of the hillside, where the Acarnanians would be more at home. This does not mean that he was intending to sacrifice the Acarnanians: only that he wanted to take the utmost advantage from the engagement of the Spartan mercenaries before committing his centre.

Philopoemen held no official position in the allied army, except perhaps as leader of the Megalopolitan cavalry in the ἐπίλεκτοι—even this is not made clear in the sources—and he clearly did not see the plan of battle in this way. What was apparent to him in his place in the centre, the closest point to the Spartan attack on the Acarnanians, was that the Acarnanians were threatened from the rear. His reaction was based on instinct rather than military discipline. He drew the attention of the Macedonian officers to the threat from the Spartan mercenaries, and suggested immediate action. Reasonably enough, as welltrained officers, they resisted this attempt from the ranks to teach them their responsibilities, and waited for the prearranged signal from Antigonus' headquarters. Before this came, Philopoemen broke ranks and led his Megalopolitans, followed by the rest

---

[1] On the dispositions, cf. Walbank, *Comm.* i. 279 f. This must be adapted to suit Pritchett's new site (see sketch map in *Studies* i. 60).

[2] Cf. Ferrabino, *AAT* 1918/19, 756 ff.

of the cavalry, to relieve the Acarnanians by a charge against
the Spartan cavalry which had been left exposed by the mercenaries' advance.[1] The Spartan mercenaries were thus forced
to retire to protect their cavalry, the pressure on the Acarnanians
was relieved, and the allied cavalry could return to its position.
In the event, Philopoemen's self-willed intervention had been
successful in allowing the Acarnanians a freer attack. But in the
long run it made little difference to the success of the attack on
Euas. For by this time the Illyrians had come round the shoulder
of the hill, and Eucleidas, instead of using the advantage which
his superior position gave him for attack, allowed the Illyrians
and Acarnanians time to reach close quarters. As a result of the
subsequent fighting the whole of the Spartan left on Euas was
beaten into retreat down the opposite slope and annihilated.

Philopoemen's effort therefore in this part of the battle was
essentially a minor episode which may have added to the comfort
of the Acarnanians and saved some lives, but had little if any
effect on the course of the battle as a whole. Polybius' account
of this—perhaps influenced by information from Philopoemen
himself—transforms it into a major part of the fighting, to the
greater glory of Philopoemen and Megalopolis. In effect, he
suggests that Philopoemen's initiative was mainly responsible for
the success of the attack on Euas, which can scarcely have been
the case.[2] But in the final assessment Antigonus was generous
with praise to Philopoemen, when he found him seriously
wounded after the later main cavalry engagement—although
Polybius' anecdote suggests that had Alexander, the Macedonian
commander of the right, been responsible for the premature
cavalry attack he would have expected to answer for his temerity.
But there is little reason to doubt the authenticity of the com-
pliment which Antigonus bestowed on Philopoemen, that he
had acted like a good general. When the battle was over Antigonus had no reason to be sparing of his praise to the wounded.
There is equally no reason to doubt that Antigonus suggested
that Philopoemen should serve him, a detail which must have
come originally from Philopoemen himself. If his tactical insight

---

[1] τοὺς ἑαυτοῦ πολίτας (Pol. ii. 67. 5; cf. Plut. *Phil.* 6. 3). These were certainly the
cavalry, not the infantry who were also close: Philopoemen, himself a cavalryman,
would not lead an infantry attack on the Spartan cavalry.

[2] Pol. ii. 67. 8. Plutarch's account (*Phil.* 6) is in the manner of an *Aristeia*, and
is accordingly confused in detail.

had been at fault, there could be no doubt of his personal courage and initiative in fighting on when his legs were transfixed by a javelin.[1]

After the success of the allies' attack on Euas, Cleomenes on Olympus in desperation launched a phalanx attack on Antigonus. The fighting here was severe, but the weight of the Macedonian phalanx, supported by the victorious right wing after its successful attack on Euas and by the cavalry, was sufficient to win the day for the allies. The Spartans broke, and Cleomenes escaped to Gytheum from where he sailed at once to Egypt.[2] The war was over. The threat to Achaea from Sparta, for the moment at least, was destroyed. The Megalopolitans could thank Philopoemen's foresight for preventing their accepting Cleomenes' friendship.

II

Philopoemen had substantially enhanced his reputation as a soldier in the war against Cleomenes, and soon afterwards he went to Crete, where he stayed for about ten years, fighting on behalf of the Gortynians. In this service he was probably associated with the interests of Philip V of Macedon, who became king when Doson died in the course of the winter after Sellasia. Philopoemen's activities in Crete require separate discussion.[3] Here it will be convenient to examine briefly events in Greece between Sellasia and Philopoemen's first federal appointment in Achaea, as hipparch in 210/09.

The members of Doson's symmachy surrounded and enclosed the territory of the Aetolian League, which had been strong enough to refuse to participate in the symmachy. Philip was only sixteen on his accession, and the Aetolians took advantage of his youth to attack Achaea, which now relied wholly on Macedon for protection. In 221 various raids against Achaea and elsewhere caused Philip's advisers to allow the symmachy to declare war on the Aetolians.[4] The threat to Achaea from Sparta was also renewed when the Aetolians made an alliance in 219 with Lycurgus, who had emerged from the chaos following Cleomenes' death as the dominant figure at Sparta. Since Philip and

---

[1] Plut. *Phil.* 6. 7–7. 1; Pol. ii. 68. 1–2.
[2] Pol. ii. 69; Plut. *Cleomenes*, 28–9.   [3] Cf. chapter III, pp. 27 ff.
[4] Pol. iv. 25. Cf., in general, Fine, *AJPh* 1940; Walbank, *Philip*, pp. 24 ff.

his advisers viewed the war against Aetolia as a whole, he spent 219 in trying to open up the western route from Macedon to the Peloponnese. As a result, Achaea was virtually left to take care of itself. Philip's subsequent winter campaign against Elis and Triphylia did not significantly alter this state of affairs, and in 218 the Achaeans were so oppressed that they agreed to pay Philip for the time which he spent in defending specifically Achaean interests. Aratus had some influence with Philip, and he tried to preserve some reality behind the façade of the symmachy; but the dominant influence on Philip was Apelles, his chief Macedonian adviser, who looked upon the symmachy simply as a weapon of Macedonian aggrandisement, much as Doson had conceived it.[1]

The effect of these two conflicting interests on Philip was confused still more in 219, when he was joined by Demetrius of Pharos, who had been driven out from his Illyrian kingdom as a result of his misinterpreting Roman 'freedom'.[2] Demetrius quickly gained influence at the court, and his arrival provided a new direction and method for Macedonian foreign policy. His own aim was the recovery of his kingdom, and by 218 he had gained sufficient support at the court to cause the Macedonians to build a fleet. Demetrius' influence distracted Philip from the Peloponnese and from Achaean problems, and despite the fact that Philip was beginning to think for himself and to break away from Apelles' dominance, Achaea was for the most part left to defend herself. In 218 a purge removed Apelles and some of his associates from the court, and although Aratus was found useful at the time, Achaea continued to be neglected during 217. In July the Nemea brought Philip to Argos. During the festival he received news of the battle of Trasimene, which excited him to the point where his interest in the Aetolian war was effectively replaced by a plan of invading Italy and joining Hannibal against Rome. The war in Greece was therefore quickly brought to an end in 217 at a conference at Naupactus. Peace was made, but Agelaus of Naupactus recognized the danger to Greece as a whole from Philip's interest in Italy when he warned the

---

[1] On this in detail, cf. Niese, *GGMS* ii. 408 ff.; Walbank, *Aratos*, pp. 126 ff. On relations between Philip, Aratus, and Apelles, cf. Errington, *Historia* 1967, 16 ff.

[2] Cf. Badian, *PBSR* 1952 = *Studies*, pp. 1–33. A briefer account in *For. Cl.*, pp. 45–6. For earlier work, cf. *Studies*, p. 25.

assembled Greeks about the 'cloud in the west'.[1] Philip nevertheless formed an alliance with Hannibal whereby Hannibal recognized his potential diversionary value. The Senate was forced
to take notice, and in 214 it stationed a fleet under M.
Valerius Laevinus in western Greece to protect the straits of Otranto. No
attempt was made to extend Roman influence in Greece until
212, when approaches to the Aetolians resulted in an alliance
which carefully emphasized that the Senate was not interested
in permanently occupying Greece: the Aetolians should have
all captured territory, the Romans all movable plunder.[2]

Once Philip's war against Aetolia was concluded in 217 he
could afford to indulge his lack of vital interest in Achaea. Subsequently his only purpose in southern Greece was to keep the
Peloponnese quiet in order that he could concentrate on his more
grandiose western plans. To this end he retained his garrisons at
Corinth, Heraea, Orchomenus, Alipheira, and in Triphylia. Yet
these proved to be insufficient when factional trouble broke out
at Messene in 215. Achaean interest was clearly deeply involved,
and Aratus travelled quickly to Messene. On his arrival he found
Ithome already occupied by Philip and Demetrius. A discussion
took place in which Demetrius urged that Macedonian interest
demanded the permanent occupation of Ithome; Aratus argued
against him that the goodwill of the people was likely to be more
effective. On this occasion Philip allowed himself to be persuaded
by Aratus, although the concession cost him little. To make up
for the absence of a permanent garrison on Ithome he asserted
himself by ravaging Messene in 214.[3] Aratus had ultimately
failed in his attempt to conceal the fact that he had made
Achaea into a Macedonian satellite. His claim to be able to
exert personal influence on Philip was finally shattered, privately
by the discovery that Philip had seduced his daughter-in-
law, publicly by the lack of interest which Philip finally showed

[1] Cf. Niese, *GGMS* ii. 459; Walbank, *Philip*, pp. 51 ff.; *Aratos*, pp. 139 ff. Pol.
v. 104 (Agelaus' speech): the historicity of this speech has been questioned by
Schmitt, *Rom und Rhodos*, p. 54, n. 1; but Roman influence in Illyria had been close
enough for twelve years to make the speech entirely plausible in outline. Cf. Walbank, *Philip*, p. 66.

[2] Cf. Walbank, *Philip*, pp. 68 ff.; Badian, *For. Cl.*, pp. 55–7; on the treaty, cf.
Badian, *Latomus* 1958; Lehmann, *Glaubwürdigkeit*, pp. 10 ff.; earlier bibliography
in *SEG* xiii, no. 382.

[3] Pol. vii. 12; Plut. *Aratus*, 50; cf. Niese, *GGMS* ii. 469–71; Walbank, *Philip*,
pp. 72–5; *Aratos*, p. 156.

in the constitutional trappings of the symmachy. The symmachy had been formed as an expression of Macedonian domination, and only briefly, while Philip was finding his political orientation, had it been anything else. When Aratus died in 213/12 in his sixteenth *strategia*,[1] Achaea had become little more than a toy in the hands of the great powers.

[1] Pol. viii. 12; Plut. *Aratus*, 53; cf. Walbank, *Aratos*, p. 157.

III

CRETAN CONNECTIONS

I

PHILOPOEMEN spent more than fifteen years[1] of his mature life in Crete, years which the literary sources virtually ignore. This must be partly due to the loss of Polybius' biography, where the events in which Philopoemen took part in Crete must have been described. But since the work was a panegyric account, which may have contained little more than a list of the hero's achievements without supplying any background material or discussion of his motives, its survival might not have provided much useful information. But there is no means of judging the value of the material in the biography, since neither Plutarch nor Pausanias made any use of it for the Cretan years, and Polybius' *Histories* ignore this part of Philopoemen's career. As far as the surviving literary sources are concerned, therefore, these two periods in Crete are a gap, which it is the purpose of the present chapter to attempt to fill.

The essential inadequacy lies in the sources. Philopoemen himself is not mentioned at all, Achaea only marginally, in the literary sources which give information about Crete at this period; and apart from the War of Lyttus, to which Polybius devotes three chapters, the internal history of Crete is just as obscure.[2] To some extent epigraphic evidence can fill the gaps in the literature; but as so often when inscriptions provide the bulk of the evidence, they are fragmentary and accordingly interpretations are uncertain. It is therefore only possible to offer a tentative reconstruction of events in Crete during these years, and of the relationship of the island to the general Greek political movements of the age. The interpretation offered here

---

[1] c. 220–210 and 200–c. 194.
[2] Pol. iv. 53–5. As far as Philopoemen is concerned, Plutarch simply records that on each occasion he returned λαμπρός—little more than conventionally 'successful' (*Phil.* 7; 14).

is an attempt to use the available material to build up some kind of positive picture of the place of some of the Cretan cities in the general history of this period, and to discover the part played by Philopoemen in the events of the years of his absence from Achaea.

At some time soon after the battle of Sellasia (222) Philopoemen went to Crete, where he remained until 211. Plutarch gives the most detailed account of the circumstances: 'Antigonus was eager that Philopoemen should take service under him, and offered him command and pay. These Philopoemen declined, chiefly because he well knew that it was naturally unpleasant and hard for him to be under another man's orders. Not wishing, however, to be inactive and idle, for the sake of training and practice in war he sailed to Crete in search of military service. In Crete he practised himself for a long time among men who were not only warlike and versed in many kinds of warfare, but also still moderate and restrained in their ways of living, and he came back to the Achaeans with such distinction that they at once made him commander of their cavalry.'[1] Pausanias merely abbreviates Plutarch's account, adding on his own initiative that Philopoemen was indignant at Antigonus' offer.[2] Clearly Philopoemen entered no agreement with Antigonus. Yet it will become clear that his later activity in Crete certainly coincided with Macedonian interests and probably cannot have been independent of them. Again, on his return to Achaea, Philopoemen attached himself to the Achaean party which was supported by Philip, and probably himself enjoyed Macedonian support. It therefore seems probable that, once he had arrived in Crete, Philopoemen found it convenient, and perhaps advisable, to associate himself with the parties which Philip supported. This association may have developed into some kind of informal representation of Philip: the tradition of the upper-class *condottieri* would make this honourable.

The exact date of Philopoemen's departure for Crete is not known. But it may have some significance that in 220 Philip sent a force from the symmachy to Crete to help the Lyttians and their allies. Included in this force were some 200 Achaeans.[3]

[1] Plut. *Phil.* 7.
[2] Paus. viii. 49. 7: τῷ δὲ Ἀντιγόνου μὲν ὀλίγον μελήσειν ἔμελλε.
[3] Pol. iv. 55. 2.

In connection with the War of Lyttus, Polybius records an internal quarrel at Gortyn between groups which he calls *neoteroi* and *presbyteroi*.[1] Since the *neoteroi* were allied with the Lyttians and the *presbyteroi* with their opponents, the Gortynian civil war must also have some external political significance. The precise meaning of the names *neoteroi* and *presbyteroi* is not clear. Van Effenterre accepts the obvious indications of the names and suggests that they represent democratic and oligarchic parties within

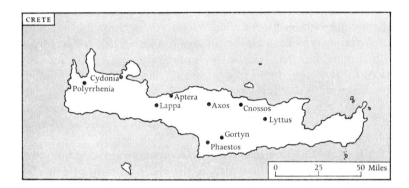

Gortyn[2]—democratic in the attenuated sense of the word forced upon the language by Hellenistic conditions: '... le terme s'oppose moins désormais à aristocratie ou oligarchie qu'aux diverses formes de pouvoir personnel favorisées souvent par les monarques dans les cités grecques.'[3] Willetts bases his interpretation on Forbes's examination of the institution of *Neoi*, and suggests that this *stasis* at Gortyn was 'a conflict between the older and younger citizens ... promoted by internal causes of which we are ignorant'.[4] Manganaro offers a geographical explanation. An inscription from Axos of about this date records a treaty between Axos and Γορτυνίοις ταὶ ἄνω πόλι καὶ ταὶ κάτω.[5] This he connects with Polybius' distinction between *neoteroi* and *presbyteroi*, and suggests that the *presbyteroi* were the inhabitants of the ἄνω πόλις (Gortyn proper), the *neoteroi* the inhabitants of the

[1] Pol. iv. 53. 7 ff.   [2] Van Effenterre, *La Crète*, pp. 165 ff.
[3] *La Crète*, p. 167.
[4] Willetts, *Aristocratic Society*, pp. 187–91; cf. Forbes, *Neoi*, *passim*.
[5] Manganaro, *Historia* 1966, 18 ff. (first publication of the inscription). The phrase quoted occurs in lines 1–2 and 3–4.

κάτω πόλις (Phaestos). The distinction between 'upper' and 'lower' Gortynians, with a specific reference to Phaestos as the lower city, is also made in a Gortynian inscription.[1]

Against Manganaro's view can be set Polybius' account of the War of Lyttus, in which he places the Gortynian civil war in Gortyn itself. At one point the *neoteroi* were expelled from the citadel of Gortyn by the *presbyteroi*; and Polybius ends his account by relating that 'the Gortynian exiles [i.e. the *neoteroi*] even seized the harbour of the Phaestians . . .'.[2] In this way he indicates that the *neoteroi* were not themselves men of Phaestos, who are here distinguished both from the *neoteroi* and from the *presbyteroi*. The civil war, therefore, took the form of a division within Gortyn— which may, nevertheless, be the 'upper city' of the Axos inscription. Of the other two explanations, Willetts's seems preferable, on the grounds that it is less precise and does not imply knowledge of Cretan affairs which we do not have. The real objection to van Effenterre's more positive view is the fact that there is no supporting evidence for it.

Although the character of the Gortynian parties cannot be certainly elucidated, the causes of the civil war may perhaps be investigated with more secure result. The War of Lyttus started as a final phase in the attempt of Cnossos and Gortyn to subdue the island to their joint hegemony. In the course of this war against Lyttus, other cities seceded from their alliance with Cnossos and Gortyn, and the civil war between the *neoteroi* and the *presbyteroi* broke out at Gortyn. It was only with Aetolian help that Cnossos and the Gortynian *presbyteroi* were able to come out on top. After this the war became more general and Lyttus was destroyed. At this point Philip intervened with his contingent from the symmachy, and the war was soon decided in favour of the dissidents from the Gortynian/Cnossian dual hegemony. At some time after this, Philip was appointed *prostates* of all Crete—clearly by the victorious party, which he had supported; and this party naturally included the *neoteroi* at Gortyn.[3]

Can this series of events provide a reason for the *stasis* at Gortyn? The domestic policy of the *neoteroi* cannot be ascertained; but it is clear that they must have opposed Cnossos and

---

[1] *Inscr. Cret.* iv. 165, line 3.   [2] Pol. iv. 53. 9 (citadel); 55. 6 (Phaestos).
[3] Pol. iv. 53–5 (events of war and Gortynian *stasis*); Pol. vii. 11. 9 (Philip's *prostasia*).

the dual hegemony, since these were supported by the *presby-teroi*. After the success of the general revolt from Cnossos and Gortyn, the Cretan *koinon*—whether founded then or earlier—seems to have been dominated by Gortyn; and this Gortynian domination lasted, though gradually fading out, into the mid-second century.[1] This Gortynian supremacy clearly means that the *neoteroi* had effectively managed to assert Gortynian hege-mony over the federation after the War of Lyttus. It therefore seems reasonable to see in the post-war *neoteroi*—whatever their position had been before the war—a group of Gortynian nation-alists and perhaps federalists, who were dissatisfied with the dual hegemony—and its implication of internal power in Gortyn for the *presbyteroi*. A revolution towards federation (or a more effective *koinon*, if it already existed), and away from the dual hegemony of Cnossos and Gortyn, would result in power at Gortyn for the *neoteroi*. In Crete as a whole, the *koinon* would be likely to look to the Gortynian *neoteroi* for leadership. For the success of the revolt meant that Cnossos' pretensions to hegemony were de-stroyed, and the prominence of the *presbyteroi* at Gortyn with them. From the point of view of the participants, this result was clearly worth fighting for, worth civil war—both for the Gor-tynian *neoteroi* and for their Cretan allies who were dissatisfied with the dual hegemony.

Philip's intervention in Crete is more easily explained. In Greece the Social War was declared in summer 220. Cnossos already had an alliance with the Aetolians which was naturally supported by her partners, the Gortynian *presbyteroi*. It is not known when this alliance had been established, but it fits con-veniently into the well-established anti-Macedonian traditions of

---

[1] The date of the foundation of the *koinon* is disputed. Guarducci (*RFIC* 1950) suggests that it was founded after the War of Lyttus, and that Philip's *prostasia* was a result of the part he had taken in founding it. Van Effenterre, on the other hand, (*La Crète*, pp. 132 ff.) considers it to be earlier in the third century: 'la fondation du *koinon* peut en somme être rapportée au troisième quart du IIIᵉ siècle' (ibid., p. 138). The date of the foundation is not strictly relevant to the present study; but the effect of the war and the intervention of Philip mark an important change in the Cretan balance of power, which van Effenterre notes. We need not re-examine all his epigraphic evidence, but his conclusion is a useful statement of the position: 'Ce n'est sûrement pas dû au seul hasard des trouvailles si nous avons aux IIIᵉ et IIᵉ siècles tant de traités où Gortyne figure et semble même souvent jouer un rôle déterminant' (ibid., p. 154). Whatever the facts about the *koinon*'s foundation, the intervention of Philip is, as Guarducci and van Effenterre would agree, a vitally important event in Cretan affairs.

Cnossos, which had sent help to the Rhodians as long ago as Demetrius' siege in 305. In the present war, 1,000 Aetolians were instrumental in driving the *neoteroi* out of Gortyn.[1] This alignment of the *presbyteroi* with the anti-Macedonian parties clearly attacked the personal position of the *neoteroi*. Their nationalist feelings may also have been offended, for comparatively recently there had been close relations between Gortyn and Macedon, as the extant treaty of alliance between Gortyn and Demetrius II shows clearly.[2] This treaty may have been made by the *neoteroi* during an earlier period of power, or by the *presbyteroi* at a time before the idea of the dual Gortynian/Cnossian hegemony became practicable. But during Doson's reign the alliance with Macedon must have been abandoned, for at the outbreak of the War of Lyttus, Gortyn—led by the *presbyteroi* —was firmly associated with Cnossos and her anti-Macedonian traditions. When the *neoteroi* were driven out of Gortyn, they had a ready-made grievance to set before Philip, which might be expected to attract the sympathy of his advisers. Macedonian interests were currently threatened by the predominance of the *presbyteroi* at Gortyn; and since war with Aetolia was now common to Macedonian interests both in mainland Greece and in Crete, the *neoteroi* presented a strong argument, which the Macedonian policy-makers accepted. They also seem to have gained Aratus' support, which no doubt accounts for the 200 Achaeans in the contingent which Philip sent from the symmachy.[3]

Philopoemen's position in these affairs is not altogether clear. He may have been simply one of the 200 Achaeans; or he may have gone to Crete independently on mercenary service, and while there have proved his usefulness to Philip and gained his support. If this latter were the case, the secrecy which Polybius seems to have observed over Philopoemen's years in Crete would be more easily explained: at the time when he was writing it was inadvisable to boast that Philopoemen had at any time been an agent of Macedon. Even the former case implies collaboration with Macedon, which may have embarrassed Polybius and have caused his silence. Further supporting the view

---

[1] Pol. iv. 53. 8–9; cf. Walbank, *Comm.* i. 509.

[2] *Inscr. Cret.* iv. 167.

[3] Polyrrhenia and Lappa, the leaders of the Cretan war effort, appealed both to the Achaeans and to Philip for help (Pol. iv. 55. 1); the influence of Aratus is implied by Pol. vii. 14. 4 and Plut. *Aratus*, 48. 3.

that Philopoemen was associated with Philip in Crete is the length of his stay—at least until 211—in an island now dominated by Philip and Philip's friends. Philopoemen must have fought on the winning side in the War of Lyttus; otherwise his position in Crete would have been intolerable after it. He must therefore have assisted the *neoteroi* at Gortyn, a conclusion which is supported by his return to Crete in 200 at the specific request of the Gortynians. He must also have supported the concurrent growth of Philip's influence and gained his recognition, for on his return to Achaea he was immediately elected to the federal hipparchy in 210/09, a year when Cycliadas, the leader of the Achaean pro-Macedonian party, was *strategos*. It therefore seems likely that he played some part in organizing the appointment of Philip to his *prostasia*. A personal connection with Macedonian interests explains satisfactorily Philopoemen's prolonged residence in Crete after the crisis of the War of Lyttus had passed. This had happened by 219, for it was then possible for the Polyrrhenians and their allies to send help to Philip and the Achaeans in Greece.[1] This recovery on the part of the federal faction in Crete, implied by the availability of Cretan federal troops for service with Philip, suggests that the force from the symmachy had been withdrawn, and throws Philopoemen's solitary position into relief. All factors seem to point to a close relationship between Philip and Philopoemen during Philopoemen's first period in Crete.

Despite his association with Philip, Philopoemen had refused service under Antigonus' command in 222. This does not mean that the above analysis of Philopoemen's relationship with Philip is necessarily wrong. Plutarch took what he found in Polybius, and this can only have represented what Polybius wished to publicize. When Polybius wrote his *Histories* he could not admit that Philopoemen had ever favoured Macedon—particularly not during the First Macedonian War—for this would have seemed to be a simple confirmation of his anti-Roman reputation, which Polybius was at pains to deny. In 222 Philopoemen himself may not have desired—for different reasons—to become known as a Macedonian collaborator. If he was to retain any hope of a later political career in Achaea, it was better to maintain an appearance of independence from Macedon. Therefore he

---

[1] Pol. iv. 55. 5.

refused to place himself under Antigonus' direct command after Sellasia and publicized his refusal. But a public refusal only meant the absence of immediate formal co-operation: nothing prevented Philopoemen from subsequently representing Macedonian interests in Crete where he could retain much of his valued independence of command. In this way he could preserve his political position in Achaea, while at the same time he gained personal benefits from his *de facto* collaboration. He was in no way abandoning Achaea, for the 200 Achaean troops showed clearly that Achaean interest was as closely involved as Macedonian in defeating Aetolian influence in Crete. Philopoemen's first period of Cretan activity could therefore be represented as patriotic service, as long as the Macedonian influence was discreetly kept out of sight.

II

When Nabis came to power at Sparta after the death of Machanidas in 207, he founded his position on mercenary support. In particular, this came from alliances with Cretan cities. In the course of time, these alliances became so close that Nabis came to control some of the Cretan cities—a control which Flamininus forced him to relinquish in 195.[1] By 204 he was strong enough to start sporadic attacks on Achaea, which continued for some years in a desultory fashion. In 200 Philopoemen held a successful *strategia* in Achaea, during which he made some attempt to reply in kind to Nabis, and probably took the first steps to guide the Achaean League towards alliance with Rome. After this *strategia* Philopoemen suffered defeat at the elections and returned to Crete, where he stayed until 194. One reason for his leaving Achaea is clear: the election defeat spelled danger, and this is discussed in detail elsewhere.[2] The reason for his prolonged absence, even though his supporter Aristaenus gained power in Achaea comparatively soon after his departure, is less clear. But it seems likely that it was a reason of policy which kept Philopoemen in Crete, although at the time of his departure he was simply making a virtue of necessity.[3]

---

[1] Pol. xiii. 8. 2; Liv. xxxiv. 35. 9.
[2] See below, ch. V, pp. 81 ff.
[3] Cf. Dubois, *Les Ligues étolienne et achaienne*, p. 74, n. 5. Also below, ch. V, pp. 81 ff.

Plutarch is supported by Pausanias when he states that Philo-poemen went to Crete in 200 at the express wish and invitation of the Gortynians.[1] From the above analysis of his relations with Gortyn during the War of Lyttus, it is clear that this invitation must have been issued by the *neoteroi*, who had been in power at Gortyn at least since the establishment of Philip's *prostasia*. Philo-poemen must therefore have been involved in fighting against the enemies of the *neoteroi*. Nabis' position in Crete may be rele-vant to this. Although it is difficult to discover any certain re-lationship between Sparta and any individual Cretan city at this time, there are some significant indications. After 200—while Philopoemen was in Crete—a war was in progress between Gortyn and Cnossos.[2] This must clearly have been, in some sense, a continuation of Cnossos' struggle for power in Crete, which twenty years before had resulted in the War of Lyttus. In the changed conditions of the time, if there was any broader political significance in Philopoemen's presence in Gortyn, Nabis' power should be found to have been centred on Cnossos or on one of her allies. The Achaean hostility of *c.* 200 towards Sparta would in that case have been mirrored in their respective Cretan alliances, as was the Achaean/Macedonian hostility to Aetolia in 220; and the presence of Philopoemen in Gortyn would provide an important link.

The few indications we have suggest that this may in fact have happened, although the known history of relations between Sparta and the cities of Crete over the previous hundred years can be reduced to two incidents. In 272 Areus II of Sparta served in Crete under the Gortynians. Not long afterwards, at the time of the Chremonidean War, the benefit was probably repaid, as Sparta seems likely to have been helped by Gortyn.[3] But in 272 and later, the Gortynian party which had the friendship of Sparta may easily have been that which, by the time of the War of Lyttus, was known as the *presbyteroi*. At the later time they were in close relations with Cnossos, co-operating in the attempt to establish the Gortynian/Cnossian dual hegemony. After Philip's

---

[1] Plut. *Phil.* 13; Paus. viii. 50. 6.

[2] Paus. viii. 50. 6; cf. *Inscr. Cret.* iv. 176; i. viii. 9 (which Guarducci dates to this time).

[3] Plut. *Pyrrhus,* 27 (Areus in Crete); cf. Cardinali, *RSA* 1904–5; van Effenterre, *La Crète,* p. 203; Guarducci, *Inscr. Cret.* iv, praef. hist. p. 20 (Gortynian help for Sparta).

intervention, the *neoteroi* had become the dominant party in Gortyn; and although there seems to have been no fighting in the island after the War of Lyttus, it has already been noticed that the hostility between the Gortynian *neoteroi* and Cnossos broke out again at about the time of Philopoemen's visit to Crete in 200. Nabis was probably of Spartan royal blood;[1] but in any case, as ruler of Sparta, he would take up traditional Spartan connections, which in the changed circumstances involved an alliance with Cnossos. This is what we would naturally expect of a Spartan ruler looking for support in Crete. Homolle has independently attempted to demonstrate this connection by suggesting that two Delian proxeny decrees should be read closely together: one is a decree for two Cnossians, the other a decree for Nabis.[2] He then suggests that this implies a connection between Nabis and Cnossos. But since both decrees are undated and otherwise unconnected, the most that can be extracted from Homolle's theory is that Nabis and Cnossos each had friendly relations with Delos at some points of time not too far apart. It would therefore be rash to accept van Effenterre's assurance that Homolle's demonstration shows any certainty in this relationship—'les Cnossiens sont sans doute parmi les amis de Nabis.'[3]

There are other indications, however, which suggest a close relationship between Achaea and Gortyn on the one hand, and between Nabis and Cnossos on the other. In the circumstances of the war which was going on in Crete between Gortyn and Cnossos until some time before 189,[4] we should consider the proxeny decree of Mycenae for Protimus of Gortyn.[5] Protimus had been responsible for an attempt to save Mycenaean *epheboi* who had been taken to Sparta by Nabis—perhaps among the 2,000 Argives taken to Sparta by Nabis in 195,[6] perhaps at some other time during the Spartan domination of the Argolid after 198. The decree must have been set up after the *epheboi* had returned, for it could scarcely have been erected while Nabis was still in control of the town. The type of relationship with Sparta

---

[1] Cf. Dittenberger, *ad Syll.* 584.

[2] Homolle, *BCH* 1896, 502 ff.; *IG* xi. 4. 716 (= Ditt. *Syll.* 584); 719.

[3] *La Crète*, p. 215.

[4] By 189 Gortyn and Cnossos were co-operating in a war against Cydonia (Liv. xxxvii. 60. 3).

[5] Ditt. *Syll.* 594; cf. *SEG* iii. 313; Boethius, *ABSA* 1921–3.

[6] Liv. xxxiv. 29. 14.

enjoyed by satellite towns during Nabis' comparatively brief period of control is illustrated by the decree of Mycenae in favour of Damocleidas the Spartan, which renews 'the right of the Spartans to share in the games which the town promotes'. This decree can scarcely have been passed voluntarily, at a time when the Spartans were likely to seize all the *epheboi* they could lay their hands on, as Protimus' almost contemporary decree shows.[1] The support of a Gortynian for the *epheboi* of an Achaean town when they were threatened by Nabis and its recognition by an honorary decree again suggest the public friendship of Gortyn for Achaea. The form of service which Protimus rendered to the Mycenaean *epheboi* is not made clear, but the demonstration of mutual goodwill is obvious.

A later example of the same friendly disposition on the part of Gortyn towards Achaea may be seen in the presence of Telemnastus of Gortyn with 500 'Cretans' as an important figure in Philopoemen's campaign against Nabis in 192.[2] Philopoemen's close personal connection with Gortyn and the importance of Telemnastus' part in this expedition strongly suggest a personal connection between Telemnastus and Philopoemen. They also imply a public connection between Achaea and Gortyn, for Polybius mentions that Telemnastus' exploits were remembered almost 40 years later, in 153, when his son was Cretan ambassador to Achaea.[3] The friendly relations between Gortyn and

---

[1] *SEG* iii. 312. Boethius, in his discussion of the historical setting of these inscriptions, is inclined to place them both after the peace of 195 (*ABSA* 1921–3, 425). His argument is that only after the restoration of 'friendly' relations between Achaea and Sparta would the Mycenaeans be willing to pass a pro-Spartan decree. This view seems naïve. The two decrees seem incompatible, and therefore incapable of having been passed under the same political circumstances. Protimus' decree must be after the loss of the Argolid by Nabis, therefore after 195: it would have been too dangerous to pass it before then. Damocleidas' decree, presupposing as it does entirely different political circumstances, must surely be dated to the period of Nabis' control of the Argolid, i.e. between 198 and 195. The indications are that it would be early in this period, for once Nabis had control the Mycenaeans would be eager to accommodate him as far as possible and as quickly as possible. There is no difficulty in this: a community did not have to be free to pass decrees honouring its masters. Cf. (for instance) *OGIS* 329 (Aegina).

[2] Liv. xxxv. 29. 1. At about this time, a Telemnastus of Gortyn, son of Antiphatas, had his statue erected by Cretan soldiers at Epidaurus (*IG* iv. 2. 244). That this was the same man is confirmed by Pol. xxxiii. 16, which gives evidence that the son of Philopoemen's friend Telemnastus was called Antiphatas—presumably, according to custom, after his grandfather.

[3] Pol. xxxiii. 16. 6.

Achaea seem demonstrated. But they also imply official Gortynian hostility to Nabis. This, in view of Nabis' known interests and interference in Crete, and in the light of the contemporary hostility between Gortyn and Cnossos, must indicate a friendship between Cnossos and Nabis, and supports what the other evidence has independently suggested.

In the light of this evidence, which demonstrates friendly relations between Gortyn and Achaea and implies a close relationship between Nabis and Cnossos (and other Cretan cities connected with Cnossos), it appears to be highly probable that Philopoemen's otherwise unnecessarily long sojourn in Crete from 200 to 194 was directed against the position which Nabis had built up for himself in the island and which he held until he was forced by Flamininus to relinquish it in 195.[1] His fighting in the Cretan war between Gortyn and Cnossos was probably directly parallel with the Achaean war effort in the Peloponnese against Nabis.

Since these connections have been established with some probability, other evidence can now be considered, which may fit into this pattern of relationships between the states of Crete and Greece. There is some evidence which points to Polyrrhenia's having had close relations with Sparta. In the middle of the third century the Polyrrhenians set up a stele to Areus II of Sparta,[2] a fact which indicates that they were anti-Macedonian at the time. As has already been noticed, Areus had also had a close connection with Gortyn. Polyrrhenia gained the support of the Gortynian *neoteroi* when leading the revolt from the Gortynian/Cnossian dual hegemony in the War of Lyttus. This leadership naturally attracted Philip's support; and the body of opinion in Polyrrhenia, which had led the revolt from Cnossos and Gortyn and had enjoyed the help of Philip's symmachy in 220, replied by taking the lead in organizing the Cretan force which was sent to Greece in 219.[3] This change from the earlier anti-Macedonian policy probably represents a change in the dominant political group in Polyrrhenia. But the change did not last long after the War of Lyttus. By the time of the *Kretikos Polemos*, which began in 204, Polyrrhenia seems to have again changed sides. In the series of decrees of Cretan cities for the *asylia* of Teos, that of Polyrrhenia is one of those in which the

[1] Liv. xxxiv. 35. 9.   [2] *Inscr. Cret.* ii. VIII. 12A.   [3] Pol. iv. 53. 6–7; 55. 5.

Macedonian Perdiccas does not appear. Holleaux, in his illuminating interpretation of these decrees, has understood Perdiccas' absence to mean that the Polyrrhenians now sympathized with Rhodes in the war which she was currently fighting with Philip.[1] If Holleaux is right, the Polyrrhenians would seem to be reverting to their mid-century attitude of anti-Macedonianism. At the earlier time anti-Macedonianism was synonymous with friendship with Sparta. If the attitude was resumed—and it would no doubt receive adequate encouragement from Nabis—a second ally for Nabis in Crete may have been identified.[2]

The *Kretikos Polemos*, which started in 204, has already been mentioned: more must now be said. Polybius has only two brief passages which shed light on Cretan affairs at this time. The first concerns Philip: '. . . he sent envoys to Crete to agitate and to gain support for the war against Rhodes.' The second passage concerns Nabis: '. . . he made common cause with the Cretans in their acts of piracy on the high seas.'[3] In addition to these, undated epigraphic evidence exists, some of which was first referred to this war by Herzog, and all of which has been often worked over since.[4] But despite the work of the scholars, this war, in course and origin, remains obscure. The epigraphic evidence has also been interpreted as referring to the war of 167 between Crete and Rhodes; and although Holleaux has put forward a very strong case for 204, which is accepted here, this is not absolutely certain. The passages of Polybius show this much: that Philip was hoping to find support among the Cretan cities for his current war with Rhodes. It has already been seen that some ten years previously he had established a *prostasia* in Crete; and it seems likely that he had maintained a diplomatic interest in the affairs of the *koinon*, and as a result of this in the Gortynian

---

[1] Holleaux, *Études* iv. 189 ff.

[2] Cnossos was also one of the cities which did not receive Perdiccas, as was Lappa which had been closely associated with Polyrrhenia in the War of Lyttus (Pol. iv. 53–5). Cnossos, it has been argued, was one of Nabis' cities, and in this case anti-Macedonian too. Polyrrhenia and Lappa (if we accept Holleaux' demonstration of their anti-Macedonian standpoint) should also have enjoyed the support of Nabis. In the cases of the other two cities, Rhaucus and Cydonia, which certainly did not receive Perdiccas, no other connection with Sparta can be traced, apart from this association with Cnossos.

[3] Pol. xiii. 4. 2; 8. 2. Cf. xviii. 54. 8–12; Diod. xxviii. 1.

[4] Herzog, *Klio* 1901–2; Cardinali, *RFIC* 1907; Holleaux, *Études* iv. 163 ff.; 178 ff.; Segre, *RFIC* 1933; Guarducci, *Epigraphica* 1940; Walbank, *Philip*, pp. 109 ff.

neoteroi. As far as Nabis is concerned, Polybius' reference does not seem to indicate his undertaking a full-scale war; this is hardly implied by describing him as supporting the pirates. It has already been shown that Nabis' interests should have been on the side of Cnossos. Philip's interests, on the other hand, should have been on the side of Gortyn and the *koinon*. That this was so is supported by Perdiccas' absence from Cnossos in the series of inscriptions from Teos. In any case, Philip's undertaking in Crete was only a diversionary move in his main struggle against Rhodes. That his intervention rapidly became less than whole-hearted seems clear from the Gortynians' request for help to Philopoemen,[1] at the time when Philip's occupation elsewhere must have left the *koinon* open to a split led by Cnossos; and of course Philopoemen's interests were opposed to Nabis'. Guarducci maintains[2] that the *Kretikos Polemos* united Philip, Nabis, and 'the Cretans' against Rhodes. But the considerations already advanced show that the issues can have been by no means so clear cut.

As has already been pointed out, an alliance between Philip and Nabis at this time would be surprising: it seems much more likely that there would be a direct conflict of interests in Crete between Nabis and Philip, rather than active co-operation. For Crete was far from being an isolated sector of war, and the position of the Cretan cities in inter-state diplomacy was not governed solely by domestic Cretan developments. The situation in the Peloponnese is also clearly relevant to understanding the relationship between Philip and Nabis. Philip was still an ally of Achaea, and as late as 200 he offered, however insincerely, to help the Achaeans in putting an end to their trouble from Nabis, which Achaea had by then been suffering for five years.[3] Without solid evidence to the contrary, the conclusion should be that no friendly relations had ever existed between Nabis and Philip. The agreement reached between them in 198/7 over the possession of Argos cannot be used to show any community of interests as early as the *Kretikos Polemos*; for on Philip's part it was only a stop-gap arrangement to spite the Achaeans, when they

---

[1] Plut. *Phil.* 13; Paus. viii. 50. 6.

[2] *Inscr. Cret.* i, praef. hist. p. 49; iv, praef. hist. p. 22. Walbank, *Philip*, p. 110, suggests also that Nabis may have been working with Dicaearchus.

[3] Liv. xxxi. 25. 4–7.

had joined the Roman alliance against him.[1] There is some evidence that Philip and Nabis were in fact opposed in the *Kretikos Polemos*; and this is connected with the Rhodian position in Crete. By tradition Cnossos was friendly with Rhodes. She had sent help in 305 when the island was blockaded by Demetrius Poliorcetes; in the War of Lyttus Rhodes had sent help to Cnossos; at the time of the *Kretikos Polemos* there is no reason to doubt that friendly relations between Cnossos and Rhodes still subsisted.[2] Since Cnossos seems to have been one of Nabis' sources of power in Crete, the common friendship of Rhodes and Nabis for Cnossos at the time of the *Kretikos Polemos* makes it plain that there is no possibility of an alliance between Philip and Nabis for the *Kretikos Polemos*.

It seems clear, therefore, that it is incorrect to speak of 'the Cretans' at this time as if they acted as one body, despite the existence of the *koinon*. The island was split into at least two camps, and one of the factors which conditioned the split was the friendship of Nabis or Philip. This aspect of the basically internal Cretan dissension was probably emphasized after Philip's failure in the battle of Chios, when his interest was forcibly shifted from the Aegean and his ability to create a balance of power in Crete destroyed. It is scarcely surprising to find Cnossos renewing her anti-Macedonian policies as soon as Rhodian support was available, for after the War of Lyttus Cnossos can only have been brought to acknowledge Philip's *prostasia* unwillingly. The support offered by Rhodes and the eagerness of Nabis to gain influence in the island must have appeared a providential combination of circumstances, of which Cnossos took full advantage. Gortyn and the *koinon* on the other hand were less fortunate in their overseas champion. Philip's interest in the Aegean was soon cut short, and they had to look for aid to Achaea and Philopoemen, who had served them adequately in his first period of Gortynian service.

A circumstance which may be connected with the Gortynian invitation is the presence of Didascalondas the Cretan in the Achaean army while Philopoemen was still *strategos* in 200.[3]

[1] Liv. xxxii. 38. 1–6.
[2] Diod. xx. 88. 9 (305); Pol. iv. 53. 1–2 (221); Ditt. *Syll.* 581, lines 74–7. Cf. Guarducci, *ad Inscr. Cret.* iii. III. 3A (*c.* 200); van Effenterre, *La Crète*, p. 214.
[3] Pol. xvi. 37. 3.

Didascalondas accompanied Philopoemen in his attack on Nabis' mercenaries at Pallene, and he was important enough to be entrusted with the command of part of the Achaean levy. This command seems to mark him out as being more than simply a mercenary captain—although there were ordinary Cretan mercenaries in Achaea in 200, as a dated inscription from Mantinea shows.[1] It is unfortunate that the man's home city cannot be discovered; but we can conclude with some certainty that it was not Cnossos or one of the allies of Cnossos: Achaea could not afford to employ mercenaries who were potentially sympathetic towards Nabis. This leads to the suggestion that he may have come from the *koinon*. The *koinon* was controlled at this time by the pro-Macedonian party, probably still led by the Gortynian *neoteroi*, and must have supported Philip as long as Philip supported it. It has been argued above that during the *Kretikos Polemos* the *koinon* was threatened by a secession movement which had the support of Sparta and Rhodes. It would therefore be entirely natural to find a representative of the *koinon* in Achaea—obviously a more than usually competent military man—in the first instance helping the Achaeans in their parallel struggle against Nabis, but really hoping to secure some help for the Cretan sector of the war. It seems possible that Didascalondas was such a representative.

There is no other information which sheds further light on relations between Achaea and the cities of Crete, but some events should be related in the light of what has been shown to be the probable reconstruction of Cretan politics. In 197, shortly before the campaign of Cynoscephalae, 500 Gortynians joined Flamininus under the command of Cydas.[2] De Sanctis argued that these Gortynians were simply a section of the 600 Cretans who were handed over to Flamininus by Nabis in the spring, after the

---

[1] Ditt. *Syll.* 600—in accordance with dating the fourth *strategia* of Philopoemen to 201/0 (cf. appendix 2 B) this inscription must be redated to that year.

[2] Liv. xxxiii. 3. 10. Cydas is a common enough name at Gortyn (cf. index to *Inscr. Cret.* iv); and further identification is hazardous. A Cretan Cydas was used by Eumenes in 169 to carry on his negotiations with Perseus (Pol. xxix. 6. 2; 7. 8; Liv. xliv. 13. 9; 24. 9). He may be the same man, as contact could have been made with Eumenes as a result of his participation in the Cynoscephalae campaign. The period of 30 years separating the two events is long, but need not wholly rule out identification. Cf. Niese, *GGMS* iii. 323, n. 1; Schoch, *RE* Suppbd. iv. 1123; he may have been *Cosmos* at Gortyn in 184 (Pol. xxii. 15. 1). Against this, cf. van Effenterre, *La Crète*, p. 264, n. 3; ibid., p. 298.

negotiations at Mycenae.[1] But the above elucidation of relations between the Peloponnese and Crete at this time makes it seem highly unlikely that Gortynians would seek service with Nabis (implying willingness to serve against Achaea), at the very time when in Crete Philopoemen was helping them to fight off the threat of Nabis' influence. Similarly, it is unlikely that Nabis would use mercenaries whose loyalty was necessarily in doubt. But in fact there is a much more compelling reason for thinking that these troops were not Nabis' ex-mercenaries. For Livy expressly states[2] that these troops were handed over at once— *datis*; and there is every reason to believe that this must be taken literally, for immediately afterwards the appearance of these very troops under Roman command was largely responsible for showing Philip's commandant at Corinth, Philocles, that Nabis had changed his allegiance. The 500 Gortynians who joined Flamininus in Phthiotis cannot therefore have been part of Nabis' 600 Cretans.

In this case, why did these Gortynians come to join the allied army? It is most unlikely that they were mercenaries unnecessarily hired by Flamininus. The answer may lie in Achaea. It will be shown below that there was no essential disagreement on policy between Philopoemen and Aristaenus at this time; and there is no reason to doubt that Philopoemen fully approved the Achaean agreement with Rome in 198. It is therefore possible to suggest that Gortyn—like Achaea, having turned anti-Macedonian after being abandoned by Philip—sent these troops on the advice of Philopoemen, who was acting in co-operation with the Achaean *strategoi* Aristaenus and Nicostratus. It seems too great a coincidence for the Gortynians independently to have decided to send these troops to join Rome, just at the time when Philopoemen might have been expected to urge this policy upon them, and when their main Greek allies the Achaeans had just pronounced their readiness to accept a treaty of alliance with Rome. It may be unacceptable to suggest that they were partly meant as a substitute for the Achaean troops which were occupied in the Peloponnese and were therefore not available to join the

---

[1] De Sanctis, *Storia* iv. 1. 78 and n. 159; accepted by Walbank, *Philip*, p. 167, n. 4; Aymard, *Premiers Rapports*, p. 147, n. 52; well discussed by van Effenterre, *La Crète*, p. 206.

[2] Liv. xxxii. 40. 4.

allied army in the north. But it does seem clear that some Achaean influence was at work, and this may perhaps be narrowed down to Philopoemen.[1]

Attention has already been drawn to the participation of Telemnastus of Gortyn in Philopoemen's expedition against Nabis in 192. This demonstrates clearly enough the continuance of the public and private connections of Achaea and Philopoemen with Gortyn. But why did Philopoemen only return to Achaea in 194, when he had been absent in Crete during some of the most momentous events in Achaean history? The continuity of friendly relations with Gortyn forbids the conclusion that he left Crete while he was still needed. The implication is therefore that the war between the Cnossians and the Gortynians, participation in which was the purpose of his going to Crete, was no longer continuing. It had certainly ended before 189, for the two cities joined forces in that year to fight Cydonia[2] —and this collaboration suggests that some time had elapsed since the cessation of active hostilities between them. The answer may perhaps be found in Sparta. If the Cnossians and their allies had relied as much on Nabis as he had relied on them, the termination of hostilities in the Peloponnese and the virtual neutralization of Nabis by Flamininus in 195 would have a debilitating effect on Cnossos' war in Crete. In particular, the stipulation in the terms of Nabis' treaty with Flamininus that he must give up his navy and all the cities he controlled in Crete would drastically alter the balance of power in Crete in favour of Gortyn and the *koinon*.[3] In these circumstances Cnossos may well have felt inclined to make peace before it was forced upon her by defeat. This feeling would naturally arise soon after Flamininus' settlement at Sparta, therefore in late 195 or early 194. This would give Philopoemen sufficient time to have ended his commitment in Crete and have returned to Achaea to spend a year or more in re-establishing his political position before he secured his election as *strategos* in autumn 193. The reason for Philopoemen's return from Crete in 194 may therefore have been that the parallel war in Crete did not continue into 194, but

---

[1] The fact that the Gortynians alone of the Cretan cities were prepared to comply with the Romans' request in 189 to free Italian slaves shows a respect for Rome which may have originated in their Achaean connections: Liv. xxxvii. 60. 4–5.

[2] Liv. xxxvii. 60. 3.   [3] Liv. xxxiv. 35. 9.

reached a conclusion by negotiation as a direct result of the enforced withdrawal of Nabis' support from the Cnossian alliance.

The honeymoon period of co-operation between Gortyn and Cnossos, which followed the peace and which is illustrated by their joint war against Cydonia, did not last long. By 184 they were again fighting against each other.[1] This war cannot have been very prolonged, for an extant decree of the *koinon* dated to 183 records a treaty of alliance with Eumenes of Pergamum: at the head of the list of subscribing cities are both Gortyn and Cnossos.[2] This implies that the differences which had given rise to the war had been settled, and that support for the *koinon* had been re-established. Philopoemen retained his close connection with the *koinon* to the end of his life. During his fatal last campaign in 182 he was supported by Cretans as well as Thracians and Achaean cavalry.[3] There is no means of telling which of the cities of Crete sent these troops; but since Cnossos and Gortyn were enjoying one of their transient periods of co-operation at this time, it seems possible that the troops were mercenaries from the *koinon*, and that the Cnossians too may have contributed men.[4] However this may have been, the presence of the Cretans shows clearly enough that Philopoemen maintained his links with Crete after his final departure in 194, and that even in his final campaign he still set considerable store by the aid of Cretan troops.

There is also evidence of friendly relations between Achaea and Aptera at the beginning of the second century, which may have been associated with Philopoemen's Cretan service. At the outset of the War of Lyttus Aptera had been among the supporters of Cnossos; but after the destruction of Lyttus, she was constrained to join the allies.[5] Towards the end of the third century, a decree of Aptera is extant which honoured Attalus of Pergamum for his services to Aptera and the *koinon*.[6] This evidence of friendship suggests that Aptera, along with Gortyn and the *koinon* (and Achaea) quickly developed friendly relations

---

[1] Pol. xxii. 15.   [2] Ditt. *Syll.* 627, with notes.
[3] Liv. xxxix. 49. 2; Paus. viii. 51. 5.
[4] Guarducci's theory (*RFIC* 1934) that the epitaph of the Cretan cavalryman Tharsymachus found near Cnossos (*Inscr. Cret.* i. viii. 33) refers to this war is given additional plausibility by this circumstance.
[5] Pol. iv. 55. 4.   [6] *Inscr. Cret.* ii. iii. 4C.

with Rome's friends when it became advisable. The mention of the *koinon*[1] suggests that at about the time when Philopoemen was in Crete defending Gortyn's supremacy in the *koinon*, Aptera was an enthusiastic member. Relations with leading Achaeans at this time were clearly good: Tison of Patrae, Philopoemen's federal navarch in 193/2, was honoured at Aptera with a proxeny;[2] and Aristaenus was probably also given the same honour.[3] Both of these men may well have been associated with Philopoemen's Cretan activities. The pro-Roman alignment of Aptera—perhaps mirroring Achaean relations with Rome—is also attested by a decree, which Guarducci dates to 189, honouring four distinguished Romans in (for Aptera) exceptionally fulsome terms.[4] The men are: L. and P. Cornelius Scipio, Cn. Cornelius Scipio Hispanus, L. Aemilius Regillus. It seems a reasonable conjecture from all this evidence that Aptera's friendship with Achaea— if not with Rome—developed from the wider implications of Philopoemen's service at Gortyn.

It will be convenient to conclude this chapter with a summary of what the above analysis has shown to be the probable course of events in the relationships between the leading cities of Crete and the Greek mainland from the time of Philopoemen's first visit. In 221 or 220 Philopoemen went to Crete, probably in some independent capacity, where, after publicly rejecting Antigonus Doson's offer of formal service under his command, he nevertheless collaborated with Macedonian interests. He may, however, have been a member of the Achaean expeditionary force, sent in 220 in accordance with Aratus' enthusiasm for the symmachy's participation in Cretan affairs. While he was in Crete Philopoemen fought for the cities which were opposed to the dual hegemony of Cnossos and Gortyn. As a result, he came into contact with the Gortynian *neoteroi*, and must have cooperated in achieving Macedonian aims. His co-operation with the *neoteroi* and sympathy for Philip's interests in the island led him to remain after the temporary emergency of the War of Lyttus had passed; and he was present—perhaps even actively

---

[1] *Inscr. Cret.* ii. III. 4C, line 4.

[2] *Inscr. Cret.* ii. III. 6E (and Guarducci's commentary); cf. Liv. xxxv. 26. 7 (Tison as navarch).

[3] *Inscr. Cret.* ii. III. 6F (and Guarducci's commentary); cf. discussion below, appendix 4, pp. 276 ff.

[4] *Inscr. Cret.* ii. III. 5A.

organizing support for Macedon—when Philip was granted the position of *prostates* by the *koinon*. As a result of the success of the Macedonian camp in the war, the *neoteroi* were restored to Gortyn, and under their leadership Gortyn became the dominant political influence in the *koinon*. Philopoemen was present throughout this development, and must have continued to be active in support of the Gortynians as well as of Philip, as Gortyn's later invitation to him suggests.

Nothing more is known about Crete until 204. In the meanwhile Philopoemen had been using Philip's support, which he had gained during his time in Crete, to establish himself in Achaea. During the *Kretikos Polemos* of the years after 204, the divergent attractions of Rhodian influence in Cnossos and Philip's in Gortyn caused a split in the *koinon*, of which Nabis of Sparta was able to take advantage. He had already re-established Sparta's traditional close links with some Cretan cities, probably including Cnossos, and the dissension in Crete as a result of Philip's war with the Rhodians seems to have given him an opportunity to confirm his hold. Philip soon began to lose interest in the Cretan war after his main effort in the Aegean had been frustrated by Rhodes' success in the battle of Chios and by the threat of Rhodian co-operation with Attalus in an appeal to Rome. As a result, his attention was totally diverted from Crete, which caused Gortyn to be faced with a secessionist movement in the *koinon*, as soon as it became clear that she had lost even the moral support of Philip. Nabis, in a parallel effort to his undeclared war against Achaea in the Peloponnese, continued his support for Cnossos. The Gortynians appealed for help to Philopoemen, the old friend of the *neoteroi*. He hesitated only as long as he was in power in Achaea: when the embarrassment of electoral defeat hung heavily on him, he accepted the Gortynian invitation. He spent the next five years, even after his supporters had recovered their influence in Achaea, trying—not very successfully, it seems, to judge by the effectiveness of Nabis' efforts in the Peloponnese —to break the Cretan source of Nabis' power.

The war in Crete was only brought to a close as a result of the peace treaty between Nabis and Flamininus, which stipulated that Nabis should give up his navy and his possessions in Crete. The fighting in Crete had, in any case, been sporadic, for Gortyn, probably urged by Philopoemen, had been able to send 500 troops to join Flamininus' army in 197 as a gesture of solidarity with the Achaean and Roman cause. After the indecisive conclusion of the war in Crete Philopoemen returned to Achaea, from where he kept up his contacts with Gortyn and regularly employed Gortynians such as Telemnastus in the Achaean army. Even twelve years after his return from Crete, at the time of his last expedition in 182, Cretan troops played an important part in the composition of his army.

IV

WAR WITH ROME

IN 211/10 Philopoemen returned to Achaea from Crete and was immediately elected hipparch of the League for 210/09. His absence from Achaea had lasted for ten years, and such sudden prominence—despite the fact that Achaea benefited from his work—requires explanation. His colleague in office, the *strategos*, was Cycliadas.[1] In 199/8 Cycliadas was expelled from Achaea as a result of his position as leader of the pro-Macedonian faction.[2] If he persisted in his pro-Macedonianism to the point where he allowed himself to be exiled for it, it seems more than likely that his association with Philip was of long standing, and that at the time of his *strategia* in 210/09 he was also a solid supporter of the Achaean alliance with Macedon. Philopoemen's association in office with Cycliadas, coming so rapidly after his prolonged absence, strongly suggests that he was running on the same ticket[3] —the two officials were elected at the same time—and that he therefore also represented a pro-Macedonian policy. It has already been shown that Philopoemen had probably been associated with Philip's interests in Crete.[4] His election together with Cycliadas suggests that this association continued after his return, and the rapidity of his election probably means that Philip's influence was actively at work in promoting the interests of his supporters. This support of Philip may provide an explanation of why Philopoemen returned from Crete at this time.

Achaea had never been strong militarily. Aratus had managed to achieve a brief period of independence by taking advantage of the weakness of Macedon under Antigonus Gonatas and Demetrius II, but the threat from Sparta under the active Cleomenes soon showed that this apparent independence and

---

[1] Plut. *Phil.* 7; Paus. viii. 49. 7 (Philopoemen). Liv. xxvii. 31. 10 (Cycliadas). Cf. appendix 2 B and *strategos*-list.

[2] Liv. xxxii. 19. 2.

[3] This is denied, for no good reason, by Lehmann, *Glaubwürdigkeit*, p. 207, n. 120.

[4] Cf. ch. III, *passim*.

self-sufficiency was a mirage. Aratus' invitation to Doson to save Achaea from Cleomenes in return for the Acrocorinth set the Achaean military establishment in its correct perspective. Total dependence on Macedon was seen to be the only route to long-term security. The bitterness of this discovery was partly disguised by Aratus' claim to be able to exercise some influence over the young Philip, but by the time of his death in 213/12 all his illusions were shattered.[1] Total military dependence on Macedon was by then undisguised, and there seemed to be little alternative. For Aratus had made no attempt to preserve even a minimum of efficiency in the Achaean army, and his colleagues and successors, both *strategoi* and hipparchs, simply followed his influential example. Polybius, for instance, describes Euryleon, the *strategos* of 211/10, as 'a timid man . . . and undisposed to warlike activities'. In another place he castigates the Achaean *strategoi* of this time for being totally ignorant of military requirements. His opinion of the hipparchs is the same: whether through sheer incapacity, or through blatant desire to be popular—with an eye to future elections—the training and efficiency of the cavalry had been almost wholly neglected.[2] Polybius may have exaggerated these deficiencies in order to make Philopoemen's subsequent reorganizations contrast more sharply with them; but the recent history of the Achaean army—particularly in the Social War—goes far to support his strictures.

Thanks to Philip's energy and activity, Achaean military incapacity had not yet proved disastrous. The Romans had been content to preserve their control of the straits of Otranto without actively extending the war. But 211 brought about a major development, when they formed an alliance with Aetolia, the main enemy of Philip and Achaea in the Social War, on the basis that the Aetolians would have all conquered territory, the Romans all movable plunder. This was rapidly followed by Roman alliances with Sparta, Elis, and Messene. The effect of this series of alliances was to recreate the alignment of the Social War, with the additional hazard of Roman intervention on the side of Philip's enemies.[3] The seriousness of this latter was further

---

[1] On this, see Errington, *Historia* 1967, 16 ff.

[2] Pol. x. 21. 1 (Euryleon); xi. 8. 1–3 (*strategoi*); x. 22. 8–10 (hipparchs).

[3] Liv. xxvi. 24. 1–4 (Aetolia); Pol. ix. 28–39 (speeches at Sparta); ix. 30. 6 (Elis and Messene). On the treaty, cf. Klaffenbach, *SDAW* 1954, no. 1; *SEG* xiii, no. 382; Badian, *Latomus* 1958, 197 ff.; Lehmann, *Glaubwürdigkeit*, pp. 10 ff.

emphasized by the replacement of Laevinus by P. Sulpicius Galba Maximus. Galba held the consulship as his first curule office in 211 : he was clearly a man with influential support, and his consular appointment to Greece demonstrates the awakening interest in the Macedonian war of an important section of the Senate.[1] These developments inevitably affected Philip's view of the war. The situation as a whole bore an embarrassing resemblance to the alignment of the Social War; and if developments occurred in the same way, he could expect to find himself increasingly confined to fighting in northern and central Greece.

For Achaea, the danger from the developing situation was obvious. The combined hostility of Sparta, Elis, Messenia, and Aetolia, now further strengthened by their Roman alliances, could not currently be faced with any confidence without Philip's continued help. At this critical moment Cycliadas and Philopoemen were elected to the highest federal offices. The crisis in which they were elected was essentially military. Yet even ten years later Cycliadas had no reputation as a military leader.[2] Macedonian influence and his own Macedonian connections are sufficient to explain his election. But the military crisis had nevertheless to be met. Philopoemen spent the year of his hipparchy in drastically reorganizing the Achaean cavalry, a reorganization which took Achaea half-way to military self-sufficiency. The wholeheartedness of his reorganization, its effectiveness, and the influential support which he clearly must have had to make it possible, suggest that Philopoemen was intended, both by Philip and by the Achaean electors, to carry it out during his year. It is perhaps possible to go further: Philopoemen's almost providential return from Crete at this critical time seems too convenient both for Philip and for Achaea for it to have been wholly coincidental. It therefore seems probable that he was asked to come back to Achaea by Philip and the Achaeans, who both, for their own reasons, required Achaea to gain a new military efficiency in face of the new danger.

The reason why the reorganization started with the cavalry clearly lies in part in the person of Philopoemen. Had it been decided that the infantry should first receive attention, the organizer of the reforms would have had to be *strategos*. But

---

[1] Refs. in Broughton, *MRR* i. 272; cf. Scullard, *Roman Politics*, p. 63.
[2] Liv. xxxi. 25. 3.

Philopoemen had held no previous federal office and had only recently returned to Achaea after an absence of ten years: it would accordingly be invidious for him to break the usual custom of holding the hipparchy first. Philip might well have hesitated before risking the loss of sympathy among his Achaean supporters which a *strategia* for Philopoemen in these circumstances would involve. The hipparchy carried less prestige, there could be no objection to Philopoemen's seeking it, and it had the advantage for Philip of making it possible for him to test Philopoemen's loyalty and effectiveness before he came to the infantry command which carried with it the presidency of the state. Philopoemen therefore began his re-organization with the cavalry, whose defects he had personally experienced before he went to Crete.

It is easy enough to understand why Philip should support and why the Achaeans should carry out Philopoemen's election as hipparch. It is perhaps less easy to understand why Philopoemen should have returned to Achaea. He had been away from Achaea for ten years, he was inevitably out of touch with federal politics—in which he had never played any part—and he had no doubt made his mercenary service financially worthwhile, both for himself and probably also for Achaea, in the tradition of upper-class *condottieri*. This last point is important, for large amounts of money would be required if a wholesale re-equipment of the Achaean forces was to be undertaken: the previous *strategoi* had reduced morale to the point where money would only with great reluctance be forthcoming from individual soldiers, who had received little encouragement from their elected leaders to take their part-time soldiering sufficiently seriously. Philip, with a full-scale war on his hands, was in no position to finance Achaea, and there is no evidence that the Achaean federal treasury had money to spare from normal sources. If Philopoemen returned and undertook the task of re-organizing the army, he must have expected to be required to spend much of the earnings of his mercenary service on this. This would not be unusual for him, for Plutarch, in discussing his military career, says that he used to spend his booty on 'horses, armour, and ransoming prisoners'.[1] If he continued this practice as hipparch, he must have anticipated substantial political rewards for it. Up to a point, political rewards could be assured in advance.

[1] Plut. *Phil.* 4. 3 .

He could be promised Philip's support and that of Cycliadas, the leader of the pro-Macedonian party in Achaea, for the first stages of his federal career, the hipparchy and his first *strategia*. But his continued political success would depend on his own efforts and on his popularity as a politician: once his immediate work was accomplished, his supporters could probably afford to abandon him, should this become desirable. It was, no doubt, pleasant for him to serve his home state as leader at a time of crisis, and in his later career Philopoemen showed that he indeed had the interests of Achaea at heart. But this patriotism had not been sufficiently potent to bring him back from Crete during the crises of the Social War.

The major difference in Achaean politics between then and now was the absence of Aratus. Aratus had dominated Achaean politics with an *auctoritas* all his own: it is no accident that few of the other Achaean *strategoi* were of any importance during the period of his dominance. Philopoemen had had no wish to be dominated by the Sicyonian. But after Aratus' death there was a power vacuum in Achaea. Aratus' presence had prevented any dominant personalities from emerging during his lifetime, and there was accordingly no one who could automatically assume his predominance after his death. The opportunity was open, if Philopoemen chose to take it, and was made the more tempting by the prospect of Macedonian support in the early years. He could clearly envisage himself acquiring, with this initial backing, an influence in his own generation comparable with Aratus' in his. Everything combined to make a return to Achaea highly attractive.

The immediate danger to Achaea from the more active Roman commitment in Greece had already been vividly demonstrated to the Achaeans in 210, while Euryleon was still *strategos*—a demonstration which emphasized the importance of Philopoemen's task. Galba had attacked and occupied Aegina, which he handed over to the Aetolians in accordance with their agreement. The Aetolians had no wish to keep the (for them) awkwardly situated island, and promptly sold it to Attalus of Pergamum for thirty talents. This transaction brought another enemy to close quarters with Achaea, and also created a refugee problem for her. Nothing could immediately be done to recover the island: the Aeginetan refugees who refused to accept Attalid rule had to take what

solace they could from exercising their Achaean citizenship in
their place of exile in the Peloponnese.[1] The threat to Achaean
security from continuing military impotence no longer needed
politicians to emphasize it. As a result, Philopoemen received
full co-operation from the Achaean cavalrymen when he instituted his new training schedule as soon as he was elected in
the autumn. He insisted on a formal training in individual and
combined manœuvres; the quality of the horses was improved,
which must have required disbursements from Philopoemen's
earnings; an *esprit de corps* was cultivated to replace the old individualistic tradition. Philopoemen's own active part in this
training programme was to visit each city in the autumn and
explain the manœuvres to the assembled cavalrymen and the
local commanders, who were expected to practise them during
the winter and to have perfected them by the spring. He then
revisited each town in order to check progress and provide solutions for any difficulties which might have arisen in the meanwhile.[2] In the spring, the whole federal cavalry force was collected
together for joint exercises and mass manœuvres, once the individual contingents had become proficient in their sectional
manœuvres. The whole undertaking seems to have been super-
vised, as far as possible, by Philopoemen himself, and no personal
effort was spared in the interests of efficiency.[3] The very thoroughness and attention to detail mark out the professional soldier,
who had earned his living by his military skills.

From the military point of view, Philip and his Achaean
supporters had chosen their man well. But the cavalry reorganization alone was not sufficient to ensure Achaean military self-
sufficiency. Philip cannot have expected this, particularly since
Cycliadas was *strategos*. It could therefore have been no surprise
when he received an anguished appeal for help from Cycliadas
in the spring of 209. Activity in the Peloponnesian sector of the
war was increasing, and Achaea was now menaced from two

---

[1] Pol. ix. 42. 5–8; xi. 5. 8 (capture); xxii. 8. 9–10; cf. Ditt. *OGIS* 281 (sale to
Attalus). Cf. Niese, *GGMS* ii. 484; De Sanctis, *Storia* iii. 2. 420–1; Flacelière, *Les
Aitoliens à Delphes*, p. 300, n. 2.

[2] Plut. *Phil.* 7. 3–5; Pol. x. 23. Philopoemen's explanation was made τοῖς τε
πολλοῖς καὶ τοῖς ἀποτελείοις (9). The ἀποτέλειοι were the local commanders of the
local detachments of the federal army (cf. Ditt. *Syll.* 600). It must be assumed that
οἱ πολλοί in this case were the local cavalrymen, to whom alone Philopoemen's
information was relevant. Cf. Aymard, *Assemblées*, p. 102, n. 1.

[3] Pol. x. 24.

sides. Machanidas had finally emerged from the political chaos
at Sparta—nominally, perhaps, as regent for Lycurgus' son
Pelops[1]—and he followed traditional Spartan expansionist policy
of mounting attacks on southern Arcadia, of which Megalopolis
would bear the brunt. At the same time, the federal authorities
were occupied in beating off an Aetolian attack which was
launched across the narrows of the Gulf. Livy does not mention
any major Achaean disaster; but appeal to Macedon was a tradition founded by Aratus, and Cycliadas was not the man to
break it. The attackers might be expected to withdraw at the
threat of Macedonian opposition, whereas Achaea's weakness
was notorious.[2]

Philip's preoccupation with his own sector of the war emphasized Achaean isolation. His operations near Lamia against a
joint force of Aetolians, Romans, and Pergamenes had produced
for him two successful encounters, with the result that his retire-
ment to Phalara encouraged the Aegean commercial states to
propose peace negotiations. As in the Social War, the renewed
fighting and the consequent general insecurity were disrupting
Aegean commerce, and the negotiations were undertaken by
representatives of Egypt, Rhodes, Athens, and Chios. On the
Aetolian side Amynander of Athamania was chosen to negotiate.
No conclusion could be reached on the spot, but a truce for thirty
days was acceptable to both sides and further discussion was
postponed *in concilium Achaeorum*, for which the place and date
were fixed. Philip then travelled to Argos where he celebrated
the Heraea, after which he went to Aegium *ad indictum multo ante
sociorum concilium*. At this meeting there was discussion about
ending the war with Aetolia and (too late) *ne causa aut Romanis
aut Attalo intrandi Graeciam esset*. Any prospect of a successful outcome from these negotiations was rapidly removed when the
Aetolians announced that they would consider peace only on
condition that Pylos be restored to Messene, Atintania to Rome,
and the Ardiaei to Scerdilaidas and Pleuratus of Illyria.[3]

[1] Liv. xxvii. 29. 9. Machanidas is called *tyrannus Lacedaemoniorum*; but Pelops
was still alive—he was killed by Nabis (Diod. xxvii. 1)—and it seems likely that he
was nominally king. Cf. Liv. xxxiv. 32. 1.

[2] Liv. xxvii. 29. 9.

[3] Liv. xxvii. 30; cf. Walbank, *Philip*, pp. 89–91. Larsen's reliance on Livy's
accuracy in this Achaean material vitiates his analysis of the technical form
of the *concilium*, and produces a tortuous explanation ('. . . a combination of an

Livy follows Polybius' hostile bias faithfully in giving the impression that the Aetolians were to blame for the continuation of the war;[1] but the view is too naïve. The chief contenders in the war were Rome and Philip, and while either of them wished to continue the fighting there could be no hope of ending the war. Rome was committed to neutralizing Macedon for as long as Hannibal was a serious threat in Italy: the Macedonian war would not be ended solely by events in Greece. The Greek commercial states might struggle as they would to get the parties to a conference; but until Rome desired peace their efforts would inevitably be futile. It is this background against which the Aetolians' demands at Aegium should be considered. We can now see them as demands formulated by agreement with Rome for the purpose of securing the continuation of the war by their certain rejection. The thirty days' truce had been a convenient way out of a temporarily embarrassing situation after the operations at Lamia: its only real effect was that Philip had squandered his success by misinterpreting the nature of the Roman commitment.[2]

By the time of the *concilium* the danger to Achaea had become even greater. In addition to the serious attacks by Machanidas and the Aetolians which had induced Cycliadas to appeal to Philip, the situation was complicated by Attalus' crossing to Aegina and by the Roman fleet's arrival at Naupactus.[3] It was now clear that the break for negotiations was merely an interlude, after which the war would continue as before. The implications for Achaea were very serious, since the chief enemy forces were now deployed around the Corinthian Gulf. Her coastline urgently required protection. Accordingly, while Philip travelled to Argos to celebrate the Nemea, he left four thousand troops and five ships as a guard for the north coast.[4] But five ships could not fight against Galba's fleet. The result was that these ships were only a nominal protection against the operation of the mobile Roman

---

extraordinary meeting of an Achaean assembly and of the *synedrion* of the Hellenic League' (*Rep. Gov.*, p. 170)) for a situation which, in political terms, is perfectly straightforward: Philip had no need to worry about Achaean constitutional niceties when his supporters were in office and needed his help.

[1] Liv. xxvii. 30. 14.

[2] Cf. Schmitt, *Rom und Rhodos*, p. 56: 'man sprach vom Frieden, ohne ihn zu wollen, und schob die Schuld am Mißlingen der Verhandlungen dem Gegner zu.'

[3] Liv. xxvii. 30. 11.   [4] Liv. xxvii. 30. 15; 17.

fleet. At the height of the Nemea Galba landed between Sicyon and Corinth with the intention of plundering this rich Achaean territory. Philip's garrison on the Acrocorinth did not act, and news of the Roman incursion was brought to Philip at Argos. It was a rare opportunity of demonstrating to the Achaeans the value of a quick and efficient army: he immediately left the celebrations with his cavalry, ordered the infantry to follow, and hurried northwards. He met the Romans foraging in undisciplined fashion and drove them back to their ships.[1] There could now be no doubt in Achaea as to the value of Macedonian support, no doubt what would be the effect of its withdrawal. But Philip's idea seems to have been that his support for Philopoemen's re-organization of the Achaean military establishment would allow him to operate in the north without sacrificing the loyalty of the Achaeans through his inability to help them. The urgency of this must have been emphasized by the threats of this year.

A further demonstration of Achaea's current reliance on Philip's military support and of the danger resulting from its withdrawal came soon after the Nemea. The Aetolian attacks on Achaea, begun in the spring, had had the effect of producing an invitation from the governing group in Elis for a permanent Aetolian garrison force to be stationed there, an invitation which the Aetolians accepted.[2] Cycliadas had made no attempt to deal with this threatening development until Philip was in a position to support him. Philip was interested in preventing Elis from becoming too active an opponent, since attacks from there would threaten the security of his own border castles at Heraea, Alipheira, and in Triphylia, on which he partly relied for keeping Achaea loyal. Joint Achaean and Macedonian retaliation was therefore arranged after the Nemea. The allied forces advanced from their assembly point at Dyme as far as the river Larisus, the boundary between Achaea and Elis. They were met there by the Elean and Aetolian cavalry which tried to prevent the invasion. Philopoemen's newly organized cavalry met its first test, and came through with flying colours. The Achaean and Macedonian cavalry soundly defeated the Elean, and Philopoemen won a personal encounter with Damophantus, the leader of the Elean

---

[1] Liv. xxvii. 31. 1–3.

[2] Liv. xxvii. 31. 9. De Sanctis, *Storia* iii. 2. 427, n. 75, is right (against Niese, *GGMS* ii. 487) that the *urbs* is Elis. Cf. Walbank, *Philip*, p. 91, n. 6.

cavalry. Philip must have taken encouragement from this demonstration of the effectiveness of the reorganized cavalry for his intention to continue his support for Philopoemen.[1]

After the cavalry battle the Eleans withdrew to their city. The invaders spent the next day inadvisedly in plundering the countryside, which had been abandoned to them. During the following night Galba introduced 4,000 Romans into the town. The first knowledge the invaders gained of the presence of the Romans was on the following day, when they tried to provoke a battle with the Eleans. In the ensuing struggle Philip was fortunate to escape with his life. Eventually a successful withdrawal was made to Dyme, during which more plunder was collected;[2] but strategically the expedition had been a failure, for the Aetolian garrison survived intact in Elis, and continued to be a threat to the western border districts of Achaea. In the south, no major action had been attempted against Machanidas, with the result that Achaea was still menaced from three sides: from the south by Machanidas, from the west by the Aetolians at Elis, from the north by the Roman and Pergamene fleets. Soon after Philip's Elean expedition the urgent need to develop the Achaean army and to cease relying on Macedonian aid was further emphasized by Philip's sudden withdrawal from operations in the Peloponnese. News of a fresh Dardanian invasion of Macedon immediately took him to the north. The comparative weakness of his resources is illustrated by the fact that he left only 2,500 *omnis generis armatorum* as protection for Achaea. These were commanded by Menippus and Polyphantas, but were not likely to give much protection against the three-sided threat from Elis, Sparta, and the fleets of Attalus and Rome.[3]

Galba at once took advantage of the Achaean predicament. After Philip's departure the Roman troops were withdrawn from Elis. On their way to Aegina, where they were to spend the winter, they retaliated against Dyme, since it had been used as a base for the Achaean and Macedonian expedition against Elis. The town was attacked and destroyed; and although it was repaired and restored to the Dymaeans on Philip's orders by Polyphantas and Menippus, its destruction was a brutal lesson on the

[1] Liv. xxvii 31. 9–11; Plut. *Phil.* 7. 6–7.
[2] Liv. xxvii. 32. 1 ff.
[3] Liv. xxvii. 32. 10.

inadequacy of relying on Macedonian support.[1] Achaean morale must have recovered a little when, towards the end of the year, Cycliadas won a battle near Messene against the Eleans and Aetolians, probably with the aid of the Macedonian troops.[2] But this small success was cold comfort in view of the ease with which the Romans had swept aside opposition to destroy Dyme. The Achaean cavalry reorganization was clearly only a first step in the right direction. It was far from being enough in itself to provide adequate all-round defence.

Despite the threatening nature of the situation facing Achaea, Philopoemen was not given the opportunity of turning his attention to the infantry section of the Achaean army in the next year, 209/8. Philip's sudden departure had perhaps left his plans for Philopoemen unfulfilled; and Philopoemen could not himself have yet acquired the personal prestige which could dominate the elections. In Philip's absence Nicias, whose background is unknown, was elected *strategos*.[3] But his military ability was no greater than Cycliadas' and events predictably followed the pattern of the previous year: the Aetolians, probably now operating from their base at Elis, were again active, while Machanidas took Tegea and attacked Argos. His success before Argos was so menacing that Nicias did not think of resisting alone: the traditional appeal was therefore at once made to Philip. Philip, as always, was ready to promise help on any appeal—and the

---

[1] The attack on Dyme is only known through later allusions. It has usually been placed in 208 (De Sanctis, *Storia* iii. 2. 427, n. 75; Walbank, *Philip*, p. 98), but the autumn of 209 is perhaps supported by Pausanias vii. 17. 5: ταύτην Φίλιππος ὁ Δημητρίου πολεμῶν μόνην τῶν Ἀχαϊκῶν ἔσχεν ὑπήκοον, καὶ ἐπὶ τῇ αἰτίᾳ ταύτῃ Σουλπίκιος ἡγεμὼν καὶ οὗτος Ῥωμαίων ἐπέτρεψε τῇ στρατιᾷ διαρπάσαι τὴν Δύμην. If this statement represents even part truth, it suggests that there was a close connection between Philip's use of the town and Galba's sacking, and does not conflict with the evidence that Dyme was still in Achaean hands and habitable at the time of Philip's expedition. The only difficulty is in finding a time when Philip could restore the town: he left Achaea after the Elean expedition and did not return until July 208 (Liv. xxviii. 7. 14 f.). Livy (xxxii. 22. 10) implies that the restoration followed soon after the destruction (*captis nuper direptisque*). The probable explanation is that Menippus and Polyphantas were responsible for the restoration on Philip's orders: Philip would still get the credit from the grateful Dymaeans.

[2] Liv. xxvii. 33. 5.

[3] Liv. xxviii. 8. 10. It may conceivably have been illegal for Philopoemen to hold the hipparchy and the *strategia* in successive years, although the evidence is only for iteration of the *strategia* being forbidden (Plut. *Aratus*, 24. 4). Stated as fact by Lehmann, *Glaubwürdigkeit*, p. 208, n. 123.

Achaeans' was not the only appeal to him at this time—but he was fully occupied in dealing with the more urgent threat to his interests from the operations of the Roman and Pergamene fleets in the Aegean. It was therefore already full summer and approaching the time of the Olympic games when he at last found time to move into the Peloponnese. In the meanwhile Achaea had to do her best to defend herself.[1]

In July Machanidas allowed Achaea some temporary relief by turning his attention to Elis, a fact which may reflect some success of Nicias' in repelling him from the Argolid. The Eleans were at that time preparing for the celebration of the Olympic games; and as Machanidas was also a member of the Roman–Aetolian alliance, he was not suspected of being a danger. Machanidas seems to have been dissatisfied with the effect of the Aetolian attacks on Achaea from Elis, and to have considered that he could put the anti-Achaean potential of the base to better effect. For anyone wishing to attack Achaea from the west, Elis was the most convenient base: in order to gain this vantage point Machanidas ignored his ties of friendship with Elis and Aetolia and took advantage of the Eleans' preoccupation with their preparations for the games to attack them.[2] Up to this time Philip had not been in the Peloponnese this year, but Machanidas had underestimated him. At the time of Machanidas' attack on Elis, Philip was at Elatea, again discussing

---

[1] Liv. xxviii. 5. 5. Nothing is known of Tegea between its capture by Antigonus in 223 (Pol. ii. 54. 6–8) and 207, when it was Spartan (Pol. xi. 11. 2). The bronze coins with *AXAIΩN TEΓEATAN* (cf. Head, *Hist. Num.*, p. 418) are undated, and accordingly offer no certain information about this period. This attack of Machanidas on Argos seems the best time for the Spartan capture of Tegea, rather than the autumn. Cf. Walbank, *Philip*, p. 98 and n. 2. The argument of De Sanctis, *Storia* iii. 2. 427, n. 75, that it cannot have been before summer 208 because Philip did not help Achaea recover it, is not persuasive.

[2] Liv. xxviii. 7. 14. Walbank (*Philip*, p. 96 and p. 304, n. 5) suggests that Achaea had gained control of Olympia by this time, and had taken over preparations for the games: Machanidas was therefore attacking *on behalf of* his allies, the Eleans. There is no support in Livy, in a Polybian passage, for this: *Machanidam Olympiorum sollemne ludicrum parantes Eleos adgredi statuisse.* If Walbank were correct, Polybius would have been sure to emphasize that Machanidas was threatening Achaea's right to superintend the games, and this must have been reflected in Livy. Niese's correction of the text (*GGMS* ii. 492, n. 1), *Achaeos* for *Eleos*—which Walbank's suggestion entails—is unnecessary. Machanidas' attack on his friends is quite comprehensible, and should not be explained away: there is probably some party significance, and the parallel with Nabis' attack on friendly Messene in 201 is close. Cf. below, pp. 79–80.

possibilities for general peace. The new threat to Elis affected
him directly, for it threatened his own strongholds at Heraea,
Alipheira, and in Triphylia. The previous year he had failed to
dislodge the Aetolians from Elis; but they were in comparatively
small numbers, and may not have been much more than an
irritant. Machanidas, however, clearly had territorial ambitions.
He was certainly active and powerful, and he had already had
successes against Achaea in southern Arcadia and in the Argolid.
Since he was closer to his seat of power than the Aetolians were
to theirs, his presence at Elis, with troops actively deployed
against Achaea, might ultimately cause the greater part of the
Peloponnese to be lost to Philip. First in the line of attack were
his own border castles. The negotiations at Elatea were therefore
broken off, and Philip hurried to Heraea. When he arrived he
learnt that Machanidas had already been repulsed, and had returned to Sparta. Since there was no advantage to be gained
from remaining at Heraea, he travelled to Aegium, where he
attended an Achaean *synodos*.[1]

Philip's border castles had a dual purpose: to keep Achaea in
place under the Macedonian hegemony, and to preserve the
Achaean borders from external attack. The castles' safety depended ultimately on Philip's readiness and ability to reinforce
the garrisons whenever danger threatened—a readiness which
the continuing conflict with Rome was making progressively
more difficult. Philip had already recognized the vulnerability of
Achaea in the new circumstances when he had supported Philopoemen's cavalry reorganization as a first step towards Achaean
military self-sufficiency. The Aetolian garrison at Elis had clearly
been a threat to the western border castles; Machanidas' attempt
on Elis again emphasized their essential isolation. Philip was
becoming every year more deeply involved in the Roman war,
and the number of his troops committed to garrison duty throughout Greece was in the region of 20,000[2]—clearly a number which
he would benefit from reducing. The protective duty of his
border castles could be replaced by encouraging efficient Achaean
self-defence; the hegemonic aspect of their duty could perhaps
be met by maintaining only the strongest and most central of the

---

[1] Liv. xxviii. 7. 14–17. On the *synodos*, cf. Larsen, *Rep. Gov.*, p. 170.
[2] List of garrisons and figure in Niese, *GGMS* ii. 600, n. 2 (20,000 to 30,000).
Griffith, *Mercenaries*, pp. 71–2, estimates at least 15,000.

castles—Corinth and Orchomenus—provided that the safe-guard was taken of having friendly *strategoi* elected in Achaea. This was the scheme which Philip now proposed to put into action. The hegemonic aspect of his castles must have aroused resistance among patriotic Achaeans, and the defensive aspect had not been prominently effective in recent years. Philip there-fore declared to the *synodos* that he intended to withdraw his garrisons from Heraea, Alipheira, and Triphylia, and restore these places to the Achaeans.[1] The offer was represented as a genuine attempt to give the Achaeans more control over their own affairs, and from the patriotic viewpoint must have been welcome. But it was also an admission of weakness on Philip's part, although he must have hoped that his maintenance of Corinth and Orchomenus would prevent Achaea from taking any great advantage. The necessary safeguard against a successful anti-Macedonian reaction in Achaea was already in existence. The scheme was therefore announced at the *synodos*, but no date was fixed for the withdrawal of the garrisons. Philip typically took advantage of his presence on the Corinthian Gulf to borrow some ships from the Achaeans in order to carry out an attack against southern Aetolia. Nicias accompanied the expedition; and although it was not of any strategic importance, substantial amounts of booty were collected. Philip's aim was, no doubt, that the Achaeans should continue to feel grateful to him for supporting them against Aetolia.[2]

The second safeguard for Philip's position in Achaea was achieved at the autumn *synodos*. Philopoemen was elected *strate-gos*,[3] and he immediately began his major reform of the infantry. Given the association between Philip and Philopoemen during Philopoemen's period in Crete, the fact that Philip had probably supported Philopoemen's election to the hipparchy in 210, and Philip's proposals to withdraw his garrisons, it seems very likely that Philopoemen was again strongly supported by Philip in

---

[1] Liv. xxviii. 8. 1–6. There is a difficulty in this interpretation, for Livy simply says, *reddidit . . . Achaeis* (6). But the cities, then with Orchomenus also, were not in fact handed over until 198 (Liv. xxxii. 5. 4). It seems unlikely that they were handed over in 208, recovered by Philip at some time later, and handed over again in 198. It seems preferable to see the 208 restoration as an unfulfilled promise. Cf. Niese, *GGMS* ii. 492, n. 3; Walbank, *Philip*, pp. 96–7; Aymard, *Premiers Rapports*, p. 59, n. 53; McDonald, O.C.T. *Livy, ad* xxxii. 5. 4.

[2] Liv. xxviii. 8. 7–10.

[3] Cf. appendix 2 B, p. 249.

these elections. The convenience for Philip of Philopoemen's immediate activities substantially supports this conclusion. Philip clearly realized, as he had since at least 210, that Achaea must achieve a measure of military self-sufficiency, for he could not himself guarantee her safety in the new circumstances. Even his garrisons were too isolated to be of much value—and in any case he could no longer afford to squander troops and money unnecessarily. However, if his withdrawal of support caused Achaea to suffer severely, she might join his opponents despite his maintaining garrisons at Corinth and Orchomenus. It was therefore vital that Achaea should become self-sufficient, and that this should be organized by a solidly pro-Macedonian man. Philopoemen had already demonstrated his efficiency, and nothing up to the present time had caused Philip to have any doubts about his loyalty. Philopoemen therefore became *strategos* for 208/7, probably with Philip's full support, almost certainly with a mandate to complete the Achaean army reorganization which he had started in his hipparchy with the cavalry.

It did not take long for Philopoemen to make his intentions clear; and the thoroughness with which he undertook the reform is impressive. Beginning from fundamentals, he scrapped the old equipment—the light but clumsy *thyreos* and short javelin, which had forced the army to fight at long range—and substituted the more solid shield and long *sarisa* of the Macedonian phalanx. In addition—a complete innovation for the Achaean militia—he introduced phalangite helmets, breastplates, and greaves. These provisions removed some of the basic weakness, and transformed the ineffective light-armed militia into a potentially strong army, which could press home an attack without fear of excessive danger to individuals. Philopoemen also made a return to the earlier Achaean practice of hiring mercenaries. It is clear, from the frequency of Achaean appeals to Philip in recent years, that a mercenary corps had ceased to be a permanent part of the Achaean military establishment: this deficiency was now repaired.[1] Once the equipment had been acquired, Philopoemen spoke at a meeting of the League, probably in the spring, and deplored the current decadence and lack of *esprit de corps* of the Achaean infantry—many members of which

---

[1] Plut. *Phil.* 9. 1–7; Paus. viii. 50. 1; cf. Kromayer–Veith, *Heerwesen und Krieg-führung*, pp. 131–2; Niese, *GGMS* ii. 495–8; Anderson, *CPh* 1967, 104–6.

must have been present. He urged a change in attitude. Polybius says that the result was an immediate change of heart among his audience—though this may mean no more than that they expressed willingness to co-operate.[1] The cost of these innovations must have been heavy, and cannot have been borne solely by the individual phalangites. The cost of the mercenaries, in particular, was solely the responsibility of the federal treasury. Yet there is no sign of financial strain in Achaea. A certain amount of money must have accrued from the Elean expedition of Cycliadas and the Aetolian expedition of Nicias, but this cannot have been wholly responsible for the influx of money. Philip cannot have provided any money: for had he been able to afford to supply the Achaean army, he must have been able to afford mercenaries for his garrisons in Achaea. As with the cavalry reorganization, we must look to Philopoemen's public and private earnings as *condottiere* in Crete as a major source of the influx of wealth. This seems to be the only adequate source of wealth available, and it is no accident, for this reason as much as the others, that Philopoemen was the man who was entrusted with the reorganization of both sections of the army.

Philopoemen did not simply trust to re-equipment and speeches to secure efficiency. As with the cavalry, he had to teach the infantry to use their new weapons, and to combine together and with the newly hired mercenaries, before they were ready for battle. Philopoemen spent eight months of his year on this training, visiting the individual cities, teaching and advising. In the spring, the whole army was collected together and put through exercises. When this was done, not only was greater efficiency

---

[1] Pol. xi. 9; Plut. *Phil.* 9. The order of events is that given by Plutarch, as Polybius' account of the rearming is lost (though it must have been before the speech, since the fragment Pol. xi. 9–18. 10, which begins with the speech and continues with the battle of Mantinea, is an unbroken account from the *Excerpta Antiqua*). Since Polybius mentions the new weapons in Philopoemen's speech (xi. 9. 4–5), the speech cannot have been made at the electoral *synodos* in the autumn (as Larsen, *Rep. Gov.*, pp. 170–1). (Larsen claims that he follows Polybius' order of events, which, he says, places Philopoemen's speech before the rearming, rather than Plutarch's, because Plutarch may have made a mistake. But although Polybius' order is not known for certain, the continuity of the fragment in which the speech is followed by the battle of Mantinea suggests that it was probably the same as Plutarch's.) We must conclude with Aymard (*Assemblées*, p. 276, n. 2; cf. p. 301) that it was either a *syncletos* or the spring *synodos* of 207, but not the electoral *synodos* of 208.

achieved, but the morale of the troops was much higher, and Philopoemen considered that it was worth while risking a battle with Machanidas. Machanidas was, this year, the sole problem for Achaea, since the Aetolians were fully occupied by Philip in the north. Philopoemen collected the Achaean army at Mantinea, and Machanidas, eager to accept the offer of a battle, which he had long been trying to provoke, advanced to Tegea. The ensuing battle resulted in a major victory for Philopoemen and his newly trained army. Machanidas pursued the Achaean mercenaries too far when they broke in the early part of the engagement, and returned to find that the rest of his army had been overwhelmed in his absence. The culminating disaster for the tyrant was his inability to break back through the Achaean lines: in attempting this, he was personally opposed by Philopoemen and killed in a hand-to-hand struggle with the Achaean *strategos*.[1]

Philopoemen naturally exploited his success. Immediately after the battle, the Achaean army marched into Tegea, which Machanidas had taken the previous year. From Tegea, Philopoemen advanced into Laconia and allowed his troops to ravage the countryside.[2] The mercenaries expected this licence to supplement their pay, and the Achaeans would be glad to take revenge in kind on Sparta. But there is no indication that Philopoemen had any intention of making Sparta a member of the League. His victory over Machanidas was immediately substantial, but not in the long term overwhelming. He did not, even immediately after the battle, consider himself strong enough to attack the city of Sparta and face Spartan desperation. His decision was clearly right. The rapid emergence of Nabis, backed by a power which maintained him as tyrant for fifteen years, indicates that a formidable section of the Spartan population still considered itself to be undefeated and solidly anti-Achaean. Had Machanidas himself not been killed at Mantinea, the battle would have been little more than a tactical victory for Philopoemen. As it was, it gave him the opportunity of following it up by ravaging Laconia, but not of seeking any kind of permanent settlement, such as he later attempted in 192. In 207 he had no opportunity

---

[1] Pol. xi. 11–18; Plut. *Phil.* 10; Paus. viii. 50. 2. Cf. Kromayer, *Antike Schlach-felder* i. 281–314; Roloff, *Probleme aus der griechischen Kriegsgeschichte*, pp. 116–41.
[2] Pol. xi. 18. 8–10.

for anything more than the immediate enjoyment of his victory, and the creation of a personal reputation for having crushed the traditional enemy of Achaea. The immediate benefits were nevertheless substantial, for the Achaean success at Mantinea coincided with a lessening of Roman interest in the war in Greece. For 207 and 206 the Aetolians were left to bear the brunt of the war effort, since no Roman reinforcements were sent to Greece for these two years.[1] This meant that Achaea was freed from attack by the Aetolians at Elis; and although Nabis must have become tyrant very soon after the death of Machanidas,[2] he was initially too heavily occupied with establishing his claim to power at Sparta to contemplate the immediate resumption of Machanidas' aggressive foreign policy.

Mantinea was an all-Achaean success.[3] Philopoemen's reputation in Achaea was made; Philip's plans had been outstandingly successful. The most obvious immediate result of the battle was the safety of the Achaean border areas from Spartan attack. Sparta was temporarily weakened, and for the moment Achaea was the unquestioned primary power in the Peloponnese. Philopoemen's army reform had, at its first real test, achieved the defeat of the major threat to Achaean safety; Roman lack of interest in the Macedonian war had removed the Aetolian threat; Philip had promised to withdraw his border garrisons. It must have seemed to the Achaeans that a new age of independence was dawning, in which Aratus' first anti-Macedonian strokes towards Achaean independence might be repeated.[4] This new situation of Achaea naturally threw the position of Philip's garrisons into relief. Of their two duties, defence of Achaea from outside danger and oppression of Achaea from inside, only the latter now remained. The significance of this must have been as clear to Philip as to the Achaeans: if his border castles were now evacuated, nothing remained but Corinth and Orchomenus to hold Achaea

---

[1] Liv. xxix. 12. 1: *neglectae eo biennio res in Graecia erant.* Balsdon, *JRS* 1954, 31, points out that this cannot mean that Galba was withdrawn, as his successor was not appointed until late 206 (Liv. xxix. 12. 2; cf. Broughton, *MRR* i, promagistrates for 207 and 206).

[2] Pol. xiii. 6. 1 (204): ἔτος ἤδη τρίτον ἔχων τὴν ἀρχήν. This means that he had established himself by mid-206 at the latest. Cf. Ehrenberg, *RE* xvi. 2. 1471, 'Nabis' (207); Niese, *GGMS* ii. 463–5.

[3] There is no evidence for De Sanctis's improbable assertion (*Storia* iii. 2. 428) that Philopoemen was supported by Macedonian troops.

[4] Cf. Niese, *GGMS* ii. 500.

firmly to alliance with him. While these might be adequate as long as Achaea was permanently weakened by a long-term border war, they could prove insufficient in the new conditions created by the victory at Mantinea, and as a result threaten the whole basis of Philip's power in the Peloponnese.

The garrisons in question were not, in fact, withdrawn until 198, when Orchomenus was also included, but we have no specific information about why or when Philip changed his mind and decided to keep them.[1] It has been suggested that, although Philip had supported Philopoemen in his army reforms, the effect of Philopoemen's success at Mantinea was greater than he had anticipated, and that instead of its simply relieving the pressure on his inadequate resources, it seemed likely to weaken the whole basis of his power in the Peloponnese. In the circumstances, it seems likely that this was the point at which Philip decided that he must retain his border castles. It was the moment when Philopoemen first saw the possibility of achieving Achaean independence, when the hegemonic aspect of Philip's border castles was both more obvious to the Achaeans and more necessary for Philip. Philip's method of recouping the prestige which he would lose by the withdrawal, by supporting Philopoemen and increasing Achaean self-sufficiency, had rebounded by its embarrassing success: it was this success which, in the event, prevented his being able to carry out the withdrawal. The result still cannot have been satisfactory, for his failure to make good his promised withdrawal can only have alienated patriotic Achaeans, who must have been stimulated by Philopoemen's success at Mantinea.

Mantinea was a major blow to Spartan power: 4,000 from the Spartan army had been killed,[2] and when Nabis had established himself as tyrant, he carried out a radical social reform in order to compensate for this loss of man-power. The most noticeable features of his social reorganization were a redistribution of wealth and the down-grading or exile of the traditional aristocracy. Polybius describes these innovations bitterly and abusively, and there can be little doubt that many of his strictures are legitimate.[3] On the other hand, Nabis' success, by whatever means,

[1] Cf. p. 62, n. 1 above.
[2] Pol. xi. 18. 10. The number is perhaps exaggerated, and must certainly include mercenaries and helots; but the loss was heavy.
[3] Pol. xiii. 6–8; cf. xvi. 13. 1–2.

in resuscitating Sparta and holding it securely in his power for fifteen years, deserves more appreciation than Polybius is prepared to give. Nabis was no doubt a tyrant, a complete autocrat; but if his success in his inevitable policy of hostility towards Achaea had not been so outstanding, Polybius' picture of his regime might have been rather different. It was in the propaganda of his opponents that Nabis' despotism became morally unacceptable, primarily because it was politically dangerous. It was politically dangerous in the first place because it was successfully established, and because it was a manifestation of the long-standing Spartan threat to Achaea, just as if Mantinea had not been. In the second place, the regime created exiles. This was morally objectionable on humanistic grounds, in that Greek democracies tended—except in times of *stasis*—to accommodate their opponents if they were willing to come to terms. Polybius' objection to Nabis is partly an expression of his dislike of this aspect of nakedly oligarchic or autocratic systems. But the exiles were also an immediate political problem for Achaea, and this has clearly sharpened Polybius' acrimony. For the problem of the resettlement of the Spartan exiles was the major issue in Achaean politics in the years following the death of Nabis and the incorporation of Sparta in the League.[1] Nabis' regime, therefore, was doubly detestable.

In 206 Philip brought his war with the Aetolians, who had become weary of waiting for Roman support, to an end *quibus voluit condicionibus*.[2] Appian records the presence of Galba at the meeting of the Aetolians in 206, at which it was decided to make peace with Philip. He tried to oppose the motion accepting the peace, but was shouted down.[3] There could be no doubt that the Aetolians were war-weary and felt disappointed by the recent inadequacy of Roman support. Philip grasped his opportunity of disrupting the ranks of his opponents by making peace with Aetolia. There is very little information in the sources about this peace, which the Romans opposed; but Philip's allies, including Achaea, must have participated in it, as must also the Greek allies of the Aetolians. This had the effect of returning the war to the situation in which it had been before the Roman alliance with Aetolia in 211: the two protagonists, Philip and Rome,

[1] Cf. below, chapters VII, VIII, IX, X, *passim*.
[2] Liv. xxix. 12. 1.
[3] App. *Mac.* 3.

were still enemies and still at war, but Rome was now again
without effective allies.[1]

Even before the peace of 206 the Senate seems to have been
impressed by Aetolian war-weariness, for it mounted a large
expedition of 10,000 infantry, 1,000 cavalry, and 35 ships, which
had already set out when the news arrived at Rome that the
Aetolians had made peace independently. This renewed Roman
activity was clearly a tardy attempt to show that the neglect
of the eastern theatre in the previous two years had not been
the result of any essential lessening of Roman interest in the
war. Philip was still the enemy, and the Senate could not easily
acquiesce, for prestige reasons, in the war's simply petering out,
without first making a demonstration of power. P. Sempronius Tuditanus arrived at Dyrrhachium at the end of 206 with
the new Roman forces. But events of the year offered no advantage to either side: the Romans were unwilling to carry on the
war without allies, and broke the deadlock by opening negotiations which led to the peace of Phoenice. There is no need here
for a discussion of the signatories of the peace. It is enough to
notice the effects of it on the Peloponnesian situation: Achaea
was *adscripta* on Philip's side—as we would expect—and on the
Roman side were Elis, Messene, and Nabis.[2] For Achaea this
formally marked the end of the war with Rome, which had not,
in fact, affected her greatly since 208. The aspects of the general
conflict which had affected her most at the height of the war
had already been removed before the final peace was made at
Phoenice: the threat from Sparta had been temporarily destroyed
by Philopoemen's victory at Mantinea; the threat from the
Aetolian establishment at Elis had been removed by Aetolian
war-weariness which culminated in the peace of 206.

---

[1] Cf. Walbank, *Philip*, pp. 99–101; De Sanctis, *Storia* iii. 2. 431–2; Niese,
GGMS ii. 500–1.

[2] Liv. xxix. 12. 3–7; cf. Walbank, *Philip*, pp. 102–3 (events of war). Liv. xxix.
12. 13–14 (terms of peace). A convenient bibliography and discussion in Balsdon,
JRS 1954, 30–4, whose argument for accepting Elis, Messenia, and Nabis seems
acceptable. Cf. Badian, *For. Cl.*, pp. 59–60.

V

THE NEW PATRIOTISM

I

AFTER Mantinea Philopoemen adopted the achievement of Achaean independence, which Philip had initially encouraged, as an active policy. This brought him into conflict with Philip and eventually induced him to look to Rome as Achaea's most likely ally when the Second Macedonian War was on the point of breaking out. Before we examine in detail the chronology of this change between 207 and 200, it is necessary to demonstrate that the change in policy was real and did actually occur.

The first evidence is Philip's attempted murder of Philopoemen, which is alleged by Plutarch. The account is undated, but the context places it around 205: 'Philip thought that if Philopoemen were removed, the Achaeans would again cower before him. He therefore sent men secretly to Argos to assassinate him. But when his plan was discovered he was wholeheartedly hated and scorned among the Greeks.'[1] Pausanias has virtually the same account.[2] Plutarch's interpretation of the attempt in this passage, that Philip wanted to curb Philopoemen's insistence on Achaean independence, suits the present thesis admirably. If Philip was prepared to go to the length of organizing the political assassination of Philopoemen, we must surely conclude with Plutarch that Philopoemen was following a policy not only of Achaean self-sufficiency but also of anti-Macedonian independence. But the matter is more complicated, for some considerations suggest that Plutarch's account of the attempted murder may be merely an unsubstantiated allegation.

In the first place, Philip showed very little interest in Achaea between his decision to maintain his border garrisons in 207 and

---

[1] Plut. *Phil.* 12. 2.
[2] Paus. viii. 50. 4 (who rationalizes, and puts the attempt at Megalopolis, Philopoemen's home city); cf. Justin xxix. 4. 11.

the renewed threat of Roman intervention in 200.[1] In itself, this is far from conclusive, for source material is fragmentary. But the fact remains that the major object of Philip's attention in these years was his attempt to expand his power and influence in the Aegean and in Anatolia, and to this aim Achaea was peripheral. The second consideration is that Philip was frequently charged with murder—so much so that Flamininus joked about it when he conferred with Philip at Nicaea in 198.[2] The joke was, no doubt, intended to refer to the habit of judicially murdering embarrassing individuals, endemic in the Hellenistic monarchies. But rumours were also current of simple political assassinations.[3] The records of these are uniformly preserved from hostile non-Macedonian sources, and in every case the evidence is such that it arouses strong suspicions that the allegations are the fabrications of hostile contemporaries. Suspicion might be even stronger in the case of Philopoemen, where the account is only of *attempted* assassination. But suspicions do not constitute solid evidence.[4]

However, the implications of the possible falsity of Plutarch's information must be explored further. Whether true or false, Plutarch must have taken his account from Polybius, and therefore it must in the first instance have come from Philopoemen himself. If it is false it can have entered the tradition in one of three ways. It may have been Philopoemen's propaganda, a complete fabrication aimed solely at discrediting Philip: but strongly against this is the difficulty of making such an accusation stick without either evidence or witnesses. We can therefore have some confidence that there was some actual occurrence which was interpreted in this way by the original of Plutarch's account. An actual attempt on Philopoemen's life could be interpreted in two ways to produce the account which Plutarch gives: either as a conscious distortion of an attempt in which Philip was not, in fact, implicated; or as the result of a sincere belief that Philip might attack him in this way. But these three interpretations all have a

---

[1] On Philip's activities during these years, cf. Walbank, *Philip*, pp. 108 ff.

[2] Pol. xviii. 7. 6.

[3] A list of Philip's alleged murder victims has been collected by Walbank, *CQ* 1943, 4, n. 3.

[4] Walbank, *CQ* 1943, and *Philip*, p. 124, n. 6, notes rightly that the source of the tradition must be contemporary, and calls it untrustworthy; but he does not argue the point.

similar significance for our purpose, for all equally imply that
at this time hostility existed between Philip and Philopoemen.
The second piece of evidence for Philopoemen's anti-Macedonian position after Mantinea is his association with Aristaenus.
Aristaenus during his *strategia* in 199/8 was responsible for exiling
Cycliadas, the leader of the Achaean pro-Macedonian party, and
for breaking off Achaea's alliance with Macedon and forming
one with Rome.[1] These facts allow no other interpretation than
that Aristaenus—for whatever reason—was anti-Macedonian
and pro-Roman at that time. His association with Philopoemen
is not usually demonstrated. The reason for the obscurity of the
close relationship between the two men in this period is that
later—after the wars with Philip and Antiochus—they were
opposed on points of principle connected with their interpretation of the Achaean *foedus* with Rome. This later opposition
crystallized in the tradition—starting with a misinterpretation
of Polybius[2]—and was reflected back into the earlier period.
We therefore find in Plutarch the incomprehensible picture of
Aristaenus helping Philopoemen in a personal matter of some
importance, although, Plutarch says, he differed from him politically.[3] The circumstances of this vital episode are as follows. When
Philopoemen returned to Crete in 200, Megalopolis was bearing
the brunt of the Achaean war with Nabis. The dominant Megalopolitan view of Philopoemen's absence was that he was deserting
his native city just at that time when his help was most needed.
It was therefore formally proposed to the Megalopolitans—no
doubt by personal opponents—that he should be exiled. Plutarch
then continues: 'The Achaeans stopped them by sending the

---

[1] Liv. xxxii. 19. 2.

[2] Cf. Pol. xxiv. 11. 3. Prima facie this refers only to the time of the wars with
Philip and Antiochus, i.e. after Philopoemen had left for Crete in 200 and after
his return. Cf. chapter XII, pp. 218 ff.

[3] Plut. *Phil.* 13. 4. Most modern scholars accept this assessment without examination: e.g. Niese, *GGMS* ii. 616, n. 1; De Sanctis, *Storia* iv. 1. 57; Niccolini, *La Conf.
Ach.*, p. 121. Aymard, *Premiers Rapports*, p. 47, n. 79, almost recognizes the in-
congruity, but defers to the solidity of the tradition. Lehmann, *Glaubwürdigkeit*,
p. 212, n. 131, attributes this information to Aristocrates of Sparta (with Nissen,
Krit. Unt., pp. 283–7), and says it is worthless. Nothing in Plutarch's account, in
fact, suggests Aristocrates as source here; and there is no reason why he should
have been. However, even if Nissen and Lehmann are correct in their unsupported
hypothesis, and Aristocrates was Plutarch's source here, his information cannot be
disregarded out of hand for this reason alone, when it seems reliable and is easily
explicable. Cf. chapter VIII, p. 145, n. 1.

strategos Aristaenus; and although he differed from Philopoemen on matters of policy, he did not allow the sentence to be executed.' Aristaenus was *strategos*, and although he intervened with the support of a federal decree, it is inconceivable that he would have done so had he not wanted to. And he cannot have been prepared to initiate extravagant federal action to preserve Philopoemen's civil rights in Megalopolis if he was opposed to him at this crucial time: for Aristaenus was quite prepared to exile an illustrious opponent, such as Cycliadas. Philopoemen therefore would not merit such federal intervention on his behalf by Aristaenus unless he was his close associate.

A further—and earlier—association of the two men can also probably be shown.[1] Some manuscripts of Polybius cite an Aristaenus—almost certainly this man—as hipparch at the battle of Mantinea in 207.[2] While this identification adds nothing to our knowledge of Philopoemen's disposition with regard to Macedon or Rome, it seems reasonable to conclude that the collegiality of Philopoemen and Aristaenus in 208/7 suggests that they also shared similar political views. We have argued that the elections for 208/7 were dominated by the *auctoritas* of Philip, who wanted Philopoemen to reorganize the Achaean infantry. If this is acceptable, the conclusion must be that Aristaenus also shared the support of Philip in 208. The implication of this is that Philopoemen was not alone in his defection from Macedon between his success at Mantinea and the outbreak of the Second Macedonian War, but was closely connected with Aristaenus throughout this period.

The third piece of evidence which demonstrates that Philopoemen was anti-Macedonian in 200, and therefore, in the circumstances of the time, pro-Roman, is his departure for Crete in 200/199. It has already been shown that Philopoemen's activity in Crete was probably connected with the Achaean war against Nabis,[3] but the events which caused his departure must be elucidated. The date and circumstances are discussed by Plutarch: 'Because he was then fighting against Cretans as a general overseas, he provided accusations against himself for his enemies, that he was running away from the war at home. But there were

---

[1] Full discussion of this in appendix 4, pp. 276 ff.

[2] Pol. xi. 11. 7; cf. Niccolini, *SSAC* 1913, 194 ff.; below, appendix 4, pp. 276 ff.

[3] Cf. chapter III, pp. 34 f.; Dubois, *Ligues étolienne et achaienne*, p. 74; Niccolini, *La Conf. Ach.*, p. 122, n. 1.

some who said that, since the Achaeans chose others as magistrates (ἄρχοντας), Philopoemen found himself without office, and simply used his leisure to meet the requirement of the Gortynians for a military leader. For he was averse to idleness and wished to keep his military skill, like any other possession, constantly in use and exercise.'[1] The accusation of his enemies is incredible: Philopoemen was a distinguished mercenary soldier and engaged in fighting in Crete. Clearly he would not simply run away from military activity. The other reason which Plutarch gives for his absence, however, is more fruitful and can be substantiated. Its implication is that this was the version preferred by his friends as a counter to the local accusation of his enemies of his abandoning Megalopolis. The point of the discussion in this case is not concerned with his political position in Achaea, but with his local position in Megalopolis: therefore it could be said, without losing face, that Philopoemen was simply using his involuntary leisure in Crete. The vague information about the events which caused this leisure may therefore be trustworthy.

Philopoemen went to Crete because (or simply 'when') the Achaeans chose others as ἄρχοντες.[2] This statement is valuable both for the date it provides and for the information it gives about the reasons for his departure. Philopoemen was *strategos* in 201/0, and was succeeded by Cycliadas (200/199) and Aristaenus (199/8).[3] If we are to take a secure date from Plutarch's statement that Philopoemen was without office and that he disliked idleness, the election of ἄρχοντες which he mentions must refer to Cycliadas' year or, at the very outside, to Aristaenus'. Aymard has already pointed out that ἄρχοντες need not mean *strategoi*, and therefore that Philopoemen's having left Achaea in 200/199 (Cycliadas' year) need not conflict with Plutarch on this detail.[4] But in itself this possibility does not constitute proof that he actually did leave at this time. However, if it is taken closely together with the fact that Philopoemen and Aristaenus were close political associates at the time, it becomes conclusive. For the election of Aristaenus in autumn 199 must be regarded as a victory for Philopoemen's party and policy, and would

---

[1] Plut. *Phil.* 13. 2–3; cf. Paus. viii. 50. 6.
[2] Plut. *Phil.* 13. 2: ἑτέρους τῶν Ἀχαιῶν ᾑρημένων ἄρχοντας.
[3] Cf. appendix 2 B, pp. 250–1.
[4] Aymard, *Premiers Rapports*, pp. 45 f. and n. 70 (and bibliography).

certainly not have the effect of giving him the leisure to leave Achaea and to fight in Crete. Philopoemen's departure for Crete was therefore certainly during the *strategia* of Cycliadas.

If Aristaenus' political success would have prevented Philopoemen from leaving Achaea, his association with Philopoemen and hostility to Cycliadas suggest that Cycliadas' election was the reason for Philopoemen's departure. Cycliadas was last mentioned by the sources during his *strategia* in 210/09 when Philopoemen was hipparch, and in 200 he was still strongly in favour of Achaea's alliance with Macedon. Opposition to Cycliadas therefore implied opposition to Macedon; and in the circumstances of the time opposition to Macedon entailed friendliness towards Rome: there was no room for neutrality. The most satisfactory conclusion therefore seems to be that Philopoemen's departure for Crete took place in 200/199, and that it was motivated by the election of his opponent Cycliadas as *strategos*. It again demonstrates conclusively that Philopoemen can no longer have supported the Achaean alliance with Macedon.

II

In the light of the change in Philopoemen's political position between his success at Mantinea and his departure for Crete in 200, an interpretation of the other known events of this period can now be offered. Philopoemen's success at Mantinea did more than simply destroy the threat to Achaea from Machanidas: it also revealed the possibility of creating a new independent Achaean power in the Peloponnese. Philip showed that he had realized the significance of Philopoemen's victory when he decided to keep his border castles, which he had previously offered to vacate. But this decision could not in itself depress Achaean morale to its feeble state before Mantinea. Philip himself had begun the discussions about the castles when he was hard-pressed in his war with Rome, and the movement towards self-sufficiency in Achaea—which he had initially encouraged—must have reacted unfavourably to his revoking his decision to evacuate them. From this point it was not a large step to contracting feelings of positive hostility towards Philip and the Macedonian hegemony. By 205 the Achaean independence movement had already attracted substantial support. In 206/5 Philopoemen was *strategos* for the second time, and at the Nemea in the summer of 205 he paraded his victorious Achaean troops to scenes of almost hysterical acclaim.[1]

In order to appreciate the full significance of this Achaean hysteria, it must be remembered that the Nemea was held at Argos. At Argos there was traditionally strong support for the Macedonian kings, which Philip in particular had cultivated by frequent attendance at the Nemea. Philopoemen's popular reception, therefore, must have seemed to a Macedonian sympathizer to be, in a sense, a usurpation of Philip's almost traditional honours at that festival. Moreover, Philopoemen's ovation was shared by the Achaean troops, who had gloriously saved their country by their successful battle without aid from Macedon, and who had become the symbol of resurgent Achaean efficiency and nationalism. This was a sharp contrast with the previous ineffective feebleness of the Achaean army, which had even made it necessary for Philip to abandon his celebrations as recently as the Nemea of 209 in order to repel a Roman attack.[2] The popular encouragement shown by this ostentatiously patriotic reception could only serve to confirm Philopoemen in his claim to Achaean independence from the Macedonian hegemony. Philip's offer to vacate the border castles in 208 in a moment of crisis had demonstrated that he felt no sentimental attachment to Achaea. He had encouraged Achaean military efficiency and Philopoemen had taken him at his word. After Mantinea Philopoemen wanted to exploit the new effectiveness of the Achaean army as a means of attaining a form of Achaean independence within the Peloponnese. Philip, on the other hand, simply wanted to put the clock back to the earlier period of unquestioned Macedonian hegemony, but without the accompanying disadvantage of Achaean military weakness. But he could not have it both ways, and the damage had already been done: Philopoemen's success in his independent Achaean action at Mantinea was clearly supported by the large numbers of Achaeans who greeted him at the Nemea in 205. Philip had shown bluntly that Macedonian interest alone ruled his relationship with Achaea: Philopoemen was now in a position in which he was prepared to show that Achaean interest, and Achaean interest alone, should rule Achaea's relationship with Macedon.

[1] Plut. *Phil.* 11.   [2] See above, p. 57.

Probably in the same year, 205, Megara was reunited with the League.[1] From the point of view of Philopoemen's nationalistic desire for Achaean expansion and independence, Megara was an important gain for Achaea, since it controlled the passage through the Isthmus. But it was also a useful propaganda gain, if Philopoemen wished to gain widespread support for his policy of emphasizing the desirability of reunifying the independent Achaea of the period before the war with Cleomenes. For this was the period of Achaean independence and freedom from the shackles of the Macedonian hegemony. The emphasis placed by the new accession of Megara on the conditions of this early period of the League must inevitably have produced the effect of further drawing attention to Philip's current disregard for Achaean feelings by continuing forcibly to maintain his hegemony over Achaea with his garrisons.

The independence at which Philopoemen aimed did not yet develop into a doctrinaire nationalism. A solid practical interest was added to his nationalism, which gave practical application to his policy. Philip had encouraged the Achaeans to defend themselves against Sparta; but despite their success at Mantinea, the threat from Sparta continued. While Philopoemen had been engaged in activities in Achaea which provided him with support for establishing a less close relationship with Macedon, Nabis had been consolidating his position in Sparta. By 204 he possessed a mercenary army, recruited in Crete as a result of close ties which he had established with Cnossos and other Cretan cities;[2] and he felt strong enough at Sparta to begin to make use of it abroad. The first move for an expansionist Sparta was traditionally towards the north, in particular against southern Arcadia. Nabis was no exception, and he now began to look for

---

[1] Plut. *Phil.* 12. 3; cf. Paus. viii. 50. 5; Pol. xx. 6. 7–8. The date is uncertain, and has been variously placed in Philopoemen's *strategiai* of 193/2, 201/0, and 206/5 (although it is not, in fact, certain that Philopoemen was *strategos*: Plutarch's anecdote only implies that the Boeotians thought he was). Aymard, *Premiers Rapports*, p. 14, n. 7, argues persuasively from Plutarch's order of events for 206/5. Cf. Niccolini, *La Conf. Ach.*, p. 106; Walbank, *Philip*, p. 165 (also 206/5). Niese, *GGMS* ii. 567, n. 2 (201/0). Beloch, *GG* iv. 2. 434; Meyer, *RE* xv. 196, 'Megara'; Lehmann, *Glaubwürdigkeit*, p. 334, n. 6 (193/2). Also possible is Philopoemen's uncertain *strategia* of 204/3 or 203/2 (cf. appendix 2 B, p. 250 and *strategos*-list), which is not ruled out by Aymard's argument. Since this is so uncertain, 206/5 is tentatively accepted here, although 204/3 or 203/2 would not radically affect the interpretation.

[2] See above, ch. III, pp. 34 f.

a *casus belli* with Achaea: in 204 he found it. Some Boeotian travellers had rested at Sparta, and before they left persuaded one of Nabis' grooms to defect and accompany them. He agreed and took with him the best horse from Nabis' stables. In itself, this did not have the makings of an international incident. But the sequel involved Achaea: the men had already reached Megalopolis before they were caught by the Spartan pursuit party. The Spartans naturally demanded that the alleged thieves be handed over, but were met with a point-blank refusal from the Megalopolitans. Megalopolis was naturally hostile towards a resurgent Sparta, and she was in any case under no obligation to hand over the fugitives who had sought asylum there.[1] Nabis did not need to take public offence at the Megalopolitan refusal unless he wanted to; and if he wanted to be provocative, a policy of appeasement by Megalopolis would not significantly delay the outbreak of hostilities. Nabis chose to regard the refusal as a sufficient pretext for an attack on Megalopolitan territory, which consisted of a raid on an outlying farm. It is not clear whether the pretext was engineered by Nabis—if so Polybius might have been expected to mention it—or whether he simply took advantage of the opportunity which was offered. In any case the slightness of the pretext makes it quite clear that he intended to provoke a war with Achaea.[2] The brief period of freedom from attack by Sparta, won for Achaea by Philopoemen's victory at Mantinea, was over. The new tyrant had established himself, and a situation as dangerous as that before Mantinea now existed. Another opportunity for the continuing practical application of Achaea's military self-sufficiency would easily be found.

The war, still undeclared by Achaea,[3] continued intermittently for the next two years, 203 and 202. No information about its events is extant, and as a result it is probably justifiable to conclude that no significant advantage was won by either side. Even Philopoemen, who was probably *strategos* for either 204/3 or

---

[1] A further factor may have been federal considerations. Since the re-accession of Megara, Achaea shared a frontier with Boeotia. It was therefore in her interest to preserve as friendly relations as possible with Boeotia.

[2] Pol. xiii. 8. 3–7. Polybius' comment (7) that Nabis had for some time been looking for an excuse to attack Achaea is entirely convincing.

[3] The formal declaration of war was not carried until the end of 200 (Liv. xxxi. 25. 3–4).

203/2,[1] must have failed to make any significant impression. If both sides were content to occupy themselves with border raids—a state of affairs suggested by the Achaeans' failure to declare war formally until 200—there could, by the very nature of the war, be very little advantage gained by either side. However, during the course of Lysippus' *strategia* in 202/1 Nabis altered his tactics. He determined to change the nature and direction of the war by striking out for a larger and firmer base of operations in the southern Peloponnese from which he could more easily attack Achaea. Following the example of Machanidas' attack on friendly Elis in 208, he launched an attack on Messene, probably with the support of the anti-Achaean party within the city.

At first he met little resistance, since he was formally an ally, attack from whom would be unexpected, and in his first approach he gained control of the whole city with the exception of Ithome. Philopoemen immediately recognized the danger to Achaea which was implicit in Sparta's possession of Messene: this would particularly affect Megalopolis, which must already have borne the brunt of the undeclared war. When Philopoemen urged Lysippus to send federal forces to prevent Nabis from occupying the whole of Messene, Lysippus was more concerned to reflect shortsightedly that Messene had joined Aetolia in 211 and had remained a member of the hostile alliance until 205. Lysippus clearly cannot have appreciated the danger to Achaea as a whole from Sparta's possession of Messene. To him it did not seem serious enough to make it worth his while bestowing the prestige of his office on an unsolicited and unapproved expedition to aid a recent enemy. In strict law, he had ample excuse for refusing Philopoemen's request. No source mentions that any faction among the Messenians formally appealed to Achaea: Plutarch states simply that Philopoemen took the initiative in urging Achaean intervention.[2] Philopoemen may, with some justification, have anticipated factional support in Messene for action against Nabis' attempted coup; but Lysippus as federal *strategos* could not legitimately interfere in the affairs of another sovereign state without receiving an appeal from some faction. At the same time, Achaea was not formally at war with Nabis. Therefore federal intervention was doubly illegitimate.

Philopoemen, however, decided to take private action. He held

---

[1] Cf. appendix 2 B, p. 250.   [2] Plut. *Phil.* 12. 4.

no federal office, therefore was not prevented from acting by any federal scruples. He could command no federal forces, but he had no difficulty in raising a force from Megalopolis, with which he marched to Messene. The threat to Achaea from Nabis' possession of Messene naturally appeared more realistic at Megalopolis than at Aegium: the proximity of the danger made action which the federal authorities considered unnecessary and illegitimate both vital and equitable. This was not the first time a sectional interest in Achaea had taken its protection into its own hands when it became clear that the federal authorities were incompetent or unwilling.[1] Nor was it the first time that a close relationship between Messene and Megalopolis had proved mutually beneficial: the refuge which the Messenians had offered to the Megalopolitans in 223, under a reversal of the present conditions, could not have been forgotten by Philopoemen.[2] Nabis was surprised by the arrival of the Megalopolitans; the anti-Spartan Messenians rallied, and as Philopoemen entered one gate, Nabis escaped from the opposite gate. There was little fighting, if we are to believe Polybius, who must be Plutarch's source; and it seems likely that Nabis, who had clearly overestimated the strength of his support within Messene, did not want to risk his forces in an encounter in which he was likely to be beaten. The arrival of Philopoemen and his Megalopolitans had prevented him from capitalizing on his initial success.[3]

The success of Philopoemen's unofficial action against Nabis must have increased his popularity in Achaea, for he was elected *strategos* for 201/0. The critical issue remained Sparta; and since Philip was fully occupied elsewhere, Achaea could be justly grateful to Philopoemen. He must have been successful enough against Nabis for it to be unnecessary for him to insist on a formal declaration of war by a federal *syncletos*, since this did not happen until the next year.[4] But his Megalopolitan origins made him take care to prevent the continuation of Nabis' attacks. He, as well as Nabis, had his Cretan connections, and he made use of them against Nabis in 200.[5] He had no scruples about striking at

---

[1] In 219 Dyme, Pharae, and Tritaea had decided to care for their own interests: Pol. iv. 60.   [2] See above, ch. II, pp. 14 f.

[3] Pol. xvi. 13. 3; Plut. *Phil.* 12. 4–5; Paus. viii. 50. 5. Cf. Niese, *GGMS* ii. 566; Niccolini, *La Conf. Ach.*, p. 109.   [4] Liv. xxxi. 25. 3–4.

[5] Didascalondas the Cretan (and probably others): Pol. xvi. 37. 3; cf. Ditt. *Syll.* 600, and appendix 2 B, p. 253.

Nabis without a formal declaration of war, and a cutting-out expedition, in which his Cretans took part, against some of Nabis' mercenaries at Pellana was so successful that Nabis waited until Philopoemen had ended his *strategia* before he started any further attacks on Achaea. Polybius gives a detailed description of the impressive way in which this expedition was assembled in secrecy before the attack. But his admiration does not reflect any major importance of the expedition itself: it is directed solely towards the technical competence which Philopoemen displayed in carrying out the complicated arrangements. Apart from this technical interest, the expedition was no more than an example of Philopoemen's continuing the war of local border raids. The only development was that Achaean retaliation was now placed on a federal basis.[1] Although the expedition was not sufficiently important to make it necessary to declare war, its success was startling in keeping Nabis quiet for the remainder of the year. Nabis was no hothead, and his two recent experiences of Philopoemen's energy and efficiency were sufficient to make him decide to wait until Philopoemen had been replaced in the *strategia* before he continued his plundering raids on Megalopolis and southern Arcadia in general. In the long term, Philopoemen's successes in quietening Nabis had little effect on the course of the war, but merely served to lull the Achaeans into a false sense of security.

It has already been noticed that Cycliadas was elected *strategos* in autumn 200 as Philopoemen's successor, and that as a result Philopoemen left Achaea for Crete. Philopoemen was, at this time, a political associate of Aristaenus, who shared his anti-Macedonianism and his friendliness towards Rome in 199. He was therefore in opposition to Cycliadas. Cycliadas' election, in fact, must have constituted a major defeat for Philopoemen and Aristaenus. The main problem about the election is to explain the political circumstances in which it became possible. Philopoemen was *strategos* in 201/0 and had some success against Nabis. This, in the normal course of events, should have been sufficient to secure the election of one of his associates as *strategos* for 200/199 —Aristaenus, for instance, was available and eligible. The other events of Philopoemen's *strategia* must therefore be examined in the light of this problem.

[1] Pol. xvi. 36–7; cf. Niese, *GGMS* ii. 566.

In spring 200, the Roman propaganda mission, which the Senate had decided to send to Greece when it determined on war with Philip, visited Aegium. The members were C. Claudius Nero, M. Aemilius Lepidus, and P. Sempronius Tuditanus, whose main purpose was to seduce Philip's Greek allies and to confirm the friendship of those states which had supported Rome in the previous war.[1] The ambassadors had already visited the Epirots, Amynander of Athamania, and the Aetolians *en route* from Italy. Before travelling from Naupactus to Athens, where they had arranged to meet Attalus, they crossed the Gulf of Corinth to visit the Achaeans at Aegium. In each place they visited their propaganda was based on the claim that Philip must 'make war on none of the Greeks'.[2] The motif appeared mild enough: the Romans (unasked, except by Rhodes and Attalus, who had suffered from Philip's activities in the Aegean) were announcing their general Protectorate of the Hellenes. The implication was that if Philip were willing to allow Greece to become a Roman protectorate without fighting for his hegemony—conditions which were clearly impossible for Philip to accept—war would be unnecessary.[3] Essentially benevolent in tone to the Greeks, the mission and its message were generally well received by the states it visited.

In Achaea Philopoemen was *strategos* when the ambassadors arrived at Aegium. Since Mantinea he had relied on the strength of the Achaean army to make plausible his claim that the Achaeans should adopt an attitude of independence from Philip, as far as the continued presence of the Macedonian garrisons allowed. In these circumstances the Roman propaganda motif was eminently suitable. The ambassadors' message, that Philip should stop making war on the Greeks, can only have produced an immediately sympathetic reaction in Philopoemen. For although the immediate points of reference in the Roman

[1] Cf. Broughton, *MRR* i. 321 and 322, n. 4 for references.

[2] Pol. xvi. 27. 2: τῶν μὲν Ἑλλήνων μηδενὶ πολεμεῖν.

[3] On the Roman propaganda, cf. Badian, *For. Cl.*, pp. 62 ff.; *Studies*, pp. 22–3. On the chronology and the purpose of the embassy, cf. McDonald and Walbank, *JRS* 1937, 189 f.; Walbank, *Philip*, pp. 313–17. The detailed problems concerning chronology and Roman policy in the years preceding the Second Macedonian War cannot be treated here: in addition to the works already cited, cf. Petzold, *Eröffnung*; Stier, *Roms Aufstieg*, pp. 87 ff.; Ferro, *Le origini della II guerra macedonica*. McDonald's review of Ferro, op. cit., in *JRS* 1963, 187 ff., contains a valuable statement of the nature of the problems and a summary of proposed explanations.

statement were clear enough in Philip's attacks on Pergamum, Rhodes, and Athens, the general implications suited his
own policy admirably. There is no evidence that his anti-
Macedonianism—shown by the alleged murder attempt—had
yet turned to pro-Romanism: there was no reason why it should
have. Yet Aristaenus in 199/8 was fully committed to joining
Rome in the new war against Philip. The most economical interpretation of the available evidence is that Philopoemen's and
Aristaenus' anti-Macedonianism first turned towards Rome
when this Roman propaganda mission called at Aegium in 200,
for this was the earliest time that the Romans and the Philopoemenists can have discovered that they shared a common
anti-Macedonianism.

For the moment there was no possibility of Achaea's taking
action against Philip, even with the promise of Roman support:
the Macedonian garrisons held Achaea by the throat. Moreover,
it was by no means certain that a majority of the Achaeans would
support a move towards finally abandoning the Macedonian
alliance, despite Philopoemen's personal influence. The positive
aspect of Philopoemen's policy—the assertion of Achaean power
in the Peloponnese against Sparta and of Achaea's right to take
independent action—was recognized as patriotic and desirable,
as his reception at the Nemea in 205 adequately shows. The
negative aspect—the anti-Macedonian aspect, which was a
natural growth from the other—was more revolutionary, more
dangerous to put into practice, and therefore less easy to demonstrate as being desirable for Achaea. The independence which
Philopoemen had achieved up to this time had been exercised
within the limits imposed by the Macedonian hegemony: it
seemed to be safe, and had, in the first instance, been encouraged
by Philip. The step now envisaged was incomparably larger, and
accordingly could be expected to attract less support. Most
Achaeans can have had little conception of the disparity between
the power of Rome and that of Macedon: even after most of the
Macedonian garrisons had been removed and at a time when
the Roman allies were blockading Corinth in 198, Aristaenus had
difficulty in obtaining a majority for his proposal to abandon the
Macedonian alliance and to join Rome.[1] But the formation of
a mildly pro-Roman group in Achaea, centred on Philopoemen

[1] Liv. xxxii. 19–23. 3.

and Aristaenus, seems likely to have taken its origin from the appearance of the Roman propaganda mission at Aegium in 200. This clearly was not a group of pro-Roman quislings. It must have been rather a group which was, at this stage, prepared to give a cautious welcome to Roman expressions of interest in Greek affairs, interest which happened to have features in common with the policy which the group had independently evolved. Philopoemen's partial achievement of Achaean independence had naturally led him to anti-Macedonianism: in this the interests of Rome coincided with his. It would not therefore be unexpected if an element of friendliness to Rome should, in the present circumstances, take its place in the policies of the Achaean independence party.[1]

If the presence of this Roman mission at Aegium in 200 was, in fact, the point of origin of the Achaean pro-Roman party, this will shed light on the circumstances of Cycliadas' election. If Philopoemen and Aristaenus at this point formed a policy which envisaged the possibility of Achaean co-operation with Rome against Philip, the form of their propaganda must have changed to suit this new development in their policy: they will not have simply kept quiet about their proposed *entente* with Rome. Cycliadas, on the other hand, was famous for only one thing: for being head of the pro-Macedonian party in Achaea.[2] And we must assume that it was this dominant feature of his political character which caused his election. The conflict between the new Philopoemenist policy and Cycliadas' traditionalism is obvious, and Cycliadas' success in the elections indicates that the new Philopoemenist policy was beaten conclusively—to the extent that Philopoemen was not prepared to continue living in Achaea with the notoriety of defeat hanging over him. Aristaenus, however, stayed in Achaea and braved the defeat. Whether he simply

[1] Aymard *Premiers Rapports*, p. 47, n. 79, suggests that Philopoemen was aiming at neutrality, (cf. Niccolini, *La Conf. Ach.*, p. 119; Hoffmann, *RE* xx. 1. 83, 'Philopoimen'). He is led to this by his failure to recognize the closeness of Aristaenus and Philopoemen. He therefore denies that Philopoemen can have contemplated an *entente* with Rome. Yet this seems to be the only satisfactory conclusion from the facts of his association with Aristaenus and his virtual exile in Crete. Justin (xxix. 4. 11), though confused in detail, may preserve the remains of an original statement of Polybius' to this effect: *Philopoemeni, Achaeorum duci, quem ad Romanos sociorum animos sollicitare didicerat, insidias praetendit* sc. *Philippus. Quibus ille cognitis vitatisque desciscere ab eo Achaeos auctoritate sua coegit.*
[2] Liv. xxxii. 19. 2.

took a less serious view of their defeat than did Philopoemen, whether he was more prepared to take risks with his political future, or whether he was simply less committed than Philopoemen since he had not been *strategos*, cannot be ascertained: but he clearly did not suffer from his decision to stay in Achaea. The fact that Philopoemen already had an attractive invitation from his old friends in Gortyn, which provided him with a patriotic excuse for choosing voluntary exile, clearly would make it easier for him to take a pessimistic view of his political future in Achaea, a view which Aristaenus may not have shared—or if he did, about which he could do little. There was no need for him to anticipate an unprofitable exile which might not become necessary.

One further event of autumn 200 tends to confirm that this interpretation of Cycliadas' election is correct. The wave of reaction against Philopoemen and Aristaenus manifested itself again, probably after the elections.[1] After the fall of Abydus to Philip—probably in September[2]—Achaean ambassadors arrived at Rhodes. Since Rhodes was taking the lead, together with Pergamum, in involving Rome in Greek affairs, the Achaeans asked the Rhodians to try to reach agreement with Philip. However, the Roman propaganda mission, which was on the point of completing its journey to Antiochus and Ptolemy Epiphanes, intervened and urged the Rhodians not to make peace with Philip without Roman consent. The Rhodians were only too glad to be reassured of Roman support, and immediately agreed.[3]

The Romans clearly opposed this Achaean attempt at conciliation because they did not want their potential allies to be neutralized. Since the Achaean embassy was so clearly contrary to Roman interests, it cannot have been sent with the agreement of Philopoemen and Aristaenus, but must represent the policy of Cycliadas and the pro-Macedonians. The precise time of year of the embassy and its chronological relation to the Achaean

---

[1] The precise time of the year of the electoral *synodos* is far from certain. Aymard, *Assemblées*, p. 262, places it normally between mid-September and the beginning of November. In the present case, therefore, the Achaean embassy could well have been after the elections.

[2] The order of events is Walbank's, *Philip*, pp. 313–17.

[3] Pol. xvi. 35; cf. Schmitt, *Rom und Rhodos*, p. 67; Niccolini, *La Conf. Ach.*, p. 119.

elections are not clear and cannot be discovered. If the embassy was sent before the election of Cycliadas, it suggests that the Philopoemenists had already, even before the elections, lost support. If it was sent after the elections—perhaps, as is most likely, by the same *synodos* which elected Cycliadas—it confirms that Cycliadas was willing to work in the interests of Philip. From the point of view of parties and policies within Achaea, this essentially anti-Roman mission to Rhodes seems to confirm what has already been established, that the support which Philopoemen and Aristaenus had attracted while their policy was based solely on their claim to patriotic independence had been lost by the end of Philopoemen's *strategia* of 201/0. The reason for this loss of support seems most likely to have been their proposed *entente* with Rome.

The ten years of Philopoemen's political career in Achaea between his two protracted visits to Crete saw a major change in his policies. In Crete until 211 he had worked in co-operation with Philip's interests, and he continued to co-operate with Philip after his return to Achaea. He probably gained his first federal offices, the hipparchy in 210/09 and the *strategia* in 208/7, with Philip's support. But the developing crisis in Philip's war with Rome made it impossible to protect Achaea effectively against Sparta. His encouragement of Philopoemen to remodel the Achaean army was too successful, and Machanidas' death at Mantinea showed the possibility of an Achaean policy which aimed at achieving local independence within the Peloponnese, independence which Philopoemen believed could be maintained by the new Achaean army. In this he was probably supported by Aristaenus. A solid barrier against achieving this limited aim was formed by the Macedonian garrisons; and it was natural that one result of their continuing potentially hostile presence should be the growth of an anti-Macedonian aspect in the policy of Philopoemen and Aristaenus. The next—and most far-reaching —development came in 200 when they realized that their anti-Macedonianism was shared by Rome. This unity of interest with Rome probably caused them to express cautious willingness to co-operate. But the active association with Achaea's recent brutal enemies which this implied caused a major political reaction in Achaea, and a surge of new support for Cycliadas' traditional policy, which was perhaps stimulated by Philip's realization of the danger implicit in success for his opponents. The Achaean embassy to Rhodes and the election of Cycliadas mark substantial defeats for Philopoemen and Aristaenus. It must have seemed that, for the moment, they had lost the struggle. Philopoemen, rightly or wrongly, decided that the safest course for him was to return to Crete. Aristaenus took a different view and stayed in Achaea as *de facto* leader of the party and representative of Philopoemen's interests in Achaea. They had taken up what seemed to their supporters to be an extreme position, and had advanced to the point where support was no longer forthcoming. Electoral defeat was temporarily the reward for their seeing the future too clearly.

III

The years of Philopoemen's absence in Crete were epoch-making for Achaea and for Greece. But since they are not central to the present theme, they need only be surveyed briefly here. Cycliadas' year was not successful. Nabis was again active, and Cycliadas could not end his threat. Even Philip's support proved a broken reed when, in exchange for an offer to undertake a war against Nabis he requested Achaean troops to guard Oreus, Chalcis, and Corinth. It was clear that they would be virtually hostages and Cycliadas felt unable to allow the Achaeans to vote on the offer. Philip's terms virtually shattered the Macedonian cornerstone of Cycliadas' policy. Building on its ruin, Aristaenus secured his own election as *strategos* for 199/8.[1] In the course of his year he established the Philopoemenist policy firmly: he defended Philopoemen's civil status at Megalopolis, had Cycliadas exiled, persuaded the Achaeans to abandon the Macedonian alliance and to replace it by an alliance with Rome. He met some entrenched opposition from those Achaeans who favoured maintaining the Macedonian alliance, but the threat from the presence of the fleets of Rome and Attalus at Cenchreae while the critical *syncletos* was in session at Sicyon made Aristaenus successful. Nabis also had no desire to appear on the wrong side in the war, and although Philip tried to use their common anti-Achaean feelings to bind Nabis to him by the gift of Argos, Nabis quickly joined Rome in spring 197. A truce for

[1] Liv. xxxi. 25. 2–11; cf. Aymard, *Premiers Rapports*, pp. 67–8.

the duration of the Macedonian war temporarily ended the Spartan threat to Achaea.[1]

In summer 197 Flamininus defeated Philip at Cynoscephalae. The Achaeans took no part in the battle, but benefited from the Roman success: until then Corinth had been kept by Philip; now it was freed from its garrison. Philip was broken. The Senate undertook to settle Greece, and sent ten senatorial commissioners. Flamininus insisted that the cities and states freed from Philip should remain free in fact, and not simply pass into the imperialist hands of the Roman allies. In this way he annoyed the Aetolians, who had expected to benefit from the joint success. Achaea did not require very much: Philip's Peloponnesian garrisons—except for Corinth—had been evacuated in 199, and the Roman commissioners confirmed Achaea in possession of the towns. Over the treatment of the other freed cities in Greece Flamininus disagreed with the members of the commission. The Senate was worried by reports of Antiochus III's successful progress through Asia Minor, and the commissioners, reflecting this disquiet, wished to retain control of at least the 'Fetters of Greece' —the Acrocorinth, Chalcis, and Demetrias. Flamininus was equally aware of the potential threat from Antiochus, but thought that Roman precautions could best be taken by ensuring the friendship of the Greeks—by demonstrating the sincerity of the Roman claim to have freed the Greeks from Philip, rather than by military occupation which would forfeit this.

Flamininus' success over the commissioners was reflected in his proclamation at the Isthmia of 196, that all the Greeks should be free. As an immediate gesture, the town of Corinth was reunited with Achaea. The 'Fetters' were retained for the moment, although by his proclamation Flamininus had committed himself to their eventual evacuation. Antiochus, however, was still the great fear; and Nabis' association with Rome during the war with Philip was not considered to be sufficient evidence of continuing Spartan loyalty. The excuse that Nabis refused to hand over Argos to the Achaeans was therefore given for a campaign to reduce Nabis. The Roman allies, led by Flamininus, invaded Laconia in 195 and stripped Nabis of his control of the perioecic towns on

---

[1] On Achaea during these years, cf. standard works, and especially Aymard, *Premiers Rapports*, pp. 1 ff.; Niccolini, *La Conf. Ach.*, pp. 119 ff.; Castellani, *Contributi*, 66 ff.

the coast, which were given into Achaean *tutela*, although they did not become members of the League. Nabis' Cretan possessions were also taken from him in the settlement. Argos was recovered by Achaea, but Nabis was allowed to retain Sparta: Flamininus' aim was to achieve a balance of power in the Peloponnese rather than a simple gratification of his allies' wishes.

The seriousness of a potential union of Nabis and Antiochus was now greatly diminished, and Flamininus had little further excuse for staying in Greece with Roman troops, if he wished to establish the sincerity of his 'freedom of the Greeks'. In Rome the struggle came at the distribution of the provinces for 194. Scipio Africanus had been elected consul for 194 as a result of the general Roman fear of Antiochus, and he made it clear that he wanted Macedonia as his province. Flamininus, on the other hand, was now more than ever committed to demonstrating the sincerity of his slogan of Greek freedom, and to the evacuation which this implied. In the event, the Senate adopted a waiting policy and accepted Flamininus' view: it determined to meet the threat from Antiochus with the primary weapon of Greek goodwill. It was therefore agreed that all Roman troops should be withdrawn from Greece. In spring 194 Flamininus called a general meeting of the Greek states at Corinth, and announced the withdrawal of the Roman troops.

Satisfied with his success, Flamininus passed through central Greece, withdrawing garrisons and establishing governments favourable to Rome. He continually emphasized the benevolence of Rome's interest in Greece, the fact that Rome and Flamininus were the only sincere liberators the Greeks had known. The Aetolians were not convinced. Even Achaea had the continued threat—though now less serious—from Nabis to temper her enthusiasm for the Roman liberation. These issues soon became major problems. But Flamininus had ended his mission. He left Greece, was greeted by the Senate meeting outside the city, and celebrated a three-day triumph. But despite the pomp of the triumph, there remained apprehension at Rome about Antiochus; and it was this crisis which revealed the weakness of Flamininus' balance of power in Greece.[1]

---

[1] For a detailed account of these years, cf. standard works, and especially Walbank, *Philip*, pp. 138 ff.; Badian, *For. Cl.*, pp. 69 ff.; Stier, *Roms Aufstieg*, pp. 119 ff.

VI

FLAMININUS

IN the spring of 193, some time after the consuls had held levies and left for their provinces, Flamininus asked the Senate for the ratification of his settlement of Greece.[1] At the time, envoys from the whole of the Greek world, Asia as well as Greece, were present, and were used by Flamininus to broadcast to the Greek world the resounding diplomatic defeat which the envoys of Antiochus suffered in interview with Flamininus and the ten commissioners.[2] It seems unlikely that the Aetolians were represented in Rome this spring, since Flamininus had probably, to some extent at least, engineered these embassies to demonstrate in Rome the breadth of his patronage, and the Aetolians would not find much welcome in such a gathering.[3]

In Greece in the meanwhile, Philopoemen had returned to Achaea, probably in the autumn of 194, when the war between Gortyn and Cnossos, which had been supported by Nabis, had been brought to an end.[4] It seems fairly clear that it is this period to which Plutarch refers, when he says that Philopoemen caused the secession of small constituent states of the Megalopolitan *koinon*, arguing that they did not belong to the city, and had not done so in the beginning. As a result of his encouraging this secession he was able to create a party to support him in federal politics.[5] A hostile faction among the Megalopolitans clearly wished to exploit the fact that Philopoemen had put personal and federal interests before Megalopolitan in 200, when he had left Achaea to fight in Crete. Soon afterwards they had tried to

[1] Liv. xxxiv. 57. 1.

[2] Liv. xxxiv. 57–9; Diod. xxviii. 15; App. *Syr.* 6; cf. De Sanctis, *Storia* iv. 1. 131; Badian, *Studies*, pp. 126–7.

[3] Cf. Liv. xxxiv. 57. 3: *benigneque omnibus responsum.*

[4] Cf. chapter III, pp. 44–5. Lehmann, *Glaubwürdigkeit*, p. 235, brings Philopoemen back from Crete only at the end of summer 193. This allows insufficient time before the elections in the autumn.

[5] Plut. *Phil.* 13. 5. Lehmann, *Glaubwürdigkeit*, pp. 253 ff., sees this encouragement of separatism as a general policy. But Plutarch's statement refers only to Megalopolis.

exile him, and had on that occasion only been stopped by federal
intervention headed by Aristaenus. This time it was necessary
for Philopoemen to weaken the whole political structure of
Megalopolis in order to regain his pre-war position.
Some of the towns which were now encouraged by Philopoemen to become independent from Megalopolis within the League
may be tentatively identified by their issues of bronze coinage,
which show this independence. It has been suggested that the
coins of those cities which are known to have been constituent
parts of Megalopolis, and for which there are independent
issues of the Achaean League period, should be attributed to
this time. These are: Alea, Alipheira, Asea, Callista, Gortys,
Dipaea, Methydrion, Pallantion, Teuthis, Theisoa.[1] But too
much reliance should not be placed on these coins. They are
certainly coins of the League; but their date within the League
period depends solely on historical criteria, not numismatic.
It is therefore not possible to demonstrate independently of the
historical argument that the issues in question are even contemporary. The firmest conclusion possible is that they would agree
well enough with the historical phenomena if they could on other
grounds be shown to have been issued subsequent to Philopoemen's return from Crete. We cannot therefore be certain that the
towns from which coins are extant were the Megalopolitan towns
which supported Philopoemen, still less that they were the only
ones to do so. For even if the coins can by some means be proved
to be significant in this context, this latter consideration is important, since we are completely dependent for information upon
the accidental discovery of the League coins from the towns:
there may well have been other towns that supported Philopoemen which either did not issue independent coinage at all, or
from which examples have not been discovered. With or without
the towns from which coins are extant, there must have been
a considerable body of support within the League, apart from
Megalopolis, on which Philopoemen could rely; and it must have
been with this more general support, and not primarily that of
Megalopolis, that he was elected federal *strategos* in the autumn of
193 for 193/2.[2]

---

[1] Head, *Hist. Num.*, p. 417. On an associated coinage problem, cf. appendix 3.
On the Megalopolitan *koinon*, cf. Paus. viii. 27. 3 f.; Hiller, *RE* xv. 1, 'Megala
Polis'.   [2] Cf. *strategos*-list and appendix 2 B, p. 251.

On the international plane, the summer of 193 passed without significant alteration in the cold-war situation between Rome and Antiochus. After the collapse of the negotiations at Rome in the spring, a Roman embassy was dispatched to Asia; but no concessions were extracted from Antiochus or his representatives. The king was unsettled as a result of the death of his eldest son Antiochus, and was not prepared to pay much attention to international affairs. When the embassy returned to Rome in the autumn, they reported simply that they had not discovered anything which could be construed as preparations for war.[1]

Although this was true enough as far as Antiochus himself was concerned, all was by no means peaceful in Aetolia. Matters came to a head at the autumn general meeting of the League, held as usual in connection with the *Thermica*.[2] Opposition to Rome had been growing in Aetolia since the settlement after Cynoscephalae, and at this autumn assembly in 193 it was resolved to send anti-Roman propaganda missions to Nabis, Philip, and Antiochus.[3] The Aetolian embassy to Nabis clearly concerned Achaea most deeply. Nabis had complied with the terms of the peace with Rome in all but one respect: he still kept a company of Cretan mercenaries at Sparta. It is conceivable that these had been hired in the course of the intervening months: they first appear in 192 when Philopoemen made his attack on Sparta. But the report of the Roman *legati* of 193 indicates that danger to the Roman settlement of Greece was anticipated from Nabis; and it seems most satisfactory to conclude that the Cretans had simply not been dismissed in 195.[4] Apart from retaining the mercenaries, Nabis had complied with the terms of the peace. No attempt had been made to regain his power in the Peloponnese, or to encroach on the new Achaean protectorate of the perioecic towns. The Aetolians might well have come to believe that Nabis' revolutionary fire, which they hoped to exploit, had been quenched, and that Nabis, far from lending support to any rising against Rome which they might contemplate, would at best be neutral, and at worst be on the Roman side.

For these reasons the propaganda mission which Damocritus led was necessary. He put his point strongly to Nabis: the Romans

[1] Liv. xxxiv. 59. 8; xxxv. 22. 1–3. Badian, *Studies*, p. 128.
[2] Cf. Larsen, *TAPhA* 1952, 1 ff.
[3] Liv. xxxv. 12. 1 ff.; cf. Aymard, *Premiers Rapports*, pp. 295 ff.
[4] Liv. xxxv. 29. 2; 22. 2.

had left Greece, and would not return just because of Nabis, whatever he might do; he should therefore try to get back the coastal perioecic towns, and with them the basis of his earlier power. It is not likely that the Aetolians sincerely believed the arguments which Damocritus advanced: at best they represented Aetolian wishful thinking. But they found an eager listener in Nabis, who was prepared to act as soon as he realized that there was moral support forthcoming from Aetolia. He had probably already been encouraging his old supporters in the maritime towns. Certainly he was quite quickly able to support or provoke *coups d'état* in those towns where his support was strongest; in others direct assassination achieved the desired results.

By the end of October Achaea had formally protested to Nabis, and had reminded him of his treaty obligations. Other more concrete steps were also taken, behind which the influence of Philopoemen, now *strategos*, can be traced: a garrison was sent to Gytheum, the most important of the coastal towns, and an embassy to Rome.[1] The establishment of an Achaean garrison at Gytheum was allowed under the treaty between Nabis and Rome as part of Achaean *tutela*; the embassy to Rome was merely a manifestation of diplomatic prudence. But it does indicate very clearly that Philopoemen's election in 193 was by no means an affront to Rome, as Aymard suggests. There is no evidence for this at this time. Philopoemen was no blind chauvinist, as Polybius makes clear in his comparison between Aristaenus and Philopoemen. He realized that there was a limit to what was possible for Achaea, even at a later time when the formal *foedus* was in operation between Rome and Achaea. In 193 no formal alliance existed between the states, yet there is no indication in any source that Philopoemen expressed any desire other than for co-operation with Rome whenever possible, as long as Roman and Achaean interests coincided, as they certainly did in this case. Assertions about a clash between the policies of Philopoemen and Rome at this time have no basis in the evidence, and are merely the stuff from which myths are made.[2]

When the Senate came to consider its foreign policy towards

[1] Liv. xxxv. 13. 1–3.
[2] Pol. xxiv. 11–13 (comparison of Aristaenus and Philopoemen); cf. Aymard, *Premiers Rapports*, p. 304, followed by Castellani, *Contributi*, 78. The most probable date for the *foedus*, accepted here, is that of Badian, *JRS* 1952, 76 ff., winter 192/1; cf. also Castellani, *Contributi*, 84–6.

the east in spring 192, the *legati* who had been to Antiochus impressed the Senate with the lack of warlike preparations by Antiochus, and no direct action was taken. But the cold war was to go on. The Achaean embassy bearing news of Nabis' recent hostility made some action both desirable and diplomatically possible. The aim was clearly to prevent the southern Peloponnese from becoming disaffected and a potential base for Antiochus under the renewed self-assertiveness of Nabis, and to reinforce Achaean solidarity by providing support on appeal in what appeared to be, at first sight, merely a local war. A. Atilius Serranus, who had originally been given Hispania Ulterior at the distribution of the praetorian provinces, had his appointment changed by a vote of the people, and was now given Macedonia and the fleet. M. Baebius Tamphilus, who had originally been given Hispania Citerior, was transferred to Bruttium. Atilius was ordered to build thirty quinqueremes, to select from the existing fleet any ships which were still seaworthy, and to enlist *socii navales*.[1]

These preparations took most of the summer; and although Atilius was ordered to go to Greece at once, it was near the end of summer 192 before he appeared off Gytheum. By this time the trouble in the Peloponnese was almost settled and Nabis was already dead. Aymard refuses to believe that Atilius had taken so long over his preparations. He assumes that he must have taken some part in the events of the year. But this is contrary to the impression which Livy gives and, for what it is worth, Zonaras' statement that he did nothing, both of which have as ultimate source the full text of Polybius. There is not even any compelling *a priori* reason for assuming Atilius' activity in Greece against the trend of the evidence. In addition to Atilius and the fleet, a propaganda mission was sent to Greece with the purpose of cutting the ground from under Antiochus' feet, by counteracting the propaganda of the Aetolians and the use they were making of Antiochus' reputation. This mission was led by Flamininus and was composed of Cn. Octavius, Cn. Servilius Caepio, and P. Villius Tappulus.[2] This was an extremely

[1] Liv. xxxv. 10. 11 (elections); 20. 8 f. (provinces). Livy has confused the appointments of Baebius and Atilius, but it is quite clear that the naval preparations should go with the fleet, and therefore are Atilius' responsibility.

[2] Liv. xxxv. 37. 3 (arrival of Atilius at Gytheum). Zon. ix. 19; cf. Aymard, *Premiers Rapports*, p. 309, n. 13; p. 310 (effectiveness of Atilius). Liv. xxxv. 23. 5 (appointment of propaganda mission).

influential mission, consisting as it did of three consulars (Flamininus, Servilius, and Villius), and a distinguished praetorian.
Of the consulars, Villius had had almost as much experience in
Greece as Flamininus himself: he was his predecessor as consul
in Macedonia in 199; in 197 he was appointed to his staff as
senatorial *legatus*; he served as a member of the ten commissioners for the settlement of Greece; in 193 he was a member
of P. Sulpicius Galba's embassy to Antiochus, from which he
had just returned.[1] The composition of this embassy shows clearly
that the Senate attached great importance to this aspect of the
cold war: Nabis might be used as an excuse for intervention, but
there could be little doubt that fear of Antiochus was behind it.
The envoys left Rome early in the year, and Flamininus was in
Greece early enough to be able to play a part in the early stages
of the Achaean war against Nabis.

As soon as the weather allowed military activity to take place,
Nabis attacked Gytheum. Also, in an attempt to repay the
Achaeans for putting a garrison into Gytheum, and to try to
persuade them to withdraw it, he ravaged some Achaean territory. Despite this, Philopoemen made no move until the Achaean
ambassadors to Rome had returned.[2] At this stage he clearly
wished to preserve as close a relationship as possible between
Achaea and Rome, even if this involved trouble for outlying
parts of Achaea: in particular, Megalopolis would be among the
first to suffer. As soon as the ambassadors returned, a *syncletos*
was called at Sicyon. At the same time an embassy was sent to
Flamininus, who had now arrived in Greece, but was still in the
north. As a result of his distance from Achaea Flamininus' reply,
that the Achaeans should wait for the arrival of Atilius' Roman
fleet before embarking on open war with Nabis, did not arrive
until the Achaean *syncletos* was already in session and likely to
decide in favour of war.[3] The delay can have been nobody's
fault: the fact that Philopoemen sent the embassy to Flamininus
at all, as soon as he heard of his arrival in Greece, shows that he

[1] For references cf. Broughton, *MRR* i, *ad ann.*
[2] Liv. xxxv. 25. 2–3; cf. Aymard, *Premiers Rapports,* pp. 301 f.
[3] Liv. xxxv. 25. 4–5: *in concilio omnium ad bellum extemplo capessendum inclinatae sententiae erant.* This suggests that Flamininus' letter did not arrive until at least the second day of the *syncletos,* when there had already been considerable discussion. Cf. Aymard, *Premiers Rapports,* pp. 304 ff. On the nature of the meeting, cf. Aymard, *Assemblées,* p. 313; Larsen, *Rep. Gov.,* p. 172.

was eager to co-operate. On the other hand, Flamininus can scarcely have calculated the travelling time of the envoys' return so exactly as to virtually ensure that his advice would be ignored. There was clearly no calculated duplicity on his part over this matter. He intended his advice to be taken seriously.

The Achaean ambassadors must have represented to him that the matter of Nabis was urgent; all the facts, with their full charge of Achaean emotion, must have been placed at his fingertips. Yet the only advice he could give was to wait for Atilius. Despite the Senate's instructions to Atilius to go to his province at once, Flamininus must have known that he was likely to be fully occupied with building ships and recruiting crews for some time. The implication of his reply therefore was that if the Achaeans themselves took no immediate action against Nabis, Gytheum would certainly be lost, and Achaea would be further laid open to attack from Nabis. Why was Flamininus willing to accept these implications? In the first place it must have been galling to him to be virtually powerless until Atilius arrived. Diplomacy without gunboats was an emasculated weapon to Flamininus. Yet his own chief task was to counteract Aetolian influence. The method he favoured was to acquire personal ties with the client states, and to secure their loyalty as a result of their gratitude for *beneficia* conferred by him. Here in Achaea he was presented with a textbook situation: the Achaeans were voluntarily humbling themselves by asking for a *beneficium*. Yet Flamininus was prevented by force of circumstances from conferring it.

The situation was difficult; but Flamininus did not even make the most of it. He refused to endorse the proposed Achaean action against Nabis because this action would necessarily be taken by the Achaeans alone without their waiting for physical Roman help—which he no doubt considered the essential guarantee of success in defending against Nabis his Roman settlement and the security of Achaea. Instead, he tried to turn back the tide of events. Whereas he might have promised the full moral support of his own authoritative presence for their militarily independent undertaking, he refused to compromise his chance of conferring a great *beneficium* by fighting the whole war for the Achaeans with Roman arms, and of effectively excluding them from playing a major part in their own defence and in the subsequent settlement. He therefore quite unrealistically told them to wait for Atilius. If they did this, of course, he would take the war off their hands: he was simply—and clumsily—trying to create an opportunity of exercising patronage where none existed on the scale which he envisaged. As a result of his clumsiness, he lost the chance of gaining the minor advantage for Rome of giving the Achaeans the backing of Roman prestige. In the event, Atilius' fleet played no part in the events of the year in the Peloponnese—as Flamininus perhaps anticipated when he insisted on the Achaeans' waiting for him. And although the Achaeans had little military success, they avoided incurring the debt of gratitude to Rome with which Flamininus had intended to secure their loyalty.

From the Achaean point of view Flamininus' advice was totally unexpected. Not only did it mean that Roman hostility would be aroused by any unilateral Achaean action to preserve their security and the Roman settlement, but it was also a personal affront to Philopoemen. So far he had scrupulously taken care to obtain Roman approval for every action he had contemplated against Nabis, and he now found his independence of action incomprehensibly withheld, apparently against the Roman interest, and certainly against his view of the Achaean. His view of Roman policy and aims must have immediately undergone a rapid change. His absence in Crete had prevented his previously experiencing Flamininus' methods in person. Aristaenus was too closely involved personally with the Spartan settlement to have done more than hint at dissatisfaction with Flamininus' methods. In any case, Achaea had so far come out of the Roman settlement well enough for it still to be possible to believe that Flamininus had some more friendly interest in Achaea than in other Greek states. When Philopoemen returned in Flamininus' absence from Greece, he can only have been presented with the situation through hearsay and through Aristaenus' already compromised ideas. Philopoemen's initial willingness to follow Aristaenus' established method of conduct is manifest in the cautious embassies to Rome and Flamininus. But the crisis in his belief in Roman generosity to Achaea rapidly arrived with the receipt of Flamininus' letter and its delaying advice.

Militarily delay was inadvisable, but unlikely to prove disastrous: Atilius' fleet, when it arrived, would quickly have secured the recovery of places lost to Nabis, and there had in any case already been delay while the embassy was sent to Rome. Admittedly this was in the winter; but a wait of a few months more—or even weeks, had they decided to wait for Flamininus' own presence—would not have had much effect on the situation. Flamininus' *auctoritas* alone might have been sufficient to end the war, even without the support of Roman troops, since he did in fact eventually intervene in the war himself and make a peace.[1] But politically the relationship between Flamininus and Achaea was radically altered by the arrival of Flamininus' letter: asked to endorse action, he had simply advised further delay. To him, Achaean desire for independent action was a new phenomenon, and he naturally acted defensively. But his letter openly demonstrated his essential Roman selfishness and lack of altruistic benevolent interest in Achaea, and its effect on Philopoemen was correspondingly disastrous. Ready to trust his experienced advisers until events proved them wrong, he had now already reached this point. The slogan 'freedom of the Greeks' did not affect Philopoemen in the same way as his fellow Achaean politicians— for even Aristaenus was politically compromised over this—since he had not experienced the mass emotions of the Isthmia of 196, the Nemea of 195, and the evacuation scenes of 194. He seems to have correctly seen no essential difference between the freedom conferred by Rome and the freedom granted by Macedon. Earlier in his career he had had some success in breaking away from total military dependence on Macedon by his success at Mantinea. He had been led to expect that the situation under Rome was different, that Rome would wholly co-operate with him. But his colleagues had been shown to be living in a fools' paradise, and their expectations had been shown to be wrong. It was therefore necessary to take immediate action in order to stake the Achaean claim to follow an independent policy in the Peloponnese. Flamininus' wish to deprive Achaea of the prestige of a potential military success was quite clear to Philopoemen. In his view, unprejudiced by close association, Rome was simply repeating the diplomacy of Philip's symmachy. Action was the way in which his experience advised him to claim political individualism.

His decision was made easier by the fact that the *syncletos* had expected Flamininus' letter simply to endorse Philopoemen's

---

[1] Plut. *Phil.* 15. 2; Paus. viii. 50 .10.

desire for action, had discussed the matter accordingly, and had almost decided on war before the letter arrived. Further discussion, inevitably conditioned by the contents of the letter, was indecisive. The opinion of the *strategos* was therefore sought. Philopoemen took his opportunity, and tactfully said that he was willing to undertake the consequences of any decision of the *syncletos*. The meeting correctly interpreted this opinion as an expression of his desire for war. The decision was then carried by a large majority.[1] Whatever decision the *syncletos* had taken would have meant compromising Achaean interests. To the mass of the *syncletos* the most immediate matter was the war with Nabis; to Philopoemen the most urgent need was to stake a claim for the right to follow an independent policy in the Peloponnese against the recently revealed machiavellianism of Flamininus. The circumstances of the arrival of the letter simply made easier the decision to fight Nabis, the conclusion to which both points of view tended.

From this time the hostility between Flamininus and Philopoemen began. The unique source of our information about this is Polybius. As a result of Polybius' own personal association with Philopoemen we find—not altogether unanticipated—some tendency to throw the blame upon Flamininus. The ill feeling between the two men seems to have first become general knowledge towards the end of 192, when Philopoemen gained greater honours than Flamininus for his war against Nabis. The record is in Plutarch, comes from Polybius, and is represented as simple jealousy on the part of Flamininus.[2] The idea of this was certainly common knowledge in autumn 192, for Polybius makes it a reason for the Aetolian attempt to seduce Achaea from Rome. He spoils the effect of this by laying the hostility at the door of Flamininus, while he still makes it an argument for the possibility of Achaean defection; but the same implication is there, that Philopoemen was hated by Flamininus. It is not made clear whether the hostility was mutual.[3] The next real evidence is not until ten years later. Deinocrates of Messene hoped to get help against Achaea from Flamininus as a result of Flamininus' hostility to Philopoemen. Again the same implication is there, again coming

---

[1] Liv. xxxv. 25. 6–10; cf. Niese, *GGMS* ii. 683; Aymard, *Premiers Rapports*, pp. 305–6.   [2] Plut. *Phil.* 15; *Flam.* 13; cf. Nissen, *Krit. Unt.*, p. 284; pp. 290 ff.
[3] Liv. xxxv. 47. 4.

from Polybius. It is nowhere stated that Flamininus' hostility was either reciprocated or justified.[1]

There was indeed, from Flamininus' point of view, some reason for him to be hostile towards Philopoemen. Philopoemen's action against Nabis, in direct contradiction to the advice of his letter, was the first occasion he had experienced such failure to appreciate the moral obligations of *clientela* in Achaea. His advice was such that, in his view, it should be quite acceptable to the Achaeans unless they *wanted* to offend him; the *strategos* could easily stifle any opposition *if he wanted to*. It must have been clear at once to Flamininus that Philopoemen was deliberately flouting the advice given in his letter. Polybius does not really clarify the situation when, apologizing for Philopoemen's action, he explains that Philopoemen really wanted to co-operate with Flamininus and wait for the fleet, but the danger to Gytheum and the Achaean garrison was too great.[2] Yet success could not be guaranteed without a fleet, and Achaea's was woefully feeble. In fact, if Philopoemen had been realistically assessing only the military situation, he should have waited for Atilius and not risked loss of men and prestige in contravening Flamininus' expressed wish. Flamininus clearly had sound reasons for believing that Philopoemen deliberately wanted to cross his plans. This in itself was sufficient to create an initial hostility. But it implied more. It implied that Philopoemen had realized that Flamininus' own schemes were not aimed solely at the benefit of Achaea. If Philopoemen was abusing *clientela*, he had now every reason to believe that Flamininus was playing a double game with Achaea. Flamininus for his part could not like the idea that this was fully recognized by the new *strategos*, whom as yet he can have known by reputation only. Philopoemen's action therefore represented both a breach of his obligations as client, and a tacit accusation that Flamininus was breaking his obligations as patron. It can now be fully appreciated that at this initial stage, before they had even met, the clash between the two self-willed and successful statesmen contained elements of great potential personal and political hostility.

If Philopoemen had no full realization of what Rome required of a client state—and there was no reason why he should have—he had nevertheless shown himself willing to accept the unspoken

---

[1] Winter 184/3: Pol. xxiii. 5. 2.   [2] Liv. xxxv. 25. 11–12.

ideal as long as it was expedient. But he also had a sound recognition of what a Greek state required of its protector. This was the
language he understood. When Flamininus refused to endorse the
proposed Achaean action against Nabis, refused even to allow his
name to be used in the Achaean cause, in Philopoemen's eyes he
was failing in his duty as protector. When Philip had failed
in his duty as protector, Philopoemen had taken successful independent action. Flamininus was now failing; the same remedy
was to be applied. So far the matter was simple, and in itself
quite sufficient to arouse a personal hostility on Philopoemen's
part, not so much because in this particular case Achaea would
suffer disaster if Philopoemen complied with Flamininus' advice
—although failure to act at once might prove politically inconvenient—but because it was a pointer to a general Roman
policy. In case of a conflict over a serious danger, Flamininus, in
Philopoemen's interpretation, had shown conclusively that what
happened in Achaea did not concern him unless Roman safety or
prestige were intimately involved. Philopoemen's awareness of
this must have troubled him. Yet Flamininus was attempting to
salvage the present situation, not in order to help Achaea—or he
would have given the weight of his prestige to immediate action
against Nabis—but simply to assert his own and Roman dominance
over Achaea, and to emphasize Achaean indebtedness to Rome.
Philopoemen had not had time to develop the consciousness of
Flamininus' prestige and the power of Rome, which other
Achaean politicians may have felt, and therefore considered immediate action against Nabis both possible and desirable, for the
very reason that he wanted to prevent Flamininus' taking undeserved advantage from delay. If there was some confusion
about the meaning of *clientela*—so far understood to Flamininus'
satisfaction by Aristaenus—there must have been full understanding by both men of the personal issues involved: and it was
from the conflict of personalities expressed in action that hostility
between the two men arose.

Polybius wrote with fuller understanding of Roman policy and
its basis in *clientela* than any of the contemporary politicians can
have had; and he seems to have felt that it was necessary to offer
a defence of Philopoemen's collision course with Flamininus. In
only one case does he imply that Philopoemen hated Flamininus,
when he (in Livy's version) says that the Aetolians sought

Achaean help for this reason after misinterpreting its effect. He does insist upon the point that the danger to Gytheum was the cause of Philopoemen's action, which, we have seen, is inadequate.[1] Similarly in the case of the Achaean navy. No acceptable reason for Philopoemen's use of the antique ships appears in Livy, and this must be because there was none in Polybius. Polybius' excuse, recorded by Livy, is the Homeric tag that Philopoemen was *Arcas, mediterraneus homo*—which is not in itself an explanation of the failure of the Achaean *strategos* in his professional duty.[2] Polybius clearly felt a difficulty which he was unwilling—or unable—to clarify. The only explanation can be that Philopoemen was in such a hurry to secure some success before Flamininus arrived in Achaea, so that he could present him with a *fait accompli*, that he was willing to take any risks. Polybian apologetics cannot excuse Philopoemen for the part he played in creating the hostility between himself and Flamininus.

Philopoemen's first action in this new Achaean war against Nabis was an attempt to relieve Gytheum and its Achaean garrison by a naval attack. The town was already besieged by land by Nabis, and it was the utter inadequacy of the Achaean navy which had made help from the Romans the more desirable in the first place. But since this was not forthcoming, and since political conditions made immediate action now essential, the best had to be made of the fleet at the disposal of the Achaeans. In this Philopoemen made the gross mistake which ruined the expedition, which resulted in giving Nabis time to take Gytheum, and which demonstrated the likely ineffectiveness of Philopoemen's hasty and ill-prepared scheme to prevent Flamininus from taking advantage of the war. Over-eager to make use of every available ship, he chose as flagship a quadrireme which had been in Achaean possession for eighty years, was completely unseaworthy, and utterly incapable of withstanding any pressure in battle. Nabis on the other hand had built some new ships since his treaty with Rome, and it was against these that the Achaean fleet would have to fight. Setting out from Patrae, the regular base of the fleet, Philopoemen sailed to Gytheum where he was met by the new Spartan ships. The antique flagship was quickly sunk, and Philopoemen escaped on another small ship. The fleet returned

[1] Liv. xxxv. 47. 4 (Aetolians); 25. 11–12 (Gytheum).
[2] Liv. xxxv. 26. 4.

discomfited to Patrae.¹ Such was the first result of Philopoemen's
badly planned naval raid, undertaken solely for urgent political
reasons. All the responsibility was Philopoemen's. It is inconceivable that if the old ship was as unseaworthy as Livy's account
from Polybius implies, he had not been warned by the admiral,
Tison of Patrae—who had to take the same risk of shipwreck. If,
on the other hand, advice had been given that the vessel would
stand the test, Philopoemen, although ultimately responsible for
the result, did have the excuse that he had been let down
by his advisers. Livy's failure to record a satisfactory reason for
the haste of the Achaean preparations and the incompetence of
Philopoemen has already been noticed. This can only be because
Polybius' own apologetics have obscured the true reason for the
haste, the decision taken by Philopoemen at the Sicyon *syncletos*
to finish the war before either Flamininus or Atilius could interfere. The item was discreditable; therefore, although it could
not be omitted, it could be glossed over with an apposite literary
quotation.

After this initial failure a land expedition was organized as
rapidly as possible. The situation of the Achaean garrison in
Gytheum had not improved, since nothing had been achieved
by the naval expedition. In anticipation of an attack by land,
Nabis had moved a third of his blockading force to Pleiae, where
he expected the attack to be launched. While a large-scale
Achaean expedition was in preparation, a night raid on these
Spartan troops succeeded in destroying their camp. Philopoemen
followed up this success by raiding Tripolis, the area of north
Laconia near Megalopolis. The Achaean garrison in Gytheum
nevertheless was still under siege; and when the main Achaean

¹ Liv. xxxv. 25. 12–26. 10; Plut. *Phil.* 14. That Patrae was the regular base of the
Achaean fleet seems fairly clear from Liv. xxxviii. 7. 2–3, and from the ships'
return to Patrae after the expedition; it is also perhaps worth noting that Patrae
was the place of origin of the admiral Tison. It therefore seems likely that the fleet
had set out from Patrae (the fact that the ancient quadrireme had been stationed at
Aegium is of little significance in this respect: it was a famous ship, and was therefore on view traditionally in the capital). The reading *Patras* (26. 9) has been questioned by Rühl (*Neue Jahrb. für Phil.* 1883), who suggested *Prasias*, on the grounds
that Prasiae was closer to Sparta for the subsequent expedition. This emendation
was accepted by Meischke, *Symbolae*, p. 59, and De Sanctis, *Storia* iv. 1. 134.
Aymard, *Premiers Rapports*, p. 306, n. 2, cannot decide between the established
text and the conjecture. But the sound judgement of Niese, *GGMS* ii. 683, n. 1,
followed by Mundt, *Nabis*, p. 13, is supported by Dr. A. H. McDonald, who has
kindly confirmed that *Patras* has full MS. authority.

expedition finally entered Laconia, before it could make contact with the enemy Gytheum succumbed to Nabis' persistence. As a result Nabis' troops were freed to meet the Achaean attack before Philopoemen realized this. He showed qualities of leadership in extricating his army from an attempted ambush close to Sparta, and proceeded to ravage Laconia, although he made no further attempt on Gytheum which, along with Sparta, remained strongly held by Nabis. Again very little of strategic value had been achieved by Philopoemen, although the prestige of his successful raiding expedition must have done something to remove the ignominy of the naval débâcle. But the result could not be denied: Gytheum was now in Nabis' hands. Since the relief of Gytheum had been the main reason stated for the whole Achaean war effort, Philopoemen could be considered to have failed.[1]

An interesting aspect of this expedition is the presence of a body of Cretans under the leadership of Telemnastus of Gortyn; and at the meeting at Tegea before the main campaign started, of *Epirotarum et Acarnanum principes*.[2] The connection between the Gortynians and Philopoemen has been discussed elsewhere, and clearly represents personal support for Philopoemen. The position of the Epirots and Acarnanians is more difficult to assess.[3] At first sight it seems that they were simply sympathizers with Philopoemen's hostility towards Nabis. They had probably

---

[1] Liv. xxxv. 27. 1–10; cf. Plut. *Phil.* 14. 4; Paus. viii. 50. 8 (night raid). Liv. xxxv. 27. 11–30. 13 (main expedition); cf. Niese, *GGMS* ii. 683–4; De Sanctis, *Storia* iv. 1. 134–5; Aymard, *Premiers Rapports*, pp. 306 ff. On the topography, cf. Loring, *JHS* 1895.

[2] Liv. xxxv. 29. 1 (Telemnastus); cf. ch. III, pp. 37–8. Liv. xxxv. 27. 11 (Epirots and Acarnanians). It has also been suggested that Eumenes was present at some stage in the operations against Nabis (cf. Aymard, *Premiers Rapports*, p. 309, n. 12, and works cited there, to which add McShane, *Attalids*, p. 139). Later in the year Eumenes was certainly in Greece (at Chalcis and Athens: Liv. xxxv. 39. 1 ff.), but he is nowhere mentioned in Livy's Polybian account of the war with Nabis. An inscription from Pergamum, however, records a dedication of spoils by those μετὰ βασιλέως Εὐμένου πλεύσαντες τὸ δεύτερον εἰς τὴν Ἑλλάδα στρατιῶται ἐκ τοῦ πολέμου τοῦ πρὸς Νάβιν καὶ Ἀντίοχον ἐπιστρατεύσαντας τοῖς Ἕλλησιν (Ditt. *Syll.* 605A). Dittenberger's explanation, accepted by Aymard (l.c.), is that the soldiers refer to a hypothetical expedition against Nabis in 192 and to that (certainly established) against Antiochus in 191. An equally plausible explanation, which also accounts for the absence of Eumenes from Livy's account of Philopoemen's expedition, is that the soldiers regarded their expedition of 195 against Nabis and that of 191 against Antiochus as two phases of the same war. Cf. Walbank, *Philip*, p. 195, n. 3.

[3] Cf. Oost, *Roman Policy*, pp. 56–8.

participated in Flamininus' war against Nabis, and may have been eager to prevent the resurgence of disruptive social forces which could be exploited by their disaffected Aetolian neighbours. But this alone does not adequately explain Livy's explicit mention of the *principes* of the Epirots and Acarnanians, and their presence only at the *concilium*. His source must have had a more lengthy account of their presence, which Livy has curtailed. *A priori* it is unexpected to find a client state, which Flamininus had probably already visited, supporting Philopoemen's independent action, of which Flamininus disapproved. It therefore seems possible that these *principes* had come as unofficial representatives of Flamininus, in a last attempt to urge Philopoemen to wait for Atilius. This would satisfactorily account for Livy's mention of them alone of the Achaean allies at the meeting at Tegea, and his failure to mention them in the actual war, for only the *principes* would have needed to travel to Achaea. In this case, Philopoemen's rejection of their representations would mark a further stage both in his commitment to the war against Nabis and in the mutual hostility between him and Flamininus.

From the point of view of the immediate aims of Achaea and Philopoemen the expedition had achieved little. From the point of view of Flamininus and Roman policy as represented by him, it was less disastrous than might have been expected. On the one hand, the Achaeans had been too successful for him to allow them the luxury of another unsuccessful expedition, and to upset once and for all the now precarious balance of power in the Peloponnese. Philopoemen may easily have contemplated this, for he must have taken encouragement from being able to deny Nabis the use of his country. On the other hand, Nabis too had had sufficient success in his immediate aims to give him some encouragement; and so far, as the Aetolians had forecast, no Roman army or navy had appeared: why otherwise had the Achaeans acted alone? Nabis could apparently look forward to fighting Achaea alone, for an expansion of his influence over the coastal towns of Laconia; and success was clearly possible, particularly if he could attract Aetolian support. But by the end of the main Achaean expedition Flamininus had arrived in the Peloponnese and had decided to intervene. He would at least be able to claim some thanks among the Achaeans for ending the war. And Nabis was in no position to refuse Flamininus' demand for a truce. He was still under treaty with Rome—even if it was somewhat strained by this time—and he had no intention of incurring more Roman interest than was absolutely necessary. Flamininus therefore negotiated a truce with Nabis, and put an end to active hostilities. Any further activity in this field would be associated with the presence of the Roman fleet of Atilius. For the moment the war was over. Its ending shows the extent to which Philopoemen had failed in his aim of gaining sufficient advantage from his independent action to restore a measure of equality to the relationship between Achaea and Rome. The truce was achieved by Flamininus alone; the peace was imposed on the Achaeans. All Philopoemen had achieved was the creation of personal animosity between himself and Flamininus.[1]

Despite Philopoemen's failure to achieve the ultimate aim of the war, his raid on the camp of Nabis' troops and his successful extrication of his army from the ambush were the first military activities of any Greek state allied with Rome, undertaken without either the physical or moral support of Rome, since Philopoemen's departure for Crete in 200. They were not particularly glorious by comparison with the Roman achievement; but they were Greek. As a result Philopoemen was 'exceptionally loved and honoured by the Greeks in their theatres'. Plutarch does not make any attempt to clarify what he envisages by this. Aymard interprets it simply as an ovation at the Isthmia, which were again due in 192.[2] The circumstances would certainly be sufficient to cause those with a taste for irony to enjoy the presence of Flamininus; and there is precedent enough for this type of ovation for military success at games—in Philopoemen's own case, at the Nemea of 205.[3] But despite the plausibility of Aymard's suggestion, it is not wholly satisfactory since it does not explain Plutarch's

---

[1] The circumstances in which this truce was negotiated are not clear, for Livy does not mention it, and we must rely on Plut. *Phil.* 15 and Paus. viii. 50. 10, who record no more than the fact. It is attractive to assume, with Aymard (*Premiers Rapports*, p. 312) and Lehmann (*Glaubwürdigkeit*, p. 236), that Flamininus intervened while the Achaean army was actually in the field, but the sources do not allow certainty for this. It is safer to conclude, as in the text, that Philopoemen had already ended his expedition unsuccessfully, and that Flamininus simply wanted to prevent another Achaean attempt on Sparta.

[2] Plut. *Phil.* 15. 1: ἐπὶ τούτοις ἀγαπώμενος καὶ τιμώμενος ἐκπρεπῶς ὑπὸ τῶν Ἑλλήνων ἐν τοῖς θεάτροις . . . ; cf. *Flam.* 13. 2–3; Aymard, *Premiers Rapports*, pp. 313 f. and n. 26.

[3] Plut. *Phil.* 11; cf. ch. V, pp. 75–6.

mention of the θέατρα. The plural form must have some significance, even if it only indicates the theatres of two or three individual Achaean towns. It may be added that Plutarch regards
these honours to Philopoemen as a significant stage in the development of hostility between Flamininus and Philopoemen,
and he is surely reflecting Polybius in this. Philopoemen was
being honoured equally with Flamininus, and Flamininus did
not like it.

Although Flamininus' most spectacular single honour was the
tremendous spontaneous reception he had received at the
Isthmia of 196, this was by no means a permanent honour,
although the memory of it might survive. Essentially it was the
rejoicing of the day; and it must be assumed that individual cities
would be prepared to show their appreciation of their benefactor
in a more permanent way. Plutarch indicates this clearly when
he says that the Achaeans decreed him many honours.[1] No civic
honour was considered more precious than an honorary decree
or a statue set up in the civic theatre. Statues seem to have been,
for the most part, reserved for poets, as in the case of Philippides,
honoured at Athens c. 287/6; but as for Philopoemen, after his
death, the Megalopolitans voted to honour him with twenty-four
bronzes, and to set up one of them in the theatre. Honorary
decrees were also regularly set up in theatres; and grants of
proedria were the commonest of all honorific theatre decorations.[2]
It is clear that something of this permanent kind must have been
bestowed on Flamininus by a grateful people. This was the
highest expression of civic gratitude, and must have been recognized as such by Flamininus. Although always ready to take
advantage of spectacular, if ephemeral, displays of public emotion,
he would be certain to appreciate fully the solid bonds of clientship demonstrated by these permanent forms of thanksgiving.
It must therefore have been Philopoemen's association with him
in this permanent type of offering, in the recognition that for
all time Philopoemen, the 'Arcadian fellow, a general merely
in unimportant border wars',[3] was being held to be his equal

---

[1] Plut. *Flam.* 13. 3. One of these honours, probably set up by Aristaenus, has
been identified by Bousquet, *BCH* 1964, 607 f.

[2] Ditt. *Syll.* 374, line 64 (Philippides); ibid. 624, line 10 (Philopoemen); ibid.
289, line 39 (Athenian decree); ibid. 374, line 66; 1003, line 15; 912, line 24
(*proedria*). Cf. Gundel, *RE* xxiv. 1075–6, 'T. Quinctius Flamininus'.

[3] Plut. *Flam.* 13. 2: ἄνθρωπον Ἀρκάδα, μικρῶν καὶ ὁμόρων πολέμων στρατηγόν.

which caused him to feel that his own honour was threatened. No Greek could ever equal his Isthmian proclamation of 196. However much acclamation Philopoemen might receive at the same festival in 192, it could not match the hysterical rejoicings in the name of Flamininus at the festival four years earlier. But in the civic honours, the plaques and statues set up in the theatres of the independent towns, his honoured status could be approached, and by being shared, lessened. He clearly had some justification for his distress; for Philopoemen was receiving these expensive honours for actions in a war in which, for the moment at least, he had failed, both in his political and military objectives; and if Plutarch's Ἑλλήνων can be taken at its face value, approval of Philopoemen's attempt to break Achaea's bonds of clientship was expressed further afield than simply in Achaea. Honours of this kind to Philopoemen in these circumstances were an insult to Flamininus and to the policy he represented. His public mission to counteract Aetolian influence was having unexpected and undesirable personal results.

Nabis was not slow to make his next move. Using the time granted by his truce with Flamininus, he appealed to the Aetolians for help. Clearly he must have known that Flamininus had only checked the Achaeans in order to wait for Atilius' fleet, and since he now considered himself to be too deeply committed to the anti-Roman camp to expect any favourable terms in a new permanent settlement—although his son Armenas and other influential Spartans were still hostages at Rome[1]—he determined to take all possible advantage from the respite granted him by the truce. To the Aetolians, however, he was by no means as desirable an ally as he had been in the autumn. Militarily Sparta had been envisaged as a hostile power constantly occupying the Achaeans. While this was still possible, the plan had lost much of its attraction since the neutralization of Nabis' forces by Philopoemen and by Flamininus' intervention. While the Aetolians could still see value in the fact that Nabis held Gytheum, the Achaeans had nevertheless prevented Nabis from becoming a major threat to their security. Unless the balance of power in the Peloponnese changed rapidly, Nabis was effectively out of action.

Politically also the situation had changed since the autumn.

[1] Liv. xxxiv. 35. 11; Pol. xxi. 1; 3. 4.

Matching Nabis' military weakness was the political effect of his *rapprochement* with Flamininus: he could not expect the Aetolians to sympathize with his motives for accepting a truce, which Flamininus did not have the power to enforce. His application for Aetolian aid after this could only attract the suspicion that he was trying to play a double game, and was therefore to be trusted by neither party. Yet the strategic arguments advanced in the autumn in favour of Aetolian possession of a friendly Sparta were still valid: Achaea should still, if possible, be prevented from taking part in a general war by having her forces occupied in a permanent struggle in the Peloponnese. The Aetolians therefore decided to assassinate Nabis and to take Sparta directly under the control of the Aetolian League.[1]

The first part of this mission was successfully accomplished. But as soon as Nabis was dead, the Aetolian forces which had been entrusted with the operation started looting the town, and enough support was gained by those who undertook to rally the Spartans to drive out the looters. Many were killed, but some managed to escape to Tegea and Megalopolis, in the hope of finding there a friendly reception for the murderers of the tyrant. But as Aetolians they found no sympathy among the Achaeans, and were at once arrested and sold into slavery. Philopoemen in this way quickly learnt of the death of Nabis, and he determined to attempt to bring Sparta into the Achaean League, before any one Spartan party could gain the support of Flamininus and fortify itself in power with his backing. This he had successfully accomplished just at the moment when Atilius' fleet arrived off Gytheum.[2] But the manner in which this union was achieved requires examination, for the new Spartan problem, starting as it does for Achaea with the incorporation of the city in the League in 192, was the main stumbling-block for the next thirteen years to a peaceful settlement of the Peloponnese. The idea of the union seems at first sight sensible enough: the main external threat to the safety of Achaea would be removed by the incorporation of Sparta in the League. Certainly the external threat disappeared. But Sparta's internal problems, originating in the

[1] Liv. xxxv. 34. 4–5; 35. 1 f. Cf. Badian, *Studies*, pp. 131–2.

[2] Liv. xxxv. 35. 1 ff. (detail of Aetolians at Sparta); 37. 1–3; cf. Plut. *Phil.* 15. 2–3; Paus. viii. 50. 10–51. 1 (Philopoemen at Sparta). Cf. Niese, *GGMS* ii. 687–9; De Sanctis, *Storia* iv. 1. 138–9; Aymard, *Premiers Rapports*, pp. 315 ff.; Stier, *Roms Aufstieg*, pp. 160 ff.

long years of factional government, became Achaea's and had superimposed on them the traditional problems of relations between Sparta and Achaea. The result was a situation even more confused and even more difficult to resolve. Two accounts of the actual business of union are extant. Livy simply mentions a council of *principes*, and says that it decided to join Achaea. He says nothing of the feelings and dispositions of the *principes* involved. In the circumstances it must be assumed that they were representatives of all factions, among which Livy did not trouble to distinguish. Plutarch, in describing the same scene, is more explicit: 'While Sparta was in a state of confusion, Philopoemen seized his opportunity and fell upon the city with an armed force. Though some Spartans were unwilling, he persuaded others and won over the city and made it a member of the Achaean League . . . Moreover, Philopoemen carried with him the *aristoi*, who hoped to find in him a guardian of their freedom.'[1] The party distinctions given here are extremely vague. The possibility must also be considered that Plutarch was merely writing such distinctions into his account as a rhetorical commonplace—although his account as a whole must depend on Polybius. Plutarch however does proceed to indicate who the *aristoi* were: among them was Timolaus, Philopoemen's guest-friend.[2] Of the two perhaps real groups distinguished in Plutarch's first sentence, the *aristoi* whose support Philopoemen gained can only be the latter group, those whom he persuaded to join the League. The former group must have had good reason for their unwillingness to be won over by Philopoemen: clearly because they saw greater personal advantage from independence, or perhaps even actual danger from the union. They can therefore probably be identified with the remainder of Nabis' supporters.

This makes it easier to identify the political standpoint of the *aristoi*. They were clearly a group which had not been as dangerously close to Nabis as their opponents: to them the submergence

---

[1] Plut. *Phil.* 15. 2: τεταραγμένης δὲ τῆς Σπάρτης ὁ Φιλοποίμην ἁρπάσας τὸν καιρὸν ἐπιπίπτει μετὰ δυνάμεως, καὶ τῶν μὲν ἀκόντων, τοὺς δὲ συμπείσας προσηγάγετο καὶ μετεκόμισεν εἰς τοὺς Ἀχαιοὺς τὴν πόλιν. . . . ἀνέλαβε δὲ καὶ Λακεδαιμονίων τοὺς ἀρίστους, φύλακα τῆς ἐλευθερίας ἐκεῖνον ἐλπίσαντας ἕξειν.

[2] Plut. *Phil.* 15. 4 ff. It will at times be convenient to refer to this group as 'Timolaus' group'. This does not necessarily imply that Timolaus actually led the group—a question which is beyond settling.

of state identity, through the abolition of the Spartan kingship and entry into the League, would not carry the same personal risks. It is true that even they had to be persuaded, but compromise for them was clearly practicable. On the other hand, they cannot have been actively hostile to Nabis or they would quickly have been forced into exile or annihilation. If they held principles about the nationalist bogy of Spartan traditions, they had already compromised them by continuing to live under Nabis' regime; and they were now ready to compromise them again. We do not hear of the exile of their current opponents, who cannot reasonably be identified with any of the groups of exiles who are so prominent later. It therefore seems likely that they were allowed to continue living in the city, although presumably prevented from active participation in the government.

The political confusion in Sparta was, to some extent at least, resolved by Philopoemen's installing in power those willing to support him and the union with Achaea.[1] In the circumstances it was natural that they should look to him for the security of the government. Against this background we should consider the offer by Timolaus to Philopoemen of the 120 talents raised by the sale of the household of Nabis. The extant accounts of this episode show no significant variation; therefore Plutarch's, which is more detailed and precise, will be the basis of the discussion.[2] It is clear that the Spartan *aristoi*, despite the support of Philopoemen, were not wholly secure in power. Philopoemen's reply, that they should rather buy up the trouble-makers who were harassing the city with their factional struggles, shows that opposition within Sparta was agitating against their government, and that this opposition must have provoked the circumstances in which the offer was made to Philopoemen, as an attempt to buy his support. The fact that it was made by Timolaus, Philopoemen's guest-friend, indicates the importance which the

---

[1] Aymard's discussion (*Premiers Rapports*, pp. 318 ff.) is vitiated by two basic faults in interpretation: (i) failure to distinguish between the various Spartan interests; (ii) willingness to assume a static policy for Philopoemen, and a static political situation in Sparta between 192 and 188.

[2] Pol. xx. 12; Plut. *Phil.* 15. 4–6; Paus. viii. 51. 2. Pausanias places the offer after Philopoemen's defence of Sparta against Flamininus and Diophanes in 191, but Plutarch makes it clear that it was a direct result of the initial establishment in power of Timolaus' group. Pausanias also makes the offer the actual household, not the money from the sale, and rounds off the figure to 'more than one hundred talents'. None of his variants are more than the inaccuracies of abbreviation.

aristoi attached to Philopoemen's support and to this attempt
to bribe him; on the other hand it also suggests that they were
not yet fully sure that they had his whole-hearted support.[1] But
Philopoemen's refusal of the bribe made it clear that he wanted
to avoid having his policies dictated to him in advance by personal ties based on financial gratitude. He clearly preferred that
they should meet the dictates of circumstances, and that he
should be free to form them in the most suitable way without
running the risk of incurring the charge of disappointing legitimate expectations based on such pervasive ties of gratitude. Nevertheless he made it clear that he was a friend of Timolaus' group
—meaning that, for the moment at least, he saw Achaean interest
as intimately associated with their retention of power—but he refused to accept unconditional advance obligations. By accepting
the gift he would have associated himself too closely with one
faction to make himself ever acceptable to the other; and he
clearly envisaged some kind of compromise as the only practicable
solution to the Spartan confusion. He wanted to leave the door
open for himself to act as mediator. If Polybius' report of Philopoemen's advice to the Spartan government at this time is
authentic—to bribe their enemies to silence rather than their
friends[2]—Philopoemen was already working towards his goal
of compromising differences between the Spartan factions in the
Achaean interest. He must have been afraid that Flamininus
would enjoy fishing in the troubled waters of Spartan politics,
and was eager to prevent this.

Soon afterwards the Achaean year came to an end with the
autumn *synodos* and the election of Diophanes as *strategos*. There
seems to be no reason why Philopoemen's support should not
have secured Diophanes' election in autumn 192: Diophanes
was a fellow Megalopolitan, and had served under Philopoemen
frequently in the various campaigns against Nabis. Nothing indicates that he had any serious difference of opinion with Philopoemen before his attempt in 191 to reorganize Sparta with the
help of Flamininus. Although this difference of opinion quickly
developed into open hostility, this development does not provide
an argument for political opposition to Philopoemen at the time

---

[1] Plut. *Phil.* 15. 5–6. The Philopoemen legend was probably responsible for the
growth of the tradition about Timolaus' conventional three visits.

[2] Pol. xx. 12. 6–7; cf. Plut. *Phil.* 15. 6.

of the elections. It would, in any case, be strange to find a political opponent of Philopoemen elected to the *strategia* at the very time when Philopoemen's own glory, and therefore influence, was at its peak.[1]

In the autumn of 192 Antiochus arrived at Demetrias. After an abortive attempt to gain support at Chalcis he went into conference with the Aetolians at Demetrias. A decision was taken to try to gain support in Boeotia, Achaea, and Athamania. In the case of Achaea, the attempt was agreed upon because of rumours circulating about the increasing hostility between Philopoemen and Flamininus, resulting from Philopoemen's independently undertaking the war against Nabis and his subsequent annexation of Sparta. The Aetolians and Antiochus clearly thought that the change of *strategos* in Achaea would make no difference to Achaean policy. But they had grossly misinterpreted the Achaean situation. For even at the time of his first difference of opinion with Philopoemen, Flamininus had had little doubt that Achaea was loyal to Rome on major issues, and he had accordingly directed the weight of his propaganda to other objects. By this time he may not have been quite sure that Philopoemen's hostility was only the result of his reaction to Flamininus' interference in the Peloponnese; but in any case it was no part of his task to take risks. He was therefore present at the Achaean *syncletos* which Diophanes called at Aegium to hear the Aetolians.[2]

This *syncletos* was a resounding success for Flamininus. The emissaries of the Aetolians and Antiochus were shown decisively that Achaea had no sympathy for their cause. At no stage of the *syncletos* did there appear any likelihood of the Achaeans' being persuaded by the dissidents. This was made absolutely clear when they went beyond simply rejecting the proposals of the ambassadors, with the declaration that they would have the same friends and enemies as the Romans. Had there been any doubt in Flamininus' mind about the essential loyalty of the Achaeans,

---

[1] Pol. xxi. 9; Liv. xxxvii. 20. 2; cf. Lehmann, *Glaubwürdigkeit*, p. 266. These passages, and the general consideration of Philopoemen's influence, seem decisive against the views of De Sanctis, *Storia* iv. 1. 169, that Diophanes was at this time 'avversario politico di Filopemene', and of Aymard, *Premiers Rapports*, p. 323 and n. 40, 'intermédiaire entre les deux politiques opposées d'Aristainos et de Philopoimen', followed by Castellani, *Contributi*, 79.

[2] Liv. xxxv. 47. 2–4 (Aetolian estimate of Philopoemen); 31. 2 (Flamininus' trust in Achaea); 48. 1 (Flamininus at Aegium).

it must have vanished now. Additionally, this Achaean declaration makes it clear that at this time no formal treaty of alliance existed between Rome and Achaea. The leading spirit behind Achaean action at the *syncletos* must have been the *strategos* Diophanes. He was of Philopoemen's party and Philopoemen's support for his actions was affirmed by Polybius when he spoke in Philopoemen's defence before the Roman commissioners in 145. There can be little doubt that Philopoemen fully supported the action of Diophanes over this declaration of war.[1]

Diophanes was also willing to back up the Achaean decision at once with arms. 1,000 Achaean troops were mobilized, and 500 each were sent to Piraeus and Chalcis as garrisons. This was done openly on Flamininus' request. Although it was in general unusual for Achaean troops to serve abroad, it was not unknown in times of exceptional circumstances.[2] The use which Flamininus was immediately ready to make of the Achaean troops suggests that he had probably exerted some behind-the-scenes pressure on the Achaean officials to propose the declaration of war, the ground for which was prepared at the *syncletos* by Flamininus' own speech. If this was so, Philopoemen must have known about it and have approved, despite the hostility between himself and Flamininus.

At Piraeus the Achaean troops successfully helped Flamininus to expel Apollodorus, the leader of the party favouring Antiochus. At Chalcis they were less successful, and seem to have incurred some disgrace, at least in the eyes of Philopoemen, who himself took no part in these military activities. They were, in fact, forced to bargain with Antiochus for their release; and as Plutarch's record of Philopoemen's reaction to this shows, he displayed the same contemptuous attitude towards Antiochus' Syrians as Flamininus had displayed at the *syncletos*: Philopoemen would have cut them off in their taverns. If this reaction is contemporary— it may be later reminiscence, perhaps to Polybius himself—it already indicates criticism of Diophanes' leadership, and perhaps reflects Philopoemen's disapproval of the growing familiarity of Diophanse and Flamininus.[3]

[1] On the significance of the declaration for the existence of a *foedus*, cf. Badian, *JRS* 1952, 76 ff. On Philopoemen's support for Diophanes, cf. Pol. xxxix. 3. 8.
[2] Liv. xxxv. 50. 3–4 (garrisons). For other Achaean service abroad, cf. Liv. xxxiii. 18 (Rhodian Peraea); xxxvii. 20–1 (Pergamum).
[3] Liv. xxxv. 50. 3–4; Plut. *Phil.* 17. 1.

Within the Peloponnese, Achaean expansionism and closeness to Rome caused apprehension elsewhere than at Sparta. Both aspects of her policy troubled Elis: on the one hand, continued Achaean expansion within the Peloponnese must eventually affect Elis. If powerful Sparta could be annexed with little immediate trouble, how could Elis expect to be able to stand alone? On the other hand, traditional ties of friendship between Elis and Aetolia still existed. In the past this friendship had repeatedly brought Elis into conflict with Achaea, and now that Aetolia and Achaea had again chosen different sides in the approaching war, conflict could again be anticipated. In winter 192/1 the only possible action for an anti-Achaean state which did not fully realize the nature of Antiochus' commitment in Greece was to enter negotiations with him. This the Eleans did, in the hope of securing protection against any possible further Achaean expansion which might be encouraged by Rome. The Elean negotiations were successful, and Antiochus sent a force of 1,000 foot soldiers under a Cretan Euphanes—otherwise unknown—to protect them. Since there is no record of any Achaean attack on Elis during 191, it is reasonable to conclude that the force of Cretans served its purpose until after Thermopylae.[1]

One other event of prime importance for Achaea, which probably occurred during the winter, was the grant by the Senate of a *foedus aequum* to the League. The reasons for accepting this date for the *foedus* are that the decision of the Achaeans to declare war on Antiochus in the autumn was of inestimable physical and propagandist value to Rome. The Senate would accordingly feel inclined to grant the *foedus* as an indication of Roman gratitude for the Achaeans' action. This fits well also with the increasing Achaean expansionist activity of summer 191, in the course of which it became necessary for Flamininus to explain harshly—but not explicitly—that the essential relationship between Rome and Achaea had not been changed by the grant of the *foedus*.[2]

[1] Pol. xx. 3; Liv. xxxvi. 5. 2–3.
[2] Cf. Badian, *JRS* 1952 (and bibliography, to which add Castellani, *Contributi*, 84 ff.).

VII

THE PROBLEMS OF EXPANSION

ROMAN policy towards the East does not seem to have created sufficient partisan feeling in Rome for it to have become the basis of major inter-party disputes.[1] The one feature of Roman politics which is in fact apparent is the remarkable lack of controversy over the major issues. Such dispute as arose was concerned with methods rather than with ends. For instance, in 196 Flamininus had had difficulty in persuading the commissioners for Greece and the Senate to accept the full implications of his policy of Greek 'freedom', to which he had personally committed himself. But this issue was not factional, and did not become so. It arose from a different assessment of the necessary strategy to be employed towards Antiochus: the potential threat was generally agreed.[2] Flamininus ultimately persuaded the Senate to accept his view by showing that this was the best policy for Rome. As far as we can tell, this was achieved without any 'party' disputes. There was no fundamental disagreement on the aims of policy between Flamininus and those who disagreed with his assessment of the position. Attempts to discover a party issue over eastern policy, a conflict between the Scipiones and Flaminini, do not seem to have any basis in the facts given by our sources, and must be to a large extent illusory. Certainly Africanus and his friends took the danger from Antiochus seriously; so aiso did the Roman people when they elected him consul for 194; but so equally did Flamininus when he envisaged Greek *clientela* as a major weapon for Rome's use against Antiochus. The majority of the Senate relied on the calmer advice of their eastern experts, and did not create a consular province of Macedonia in 194, clearly because they considered this the best policy.[3]

---

[1] Despite the attempts of modern scholars to find this: cf. Scullard, *Roman Politics*, pp. 110 ff.

[2] Cf. chapter V, pp. 88–9.

[3] Liv. xxxiv. 43. 1 (election of Africanus); 4 ff. (provinces); cf. Badian, *Studies*,

When the threat of real danger from Antiochus appeared in 192, Flamininus' propaganda mission of eastern experts was sent to Greece by the Senate. There can be no possibility of finding a party issue in this. Flamininus was no longer an evacuationist: his hope was that the beneficial results of his policy of evacuation would now be found. The Senate's reaction to the threat was based solely on its assessment of the situation, and it sent the best men for the job. As events took a more serious turn, it became necessary to send a consular army to Greece in 191. It happened that M'. Acilius Glabrio was successful at the consular elections for 191, probably helped by the prestige of the Scipiones, and he was sent to Greece to deal with Antiochus. But despite this election it would not be justified to assume that opposition at the elections was based on a different policy to be pursued towards Antiochus. Reports on the state of affairs in Greece came from Flamininus' mission, and the advancement of the date of the consular elections for 191 must have been decided as a result of information received from him. Clearly Flamininus, as much as the Scipiones, fully appreciated the need for a Roman army in Greece. His earlier policy of evacuation cannot now be attributed to him, for he continued his work in Greece in full co-operation with the consul. Again, there can have been no conflict of policies at the elections: only the usual conflict of persons. And this seems to have continued to be the case with regard to eastern policy throughout the period.[1]

In spring 191 the new consul M'. Acilius Glabrio arrived in Greece with M. Porcius Cato on his staff. One of Cato's first tasks was to undertake a minor propaganda mission for Glabrio. From the Roman base at or near Corinth he paid visits to that city, to Patrae and to Aegium, before leaving the Peloponnese for Athens. The purpose of these visits was probably no more than to announce the arrival of the new consul in Greece at the principal centres of population. The presence of the consular army which Cato announced was a confirmation of the Roman

pp. 122 ff. Welles, 'Greek Liberty', *JJP* 1965, 30, remarks that modern historians have failed to give proper weight to the political consequences of the Greeks' ignorance that, to the Romans, recognition of a *civitas* as *libera* carried with it the notion of patron–client. He seems to be unaware of Badian's ground-breaking studies in this period: *Foreign Clientelae* was published as long ago as 1958.

[1] Liv. xxxv. 23. 5 (Flamininus' commission); 24. 1–3 (early elections); 24. 5 (election of Glabrio).

commitment to help their allies against Antiochus, a physical demonstration that the war was not going to be fought solely by allied arms and Flamininus' propaganda. The very presence of the brash Cato straight from Rome would be quite sufficient to show the cities he visited that his was a wholly Roman commitment. Cato visited the convenient coastal towns; perhaps another legate visited the southern Achaean cities.[1]

During the spring and early summer, events in the north developed and culminated in the defeat of Antiochus by Glabrio at Thermopylae, probably in May. After the capture of Chalcis by Antiochus the previous autumn, the Achaeans played no part in the war. In the Peloponnese, however, there was considerable activity. Early in 191 Diophanes was faced with violent disaffection at Sparta. Plutarch's account is straightforward: Diophanes heard that the Spartans were undergoing another revolution, and he determined to punish them. They were disposed towards war, and were throwing the Peloponnese into confusion. Philopoemen tried to prevent Diophanes from interfering by calling his attention to the broader issues involved, in connection with the presence of Antiochus in Greece; but Diophanes took no notice, invaded Laconia in company with Flamininus, and marched on Sparta. Philopoemen rushed to Sparta, organized opposition to Diophanes and Flamininus, and successfully prevented them from entering Sparta. As a result, he ended the disturbances in the city and restored the Spartans to the League, in which they had been from the beginning. Plutarch makes no attempt to analyse either the party groupings at Sparta which led to this violence, or the motives of Diophanes, Flamininus, or Philopoemen for their actions; and Pausanias' even briefer account is of no help in this. But we must attempt to elucidate these matters, as they are fundamental for understanding Achaean politics at this period.[2]

Philopoemen's settlement of Sparta the previous autumn had confirmed Timolaus and the *aristoi* in power with the support of

---

[1] Plut. *Cat. Ma.* 12. The order of the towns in the text is Plutarch's. Aymard, *Premiers Rapports*, p. 329, n. 25, unnecessarily wishes to alter this to fit the route of a traveller from Italy. Plutarch does not say that Cato was *en route* from Italy. On the legal aspect of these visits, cf. appendix 6, p. 282.

[2] Plut. *Phil.* 16. 1–2; cf. Paus. viii. 51. 1; Niese, *GGMS* ii. 715 f.; Aymard, *Premiers Rapports*, pp. 330 ff. (both emphasize the Spartan desire for restoration of the coastal towns, which neither source mentions).

Achaea and Philopoemen. But their position was by no means secure, as their attempt to buy Philopoemen shows. Political difficulties at Sparta, therefore, must have arisen primarily from the conflict between the *aristoi* and Nabis' party. When Plutarch says that the Spartans were disposed towards war, his statement must be interpreted in the light of the party groupings. It must mean, in fact, war against the League, and this is made quite clear by Plutarch's subsequent statement that Philopoemen rejoined the city to the League.[1] This hostile activity towards the League, therefore, cannot have been by Timolaus' group, whose interest was intimately connected with their association with the League, but it must indicate that they had been overthrown and replaced by the anti-League party.

The reactions of the Achaean politicians to this news were varied. Philopoemen must have wanted to intervene on behalf of Timolaus and his own settlement, but he was no longer *strategos*. Diophanes must equally have wanted Sparta to remain in the League; but he cannot have shared Philopoemen's eagerness to save his prestige. Flamininus also had to be considered; and Diophanes may have been unwilling to act at first without Flamininus' approval. Flamininus was hampered by the fact that he was not a free agent, and had to take due consideration of the possible effect of his action on the war against Antiochus. For this reason, the general disturbance in the southern Peloponnese was dangerous, and could not be allowed to continue. But his personal feeling also had to be considered: he was tied to supporting the Spartan participation in the League, for otherwise he would get no support from either Diophanes or Philopoemen. His ideal of a balance of power in the Peloponnese had in any case only been viable while Nabis was alive. On the other hand, he was by no means tied to the support of Philopoemen's friends in Sparta. His connections of *clientela*, resulting from his defeat of Nabis, were with the tyrant's party, and it was still his view of Roman interest to keep Achaea fairly weak. If this could no longer be achieved by maintaining another power to hold her in check, it could perhaps be achieved more subtly by encouraging domestic trouble within the League.

---

[1] Plut. *Phil.* 16. 1–2. Aymard, *Premiers Rapports*, p. 334, n. 12, doubts (strangely) the certain implication of Plutarch's statement, that Sparta had been out of the League.

His aim therefore seems to have been at the same time both to destroy Philopoemen's prestige and to realize his new conception of a new larger but weaker Achaea by reuniting Sparta with the League—but under the local government of the party hostile to Achaea.

Diophanes' reaction is demonstrated by his joint expedition with Flamininus to Sparta. His motives for co-operating with Flamininus against his old colleague Philopoemen may have been mixed. His dedication, seen by Pausanias, proclaimed that Diophanes was the first man to unite the Peloponnese under Achaean control. He was clearly proud of his achievement, and this should probably be seen as the chief aim of his policy in 191.[1] He may sincerely have been convinced that his aim—in which he was directly competing with Philopoemen—could only be achieved in his year with the full co-operation of Flamininus, and it is possible that he had an informal agreement with Flamininus to this effect. This clearly differed from Philopoemen's view, but its immediate effect would be to cause him to support Flamininus at Sparta, for since Sparta had seceded from the League Diophanes would be able to claim to have restored it. At the same time he would himself replace Philopoemen as the League patron of the Spartan government.

In this context Philopoemen's violent objection to Diophanes' interference in Laconia should be interpreted. He cannot have favoured complete Achaean inaction, as Plutarch suggests, for his Spartan friends had been ousted by the anti-Achaean party. But he did have violent feelings about the action which Diophanes was contemplating. These will have been both personal and public: personal, because of his connection with the original settlement and with Timolaus' government; public, because, with his generally sceptical view of Flamininus' activities, he probably understood what Flamininus was trying to do. As long as Timolaus' group was in power at Sparta, Achaea had no need to

---

[1] Paus. viii. 30. 5. Aymard, *Premiers Rapports*, p. 335, n. 15, rejects Schorn's interpretation (*Geschichte Griechenlands*, p. 289) that Diophanes wanted to equal Philopoemen's glory—an obvious personal motive—in favour of his application of Polybius' biased judgement of Diophanes at another time as στρατιωτικώτερος ἢ πολιτικώτερος (xxii. 10. 4). In fact, everything known of Diophanes, supported by his inscription, suggests that Schorn was exact in his understanding. On Pol. xxii. 10. 4, cf. ch. IX, pp. 167–8. Polybius himself (ii. 40. 2) claims the achievement of Peloponnesian unity for Philopoemen.

exert pressure on the recognized government to keep Sparta within the League: if any intervention were necessary it could be represented as action on behalf of the legitimate Spartan government against dissident factions. With the elevation of an anti-Achaean group to power, and with a limit artificially placed on their freedom by the requirement that they would have to belong to the League, future relations between Achaea and Sparta would inevitably be confusion worse confounded—a state of affairs which Flamininus desired, as it would keep Achaea occupied and comparatively weak, while at the same time it would give him the prospect of regular intervention and provide him with frequent opportunities for demonstrating in Rome the breadth of his patronage.

These considerations, when added to his desire to prevent Flamininus and Diophanes from gaining undeserved prestige from upsetting his own settlement, made Philopoemen decide to ignore the possible consequences of opposing the *strategos* and Flamininus at Sparta: his prestige—and therefore his political career—was at stake. If it came to justification he could represent his action as support for the legitimate and recognized government against internal rebels whom the powers of the League were supporting. He arrived at Sparta before Flamininus and Diophanes, and had time to organize his friends into resistance before they arrived. It seems unlikely that there was any actual fighting before the city: Philopoemen no doubt organized his Spartan government troops and his propaganda sufficiently well to make this politically undesirable for Diophanes and Flamininus, who had no alternative but to withdraw. They had suffered a major political defeat. The compromise which they had intended to offer to the tyrants' party had been given no opportunity of being put into practice.

Philopoemen's action cannot be judged by the criterion of absolute legality, for legality had become a weapon of the political conflict. He had certainly opposed the *strategos* and Flamininus; but because he was successful he did not suffer for his rashness. Diophanes and Flamininus had set out to restore Sparta to the League and to prevent general trouble in Laconia. They could not in equity complain when Philopoemen, although acting unofficially, had achieved precisely this result. Plutarch is quite explicit on this point: Philopoemen calmed the city and restored it to the League. He had fulfilled his obligations to his friends, preserved his prestige by protecting his settlement, and robbed Flamininus and Diophanes of their political spoils by achieving their ends without using their methods—methods on which Flamininus at least had privately placed equal importance. Furthermore, his solution was likely to be far more popular among the Achaean voters than Flamininus' solution, made official by Diophanes' endorsement, which favoured Nabis' ex-supporters. He was successful, therefore he could not be punished for his action. He was successful because he had the propaganda of legality on his side, and had managed to depict the official federal action as the destruction of the legitimate Spartan government. Flamininus was not prepared to resort to naked power-politics, and therefore had to concede defeat. Had Philopoemen failed, the full force of Achaean legalistic propaganda would no doubt have been turned against him, and his political career would have come to an abrupt end.

Philopoemen's action clearly could not improve his relations with Flamininus, which had already begun to deteriorate the previous year. It also marks his first break with Diophanes, which resulted in Diophanes' associating himself with Aristaenus—who had also had no major difference of opinion with Philopoemen before his return from Crete—in the opposition to Philopoemen which flourished in the next decade.[1] But this incipient hostility did not prevent Diophanes from continuing to pursue the policy of expansion which he shared with Philopoemen. A short time after Thermopylae the island of Zacynthus, which had been held during the war for Amynander of Athamania by Hierocles of Agrigentum, was bought from Hierocles for Achaea by Diophanes. At about the same time, negotiations which had been in progress with Messene broke down. At Elis Achaean negotiators received a more favourable reply. The Eleans clearly had nowhere to turn for help against Achaea now that Antiochus was defeated, and the Achaean purchase of neighbouring Zacynthus, their closest off-shore island, could not make them feel more secure. It was therefore a matter of expediency that they should now be willing to allow negotiations with Achaea to proceed on a more friendly basis.[2]

[1] Cf. Pol. xxii. 10. 4 f.; Liv. xxxviii. 32. 6–7.
[2] Liv. xxxvi. 32. 1 (purchase of Zacynthus); 31. 1–4 (Elis and Messene).

For the moment, however, it seemed that Diophanes might have more success in gaining new adherents to Achaea if he applied pressure to Messene. After Thermopylae, military action against Messene seemed quite legitimate, since the Messenians were known to have favoured Antiochus, although they had not actually taken an active part in his support. Diophanes may legitimately have felt that extreme measures were justified in treating this potential enemy.[1] Accordingly he led the Achaean army against Messene and made preparations to besiege the town. But he had not consulted Flamininus. This omission may have been deliberate, for his flirtation with Flamininus' policies at Sparta had not had the success he desired, and he may have been disillusioned by this failure. He could always argue, if necessary, that the *foedus* granted Achaea the right to independent action. The Messenians, however, in the current situation were more willing to admit the importance of Flamininus' intervention in any Peloponnesian settlement, and accordingly appealed to him while he was at Chalcis. They offered to open their gates to the Romans, but not to the Achaeans. Flamininus hurried to Megalopolis and ordered Diophanes to stop the fighting. Diophanes, probably relying on the recent *foedus* to support his desire for Achaean expansion, had not expected a demand in these naked power-political terms, and felt obliged to acquiesce in Flamininus' demands. He played no part in the subsequent discussions about the settlement of Messene, and had no alternative to accepting what Flamininus imposed. The terms were, in the event, mostly favourable to Achaea: the chief point was that Messene was to be united with the League. The sting in the tail came with the stipulation that her exiles were to be taken back and disputes referred to Flamininus.[2]

From the Achaean point of view this settlement was acceptable, although the restored exiles might prove troublesome. Diophanes was deprived of the glory of having achieved it himself but could scarcely object on that account. Flamininus had been placed in an awkward position by Diophanes' independent action against Messene, yet he managed to create from the difficulty both a suitable immediate compromise and a new general policy for the future. He had little alternative to granting Diophanes Messene. Diophanes was a useful man to Flamininus, and he had to be

---

[1] Liv. xxxvi. 31. 2: *cum Aetolis sentiebant.*   [2] Liv. xxxvi. 31. 5–9.

THE PROBLEMS OF EXPANSION

conciliated after being prevented from fighting against Messene. If Messene had been left weak and independent, Philopoemen would certainly have taken the city in his next *strategia* without asking Flamininus' permission, with the result that Flamininus would have been robbed of a chance of extending his *clientela* both in Messene and in Achaea. His settlement of Messene marks an important new phase in Flamininus' policy of creating internal discord in a city which he united with the League. At Sparta he had failed in his attempt to achieve this by being unable to change the pro-Achaean government. At Messene for the first time he tried to achieve it by insisting on the restoration of exiles—who at Messene were already his clients.[1] This became an equally potent cause of civil disturbance, and it had the additional propagandist benefit of having equity on its side. At Sparta the lack of equity in his solution had contributed to his enforced acknowledgement of defeat by Philopoemen. After his settlement of Messene, the more satisfactory slogan, 'the restoration of the exiles', becomes the chief theme of Roman policy towards Achaea.

From the point of view of Flamininus' own relations with Messene his settlement was also satisfactory, although before this becomes clear it is necessary to identify the Messenian political groups. The only extant account of the events of 191 is that of Livy, which distinguishes two groups of Messenians: those holding the city, who offered *deditio* to Flamininus, and the *exules*, who were restored as a result of the settlement. The only Messenian politician whose name we know at this period is Deinocrates. It is therefore convenient to examine Messenian party groupings as they affected him.

In 195 Deinocrates had been leader of the Messenian contingent to the allied forces in Flamininus' war against Nabis. As a result of this he had become intimate with Flamininus.[2] The conclusion is therefore fairly safe, that the party represented by Deinocrates had been in power in Messene in 195. The next

---

[1] See below.

[2] Pol. xxiii. 5. 2: ἐγεγόνει γὰρ αὐτῷ συνήθης κατὰ τὸν Λακωνικὸν πόλεμον. The Λακωνικὸς πόλεμος can only be that against Nabis in 195: Flamininus' expedition of 191 with Diophanes was not an allied joint venture—and scarcely even a πόλεμος. That Deinocrates was the official representative of Messene in 195 seems clear from the concessions granted to Messene in the settlement: Liv. xxxiv. 35. 6; cf. Seeliger, *Messenien*, p. 18.

information about Deinocrates is from winter 184/3, when he appeared in Rome, and looked to Flamininus for support against Achaea for Messenian independence. The basis for this hope was his long-standing friendship with Flamininus, which had been formed in 195 and presumably continued unbroken until 184/3. This, at least, is the impression which Polybius' account gives. In it Deinocrates assumes automatically that his bond of *clientela* with Flamininus will work satisfactorily in his favour. Certainly no doubt was in his mind that their ten-year-long friendship had altered in any way, or that anything had intervened which would make the answer to his request for help seem at all doubtful to him.[1] This later trust in the solidarity of *clientela* is important in considering the groupings of 191. For if Deinocrates' group had held the city in 191, they must inevitably have felt that the foundations of the *clientela* existing between Flamininus and Deinocrates had been betrayed by Flamininus: *deditio* was offered to Flamininus in all good faith. But the result was that the worst fears of the *dediticii* were realized: enforced membership of the Achaean League, which it was the very purpose of their *deditio* to avoid, and the enforced restoration of the exiles, who in the nature of things must have been their political opponents.[2] This was scarcely the way in which Deinocrates would expect *clientela* to work. It did not augur well for his future relations with Flamininus. Yet there is no hint in 184/3 that any such betrayal had taken place.

From the earlier and later relationship between Deinocrates and Flamininus we would expect the benefit of the settlement of 191 to have accrued to Deinocrates' party. In the actual settlement, the group which certainly gained the greatest benefits was the group of exiles, not the group of *dediticii*. It has been shown that there are reasons connected with Flamininus' developing policies which made the restoration of the exiles at Messene desirable for its own sake. But a personal link between Flamininus

---

[1] Pol. xxiii. 5.

[2] Roebuck, *Messenia*, p. 92 and n. 117, thinks that the Messenians' offer of *deditio* was not accepted: 'The sequel of Livy's account shows that Flamininus himself made final arrangements for Messene's entrance into the League; had he accepted the surrender on behalf of Rome he could scarcely have done this, although a Roman commander who accepted *deditio* had wide powers . . .' This misunderstands the nature of *deditio*, which was essentially an agreement between the Roman commander and the *dediticii*. Cf. Heuss, *Völk. Grund.*, p. 60.

and the exiles should not be discounted on these grounds. If we discard the identification of Deinocrates with the *dediticii* and examine the alternative, the difficulties are much less. If Deinocrates was one of the exiles, there is no need to look upon Flamininus' action in 191 as being contradictory to his friendship with Deinocrates, which dated from 195. It also shows more clearly the solid basis for the hope which Deinocrates showed in 184/3.

The main difficulty in this identification is that we know nothing of the change of circumstances which turned Deinocrates from leader of his countrymen in 195 to exile seeking restoration in 191. In itself the change is hardly surprising; nor is the fact that we hear nothing of it, for the sources have no special interest in Messenian politics. Nevertheless, the difficulty remains in some degree unless a change in general circumstances can be found to support the hypothesis: it is clear that neither the *dediticii* nor the exiles were in favour of union with Achaea, so that this cannot have been the issue over which they split.

The single most important issue facing the states of Greece between 195 and 191 was the attitude to be taken towards the Aetolians and Antiochus. This was a particularly vital issue for Elis and Messene, which were old allies of Aetolia and Rome. Elis had quickly made her decision, and a Syrian-paid garrison was accepted into the city. Messene was not openly committed to the same extent, but this does not mean that the issue was not alive.[1] It is not possible to envisage Deinocrates' recommending any other policy than that of closer union with Rome. In autumn 192, before it was known how fully the Senate was committed to the war with Antiochus, and when Antiochus was already in Greece, this may have appeared a dangerous course. When the Syrian garrison came to Elis it was impossible. Deinocrates must have seen great personal advantages in a close

---

[1] Well seen by Seeliger, *Messenien*, p. 19, but denied by Aymard, *Premiers Rapports*, p. 341, n. 14, on the grounds that this would have interested Livy, who would therefore have been bound to include it. But Livy has already sufficiently indicated that Messene was an Aetolian sympathizer. Aymard prefers to refurbish the oligarch/democrat division at Messene, for which the only evidence seems to be Pausanias' description of Deinocrates as δυνατὸς χρήμασι (viii. 51. 7). This view was apparently founded by Freeman, *History of Federal Government*[2], p. 505, and became standard when accepted by Colin, *Rome et la Grèce*, p. 227, and Niccolini, *La Conf. Ach.*, p. 157. Cf. Roebuck, *Messenia*, p. 95, n. 126; Lehmann, *Glaubwürdigkeit*, pp. 182-3. It is no longer tenable.

relationship with Rome. He also seems to have had a more realistic understanding of Roman power than his opponents. When
Diophanes opened negotiations with Messene, it was known
that the group which formed the government was in favour of
Antiochus. It therefore seems most likely that Deinocrates had
been forced into exile over this issue.

Deinocrates' presence among the exiles made possible a settlement of Messene which must have been a cause of high satisfaction to Flamininus. We have already seen how the settlement
suited his Achaean policies. Similar considerations must have
been at work in his relations with Messene. Here also the settlement was a compromise by the friends of Rome: Deinocrates
and his fellow exiles were restored, but they cannot have liked
Messene's being united with Achaea. The *dediticii* who had
favoured Antiochus were weakened both by the union with
Achaea and by the restoration of their opponents: their relations
with Antiochus ensured that they gained no compensating advantages. All advantages gained by the various interests in
Achaea and Messene could be claimed by Flamininus as mani-
festations of Roman generosity—and as a (somewhat heavy-
handed) demonstration of how *clientela* worked. All disadvantages
and difficulties could be laid at the door of local party squabbles
and the necessity for compromise in the general interest. The
settlement was a neat distribution of *beneficia* to those willing to
compromise. But as so often—as Flamininus no doubt realized
—the compromise satisfied none of the participants, and Messene
was a satisfactorily recurring problem for Achaea for the next
twelve years.

After he had imposed his settlement on Messene, Flamininus
made it known to Diophanes that he wanted him to call a *syncletos*. When the meeting assembled, despite his recent acceptance
of the accession of Messene to the League, Flamininus made
it quite clear that Rome was not prepared to allow Achaean
expansion to continue indefinitely: within the Peloponnese—a
concession to Diophanes' aims, and a bid for his support—it
could be acceptable; outside the mainland was out of bounds.
The matter which produced this crisis was that of Zacynthus,
which had recently been bought by Diophanes. Flamininus used
the simile of the tortoise's vulnerability, once its head was out
of its shell, to demonstrate that Achaea must keep within the

Peloponnese. But in fact there had been some sharp practice in the purchase of the island, which Flamininus could legitimately claim as Roman by virtue of the defeat of Amynander before it had been bought by the Achaeans. There was clearly some truth in his claim, and Diophanes must have realized the possibility of the charge when he bought the island. At the *syncletos* however he vainly insisted on the legitimacy of his own action, against the arguments of Flamininus and of an unidentified group of *quidam Achaeorum*.[1]

The main issues arising from Livy's narrative of the *syncletos* are the identification of these *quidam Achaeorum*, and the reasons for Diophanes' violent reaction to Flamininus' interference over Zacynthus, at a time when we would expect him to have been coming closer to Flamininus' policy for Achaea. Relations between Philopoemen and Diophanes must have been openly hostile after their opposition at Sparta. Yet it is clear that they both believed in the possibility and desirability of annexing new territory. The growth of personal antipathy between the two men was no reason for Diophanes to change the policy in which he believed and to which he was politically committed. The Messenian affair shows this clearly, and Zacynthus is in this pattern. Diophanes had again tried to present Flamininus with a *fait accompli*. Now that this had failed, he had no alternative but to defend his purchase of the island, in which his personal prestige was deeply involved. He had lost little by complying with Flamininus' order over Messene, since it had arrived before any conclusion had been reached. With Zacynthus, the situation was different: an already-existing Achaean settlement, to which Diophanes had committed himself, was to be overturned. However much Diophanes may have been willing to co-operate with Flamininus in general, he was already too deeply involved on the opposite side on this issue to be able to do anything but defend his position. If he did not have any hope of winning, he could at least hope to take some advantage from demonstrating his patriotism.

The Achaean opposition to Diophanes, which Livy leaves anonymous, cannot be certainly identified. Since Livy does not name the spokesmen, Polybius may not have done so either. If this were

---

[1] Liv. xxxvi. 31. 10–32. 9; cf. Aymard, *Premiers Rapports*, pp. 350–1; Lehmann, *Glaubwürdigkeit*, pp. 266 ff., esp. p. 270.

so, it would immediately arouse suspicion. The activity of the opposition spokesmen at the *syncletos* was confined to attacking Diophanes in person, and to dissociating themselves from his action: *et initio eam se rem aspernatos testabantur et tunc pertinaciam increpitabant praetoris.*[1] Livy does not suggest that there was any general sympathy for Flamininus; he makes it quite clear that this specific issue was the object of their hostility to Diophanes— *eam rem.* It is clearly possible that Livy has here recorded a piece of deliberate concealment by Polybius. Were the *quidam* Philopoemen and his supporters, using the Zacynthus issue—which was already lost—to destroy Diophanes politically, just as Diophanes had attempted to destroy Philopoemen politically over Sparta? This would certainly make sound political sense. The difference of opinion cannot have been over the ideology of expansion, since this was apparently agreed by all groups. But it could clearly have been a personal matter of this nature. Philopoemen may even have attracted support *on this issue* from the more moderate Achaeans who were unwilling to act independently of Flamininus.[2]

Diophanes was badly disappointed if he hoped that his display of patriotism in a lost cause at the *syncletos* would compensate for his earlier failure at Sparta, and create sufficient influence in his own right to prevent Philopoemen's election as *strategos* at the *synodos* which followed soon after. Philopoemen was elected, and at the electoral *synodos*[3] itself again conflicted with Flamininus. Diophanes, on the other hand, was not, as far as we know, ever again elected *strategos*. His future lay in a policy of close co-operation with Rome, into which he was driven in order to provide an alternative policy to the more openly independent action of Philopoemen's group. He had forfeited Philopoemen's trust, and with it participation in his party, by his stab in the back at Sparta, when he deserted Philopoemen for Flamininus. Nevertheless, despite his ultimate failure in federal politics, he did succeed in unifying the Peloponnese under Achaea. His statue proclaimed this until imperial times. But as far as we know, his

---

[1] Liv. xxxvi. 32. 4.

[2] Among them may have been included Aristaenus, as Aymard, *Premiers Rapports*, pp. 350–1.

[3] By this time it was probably about September, the time of the autumn *synodos*, therefore the time of the elections. Cf. Aymard, *Premiers Rapports*, p. 352, n. 2; Larsen, *Rep. Gov.*, p. 173; below, appendix 2 B, pp. 251 ff.

political unreliability disqualified him from playing an important part in administering his achievement.[1]

A further attempt to assert Roman patronage in Achaea was made at the autumn *synodos* of the League at which Philopoemen was re-elected *strategos*. Flamininus had convinced Glabrio of the value of his Peloponnesian policy, and both came to Aegium. Since the spring, Flamininus had discovered a new diplomatic weapon for harrying expansionist Achaea in the numerous exiles in the Peloponnese. The restoration of the exiles had been accomplished at Messene. Now it was to be introduced at Sparta. Large numbers of exiles had been created by the various extremist regimes of the Spartan revolution : Flamininus did not distinguish between the various groups, but simply insisted on wholesale restoration.[2] They had become his clients at the time of his expedition against Nabis in 195;[3] but until his restoration of Deinocrates and the other exiles to Messene he had not formed any policy which involved their restoration. This was advanced for the first time at the autumn *synodos* of 191, and naturally met violent opposition from Philopoemen. His argument, recorded by Plutarch, was that he wanted the exiles to owe their gratitude for their restoration to Achaea and Philopoemen, not to the Romans.[4] The issue is very clearly formulated, for it was clearly understood by Philopoemen: he knew well that Flamininus stood to gain from the restoration of the exiles the advantages which he had failed to achieve by his earlier attempt to change the governing party. His own direct public and private interest was to prevent Flamininus from achieving this, to prevent him from causing discord within the League and from increasing his own influence at Sparta at the same time. If the Romans should insist on a restoration, Philopoemen realized that he would ultimately have to submit. But he clearly hoped that he could manipulate the circumstances in such a way that the patronage of Achaea and Philopoemen would achieve the result, not that of Rome and Flamininus. But the point of submission had not yet been reached. The matter had just been broached, and there was still time to see whether the Senate would endorse its

representatives' demands. For the moment Philopoemen managed
to persuade the *synodos* to postpone a decision.[1]

The other matter discussed at the *synodos* in which the Romans
were interested was the accession of Elis. The Eleans as much
as the Achaeans had every reason for wishing to prevent the
Romans from exercising their patronage. They had much to gain
if they succeeded, for they had been open supporters of Antiochus, and could therefore be regarded by the Roman Senate as
defeated enemies. The position which they took up was based on
the consideration that if they joined the League voluntarily, they
might avoid Roman retaliation—the importance of which was
vividly brought home to them by the fate of the Messenians, who
had been in a similar situation. Flamininus' treatment of Messene,
in particular his restoration of the exiles, could scarcely be expected to encourage other states to put themselves into his hands.
Since the Eleans had no alternative to joining the League, they
naturally wanted to do so on the most favourable terms possible.
This clearly meant without Roman interference. They stated
their position clearly; and the *synodos* recognized the coincidence
of Achaean and Elean interests—perhaps again advised by
Philopoemen's experience of Flamininus' diplomacy of patronage.
The meeting accepted the Eleans' statement. Flamininus and
Glabrio had again been deprived of a chance to assert their
patronage, had again been frustrated by Philopoemen, who was
this time aided by Elean suspicions. The continuation in useful
diplomatic life of the slogan of Greek freedom depended on the
absence of Roman demands in terms of power politics. Accordingly the Romans had no alternative but to accept their defeat.

The formalities of the union of Elis with Achaea were probably
carried out at once, if we may accept as the whole truth the claim
on the base of Diophanes' statue, that Diophanes was the man
who first unified the Peloponnese under the Achaean League.
There is no good reason for rejecting this claim except for Polybius' generalized statement in Philopoemen's favour; and since

---

[1] Aymard argues that this policy must have been passed down to Flamininus
by the Senate, but he does not offer any conclusive argument. The usual practice
was for the man on the spot to formulate a policy in good faith, which was then
approved and adopted by the Senate, and it seems likely that this was the procedure
in this case. Aymard's attempt to prove his point (*Premiers Rapports*, pp. 356 f., n. 1)
by arguing that Pol. xxi. 1 refers to summer 191 is not convincing. See appendix
8, pp. 286–7.

Diophanes' year must have ended at, or soon after, the *synodos*, the union was probably arranged and ratified at this *synodos*.[1]

Opposition over internal Peloponnesian matters did not mean that Philopoemen considered it necessary to refuse all co-operation to the Romans. During the following winter an Achaean force ravaged the south coast of Aetolia. This seems to have had little effect on the general course of the war, but it illustrates that Philopoemen's willingness to co-operate with Rome on the major issues was not affected by his opposition to Roman interference in the Peloponnese.[2]

---

[1] Liv. xxxvi. 35. 7; cf. Pol. ii. 40. 2 (Philopoemen); cf. Aymard, *Premiers Rapports*, pp. 353 ff. Another matter in which Diophanes perhaps concerned himself was the negotiation with Glabrio for the resettlement of the Elateans, who had taken refuge at Stymphalus when their city was destroyed, probably by the Aetolians. An inscription from Stymphalus records the event (*SEG* xi. 1107): the interpretation accepted here is that of Passerini, *Athenaeum* 1948; also accepted by Lehmann, *Glaubwürdigkeit*, pp. 120–5. But cf. Mitsos, *REG* 1946/7; Accame, *RFIC* 1949 (both argue unconvincingly that Elatea had been destroyed by the Romans). It is not clear whether the Diophanes mentioned (line 12) as envoy to Glabrio is the *strategos*. Against the identification is the fact that the Diophanes of the inscription was sent by the Achaeans outside the Peloponnese on relatively unimportant business, which the *strategos* would not normally undertake in person. However, this mission could have been in the interval between the end of his *strategia* and Glabrio's departure from Greece.

[2] Liv. xxxvii. 4. 6.

VIII

SPARTA

FLAMININUS' policy towards Achaean domestic affairs took a new turn in winter 191/0, when his intention to restore the Spartan exiles was given the seal of senatorial approval. The occasion was the reception of an embassy from the Spartan government which enquired about the possibility of the Senate's restoring the five Spartan hostages who had been taken by Flamininus in 195 after his war against Nabis. They also asked whether the coastal towns which had been placed under Achaean *tutela* at the same time could now be restored to Spartan control. The Roman reply was non-committal on this issue: the Senate would give instructions about the coastal towns to envoys who were being sent to Greece. As far as the hostages were concerned, there was need for further consideration. Flamininus' policy then showed itself, in its new senatorial guise, when the Senate ended the interview by asking the Spartans why the 'old exiles' had not yet been restored, now that Sparta was free. The reply of the embassy is lost.[1]

The presence of this embassy at Rome is of great importance for understanding the fluid situation at Sparta. It was clearly a Spartan government embassy: Polybius would not otherwise have called the ambassadors simply Spartans (Λακεδαιμόνιοι). But their requests—particularly that about the hostages—seem directly contrary to the interests of Timolaus' group. Clearly they cannot have been responsible for the embassy. The only possible conclusion seems to be that they had been overthrown at some time between Philopoemen's defence of Sparta in spring 191 and this embassy of winter 191/0. In the first place the embassy was contrary to the convention included in the Achaean *foedus* with Rome, which prevented a constituent state from petitioning the Senate.[2] Timolaus' group would certainly have acted legally, through their protector Philopoemen, and Philopoemen certainly would not have sanctioned these requests. Again, although

---

[1] Pol. xxi. 1. Cf. appendix 8, pp. 286-7.   [2] Cf. appendix 6.

Timolaus' group may have wanted the restoration of the coastal towns, it could have no interest in asking for the restoration of the hostages taken from Nabis: they included Armenas, Nabis' son, and must have been all five strong supporters of the tyrant's party.

Just as significant is the terminology of the Senate's reply. For the first time, the phrase 'old exiles' (ἀρχαῖοι φυγάδες) is used in connection with the Spartan exiles. At the *synodos* only *exules* (without modification) were considered to need restoration. This refinement of terminology must imply that there were now at least two groups of exiles;[1] and of these, the Senate was not concerned with the 'new exiles'. Since this distinction first appears between the Achaean autumn *synodos* of 191 and the winter audience of the Spartans at Rome, the creation of the 'new exiles' must have taken place in that period. Since the demands of the embassy in themselves suggest that there had been a change of government between the spring and the winter, it is an economical hypothesis to conclude that the 'new exiles' had been created by this change of government, and that they were therefore Timolaus' group.

It could, perhaps, be argued against this view that Livy's failure to specify 'old exiles' is not decisive for a change of Spartan government between the *synodos* and the winter. He could be, perhaps, simply using imprecise language. This objection, however, involves explaining the creation of the 'new exiles' before the *synodos*. The only occasions when it is known that there was trouble in Sparta between the death of Nabis—the *terminus post quem* for the creation of 'new exiles'—and the *synodos* of autumn 191, were at the time of Philopoemen's original settlement, and at the time of his interference in spring 191. On neither of these occasions were his opponents driven into exile. The original settlement involved 'persuading some, compelling others', but not exiling them, as is clear from the trouble which Timolaus' group had in maintaining themselves in power after the

---

[1] The distinction was appreciated by Niese, *GGMS* ii. 716, n. 3, although not elaborated, but is surprisingly denied by Aymard, *Premiers Rapports*, p. 359, n. 9. Shimron's suggestion (*CQ* 1964, 238, n. 4) that the 'old exiles' are simply exiles from Cleomenes' time seems prima facie unlikely. The phrase seems in the first instance to have been the Senate's, and it is difficult to believe that the Senate would trouble to distinguish between already existing groups of exiles. Newly created exiles are clearly a different matter.

settlement. Similarly, at the time of Philopoemen's intervention no exiles were created. If exiles had been created then, they would have been the anti-Achaean group, the party which was opposed to Timolaus' and whom Flamininus intended to install in power instead of Timolaus' group. In winter 191/0 this group was responsible for the request to the Senate for the restoration of the hostages. Therefore they must have been themselves restored at some time between Philopoemen's intervention and their winter appeal to Rome. The only occasion in this period when Spartan exiles are mentioned is at the Achaean autumn *synodos*, where Flamininus and Glabrio demanded the restoration of the *exules*. If the anti-Achaean group had been exiled at Philopoemen's intervention, they must have been restored now to be able to send the embassy to Rome the following winter. But Philopoemen refused to restore the *exules* at the *synodos*. Therefore the exiles in question at the *synodos* cannot have been the tyrant group, who must accordingly have been at Sparta all along. We can therefore have confidence in Livy's statement that only unspecified *exules* were involved in the discussions at the *synodos*, and in our conclusion from this that the distinction between Livy's *exules* of the autumn and Polybius' 'old exiles' in the winter is a genuine distinction. It must be due to the creation of 'new exiles' between the two events. These 'new exiles' were most probably Timolaus' group.

The circumstances of the change of government cannot be certainly ascertained. But the fact that the embassy was so quickly dispatched to Rome suggests that Flamininus may have had a hand in it—this time, perhaps, forestalling Philopoemen's attempt to prevent the *coup d'état*. Equally suggestive of Flamininus' interference is the fact that the Spartan hostages—except for Armenas, who did not long survive—were in fact released soon after the embassy had been received.[1] The survivors of Nabis' party were his clients; and he was more than ever attached to them after being frustrated by Philopoemen in the spring. It seems quite likely that, without physical interference on his part—which could again be anticipated and perhaps frustrated by Philopoemen—he had continued throughout the year to encourage his Spartan friends, and had offered them diplomatic support and recognition by the Senate as the legitimate

[1] Pol. xxi. 3. 4.

government. Hence their haste in sending the embassy to Rome before Philopoemen could interfere. But the question of the mass of exiles created by the tyrants from Cleomenes onwards—now described by the Senate *en bloc* as 'old exiles' to distinguish them from Timolaus' group—was still a hare worth pursuing. Despite the change in Spartan government—enough in itself to create infinite discomfort for Achaea—the Senate seized upon the cause of the 'old exiles': it had the supreme advantage of being at the same time the cause of equity and of convenience.

Information about Achaean policy on wider issues at this time is sparse; but what there is confirms that Philopoemen's group was still willing to offer full co-operation to Rome and Rome's allies on major issues outside the Peloponnese. In spring 190 an embassy arrived in Achaea from Eumenes of Pergamum seeking help and confirmation of his alliance. The Achaeans did not hesitate. A *syncletos* at once confirmed the alliance and 1,000 Achaean infantry and 100 cavalry were sent to Eumenes under Diophanes. Diophanes must have been a political embarrassment to Philopoemen this year. But Diophanes was a competent soldier. It seems likely therefore that Philopoemen made use of Eumenes' claim on the alliance to remove the potential political trouble-maker, by sending him with the expeditionary force. This was still in Asia in the autumn and formed part of Eumenes' contingent at Magnesia.[1] No information is preserved about Achaean activity for the remainder of 190; but in spring 189 she continued her participation in the Roman war-effort against Aetolia. Achaean troops co-operated with Pleuratus of Illyria in a ravaging expedition against the south coast of Aetolia. It seems to have had little success or effect on the course of the war. In the autumn, after the beginning of the Roman siege of Same in Cephallenia, Achaean *funditores* from Aegium, Patrae, and Dyme were present with the consul M. Fulvius Nobilior. Livy, taking his information from Polybius, is careful to point out that there is no political significance in the choice of these towns: it was simply that they provided the best slingers because of the pebbly beaches! Apart from these incidents of participation

---

[1] Pol. xxi. 3b (dispatch of Diophanes). Liv. xxxvii. 20; 39. 9; cf. App. *Syr.* 31; Ditt. *Syll.* 606 (Magnesia): the problem of the numbers should be resolved by accepting Livy (Polybius). Cf. De Sanctis, *Storia* iv. 1. 199, n. 136. On the Achaean alliance with Eumenes, cf. appendix 5, pp. 280–1.

in the general war, nothing more is known of Achaea until autumn 189, when internal troubles again broke out at Sparta.¹ The course of these troubles and the manner of their settlement are related by Livy. Although his narrative material is from Polybius, and is therefore in general trustworthy, the chronology is very confused. This confusion has led to great differences in interpretation; and not until Holleaux treated the problem did the chronology become clear. Since his fundamental study raises no disagreements about chronology, a detailed repetition of his arguments would be otiose. However, a résumé of his results is necessary to provide a basis for examining the events themselves as they affected Achaea.²

M. Fulvius Nobilior laid siege to Same about the beginning of October 189. The siege had lasted four months—a round figure—when it ended towards the end of January 188. Once the siege was under way, Fulvius left Same for Rome to conduct the elections: this was towards the end of October. After supervising the elections he returned to Same, where he arrived in mid/late December, and where he stayed for the remainder of the siege. In the Peloponnese Philopoemen was elected Achaean *strategos* at about the time of the beginning of the siege. Shortly after this 'the Spartans' attacked 'the exiles' at Las, 'the exiles' appealed to Achaea, and a *syncletos* demanded satisfaction from 'the Spartans': the surrender of the ringleaders.³ A massacre followed at Sparta of those 'Spartans' who favoured compliance with the Achaean demand. This was accompanied by a decree which unilaterally declared Sparta independent of the League, and by an appeal to Fulvius. Fulvius however by this time had left Same to conduct the elections. Another Achaean *syncletos* now declared war on Sparta, and hostilities began on a small scale, but were prevented from becoming general by the onset of winter. At the same time Philopoemen allowed it to be known that he intended to propose a law making the meeting-place of the *synodos* variable: the people of Aegium, whose monopoly this was, felt their privilege threatened, and also appealed to Fulvius. This appeal also arrived at Same in Fulvius' absence.

After the return of Fulvius, the siege occupied him fully until

¹ Liv. xxxviii. 7. 2–3 (operation with Pleuratus); 29. 3 f. (Cephallenia).
² Liv. xxxviii. 30–4; Holleaux, *Études* v. 249–94.
³ Cf. also Aymard, *REA* 1928, 14 ff.

its end. Meanwhile the Achaean *damiourgoi* announced the regular first *synodos* of the year for February, to be held as usual at Aegium. In order that his proposal to make the place of the *synodos* variable might be discussed before the *synodos* took place, Philopoemen summoned a *syncletos* at Argos. Fulvius, as soon as he was able to attend to the accumulation of Peloponnesian affairs, came first to Aegium; but when he discovered that the regular *synodos* was being preceded by a *syncletos*, he continued to Argos. There he found little opposition to support, and Philopoemen's proposal was successfully passed.[1] Another *syncletos* was then summoned, this time to Elis, to discuss the Spartan question—by this time it must have been late February—and at this second *syncletos* Fulvius advised sending ambassadors to the Senate. Lycortas and Diophanes were duly dispatched, and had probably returned to Achaea by the end of April. In May, after their return, Philopoemen was joined by large numbers of 'exiles' when he led the Achaean army against Sparta. At Compasion, he met the leaders of the 'Spartans', and in a riot some were killed; the next day others were judicially murdered. A settlement of Sparta was then carried out, which was quickly approved by a *syncletos* which met at Tegea.

This chronology is the basis of the following discussion. Two matters require further investigation: Philopoemen's successful proposal to alter the Achaean constitution over the place of the *synodos*, and the events at Sparta. They will be discussed in that order.

Aegium had been virtually the capital city of the early Achaean League. It was the centre of Old Achaea and was easily accessible from each of the original Achaean cities. For this reason the regular *synodoi* had always been held there, and the Aegienses had come to regard the monopoly as their right and privilege. They no doubt found economic advantages in being hosts to the *synodoi*; but additionally they must have acquired prestige within the League, and the possibility—not to be discounted—of exerting

---

[1] On this interpretation of the *synodos* and *syncletos*, cf. Badian and Errington, *Historia* 1965, 13 ff. (and bibliography). Lehmann, *Glaubwürdigkeit*, pp. 251 ff., esp. p. 253, n. 225, disagrees with our conclusions and gives the traditional version of opposition between Philopoemen and the *damiourgoi*. But he does not meet our arguments: he takes no account of Livy's confused chronology—which cannot be doubted—and other confusion stemming from this, and seems to be unaware of Holleaux's article. His version is therefore fundamentally unsatisfactory.

unofficial local influence on decisions to be taken in the *synodoi*: influence clearly was not solely dependent on a predominance in voting. As the League expanded, and as the weight of population became increasingly Arcadian rather than Achaean in the strict sense, it must have become increasingly inconvenient to retain Aegium as the invariable meeting-place of the regular business *synodoi*. This may have seemed the more important since Megalopolis was providing a larger proportion of leading Achaean statesmen than any other single city—to our knowledge, Philopoemen, Lycortas, and Diophanes.

There were also occasions which could be clearly envisaged when it might be more efficient to hold a *synodos* elsewhere than at Aegium; and this type of consideration seems to have been behind the reform of 188. Variations, of course, opened the possibility of manipulation, in order to subject the members of the *synodos* to local influence in the case of specific local issues, as was already the case with the *syncletoi*. However, there is no evidence that this occurred. Of the seventeen recorded *synodoi* after the reform,[1] four were held at Megalopolis, three at Corinth, two at Aegium, one at Sicyon, and seven at places unknown. This scarcely suggests regular manipulation by dominant local interests, although such a small, scattered sample of meetings does not allow a definite conclusion either way. It is clear, however, that Aegium was by no means excluded by Philopoemen's law. Fulvius had initially supported the opposition of the Aegienses. In addition to his natural desire to offer help on appeal, his support had been soundly based on the obvious convenience for the Romans of knowing that Achaean *synodoi* would regularly take place only at one convenient coastal town—though in fact most Roman ambassadors were received at *syncletoi*. But this objection seems in practice to have been met: the only two known *synodoi* after Philopoemen's law at which Romans were present were held conveniently at Aegium.[2] Accordingly, in the absence of evidence to the contrary, it seems that efficiency and privilege-breaking were the chief aims of the reform. There is no evidence to suggest that the possibility of manipulation which it created was regularly abused. This seems indicated also by the fact that

---

[1] Larsen, *Rep. Gov.*, pp. 175 ff.
[2] On Romans at *syncletoi*, cf. Larsen, *Rep. Gov.*, appendix *passim*; at *synodoi* after 188: Pol. xxviii. 3. 7–10 (in 170); Pol. xxxviii. 10 (in 147).

there was little opposition to Philopoemen's proposal when the *syncletos* met at Argos. There is no need to detect corruption in the haste of his summoning the *syncletos*. In order to prevent the matter from being discussed at the *synodos*, which was already announced, in the hostile atmosphere of Aegium, it was essential to hold the *syncletos* both before the *synodos* and at a distance from Aegium. Hence Argos and the haste. There was naturally opposition from the Aegienses; but it did not obtain sufficient support to make Fulvius consider staking Roman prestige on what appeared to him to be a lost cause: it was clearly a victory for the better cause.[1]

The evidence of these same chapters of Livy is the first detailed indication we have of how matters had developed at Sparta since the embassy to Rome of winter 191/0. Flamininus' policy of re-integrating the 'old exiles' had been heavily emphasized by the Senate in 191. In 190 another Roman mission was sent to Greece which carried instructions about the Laconian coastal towns. Nothing is known of the composition or task of this embassy in detail; but it seems very likely, from the circumstances in which it was appointed, that its instructions would include a further emphasis on Roman insistence on restoring the Spartan exiles.[2] Philo-poemen must again have offered resistance to this statement of Roman policy, as he had to Flamininus and Glabrio at the *synodos* in 191, for nothing suggests that the 'old exiles' were restored before 188. At the same time, Philopoemen must have realized that, if the problem of the exiles really reached crisis point, the Senate could insist on their restoration, and he would have to agree. He must, therefore, by this time, have been trying to find a formula which would both discourage further Roman intervention and save Achaean face. His action in 188 shows that by this time he thought the formula had been found.

Livy's account is supplemented in one detail by a very fragmentary passage of Polybius, in which he says: 'It was good to restore the captive exiles (τοὺς αἰχμαλώτους φυγάδας) to Sparta, and expedient to humble the city of the Spartans by driving out those who had borne arms for the regime of the tyrants.' Livy confirms that the *externi auxiliares* were expelled, but says nothing about the 'captive exiles'.[3] It is clear that those who had continued

---

[1] Cf. Badian and Errington, *Historia* 1965, 13 ff.   [2] Pol. xxi. 1. 3.

[3] Pol. xxi. 32c. 2: καλὸν μὲν γὰρ τὸ κατάγειν τοὺς αἰχμαλώτους φυγάδας εἰς τὴν

to employ the mercenaries who had supported the tyrants must be the remnants of Nabis' party, the men who had sent the embassy to Rome in winter 191/0. From Philopoemen's expulsion of these mercenaries it is clear that Nabis' party must have been the government in power. Accordingly, between autumn 191, when Timolaus' group was overwhelmed, and autumn 189, when these new troubles began, the party in power at Sparta had not changed.

Polybius' description of the exiles whom it was worthy of Philopoemen to restore as 'captives' does not allow a wholly satisfactory explanation. He clearly uses the term to distinguish a particular group of exiles, but he does not make it clear whether he wishes to distinguish one group from among the 'old exiles', or a separate group in contrast to the whole mass of 'old exiles'. It may be best to approach the difficulty from the point of view of general probability. Polybius' own bias in favour of Achaea and Philopoemen suggests that he would approve most of all of the restoration of that group of exiles which favoured Achaea and Philopoemen: the group associated with Timolaus. His ambiguity in this passage may be deliberate, for he certainly had a misleading statement which Livy translated: *Philopoemen praetor iam inde ab initio exulum causae amicus.*[1] If this phrase is supposed to refer to the 'old exiles' alone it is patently untrue. If on the other hand it refers to exiles in general—among whom were now Timolaus' group of recent exiles—it can be ambiguously interpreted to include both Timolaus' group and the 'old exiles'. To some extent this might be aimed at saving Philopoemen's reputation as a humanitarian, although in the event it does not enhance that of Polybius as a wholly honest historian. We may therefore tentatively prefer this explanation of 'captive exiles', and assume from the terminology that at first some members at least of Timolaus' group had been taken prisoner by their opponents before escaping. Presumably they chose as their place of exile, among other places, Las. For the events stemming from the violence of the Spartan government's attack on Las were the

Σπάρτην, συμφέρον δὲ τὸ ταπεινῶσαι τὴν τῶν Λακεδαιμονίων πόλιν, ⟨ἐξηλάσαντ⟩α τοὺς δεδορυφορηκότας τῇ τῶν τυ⟨ράν⟩ν⟨ω⟩ν ⟨δυναστείᾳ.⟩ On text, cf. appendix 7, p. 284. Liv. xxxviii. 34. 1 (*externi auxiliares*).

[1] Liv. xxxviii. 31. 1. This phrase, interpreted out of context, has led to failure to understand Philopoemen's attitude to the exile problem. Cf. Niese, *GGMS* ii. 715; Aymard, *Premiers Rapports*, pp. 321, 338.

occasion for the Achaean declaration of war on Sparta. The issue of the 'old exiles' was certainly alive, as the Senate had recently made quite clear. But it could not have aroused such violence as that of the comparatively recently expelled pro-Achaean government. The appeal of these exiles in Las to Achaea after the Spartan attack also tends to support the view that they were not 'old exiles', but those whom Polybius describes as 'captive exiles': the 'old exiles' could not have anticipated much support from Philopoemen, despite the fact that Las was still in Achaean *tutela*. On the other hand, the appeal of the Spartan government to Fulvius against Achaea, after slaughtering the remaining pro-Achaean elements in Sparta, shows clearly that this group had great trust in the protection of Rome—protection which had first been demonstrated by Flamininus—to such an extent that they expected Rome to support them against Achaea.[1]

It is now possible to understand the nature of the compromise by which Philopoemen was able, as a by-product of helping Timolaus' group—which he had supported throughout at Sparta: *iam inde ab initio exulum causae amicus*—to restore the 'old exiles' in accordance with the policy of Flamininus, and to prevent Flamininus from gaining the patronage of the restored exiles which he had hoped to acquire for the Senate. Philopoemen had been forced to compromise: ideally he could not desire to bring to Achaea the additional trouble which could be expected from the restoration; but here Philopoemen ultimately had no choice, if the Senate chose to insist. His aim was therefore to gain as much advantage as possible by stealing the Senate's policy and to take the credit for it.[2] The attack on Las in autumn 189 by the government of the tyrant party must have been primarily aimed at annihilating the remaining members of Timolaus' group. The appeal to Philopoemen, which first involved Achaea again in Sparta's internal troubles, will have been by Timolaus' party. Philopoemen responded, as expected, by demanding the surrender of those of Nabis' group who were responsible. The result

---

[1] Liv. xxxviii. 30. 9 (appeal of exiles to Achaea); 31. 5–6 (appeal of government group to Rome).

[2] Pol. xxii. 11. 7 makes it clear that the old exiles were in fact restored in 188. Cf. Liv. xxxix. 36. 14 (Areus and Alcibiades); Pol. xxiii. 4. 2–3 (where the complaint of the 'old exiles' is not that they had not been restored, but that their settlement after restoration was unsatisfactory).

of this demand was a further anti-Achaean demonstration at Sparta, the murder of thirty Achaean supporters, secession from Achaea, and appeal to Fulvius. Some fighting followed the subsequent Achaean declaration of war, but winter froze the *status quo.*

The Achaean ambassadors to Rome, sent on the suggestion of Fulvius in the spring after the *syncletos* at Elis, were Lycortas and Diophanes. Lycortas represented the well-established view of Philopoemen, that the Achaeans should be allowed to decide matters at Sparta in accordance with the agreement whereby the city had originally entered the League, and with their own laws. This view represented the issue as a purely internal Achaean matter of no interest or importance to the Senate. It implied that the intervention of Flamininus and the interest he had developed in the Spartan question were illegitimate. Diophanes' position was that which he had first taken up in spring 191. In 191 he had allowed that Flamininus might have a legitimate interest in Sparta, and he had committed his support on this. The same point of view was expressed by him now at Rome, that the Senate should have the first and last words on the Spartan question—a view which ten years later Callicrates persuaded the Senate to accept. He recognized—as did Philopoemen—that in the last resort the Senate could insist irresistibly that its requirements be carried out. He differed from Philopoemen in much the same way as Aristaenus did: he hoped that by acceding to, and going half-way to meet the inevitable, he might make the inevitable less disastrous in its effect.[1]

The result of these Achaean representations was that the Senate decided to preserve the *status quo*: *novari nihil de Lacedaemoniis placebat*, although, according to Livy, *magnae auctoritatis apud Romanos tum gens Achaeorum erat.* It is clearly true to some extent that the Achaeans had unusual influence at Rome, although this did not mean that the dominant Achaean group could get everything it wanted from the Senate. This is made clear in the Senate's reply, which favoured neither side. *Magnae*

---

[1] Liv. xxxviii. 32. 6–10 (Achaeans at Rome); cf. Pol. xxiv. 12–13 (comparison of Philopoemen and Aristaenus); xxii. 10. 14 (unanimity of Aristaenus and Diophanes). The *foedus* to which Lycortas refers (Liv. xxxviii. 32. 8) is more likely to have been the agreement between Sparta and Achaea than the Achaean *foedus* with Rome, since Lycortas' whole emphasis is on the fact that this is an Achaean internal matter. Cf. Niese, *GGMS* iii. 44; Lehmann, *Glaubwürdigkeit*, p. 237, n. 189.

auctoritatis means, more precisely, that a comparatively large body of senators had been recently involved in Achaean affairs, and understood the issues. Also the Senate as a whole had been grateful enough to the Achaeans for their declaration of war against Antiochus to grant them a *foedus aequum*. Since then, Achaea had supplied contingents of troops against the Aetolians, and had helped Eumenes before Magnesia. Achaean *auctoritas* was based solidly on the Senate's recognition of the value of these *officia*. Nevertheless, the Senate expressed its view of the essentially peripheral nature of its involvement in Achaean affairs, now that Antiochus was finally defeated. As long as Achaea remained comparatively quiet and played its part as Roman client, the Senate did not care unduly what action was taken at Sparta. The result of this reply was that both the Spartans and Philopoemen were equally able to argue from its ambiguity that the Senate had given them each the right to their own way : the only clear outcome was that the Senate had no intention of intervening openly in the way Diophanes had requested.[1]

In May, after receiving the Senate's reply, Philopoemen assembled the Achaean army, and accompanied by large numbers of exiles—certainly Timolaus' group, but at least some of the 'old exiles'—made his way to Compasion in Spartan territory.[2] Secession was a major federal offence, and he demanded the surrender of the leaders who had been responsible. A conference was arranged, and eighty Spartans accepted Philopoemen's pledge of safety. As they approached the Achaean camp they were given a hostile reception by the groups of exiles, and although Philopoemen himself and Achaean officials tried, at this stage, to honour Philopoemen's pledge of their safety—though this may be simply Polybian apologetics—seventeen were stoned to death on the spot by the exiles, all of whom had feelings of great personal hostility to the leaders of the tyrants' party. The next day the remaining sixty-three were given a summary trial and executed.[3] It would be difficult to defend this breach of Philopoemen's pledge of safety at the time of the conference, whereby normally accepted diplomatic procedure was sacrificed to

---

[1] Liv. xxxviii. 32. 9–10.
[2] Liv. xxxviii. 33. 4–5. The 'captive exiles' were restored (Pol. xxi. 32c. 3), therefore must have been present at Compasion. At least Areus and Alcibiades of the 'old exiles' were present (Liv. xxxix. 36. 14–16).
[3] Liv. xxxviii. 33. 6–11; Plut. *Phil.* 16. 3; Paus. viii. 51. 3.

temporary political advantage. Even Polybius—judging from Livy's version and from the fragments of his own account—contented himself with simply retailing the facts and expressing his own opinion in a rhetorical commonplace: it was good to restore the 'captive exiles', expedient to humble Sparta by expelling the tyrants' mercenaries. He says nothing in his brief extant (but admittedly extremely fragmentary) discussion to justify these murders. To Philopoemen, the expediency of taking the advantage offered must have seemed to outweigh any moral aspects of his action. The possibility of finally resolving the Spartan problem must have already seemed to be at hand: the annihilation of the leaders of the tyrants' party would make the restoration of Timolaus' group easy; with these friends of Achaea could go the 'old exiles', thus removing a source of Roman interest and a potential area of disagreement. Both groups of restored exiles in Sparta would then be so closely attached to Achaea and to Philopoemen by ties of gratitude that future serious trouble would not be expected.

With these considerations to the fore, it was no doubt easy enough for interested parties to condone the pseudo-judicial massacre. The only extant fragment of a non-Achaean account is that preserved by Plutarch of the Spartan historian and antiquarian Aristocrates. Aristocrates' version is that Philopoemen killed three hundred and fifty Spartans, whereas Polybius' figure in Livy is only eighty. Aristocrates' figure must therefore either be exaggerated or include figures which Polybius failed to record. There may, for instance, have been a continuation of the massacre once Philopoemen had gained control of the city, the casualties from which Polybius discreetly failed to include in his figure for Compasion. On the other hand, Aristocrates' figure may have been deliberately exaggerated in order to vilify Philopoemen and Achaea—although in this case an even larger figure might perhaps have been expected. The choice between the two figures must be largely *a priori*, in which case Polybius' reputation for accuracy must not be allowed to prejudge the issue in his favour: we have insufficient information on which to form any judgement about Aristocrates' historical tendencies.[1]

---

[1] Plut. *Phil.* 16. 3; *FGH* iii, no. 591. The fragments and testimonia are insufficient to allow the acceptance of Aymard's judgement of Aristocrates as 'auteur d'assez faible valeur' (*Premiers Rapports*, p. 330, n. 1; cf. Stier, *Roms Aufstieg*, p. 174, n. 136, 'der

The settlement imposed by Philopoemen at Sparta after the massacre at Compasion was the origin of substantial future troubles for Achaea. For the violence of the settlement had sacrificed, to some extent, the goodwill of all Spartan parties. Philopoemen ordered the city walls to be torn down, the mercenaries who had supported the tyrants and their successors, and those helots who had been enfranchised by the tyrants, to be expelled. Neither the ordinary citizens nor the returning exiles would have much quarrel with this, although a source of future trouble might arise in the ex-helots, particularly since those who refused to leave Laconia—some three thousand—were sold as slaves in Achaea, and a portico was built at Megalopolis with the money realized. But all Spartan parties might justifiably have felt offended at the remaining provisions of the settlement. For the traditional Spartan institutions were abolished, including— perhaps most significantly—the *agoge*. This clearly struck at the heart of the traditional Spartan state of the days of independence. The substitution of the Achaean system of education could have been consolation to neither group of exiles, nor to the remaining population of Sparta.[1]

These issues might affront Spartan municipal pride. But the problem which most affected the everyday lives of the largest numbers of the remaining population and of the exiles themselves was the problem of reintegrating the 'old exiles', and, to a lesser extent, Timolaus' group. Philopoemen made no attempt to solve this problem. The property of the murdered and dispossessed of the tyrants' party was available; the money from the sale of the three thousand ex-helots would certainly have gone far to alleviating the real physical problems associated with the restoration.

spartanische Tendenzhistoriker'). Polybius' own natural bias must be taken into consideration. There was later a group of Spartans which Polybius (xxiii. 4. 5) describes as ἀπὸ δὲ τῶν τεθανατωμένων καὶ τῶν ἐκπεπτωκότων κατὰ τὰ τῶν Ἀχαιῶν δόγματα. This description clearly suggests that further judicial proceedings were in fact carried out after Compasion, with the result that the actual number of persons condemned in the whole of the settlement of Sparta was far higher than Polybius' eighty, which only includes the deaths of the two days. Aristocrates' figure therefore cannot simply be ignored (with, e.g., Niese, *GGMS* iii. 45). Pausanias' account (viii. 51. 3) is briefer than Plutarch's and contains some variations: he mentions no deaths at all, says three hundred were 'expelled from the Peloponnese', and agrees that three thousand helots were sold. Where Pausanias' figure for expellees comes from is obscure: perhaps a confused attempt to combine Aristocrates' and Polybius' figures from Plutarch.

[1] Liv. xxxviii. 34. 1–9; cf. Chrimes, *Ancient Sparta*, pp. 43 ff. and esp. pp. 46–7.

Yet Philopoemen squandered this invidiously on a portico at Megalopolis, emphasizing—if this was still necessary—the total submergence of all Spartan interests in those of Achaea.[1] By this ill-considered victory display he had forfeited his opportunity of solving the problem which was to vex Achaea for the next nine years. The weakest point in his compromise with Roman policy was that Achaea was now burdened with the problem of rehabilitating the Spartan exiles; he had rashly thrown away his chance to eradicate this weakness. Although there can be little excuse for this major failure of statesmanship, it is perhaps possible to discern the reason for it. In the fragmentary passage in which Polybius analyses Philopoemen's motives, he seems to provide Philopoemen's reasons for not using the available money to help the exiles: he realized that money was necessary to restore the monarchy; therefore he prevented money from becoming easily available.[2] This consideration is clearly crucial, for it provides a perfectly adequate reason for Philopoemen's short-sightedness. His mind was fixed solely on the prevention of a restoration of the Spartan monarchy, for since the time of Cleomenes this had been the major problem for Achaea. It is easy enough in this context to understand his failure to realize that the question of the monarchy had already been settled by his own massacre of the tyrants' party. It had, in fact, been replaced by the exiles' prosecution of their dissatisfactions, which, in the new conditions of the Senate's willingness to interfere, were equally unsettling for Achaea. Philopoemen's lack of magnanimity in victory insulted his friends, and gave immediate point to agitation by all parties and interests at Sparta for a new and more satisfactory settlement.

---

[1] Liv. xxxviii. 34. 7.
[2] Pol. xxi. 32c. 4; cf. appendix 7, pp. 284–5.

IX

THE *PAX ACHAICA*

THE solution of the Spartan problem, put into effect by Philopoemen in his settlement after Compasion, offended too many interests at Sparta to have any chance of being widely supported. As soon as the character of the settlement became clear to the Spartans, objections were raised. Polybius records an embassy to Rome by 'some elements in Sparta who were dissatisfied with what had happened, and who considered that the power and *prostasia* of Rome had been weakened by Philopoemen'. In Rome, when received by the Senate the following winter, they appealed against Philopoemen's settlement, in the hope of inducing the Senate to interfere and to alter its terms.[1] Who were these dissatisfied men, surprisingly left anonymous by Polybius, who were so quickly ready to appeal to Rome against Achaea? The possibilities are that they were either one of the exile groups, or the remains of the tyrants' party, who had escaped Achaean violence. Neither group of exiles would be expected to throw their gratitude for their restoration to the winds immediately after they were restored. The pro-Achaean group with which Timolaus had been associated could not expect any benefit from an appeal to Rome; the 'old exiles' might be expected, at least for the first six months of their restoration, to withhold their complaints until they saw more clearly what their position would be. Had the 'old exiles' turned ingrate so rapidly, we should have expected Polybius to say so in unambiguous language. But he does not mention their dissatisfaction until 185/4.[2]

The one aspect of the settlement which caused the greatest distress at Sparta, according to Livy, was the restoration of the

---

[1] Pol. xxii. 3. 1–4. Wunderer's conjecture, which Büttner-Wobst prints at 3. 1, Λακεδαιμονίων for the MSS. 'Ρωμαίων, deprives the sentence of much of its point. Cf. Badian, *For. Cl.*, p. 91, n. 2. On the date of the embassy, see appendix 2 B, pp. 255 ff.

[2] Pol. xxii. 11. 7.

exiles. Accordingly, those who suffered most from the restoration of the exiles would feel the greatest and most immediate dissatisfaction with the Achaean settlement. Any survivors of the tyrants' group, which Philopoemen had overthrown and almost annihilated, would clearly suffer the greatest loss. They also had been the group most closely attached to Rome. Flamininus had supported them in 191; the Senate had granted them the restoration of the hostages in 190, and had left them in power; when threatened by Philopoemen the previous autumn, they had been responsible for offering the city to Fulvius. It would clearly be natural for them—much more than for any other identifiable group—to appeal quickly to Rome. Their position had been overthrown; and with it, they could claim, the Roman *prostasia*, which had most recently been given form in the ambiguous reply of the Senate to the envoys from Achaea and Sparta in spring 188, which tried to preserve a stable situation in the Peloponnese. The Spartan government of the time naturally interpreted this as a continuation of Roman patronage in their favour, and a confirmation of their right to rule Sparta. In these circumstances their overthrow must have been in itself sufficient provocation for an appeal to the Senate which, they might argue, should feel as offended as they themselves. It therefore seems clear that this hasty appeal to the Senate must have been by those members of the tyrants' party who had survived the massacre at Compasion. That there was such a group as late as 184/3—then in exile—is clear from Polybius' description of Chaeron at Rome at that time as a representative of 'those who had been condemned to death and those expelled in accordance with the Achaeans' decrees'.[1]

As soon as Philopoemen learnt that this Spartan embassy had been sent to Rome, late in his *strategia*, he immediately sent Nicodemus of Elis to represent the point of view of the Achaean government.[2] The urgency with which Philopoemen sent Nicodemus must clearly have been conditioned by the fact that the Spartan embassy was instructed by the anti-Achaean group. For the Spartans would be sure to emphasize their own interpretation of the Senate's reply to the Achaean and Spartan envoys in the

---

[1] Pol. xxiii. 4. 5: ἀπὸ δὲ τῶν τεθανατωμένων καὶ τῶν ἐκπεπτωκότων κατὰ τὰ τῶν Ἀχαιῶν δόγματα.

[2] Pol. xxii. 3. 4. On the chronology, see appendix 2 B, pp. 255 ff.

spring of 188. And since the recent history of the relations of this group with the Senate might lead the Achaeans to expect that the Senate would show the Spartans favour in this case also, it was necessary to make clear the Achaean point of view, that Philopoemen's interpretation of the ambiguous *Senatus Consultum* was just as reasonable as the Spartans'. If the Senate had been prepared to accept the situation existing in the spring of 188 for the sake of stability—the declared policy of their reply—they should be equally prepared to accept the situation existing in the autumn of the same year. For the Spartan situation in the autumn, ought, in the Achaeans' opinion, to have seemed to the Senate to have improved on that of the spring, as a result of Philopoemen's fulfilment of the Senate's frequently emphasized aim of restoring the 'old exiles'. Additionally, the Achaeans were, on their interpretation of their *foedus* with Rome, free and equal allies of the Romans, and ought therefore to have attracted more benevolent attention from the Senate than the disreputable remains of the troublesome tyrants' party.

From the Senate's point of view, the Achaeans were no more than clients who, blinded by their apparent legal rights, failed to recognize their extra-legal moral obligations. As a result, the Senate was for some years after the final defeat of Antiochus and the Aetolians unable to form a positive policy, in the absence of immediate active interest in Greece, which made Roman expectations sufficiently clear to the client states which had supported them in the wars. For as long as Flamininus was active in Greece, it had been possible for him to find solutions to problems which had arisen among the clients of Rome, whom circumstances had also made his own personal clients. Latterly, the undoubtedly equitable demand for the restoration of the Spartan 'old exiles' had given direction to senatorial policy towards Achaea. The Senate had neither the need nor the desire to interfere physically in Greece; but the cause of the Spartan 'old exiles' had given it an opportunity of exercising patronage, and, as the senators thought, of making it abundantly clear that in practice the Achaeans were expected to meet Roman requests. The Achaean opposition had been unexpected. But the repetition of the policy had served to maintain in clear outline the relationship which the Senate required. When Flamininus finally left Greece in autumn 191, this connecting link, which had until now given a continuity to Roman policy towards Achaea, was broken, and the rapid change of circumstances at Sparta radically altered the Peloponnesian situation. The Senate still wished to emphasize the client–patron relationship; but Philopoemen had shattered the possibility of making this generally comprehensible to the Achaeans by virtually cutting out Diophanes, who had seemed to understand *clientela*, from influence in Achaea, and by his implementation of Roman policy in the restoration of the 'old exiles'. This latter effectively achieved what had been understood by the Achaeans to be the aim of senatorial policy.

As long as the problem of the 'old exiles' had remained unsolved, senatorial policy had appeared consistent and purposeful —so much so that Philopoemen had found no alternative to stealing the Senate's thunder. The real desires of the Senate, however, for stability on the one hand, and responsible *clientela* on the other, were far from being fully comprehended by the Achaeans. But once this problem of the exiles was solved, however inadequately, the continual, but non-committal and ineffective, partisan interference with the detail of Achaean politics by the Senate and its representatives—the only way in which the desired relationship could now be asserted—eventually revealed to Philopoemen the limitations imposed on the Senate by its own code of conduct, and seems to have led him to exploit the situation. It took Callicrates, after Philopoemen's death and after years of confusion, to give renewed direction to senatorial policy by urging further and more brutal interference.

This initial confusion in the minds of the Achaeans as to the real aims of senatorial policy, followed by Philopoemen's understanding and exploitation of it, is one of the touchstones by which relations between the Senate and the Achaeans in the 180s should be interpreted. The other is the apparently directionless drift of the policy itself, which resulted from an essential lack of interest in Achaea after the crises of the wars against Philip and Antiochus. This first becomes clear in the Senate's reply to the envoys sent to Rome by Achaea and Sparta, with the encouragement of Fulvius, in spring 188. The Senate's answer to the problem was simply to preserve the existing situation: *novari nihil de Lacedaemoniis placebat*.[1] Sufficient survives of a corrupt and fragmentary passage of Polybius to see that the Senate showed the same attitude

---

[1] Liv. xxxviii. 32. 9; cf. chapter VIII, pp. 143–4.

in its reply to Nicodemus in winter 188/7: they disapproved of
the destruction of the walls and of the murders at Compasion,
but would not interfere with any detail.[1] Circumstances compelled the senators to express disapproval: Philopoemen had
acted violently and wilfully, in contravention of senatorial advice
for inaction; the offended parties at Sparta were Rome's clients,
and had appealed for support. The Senate had to pay lip-service
to this moral commitment. But the 'old exiles', also Roman clients,
had been restored in accordance with Roman policy and no disapproval could be expressed about this, as Philopoemen had
anticipated. The Senate therefore formally expressed its disapproval of the most obviously factional and violent—therefore
controversial—aspects of Philopoemen's settlement, the destruction of the walls and of the Lycurgan constitution,[2] and the mass
murder at Compasion. But it was satisfied with this ineffective
paternal admonishment, and expressed no intentions for the
future, to which it might be held morally committed by any
interested party. Peace, stability, and the due recognition of
clientela were the aims; therefore the Fathers would not do anything to alter the new established situation. Perhaps taken by
surprise, and found without a positive reaction to this conflict of
petty clients' claims, they could only repeat their disinterested
plea for inaction of the previous year. The Spartan mission had
little more success in eliciting positive support for their new situation. After a delay, they managed to obtain a letter to the
Achaeans from the consul M. Aemilius Lepidus. But it contained
little comfort. It was no more than a repetition of the Senate's
non-committal attitude: the Achaeans had not handled the
Spartans correctly.[3] It is not surprising that when the Achaeans
received their report from Nicodemus they simply let the matter

---

[1] Pol. xxii. 7. 6: δυσαρεστοῦνται μὲν καὶ τῇ τῶν τειχῶν συντελέσει* καὶ τῇ καταλύσει
* * * τῶν ἐν τῷ Κομπασίῳ διαφθαρέντων, οὐ μὴν ἄκυρόν τι ποιεῖν. Cf. Diod. xxix. 17.

[2] The *lacuna* in Pol. xxii. 7. 6 must have contained some mention of this (as in
Büttner-Wobst's conjecture).

[3] Pol. xxii. 3. 3: οὐκ ὀρθῶς αὐτοὺς κεχειρικέναι τὰ κατὰ τοὺς Λακεδαιμονίους.
The letter was probably written not long before Lepidus departed for his province. He clearly did not want to commit himself until he knew the attitude of the
Senate as a whole, which he simply echoes. Cf. Niccolini, *La Conf. Ach.*, p. 150.
Castellani, *Contributi*, 90, by following Aymard's chronology (cf. appendix 2 B,
pp. 255 ff) makes Lepidus' letter precede the Senate's reply to Nicodemus by nearly
a year. No satisfactory explanation is available for this delay, which becomes simply
'altro segno del disinteresse dei Romani'.

pass without opposition or discussion. It must have seemed a clear victory for Philopoemen, openly acknowledged by the Senate.

Probably during this same *strategia* of Philopoemen, trouble between Achaea and Boeotia broke out, which reached serious dimensions. The Achaeans and the Aetolians had been urged by the Senate to act as dutiful clients, and to insist that the Boeotians comply with senatorial policy and restore Zeuxippus, another of Flamininus' friends. The Achaeans had initially responded by sending an embassy which urged the Boeotians to do this. But at the same time they determined to make use of their role as Roman agents to employ Roman prestige in their own favour in connection with a purely local issue. Several lawsuits to be settled in Boeotian courts between the Megarians—members of the Achaean League since 206/5—and the Boeotians were outstanding, which the Boeotians were reluctant to settle. Since this was apparently a federal matter, the Achaeans, at the same time as they presented the Senate's request about Zeuxippus, asked that these local lawsuits should be settled by the Boeotians. This was agreed, but the Boeotians did nothing. Philopoemen then allowed the Megarians to lay hands on Boeotian property, whereupon the situation rapidly became critical. Polybius says that if the Senate had pressed the restoration of Zeuxippus on the Boeotians at this point, there would have been war; and the situation was only eased, on the Achaean side, by the Megarians' stopping their raids, and on the Boeotian side by the settlement of the lawsuits.[1]

This easing of tension was the result of a compromise. But from the Achaeans' point of view the outcome was entirely satisfactory, for it was the Roman policy which had suffered in the compromise. By tacking the local matter of the Achaean lawsuits on to the Roman request about Zeuxippus, Philopoemen had created a tension which made it impossible for Roman policy with regard to Zeuxippus to be fulfilled. It seems fairly clear that Philopoemen, when he realized that he could not enforce both the Roman and the Achaean demands, must have deliberately decided that the Roman policy was to be sacrificed in favour of the compromise which settled the Achaean lawsuits. The result was a bargain between the Achaeans and the Boeotians for the better interest of both parties. The Boeotians must have had much the same objections to restoring Zeuxippus as

[1] Pol. xxii. 4. Cf. Niese, *GGMS* iii. 16–17, who places the events in 186.

the Achaeans had had to the restoration of the Spartan 'old exiles'. Philopoemen was only acting as agent for Rome in this matter and presumably felt no personal commitment to achieving the aims of Roman policy. He must have seen Achaean interest in the first place in settling the Megarians' complaints, in the second place in maintaining generally good relations between Achaea and Boeotia. In the present circumstances neither of these aims could be achieved by insisting on Zeuxippus' restoration; both were achieved by his neglecting it. The aims of the Senate, which had been the reason for opening the original negotiations, were lost in the diplomatic mêlée. Since the Senate's policy of restoring Zeuxippus was essentially Flamininus', it must have appeared to him in Rome that the Achaeans' preoccupation with their own local problems, and their failure to recognize the priorities expected of a client, were again—it must have seemed deliberately —frustrating his policies. This impression can only have been reinforced by the fact that it was again Philopoemen who was responsible for opposing Flamininus.

Again, probably in this same *strategia*, Philopoemen clashed with the policy of Flamininus, this time over Messene. He is alleged to have interfered with the terms of the *diagramma* which Flamininus had issued at the time of the Messenian settlement in 191. This document was probably a comprehensive regulation of the whole settlement, the basis of which Livy gives when he describes how Messene was treated in his account of 191.[1] The circumstances in which we learn about Philopoemen's amendment of the *diagramma* are as follows.[2] When the Roman embassy headed by Q. Caecilius Metellus was entertained in Achaea in 185, accusations of responsibility for the current discontent in the Peloponnese were levelled at Philopoemen by Diophanes. Disputes had arisen, it was alleged, about the Messenian exiles, and in particular about Flamininus' *diagramma* and Philopoemen's amendment. What had this amendment involved, that it should cause serious disputes? Roebuck rightly dismisses the view that it was a constitutional move in a democratic direction, but fails to suggest an alternative. Some attempt, however, to discover the scope of the amendment must be made. It seems

---

[1] Liv. xxxvi. 31. 9.

[2] Pol. xxii. 10. 1–6. On the general nature of this type of *diagramma* see Welles, *AJA* 1938.

fairly clear that the establishment of effective democracies was not a live issue in Achaea (or elsewhere in Greece) at this time— if for no other reason than that Nabis' propaganda must have made democracy a dirty word. If, then, we agree with Roebuck in rejecting the view that Philopoemen's amendment was a change to democracy, what was its effect?[1]

In the circumstances, his most likely action would have been an attempt at securing, in some way, greater Achaean control over Messenia. This was certainly desirable, for Messene was an unwilling member of the League. Neither the restored exiles nor the party in power in 191 had wanted to be united with Achaea in the first place. The result of Flamininus' original settlement, from the Achaean point of view, must therefore have been unsatisfactory, although at the time Diophanes, given no alternative, had accepted the terms.[2] Added to this problem of relations between Messene and the League was the internal Messenian problem of reintegrating the exiles. As at Sparta, union with the League had made the integration of exiles an Achaean problem, which the hostility of both parties to Achaea must have made both more difficult and more essential to solve. Two methods of gaining greater Achaean control were feasible: the establishment of a group in power in Messene which, for the sake of Achaean support in internal matters, was prepared to compromise its essential opposition to union with the League—as with Timolaus' group at Sparta in 192; or some enforced alteration in the terms of the agreement uniting the city as a whole to the League. This latter could only have contravened the terms of Flamininus' *diagramma* if the specific terms of Messenian entry into the League had been detailed in it. In itself this must have been an intrusion

---

[1] Roebuck, *Messenia*, p. 95, n. 126. Aymard, *Premiers Rapports*, p. 365, n. 26, does not speculate about the nature of the amendment, but suggests: 'en 191/190 cette intervention est à sa date logique et normale'. However, he cites no evidence to support this. Philopoemen's fifth *strategia* is also supported by Seeliger, *Messenien*, pp. 19–20 (although he dates this to 190/89). This cannot be correct. In spring 188 Diophanes was in Rome opposing Lycortas and Philopoemen (Liv. xxxviii. 32. 6–7); and although the main point at issue was Sparta (as it was also in 185), Diophanes would have been certain (as in 185) to have raised the matter of Messene if Philopoemen's amendment had at that time already been put into effect. Since he did not, the amendment must be placed after spring 188. Aymard and Seeliger are clearly right in agreeing that Philopoemen must have been *strategos* at the time. Since we have no evidence for his holding a *strategia* between 189/8 and 183/2, it seems best to place his amendment in his 'reform year', 189/8.

[2] Cf. above, chapter VII, pp. 123 ff.

into the League's internal affairs, although, from Flamininus' point of view, it was easily justifiable by the Messenian *deditio* and by the necessity, after the conclusion of the Achaean *foedus* and the events of the year, of demonstrating to the Achaeans the nature of *clientela*. But perhaps more likely, since the dispute in 185 was essentially about the exile problem, is that the *diagramma* had contained some specific political safeguards for the restored exiles—Flamininus' friend Deinocrates and his associates—within Messene. This was clearly not overstepping the bounds of equity or interfering excessively in Achaean affairs, since Messene had offered *deditio*, and all parties were Flamininus' clients.

But if Flamininus could claim the right to interfere in this way on behalf of his friends, it was equally possible for Philopoemen, as *strategos* of the League, to argue his right to interfere on behalf of his. For where Achaean interest was so deeply involved, Philopoemen could argue that his interpretation of the constitutional rights of one section of the Messenian community had as much claim to validity as Flamininus' interpretation of the rights of another section. If Deinocrates had been established in power by Flamininus' action, he could be disestablished by Philopoemen's. Action of this kind was particularly likely in the political atmosphere of Achaea in 188, after the apparent solution of the Spartan problem. One detail which, if connected with the present context, suggests that Philopoemen's action was aimed specifically at Deinocrates, is Plutarch's explicit statement that there was personal hostility between the two men. This shows at its most extreme in the apparent reluctance of Deinocrates to use Philopoemen as a bargaining counter in 182 after he had captured him. The Achaean view of their hostility is equally clear from the rumours, freely circulating among the Achaeans after Philopoemen's death, that Deinocrates had poisoned him— recorded uniformly in all sources, which depend on Polybius.[1] There is ultimately no means of testing Polybius' evidence on the matter of fact; but true or false, it has the same significance for the present purpose: the rumours were considered believable, and therefore illustrate that it was common knowledge in Achaea that there was a violent personal hostility between the two men. The origin of this becomes much clearer if Philopoemen's

[1] Plut. *Phil.* 18. 3 (personal hostility); Liv. xxxix. 50. 7–8; Paus. viii. 51. 7; Plut. *Phil.* 20; Pol. xxiii. 12. 3 (poisoning). Cf. below, chapter X, pp. 190 ff.

amendment is interpreted as a measure which removed the safeguards which Deinocrates had enjoyed in Messene by the terms
of Flamininus' *diagramma*.

If this interpretation of Philopoemen's amendment of the *diagramma* is acceptable, it fits well with the pattern of Philopoemen's
activity in this *strategia*. His aim was clearly to solve every outstanding problem connected with Achaean predominance in the
Peloponnese which might invite Roman intervention. He had
actually been prevented from claiming to be the unifier of the
Peloponnese; for in that race Diophanes had already scrambled
home in his *strategia* of 192/1 with the support of Flamininus,
and removed the prize from the competition—although Polybius allows no credit to Diophanes.[1] But problems remained;
and Philopoemen could stress the inadequacy of Diophanes'
superficially glorious achievement by drawing attention to the
problems left unsolved, and by providing independent Achaean
solutions to them. Despite Polybius' efforts, he could not oust
Diophanes from his claim to fame; but he could prevent him from
benefiting from his personal disloyalty. Philopoemen could prevent Diophanes from claiming that he was the only successful
expansionist. At Sparta, therefore, he had tried to solve the
problems by the annihilation of his most outstanding opponents,
by the forcible restoration of those likely to support Achaea, and
by a concession to equity which was intended to destroy the
Roman claim to interference. In Boeotia he had been prepared
to provoke serious trouble in order to settle the Megarian lawsuits. In these circumstances it would not be at all surprising to
find him interfering with Flamininus' settlement of Messene in
favour of a group more ready to co-operate with Achaea, thus
reducing the prestige which had been built into Deinocrates'
position by Flamininus.

Despite this independent activity throughout his year, usually
in conflict with the spirit of declared senatorial policy and that
of Flamininus, Philopoemen does not seem to have won general
approval in Achaea. This was made quite clear at the time of the
elections when Aristaenus, who must have disapproved of the
clumsiness of Philopoemen's non-compliance with Roman wishes,
was elected *strategos*.[2]

[1] Pol. ii. 40. 2.
[2] On the chronology, see appendix 2 B, pp. 259 ff.

Aristaenus has been shown above to have been a supporter of Philopoemen before Philopoemen's second visit to Crete in 200.[1] Polybius, however, after the death of Philopoemen, contrasts Aristaenus' policy with that of Philopoemen; and the period to which he refers is that after Philopoemen's departure to Crete in 200.[2] We must conclude from this that at some time between 200 and Philopoemen's death, Aristaenus and Philopoemen began to differ. The issue on which they differed was Achaean policy towards Rome, on which Aristaenus was more willing to compromise than was Philopoemen. We have seen how Philopoemen's hostility to Flamininus and his suspicion of Roman policy only began during his *strategia* in 193/2.[3] Before this, he must have remained in broad agreement with Aristaenus, who had developed his reaction to Roman policy during Flamininus' wars with Philip and Nabis. From this time onwards, the divergence was Philopoemen's. His policy developed in such a way that he cannot have expected Aristaenus, any more than Diophanes— though for different reasons—to continue to give him full support. Moreover, this divergence of opinion must have been further emphasized when Rome granted Achaea her *foedus*; for to Philopoemen this simply legalized his view of Achaean independence. Aristaenus, as is clear from Polybius' assessment, did not and could not follow Philopoemen. It is therefore necessary to view the election of Aristaenus to the *strategia* of 188/7 as a defeat for Philopoemen's group. Aristaenus must have had large support for his more co-operative programme from those vested interests, more interested in stability than independence, which must have been afraid that Philopoemen was being unnecessarily provocative in his interpretation of Achaean rights under the *foedus*, and was prejudicing the stability which was essential for commercial activity. Despite the violence used at Sparta, by the end of his *strategia* it must have been already clear that Philopoemen's settlement had not created the general peace and stability which they needed, and that it was by no means generally acceptable as the last word on the problem by those most intimately concerned. If he claimed this, it could already be shown to be otherwise. He was therefore unable to have one of his close supporters elected *strategos* for 188/7. Aristaenus thus broke for the first time

---

[1] pp. 72 ff.   [2] Pol. xxiv. 11-13; cf. below, chapter XII, pp. 221 ff.
[3] pp. 97 ff.

the dominant position which Philopoemen had held since his return from Crete.

The one event which we know occurred in Aristaenus' *strategia* in 188/7 was the *synodos* held in the late summer at Megalopolis. At this *synodos* several embassies from foreign powers were received, and Achaean ambassadors returning from missions abroad made their reports. The first report was from Nicodemus of Elis, whom Philopoemen had sent to Rome, who brought the news that although the Senate was dissatisfied at Philopoemen's action at Compasion, it did not intend to do anything. No decision or action seemed necessary from the Achaeans, and the matter was passed over.[1] It must have seemed that Philopoemen had been successful with his *fait accompli*; and Aristaenus was not the man to shrug off obvious Achaean advantage by making an issue of the Senate's reply for personal political reasons. It was clearly wiser to accept the rebuke along with the declaration of Roman non-interference. Aristaenus, as much as Philopoemen, wanted to give the Spartan settlement every chance of success. The fact was that if it failed—as already seemed possible —no Achaean politician had an acceptable alternative to offer. Nicodemus' report therefore attracted no discussion.

After Nicodemus, envoys from Eumenes of Pergamum were received: they offered to renew the existing alliance, and announced that Eumenes offered the Achaeans 120 talents, which he intended should be invested and the interest used to provide a payment for those attending the *synodos*. Polybius then gives details of the debate which followed the offer. Considerable opposition was aroused among the Achaeans. Apollonidas of Sicyon argued that, although the amount of money offered was suitable to the dignity of the Achaeans, the purpose for which it was offered was disreputable, and even illegal. He cited an Achaean law which prevented individuals or officials from taking presents from any of the kings; and argued that if Eumenes' gift were accepted, all members of the *synodos* would be openly admitting that they were being bribed. Now it was Eumenes offering money: soon it would be Prusias and Seleucus, and the Achaeans would be equally bound by gratitude to each of them. The gift should therefore be refused. The second speaker was Cassander of Aegina. Aegina had been in Pergamene hands since the first

[1] Pol. xxii. 7. 5–7.

Macedonian War, and Cassander argued that to accept Eumenes' offer would be to acquiesce in his continued possession of the island. The *synodos* then unanimously rejected Eumenes' offer.[1]

Aegina had been a Pergamene possession for more than twenty years; there was little prospect of its being returned to Achaea; yet it was still claimed as Achaean, still the exiled Aeginetans exercised their Achaean citizenship. Although we hear nothing about the effect of this issue on Achaean policies until 187, it was clearly kept alive, in much the same way as contemporary claims of the same type are maintained as long-term policies. Achaea had not been rash enough to commit herself to the equivalent of a Hallstein doctrine, but tempered Aeginetan emotion with diplomatic good sense. Nevertheless, the Aeginetan lobby was clearly of some strength, and with reason: for the completeness of the control which the Pergamene governors exercised over Aegina must have found its emotional reaction in an Achaea which still affected political independence. Even if this was occasionally circumscribed, Achaea maintained her pretensions, and opposition to the conditions illustrated by the Cleon inscription must have been entrenched.[2]

This maintained hostility to Pergamum on the local issue had not resulted in doctrinaire blindness on the broader. It had not prevented the formation of an alliance with Attalus, nor action on it when requested by Eumenes. But political conditions in Greece had changed since the defeat of Antiochus and the final withdrawal of Roman troops, and the fulfilment of Roman wishes no longer directed Achaean foreign policy. Eumenes had made good use of the Achaean troops which had been sent to him in 190; and as a result of the Roman victory over Antiochus at Magnesia—in which the Achaeans had served with Eumenes— he had received large territorial accessions in Asia Minor. Although there is no reason to assume that the Achaean troops had not been paid by Eumenes—perhaps through Attalus[3]—it was clearly in his interest that Achaean troops should continue to be available in the future, perhaps to defend his new possessions, perhaps to gain more. His treaty with the Achaeans, which had already proved so unexpectedly useful, was therefore to be renewed; and as an attempt to commit Achaea to his support for the future, he offered 120 talents to the *synodos*.

[1] Pol. xxii. 7. 8–8. 13.   [2] Ditt. *OGIS* 329.   [3] Cf. Ditt. *Syll.* 606.

The Achaeans reacted to this in exactly the same way as Philopoemen had acted when Timolaus had tried to buy his support at Sparta. Aristaenus had no desire to compromise Achaean foreign policy in advance, and there is no reason for believing that Philopoemen would have acted differently. Apollonidas' reference to Prusias and Seleucus voiced the fear that the Achaeans might find themselves intimately tied to the support of conflicting interests in Asia once a precedent was set by the acceptance of Eumenes' offer. The Senate's new non-committal policy could not be expected to help them to decide the correct course of action. Accordingly, if freedom was to be maintained in policy-making, it was clearly necessary that no compelling ties of gratitude should be contracted with foreign powers. Apollonidas did not make explicit the disfavour which an Achaean might feel for being bound to Eumenes in particular in this way: he contented himself with objecting to the precedent which it would set. But he must also have had in mind that Aegina had been bought by Attalus, with notorious consequences. In the circumstances no free Greek, with any claim to freedom of action, could have allowed himself to act otherwise than in opposition to this flagrant example of Pergamene cheque-book diplomacy. His advice was popular, and he could support it with legal and moral arguments by his appeal to the Achaean law and the rectitude of the *synodos*—which could no doubt have been quietly set aside, had interest lain in that direction. But this did not prevent him from concluding with a violent personal attack on Eumenes: he called on the Achaeans not only to repudiate the offer, but also to hate Eumenes for the intention behind his gift. Cassander appropriately did not have the same hesitations as Apollonidas, but came straight to the point, stressing the fact that Aegina had been bought. In the circumstances it was not surprising that the *synodos*, swayed by these emotional appeals —which in this case had hard-headed politics behind them— unanimously voted for the rejection of Eumenes' offer. This probably also meant the end of the alliance.[1]

There may also have been sound domestic reasons for the

[1] Despite Polybius' ἀνενεώσαντο (xxii. 7. 8). Cf. De Sanctis, *Storia* iv. 1. 238; McShane, *Attalids*, p. 164 and n. 51. There is no need with De Sanctis (loc. cit.) and Niccolini, *La Conf. Ach.*, p. 151, to interpret this as an anti-Roman move: the Achaeans had sufficient cause of grievance against Eumenes simply in his capacity of king of Pergamum and lord of Aegina.

synodos' rejection of Eumenes' offer. There was no payment for attendance at the meetings of the *synodos*.[1] Therefore only those who could afford to finance themselves were able to play any large part in federal politics. This ensured that the administration of the League remained solidly middle- and upper-class. If the *de facto* requirement of financial independence were removed by Eumenes' gift, it might easily open the way for lower-class demagogues to play a serious part in federal politics, to the exclusion of some of the more respectable but less talented middle-class members. This prospect would naturally arouse immediate opposition from the capitalist classes, whose wealth made it possible for them to participate in the business of the League. We must therefore see these vested political interests also at play in the rejection of Eumenes' offer, which made Cassander's emotional appeal about Aegina and Apollonidas' general foreign-policy considerations coincide to a large extent with personal interest.[2]

The same *synodos* was immediately given another opportunity of emphasizing the Achaean desire to maintain unimpaired the possibility of forming an independent foreign policy, unhindered by any moral commitments. When Seleucus' envoys were received to discuss the renewal of their treaty, they offered a gift of ten warships, which would have made an important addition to the Achaean navy. Seleucus' motive was quite clear, for it was obviously in the interest of the new king to make an early attempt at securing the goodwill of one of the more important Greek clients of Rome. From his point of view, his offer of the ships was in itself modest, and unlikely to create the invidious impression of an attempt at buying Achaean support. But Eumenes had already aroused Achaean suspicions of this kind of offer, and the same considerations had to be made by the Achaeans with regard to Seleucus' offer as with Eumenes'. And although the alliance was renewed—a token of friendship and a safeguard for the future—the gift of the ships was rejected.

Although the rejection of the gifts offered by Eumenes and

---

[1] Cf. Aymard, *Assemblées*, pp. 331 f.; above, chapter I, p. 6, n. 3.

[2] Larsen, 'Roman Greece', in Frank, *Economic Survey* iv. 366–7, suggests that the size of Eumenes' gift would have the effect of depressing interest rates in Achaea, and would thus cause the commercial classes to oppose the offer. But since background information about the Achaean commercial scene is totally lacking, this must remain mere speculation.

Seleucus represented successes for Aristaenus, they were not controversial or factional successes, for there is no reason for believing that Philopoemen would have advised differently. But Aristaenus did have a major party-political success at the *synodos*, which was gained at the expense of Philopoemen's group. Towards the end of Philopoemen's *strategia* in 189/8 he had sent Lycortas and two Sicyonians, Theodoridas and Rhositeles, to Alexandria, in order to negotiate the renewal of the current Achaean alliance with Egypt. Lycortas had returned in time to make his report at this *synodos*, and he was accompanied by Egyptians bringing gifts from Epiphanes, which consisted of 6,000 bronze peltast shields and 200 talents of coined bronze.[1] The negotiations seemed to have been ostentatiously successful, and the alliance had been sworn. A new diplomatic triumph for Lycortas and Philopoemen's party had clearly been gained, which only required the formality of ratification by the *synodos*. Epiphanes' gifts were offered in an essentially different spirit from those of Eumenes and Seleucus, for throughout a great part of the third century Achaea had received subsidies from Egypt, for as long as Achaean and Ptolemaic policies coincided.[2] In the second century Egypt still maintained a naval station in Achaean territory at Methana,[3] and this must have been countenanced by the Achaean authorities, on the 'sovereign base' principle. We hear of no agitation to have the base removed—such as there was against Eumenes' continued possession of Aegina—and must conclude that it was generally accepted by the Achaeans without opposition: it no doubt brought some prosperity and employment to a remote part of the Argolid. The Egyptian gifts would not therefore be considered to have 'strings' attached, but were rather offered in the spirit of the third-century subsidies, and therefore, even in second-century conditions, were likely to prove more acceptable.

After Lycortas had made his report, Aristaenus opened the discussion. He saw in these apparently successful negotiations of Lycortas and his colleagues an opportunity to blur the image of active efficiency which Philopoemen was trying to create for his

---

[1] Pol. xxii. 3. 6 (dispatch of embassy); 9. 1–12 (return and discussion).
[2] Plut. *Aratus*, 14. 1; 24. 4; 41. 3.
[3] Ditt. *OGIS* 115; perhaps = Arsinoe in the Peloponnese, cf. *OGIS* 102, line 12, and Dittenberger's n. 7; Robert, *Hellenica* xi. 157 ff.

group. On a point of information, he asked which of the many alliances which the Achaeans had had with the Ptolemies at various times—each inevitably containing widely differing terms —had been renewed by Lycortas. On the face of it, the inquiry was reasonable enough, for Aristaenus as *strategos* clearly needed such information. But he must have suspected some irregularity when he was prepared to make an issue of this at the *synodos*. He must already have undertaken some research into the Achaean archives to discover the state of the alliance before Lycortas was sent to Egypt. As a result of this investigation, he must have realized that Philopoemen had not made such a thorough examination, and that he therefore had a great opportunity to shatter public confidence in Philopoemen's group. The result of his apparently ingenuous question was highly satisfactory; for neither the Egyptian ambassadors nor Lycortas was able to answer. Attempts to make light of the matter by treating it with good-humoured levity did not deceive the *synodos*, some members of which must have been prepared for Aristaenus' manœuvre. Philopoemen, whose was the ultimate responsibility, was also unable to clarify the issue. Aristaenus was in sight of a major political success. As *strategos*, he refused to allow the *synodos* to ratify the alliance. A final decision was accordingly shelved. Even Polybius records that Philopoemen and his associates were generally considered to have failed to take sufficient care over public matters which had been entrusted to them; and that Aristaenus acquired the reputation of alone knowing his business.

Aristaenus had scored a major success over Philopoemen, who was, at least temporarily, discredited. Yet we should not conclude from this that Aristaenus was necessarily opposed to the continuation of friendly relations with Egypt: had this been so he could have organized a speaker to oppose the Ptolemaic possession of Methana. The fault which he had revealed was as much a fault of the Alexandrian chancellery as of the Achaean *strategos*; and his refusal to give *carte blanche* to the negotiators was only statesmanlike caution. Clearly he was simply using the issue— which was not of any great urgency—for immediate political advantage, but without prejudice to the ultimate result. In fact, the alliance was not concluded in the immediate future, but was delayed until Lycortas himself could successfully complete the negotiations, probably in his *strategia* of 185/4: he was quite as deeply committed to this alliance as Philopoemen, and would be likely to settle the issue as soon as he was given the chance.[1] Aristaenus, on the other hand, had every interest in making political capital by postponing the negotiations, in order to emphasize that the inefficiency of Philopoemen's party was responsible for depriving Achaea of the security of the Ptolemaic alliance and the enjoyment of the gifts. As far as the gifts were concerned, since they were essentially different in intent from those of Eumenes and Seleucus, they were accepted when Lycortas' negotiations on the alliance were finally successful.

Aristaenus had shown himself at the *synodos* eager, as far as possible, to preserve a non-aligned Achaea. Fulfilment of the terms of a general alliance with any power depended, as always, on the circumstances of the moment, and on the effect of the proposed action on the immediate policies of the states concerned. The terms of such a relationship were by no means as binding as the more strictly moral ties, which would have been contracted by the acceptance of a large donative from a king. Apollonidas was certainly correct when he argued that the Achaeans would feel that they had been bought—and moreover, the donor would expect them to feel this. As a result, the obligation from acceptance was felt to be more compulsive than that from a formal legal alliance. There could be no doubt that Aristaenus carried a majority of the *synodos* with him in rejecting these propositions, and it is likely that this included Philopoemen. On the other hand, Philopoemen had suffered a major defeat through Aristaenus' demonstration of his reckless inefficiency over the Egyptian alliance; and other members of his group must have shared his discredit. On this ground alone, therefore, it would be surprising to find Philopoemen or one of his party elected to the *strategia* for 187/6. In addition to the Egyptian business it might be expected that a further tactless *strategia* of Philopoemen would lead to a further deterioration in relations with Rome. If, despite these considerations, Philopoemen was the unknown *strategos* for 187/6, he did not long retain his ascendency, for Aristaenus was re-elected as soon as was legally possible, in 186/5.[2]

In 185, in the course of Aristaenus' fourth *strategia*, relations with Rome again assumed a preponderant importance for

---

[1] Pol. xxiv. 6. 5. Cf. De Sanctis, *Storia* iv. 1. 146, n. 20.
[2] On the *strategos* and the chronology, see appendix 2 B, pp. 259 ff.

Achaea. Q. Caecilius Metellus came to Achaea after spending
some time in Macedonia collecting complaints against Philip.
It was July, and the time of the Nemea, when Metellus arrived
in Achaea. The Achaean magistrates therefore assembled to meet
him at Argos.[1] Metellus had no official letters from the Senate
to Achaea; therefore it seems likely that the visit to Achaea was
no part of his original instructions from the Senate. The purpose
of his visit seems to have been little more than to impress the
Achaeans with his own importance, and to assert Roman
patronage after an interval of two years. Aristaenus, as much as
Philopoemen, had attached more importance, in his interpretation of the Senate's reply to Nicodemus in 187, to its declaration
that it intended to take no action on the Spartan settlement,
than to the clause of its reply which deplored the Achaean
violence. At the time, wishful thinking had made this seem less
relevant, since no action was required. As a result, no action
had been taken by the Achaeans in the intervening period, except
such as was necessary to continue the process of Spartan integration into the League. But to a Roman, with Metellus' apparent
intention of interfering in Achaea for interference's sake, this gave
a useful opportunity. It seemed to allow him to ignore the more
moderate and negative aspect of the original senatorial declaration, and to draw attention to the positive aspect, that which the
Achaeans had so far ignored.

It was with this that the conference opened. Metellus repeated
in his own words the Senate's disapproval of the Achaean violence
at Compasion; but he went further than the Senate, which had
required no action: Metellus also urged them at some length to
correct their former mistaken conduct.[2] His demand took the
Achaeans by surprise. Nothing had led them to think that the
Senate's attitude had changed since 187. Yet here was Metellus
recklessly demanding that they reopen the whole Spartan question, a demand which, if pressed into action, would destroy
everything which had been achieved by the relative stability of
the past two years. Aristaenus, the *strategos*, remained silent.
Polybius gives his own interpretation of this: 'It was clear from
his silence itself that he was displeased with the settlement and

---

[1] Pol. xxii. 10. On the date of the Nemea, 18 Panemos = early July, cf. Boethius, *Der argivische Kalender*, p. 51; cf. appendix 2 B, pp. 259 ff.
[2] Pol. xxii. 10. 2.

sympathized with what Metellus was saying.'[1] This interpretation, in fact, is precisely the opposite to what we would expect
Aristaenus' true motives to have been. Had he been so grossly
dissatisfied with the Spartan settlement as to approve (even
tacitly) of Metellus' demand for new action, he could have
taken steps to alter it in one of the two *strategiai* which he himself
had held since the settlement in 188; and he would have been
assured of senatorial approval had he undertaken this. Yet he
had accepted fully every implication of Philopoemen's settlement by his failure to attempt to reverse it: the presence and
complaint of Metellus are sufficient proof that no change had
been contemplated. Had Aristaenus wished to express satisfaction
at Metellus' demands, his silence would have been the worst
possible way of showing Metellus that he agreed with everything
he said. In the circumstances, Aristaenus' silence shows clearly
enough that he considered himself to be tarred with the same
brush as Philopoemen on this issue. Since Metellus was not ex-
pecting open opposition, Aristaenus as *strategos* clearly thought
it politic to keep quiet about his real feelings, in the knowledge
that he would only antagonize Metellus by expressing them and
by giving them the air of an official statement. Protestation of
what the Achaeans thought the Senate had meant in 187 had
no value, even as a face-saving argument, when confronted with
the text of the Senate's reply and with Metellus' interpretation
of it. Silence was the only possible course for Aristaenus.

Diophanes, however, in sharp contrast to Aristaenus' reticence,
rushed in with personal charges against Philopoemen. Aristaenus
had accepted Philopoemen's settlement of Sparta; since 191
Diophanes had been unable to gain any official position from
which he could commit himself to any course; and this must have
angered him. But Diophanes had suffered more than political
eclipse: in addition to being kept out of further office, he had
been personally offended by Philopoemen's interference with
Flamininus' settlement of Messene, in which he had played an
important part. Diophanes therefore had adequate private reason
for feeling aggrieved at Philopoemen, and he was prepared to
give voice in support of whoever attacked Philopoemen. Metellus'
reproaches were precisely the stimulus which Diophanes needed:

[1] Pol. xxii. 10. 3. Polybius' implications are accepted as justified by Lehmann,
Glaubwürdigkeit, p. 263.

he was hurt, and did not consider the more distant effects of his self-defence. It is this kind of behaviour which Polybius had in mind when he described Diophanes, at this time, as an inadequate politician, a character more soldierly than diplomatic.[1] Diophanes expressed full agreement with Metellus' condemnation of Philopoemen's action at Sparta, and added his private complaint about his treatment of Messene. Personal rancour had now broken the unified front which the Achaeans had so far presented to Metellus. Had Diophanes kept his personal complaints to himself, Metellus would have been content with the satisfaction of impressing himself on the Achaeans by administering his rebuke. The Achaeans would have accepted this in silence, and have continued their inaction. Honour on both sides would have been satisfied.

The possibility of this satisfactory outcome was destroyed by Diophanes' indulging his personal interest in Messene and personal hostility towards Philopoemen. Metellus at once noticed the dissension, and, seeing the possibility of making a greater personal effect, put on a show of anger at the fact that the Achaeans had not yet taken any action over Sparta. The calmness of the meeting was shattered; personal hostilities had been allowed to guide action. Metellus' new speech provoked Philopoemen's party. Successive speeches by Philopoemen himself, Lycortas, and Archon defended the Spartan settlement, and emphasized the supreme importance of allowing the current stable conditions at Sparta to continue. Despite Diophanes' tirade, it became clear that the meeting as a whole approved the maintenance of the settlement, and Metellus realized this. He again showed anger at the frustration of his efforts, for, since his reliance on the disagreement evidenced by Diophanes' speech, he was more than ever committed to forcing positive action from the Achaeans. He could not have immediately realized that Diophanes was in a minority of one, and proceeded to demand a *syncletos* to hear his point of view. He no doubt hoped that the larger meeting would be less mindful of the broader political implications for Achaea, and pay more serious attention to his bluster. But the Achaean magistrates were equal to the occasion, and replied by demanding to see his written instructions from the Senate, in accordance with which he would

[1] Pol. xxii. 10. 4: ἄνθρωπος στρατιωτικώτερος ἢ πολιτικώτερος.

have had the right to be considered an official ambassador. In support they quoted the Achaean law on the subject, which forbade the official reception by a *syncletos* of Roman envoys who were without written instructions from the Senate.[1] Metellus had none, and saw himself beaten: frustrating indeed for the Roman, using his initiative and already exceeding his instructions, to find the internal laws of the client state interfering with his wishes, which he considered a higher legality. Achaean exploitation of the terms of their *foedus* was complete. Metellus was powerless to do anything about it. In an attempt at rescuing what remained of his dignity, he stormed out of the meeting before a formal answer to his initial request had been given.

Aristaenus, as *strategos*, must have been more deeply involved in the rejection of Metellus' request than any other Achaean; yet he receives no credit for this from Polybius. Yet despite Polybius' unfavourable picture of Aristaenus at this meeting, this was not his own considered verdict. For the latter, we must look at the comparison which he makes later between Aristaenus and Philopoemen. There his conclusion is that Philopoemen's policy was καλή, Aristaenus' εὐσχήμων, and both ἀσφαλεῖς.[2] This judgement disallows any suspicion of traitorous behaviour, such as he implies in his account of the meeting at Argos; and since the *syncrisis* must represent Polybius' quietly considered opinion, the earlier account can only represent contemporary propaganda. The reason for his including the unfavourable assessment in his work probably lies in Polybius himself and in his political associates. At the time of the meeting at Argos, Polybius cannot have been much more than 20 years old, an age at which he might easily have been ready to accept the versions of events and assessments of characters which Philopoemen and Lycortas found it convenient to propound. When he later came to write about these same events, Polybius could not be *sine ira et studio*: he had been involved—even if only as a passive recipient of the propaganda—and would tend to react towards the events in retrospect in the same way as he had at the time. His comparison of Aristaenus and Philopoemen shows a different kind of approach. There he was judging policies in general terms, with a different point of reference. He was accordingly able to reach a better-balanced and less partisan conclusion.

---

[1] Pol. xxii. 10. 12. Cf. Larsen, *Rep. Gov.*, pp. 89 f. [2] Pol. xxiv. 13. 8.

Nevertheless, despite his independent view of Aristaenus'
career, Polybius colours his picture with Lycortas' tints when he
adds at the end of the *syncrisis* that 'a rumour was current that
Aristaenus was more favourably disposed to the Romans than
was Philopoemen'.[1] Although Polybius seems to be trying to dis-
sociate himself from the rumour, he had no reason to record it
at all if he considered it to be wholly false. It is clear that even
in this attempt at dispassionate comparison, his father's political opposition affected Polybius' judgement. The differences in
policy between Aristaenus and Philopoemen were, in fact, differences of method rather than of end, as Polybius' analysis shows
clearly. But since the main political difference had to be sought
in the emphasis placed on a personal interpretation of τὸ καλόν
vis-à-vis τὸ συμφέρον passions ran high, and control of the source
of long-term propaganda—Polybius himself—has been sufficient to achieve the permanent misrepresentation of a statesman
who was as loyal and patriotic as any of his contemporaries.[2]

Although Polybius was clearly capable of discarding contemporary propaganda, it is nevertheless this which has most affected
his account of Aristaenus. In the propaganda of the Philopoemenists, Aristaenus was Philopoemen's opponent, therefore capable
of no patriotic action. Yet if we reject Polybius' partisan interpretation of Aristaenus' action at Argos, nothing remains which
suggests that Aristaenus was in any way inferior to Philopoemen
in his patriotic desire to maintain intact the vital Spartan settlement. Aristaenus had the company of Philopoemen, Lycortas,
and Archon when he kept quiet at Metellus' initial demand; yet
Aristaenus alone is branded as a sympathizer by the propaganda.
When the silence was broken by Diophanes, Aristaenus did not
reply: but sufficient was said by Philopoemen, Lycortas, and
Archon to make it unnecessary for the *strategos*—who was probably chairman—to add anything, which would only have the
effect of prejudicing Metellus further against him. The significant
fact is surely that Aristaenus could probably have refused to put
the question of Metellus' demand for action at Sparta to the
vote, had he disapproved of its inevitable rejection. Again, Aristaenus as *strategos* must have been the man who cited the law

[1] Pol. xxiv. 13. 10.
[2] Pol. xxiv. 11–13 (*syncrisis*); cf. chapter XII, pp. 224 ff.; De Sanctis, *Storia* iv. 1.
240. Castellani, *Contributi*, 92–3, takes no account of Polybius' bias.

to Metellus, which refused him a *syncletos*. Yet Polybius passes over in silence the lead which he must *ex officio* have taken in this. In his account, the refusal of a *syncletos* was made by the sum total of the magistrates, a lack of detail which makes a strange contrast with his account of the *synodos* at Megalopolis in 187, where personalities are named explicitly on each issue. It seems clear that Polybius is simply retailing propaganda, in which Aristaenus' part was consciously concealed in favour of the members of Philopoemen's party who were named individually.

Aristaenus was a serious political danger to Philopoemen because he was successful. He had gained two *strategiai* at the expense of Philopoemen's group, and his policy was close enough to Philopoemen's to make the latter appear simply the more dangerous version. It was necessary to discredit him if the Philopoemenists were to survive as an effective group, and they seem to have chosen this meeting at Argos as the crisis point. It is not altogether clear why they thought Aristaenus could be successfully misrepresented. The method is clear enough: to discredit him by bracketing him with Diophanes as an unpatriotic Romanophile, which Diophanes' convenient outburst at Argos made easier. Since his *strategia* of 192/1, Diophanes had moved into a position of severe opposition to the Philopoemenists, and seems to have begun to realize that, in the long run, only compliance with Roman requests and a non-partisan settlement of Sparta and Messene was a viable policy. But Diophanes' policy became effective in Achaea only after the death of Philopoemen, when Callicrates adopted it. In 185 it was traitor-talk. It is not clear how the propaganda was able successfully to associate Aristaenus with this currently disreputable policy. Polybius says that 'the Achaeans' accused Aristaenus and Diophanes of having invited Metellus, and in 188 Fulvius.[1] It seems clear that 'the Achaeans' in question are no other than Philopoemen's group. But it is one thing to raise a rumour, another to make it stick as a reputation. And Aristaenus must have been vehement in his counter-propaganda. It seems an insufficient explanation of Philopoemen's success simply to assume that the *strategos* failed to counteract this hostile propaganda adequately, although it was demonstrably untrue.

The Philopoemenists' suspicions of Diophanes may bear some

[1] Pol. xxii. 10. 14.

relation to the facts, for Diophanes was a self-confessed Romano-phile. But we cannot assume that Aristaenus courted disaster by inviting Metellus to make his disastrous appearance at the meeting of magistrates. Nevertheless, the propaganda's effectiveness and the fact that the Philopoemenists chose this issue for the struggle with Aristaenus suggest that there may have been some awkwardness about Metellus' visit, which prevented Aristaenus from defending himself effectively against the propaganda. The year was a Nemean year, and the crucial meeting took place at the time and place of the Nemea. This suggests that Metellus was probably in Argos primarily for the celebration of the festival. Aristaenus was *strategos*, and therefore must have been responsible for entertaining him. It seems unlikely that Metellus would simply appear at the festival—a visit to Achaea was not on his official itinerary—without a specific invitation. But there is no difficulty in this, for it is likely that, as the official Roman representative in Greece, he would be given an invitation as a matter of normal diplomatic courtesy. If so, the invitation must have been issued by the *strategos* Aristaenus.

If this hypothesis is correct, it will help to reveal the awkward situation which prevented Aristaenus from adequately countering the propaganda of the Philopoemenists. For it would mean that he could not deny that he had invited Metellus to Achaea, although his invitation was for a different purpose. Aristaenus clearly had not wanted him to speak to the magistrates; but once in Achaea, Metellus could be approached by any dissident parties —whether Diophanes or some Spartan group[1]—and request a meeting. In the circumstances, Aristaenus could not refuse. The innocent formal invitation to the Roman ambassador to attend the Nemean celebrations was turned by the Philopoemenists' propaganda into a plot to overthrow the patriotic policy. Aristaenus was branded with Diophanes.[2] The slander is manifest. Yet it succeeded; the charges stuck; and the disreputable manœuvre ended Aristaenus' political career. From this time he disappears from Achaean history, and the party of Philopoemen, now entrenched as the only patriotic group, remained in power until Philopoemen's death removed his *auctoritas*.

[1] Cf. Paus. vii. 8. 6.

[2] Lehmann, *Glaubwürdigkeit*, pp. 263, 275, accepts Polybius' account of the meeting at its face value, and depicts Diophanes as a consistent supporter and associate of Aristaenus. This is never explicitly and unambiguously stated by Polybius.

X

CRISIS

THE visit of Metellus and the support given him by Diophanes gave an ideal opportunity to the Philopoemenist
propaganda machine. When it set to work after Metellus'
departure, it is not surprising to find that Lycortas was elected
strategos for 185/4.[1] Lycortas' year saw various developments, both
in the situation at Sparta and in relations with Rome, all of which
stemmed from the rebuff of Metellus. The Achaeans realized
that, although Metellus had not had formal letters from the
Senate authorizing him to interfere in Achaea, and although
the Achaeans seemed to themselves to be fully justified by their
law in refusing him a *syncletos*, it was likely that he would complain to the Senate about the lack of co-operation he had met
when he visited Argos. In order that his misrepresentation should
not pass unnoticed, Apollonidas of Sicyon was sent to Rome to
represent the Achaeans. It is not clear whether he was sent by
Lycortas or by Aristaenus: he had led the opposition to Eumenes'
offer in 187, and may have belonged to Aristaenus' group. But
the evidence of the meeting at Argos shows that there was little
serious disagreement in Achaea—except for Diophanes—on the
issue of Sparta. Apollonidas' defence of the settlement in Rome
would be equally appropriate whichever *strategos* had sent him.[2]

Two aspects of the Achaean reception of Metellus were discussed by the Senate: the problem of Sparta, and the Achaeans'
refusal to summon a *syncletos* for him. These were treated
separately. Over the refusal of the *syncletos*, Apollonidas based his
defence on the same argument as Aristaenus had used to foil
Metellus at the meeting: the citation of the Achaean law limiting
the *syncletos* to discussing alliances, war, or letters from the Senate.
Against this legal argument Metellus made a general accusation
of Philopoemen and Lycortas—and presumably of Aristaenus,
although Polybius makes no mention of it—and expressed
dissatisfaction at the state of the Spartan question. In contrast

[1] Cf. appendix 2 B, p. 262.   [2] Pol. xxii. 11. 6; 12. 1; 12. 5–10.

with the violence of Metellus' language, the Senate's reply was
studiously moderate: it impressed upon Apollonidas that fitting
reception should always be given to Roman representatives 'as
the Romans do to ambassadors who visit them'. This statement
did no more than emphasize the importance, for any diplomatic
exchange, of the grant of reciprocal facilities. No attempt was
made to come to terms with the Achaean law: this was a question
which the Senate evaded. It was quite within its power to re-
commend that the law be altered, that special exceptions should
be made in the case of Romans. Yet it did not. It seems clear that
the Senate did not think that it was publicly affected by the rejection of Metellus' demand, which it had not authorized. Metellus'
private commitment was politely disowned by the Senate, with
a mild attempt at saving face by the citation of general principles
of diplomatic communication. The Achaean law could clearly be
useful to the Fathers if they wanted to keep their legates strictly
in check, if they wanted to preserve the possibility of rejecting inconvenient public involvement when private prestige had
been unofficially and unnecessarily committed.[1] The Achaeans
realized that the Senate was not prepared to take full responsibility for every rash private action of its diplomats, which did
not concern it, and the law probably remained on the Achaean
statute book.

In the case of Sparta, however, the new commitment which
Metellus had undertaken could not be shrugged off so easily, for
here he had simply given new emphasis to already declared
senatorial policy. The fact that he had re-awakened awareness
of the matter, when the Senate would have preferred to let it lie
dormant, was irritating, but in this case irrelevant, for here his
private action necessarily involved public commitment. The
situation was also complicated by a new factor, for which Metellus
was wholly responsible. His expression of interest in Sparta had

---

[1] A similar interpretation should be given to the *senatus consultum* drawn to the
attention of the Greeks by C. Popillius Laenas and Cn. Octavius in winter 170/69,
which instructed the Greeks not to provide troops to a Roman commander unless
he possessed a *senatus consultum* explicitly authorizing this (Pol. xxviii. 13. 11; 16. 2; cf.
Liv. xliii. 17. 2). The usual interpretation of this (cf. Meloni, *Perseo*, pp. 270–1, and
bibliography cited there) has been that the Senate merely wished to recover Greek
goodwill before the war with Perseus. But an equally important consideration may
have been the Senate's own insistence, in view of recent events, on the Senate
oligarchy's corporate control of all foreign policy—the same consideration which
perhaps led to its disowning Metellus in 185/4.

encouraged Areus and Alcibiades, two of the 'old exiles', who were dissatisfied with their reception at Sparta, to go to Rome. Their names are clearly significant of their Spartan royal background; and their aim was to re-establish a glorious and independent Sparta—in which the chief glory would fall to them. They were unwilling to be 'grateful' to the Achaeans, the traditional enemies of their city, for their restoration, for this would have meant acquiescing in Achaean control.[1] But they had taken no action until Metellus had inadvisedly expressed renewed Roman dissatisfaction at Philopoemen's settlement. The glory-seekers leapt at the chance, and hastened to Rome, where they were received by the Senate and disputed with Apollonidas' legation. Part of Apollonidas' mission was to attempt to improve Achaean relations with Rome over Sparta; and he conceived of this as a simple explanation to the Senate that matters could not have been better managed than by Philopoemen. The presence of Areus and Alcibiades at Rome, and their statement of the policy they represented, constituted an open denial of the truth of Apollonidas' statement, and consequently removed a great deal of credibility from his arguments. Faced with two such diametrically opposed views, and with the consideration that Metellus had already committed Rome to new activity on the Spartan question, the Senate had little alternative but to add Achaea to the terms of reference of the mission which was again to investigate Macedonia in 184, this time headed by Ap. Claudius Pulcher: there would be no doubt about Pulcher's having written instructions to visit Achaea.[2] This decision preserved the Senate from committing itself to a course of action based on insufficient evidence, and from admitting that it had no immediate and urgent policy towards Achaea. On the other hand, it allowed the continuation of its non-committal apology for a policy of merely asserting legitimate interest in client Achaea—which Metellus had embarrassingly again brought to light.

Areus and Alcibiades did not represent all the restored 'old exiles', but were an extremist splinter group. Their complaints before the Senate concerned the power and status of their city which had been shattered in Philopoemen's settlement. They

[1] Achaean reaction was based wholly on their failure to show due gratitude: Pol. xxii. 11. 8; Liv. xxxix. 35. 6–8.
[2] Pol. xxii. 11. 7; 12. 1–4.

argued their desire for a free Spartan state, free of all the limitations which the federal mechanism inevitably imposed on them.
In particular, the necessity to act, both publicly and individually
—like the other cities of the League—in accordance with the
regulations laid down by federal magistrates, was felt to be irk-
some. When Apollonidas returned to Achaea and announced
that Pulcher had been given explicit instructions to deal with
Achaea, and that Areus and Alcibiades had been received by the
Senate, where they had apparently found favour, Lycortas decided that a *synodos* should discuss all issues which might be raised
by Pulcher when he addressed the *syncletos*, and should decide
as far as possible what line the Achaeans should take. The one
great issue was clearly Sparta and the action the Achaeans should
take over the sectional appeal of Areus and Alcibiades to the
Senate. The ties of gratitude, with which Philopoemen had hoped
to hold the support of the 'old exiles', after their restoration, had
not proved as strong as expected; and the *synodos* fully expressed
its indignation that due gratitude owing to Achaea from this
section of the 'old exiles' had not been shown. Passions became
inflamed at the fact that Areus and Alcibiades, through their
traditionalist independent view of Spartan policy, were inviting
Roman intervention, which might easily result in the loss of
Achaean freedom of action. Instead of quietly attempting to work
out a solution to this new facet of the Spartan problem and its
implications with regard to Achaean relations with Rome, the
meeting allowed emotionalism to take the upper hand, and
Areus and Alcibiades were condemned to death.[1]

There was little reason behind this. It must have been apparent
that a solution could not be reached in this way which would
satisfy the Senate. For even if it remained essentially indifferent
to Achaean affairs, Metellus' action and the appeal of Areus and
Alcibiades had made it necessary to act in order to save face.
Moreover, Sparta was the one Achaean issue on which the Senate
had continued—even if in a desultory manner—to assert its
interest. The purpose of the *synodos* had been to form a policy:
ideally, it had been to find a means whereby a satisfactory compromise could be reached, which would have allowed the Senate
to extricate itself from its support of Areus and Alcibiades, without severely damaging Philopoemen's Spartan settlement. It had

---

[1] Liv. xxxix. 35. 5–8; cf. Pol. xxii. 11. 8.

ended by destroying the possibility of a reasonable compromise policy's being formed. Lycortas was now condemned to face Pulcher at the *syncletos* with a mandate to defend this extreme position.

But worse was to come. When Pulcher arrived at Cleitor, where the *syncletos* had been summoned for him, he was accompanied by Areus and Alcibiades. Pulcher began with what had by now become almost the traditional statement of Roman policy, the condemnation of Philopoemen's settlement after Compasion. Reply was made by Lycortas on behalf of the Achaeans. The speech in Livy cannot represent the actual words of Lycortas. A detailed examination is therefore valueless for the present purpose; but Pausanias confirms that the spirit of the speech is correctly given by Livy. It was in full accordance with the views of the most extreme members of Philopoemen's party, and in no way suited to the delicate diplomacy which the situation required. Lycortas went so far as to suggest that the real responsibility for the present dissatisfaction lay in the ineffectiveness of Roman policy on the Spartan issue in 189, in the already existing *stasis* at Sparta, and in the ingratitude—this could never be forgotten by Philopoemen's group—of Areus and Alcibiades. Had Lycortas given up all hope of reaching a negotiated settlement, and determined merely to establish his reputation locally as a patriot, he could not have spoken less relevantly. It was a reaction which found its stimulus in frustration and despair.[1]

The reaction of the mildest Roman could not have been favourable—and Pulcher did not lack the usual Claudian consciousness of his *dignitas*. In practice, the only wise course for the Achaeans would have been to repeat the silence which had initially greeted Metellus the previous year. No speech, however conciliatory, could have affected the preconceptions which conditioned Pulcher's expression of Roman requirements. However reasonable Lycortas' defence might appear to be from the Achaean point of view, the very fact of his daring to make it showed the Roman that the essential nature of the client–patron relationship between the two states was being flagrantly violated by the Achaeans. In the circumstances the speech was irrelevant—and worse, insolent and provocative. Roman policy could not take its arguments

---

[1] Liv. xxxix. 36. 1–2 (Areus and Alcibiades); 3–4 (Pulcher's disapproval); 36. 6–37. 17; cf. Paus. vii. 9. 4 (speech of Lycortas).

into consideration, and its content was duly ignored by Pulcher. His subsequent statement was that, although it was in his power to treat the Achaeans however he wished—a more than usually naked statement of what *clientela* could mean to a Claudian— he would be happier if the Achaeans could be persuaded to act without compulsion, in accordance with the normal client's desire to perform *officia*. The threat frightened the meeting. Faced with no alternative, it could only comply. The Achaeans did not realize that the words themselves in Pulcher's reply to Lycortas were the only reality: the threats they expressed were mere bluster. There was no likelihood of physical intervention by the Senate to force a new settlement at Sparta, as the magistrates at Argos had realized when confronting Metellus the previous year. The larger *syncletos*, however, could be stampeded by threats, as Metellus had hoped, and as the present case demonstrated: Pulcher was therefore able to have his way. Lycortas could do nothing, despite his more realistic appreciation of the extent of senatorial commitment. The *syncletos* gave Pulcher *carte blanche* over Sparta; but the only specific action taken was to rescind the recent condemnation of Areus and Alcibiades by the *synodos*. Pulcher was satisfied to have impressed the Achaeans with their real status, and was careful to avoid involving the Senate in any complications relating to specific details of the Spartan settlement.[1]

Pulcher drove home his point about Roman supremacy in the *clientela* relationship by granting the Spartans dispensation from the terms of the convention which regulated the dispatch of embassies to Rome, and giving them permission to send envoys.[2] They were ready to take full advantage of this, and four separate groups of Spartan envoys, each representing different policies and interests, were dispatched to Rome and received by the Senate in winter 184/3. The readiness of the Spartans to act in this way suggests that there was general dissatisfaction in Sparta at the way in which Areus and Alcibiades had managed to obtain factional advantage by having established close relations with important senators. But there is no evidence which suggests that Pulcher allowed the Spartans to secede from the League.[3] The

---

[1] Liv. xxxix. 37. 18–21. Cf. Niese, *GGMS* iii. 48–9; De Sanctis, *Storia* iv. 1. 241; Castellani, *Contributi*, 96 f.   [2] Paus. vii. 9. 4. Cf. appendix 6, p. 282.
[3] As Niccolini, *La Conf. Ach.*, p. 154; De Sanctis, *Storia* iv. 1. 241.

fact that he gave them permission to send ambassadors to Rome clearly suggests that he was not prepared to take any decision on details which would commit the Senate in advance to a new controversial settlement. Despite his emphasis on his general ability to take unlimited action regarding Achaea, he did not in fact do more than state this position. The federal authorities, representing Philopoemen's party, sent Xenarchus to Rome to negotiate the renewal of the *foedus*, and to continue Achaean representation at the discussion on Sparta.[1]

It is fortunate that Polybius' own account of the Spartan envoys and the policies which each represented is extant, since Livy's is summary.[2] It is therefore possible to discover more accurately the recent course of Spartan history. The first group (in the order in which Polybius describes them) was headed by Lysis. They represented 'old exiles', and predictably wanted total restoration of all their property.[3] This was the traditional and expected demand of the restored exile, and Lysis must have represented the largest proportion of the 'old exiles'. Also represented was the royalist splinter group, again headed by Areus and Alcibiades. Instead of simply opposing Achaean restrictions on Spartan independence, their policy had now assumed the more positive form of a desire to re-establish a large, active, citizen body. Their specific proposals were a compromise on the main 'old exile' demands, in favour of this positive policy: that property to the value of a talent should be restored to the 'old exiles', and that the remainder of the money made available by the redemption of the exiles' property should be used to enfranchise 'those worthy of citizenship'.[4] This scheme looks very like a revival of Cleomenes' plan for a resurgent Sparta, although it is unlikely

---

[1] Pol. xxiii. 4. 11.   [2] Pol. xxiii. 4; cf. Liv. xxxix. 48. 2–4.

[3] Pol. xxiii. 4. 2: φάσκοντες δεῖν ἔχειν αὐτοὺς πάσας τὰς κτήσεις, ἀφ᾽ ὧν ἐξ ἀρχῆς ἔφυγον. Büttner-Wobst conjectures Κλῆτιν for the leader of the delegation instead of the MSS. Λῦσιν, because Cletis is mentioned at xxiii. 18. 5. This is unnecessary when we consider the rapid turnover of Spartan politicians at this period (see appendix 9). Dr. B. Shimron (in a private letter) suggests that Lysis' group represented the descendants of the 'old oligarch' opponents of Cleomenes. This is possible. On the other hand there must have been numbers of exiles created by the factional struggles after Cleomenes' death and by the regime of Machanidas (now all together considered as 'old exiles', together with the exiles from Nabis' time), which would tend to blur precise distinctions after more than 40 years. The total restoration of property was the regular demand of the restored exile and cannot in itself be taken to describe any particular group: cf. Ditt. *OGIS* 2 (Mytilene); *Syll.* 306 (Tegea); Michel, 417 (Calymna).   [4] Pol. xxiii. 4. 3.

that Areus and Alcibiades represented an actual body of exiles from that time. Their policy was nationalist, and therefore was opposed by the other 'old exiles', who were primarily interested in recovering their private property. This sufficiently explains the existence of divided interests among the 'old exiles' and the creation of this 'royalist' splinter group.

The ideas of Areus and Alcibiades show strong anti-Achaean bias, and a traditionalist desire for Spartan independence, which is in sharp contrast to the narrowly personal motives of the other groups. But their demand was so out of keeping with the reality of the changed circumstances that, in the form in which it was stated, it could not now find acceptance, or even serious support, in the Senate, whose aim was to solve problems, not to create more. The method by which Areus and Alcibiades proposed to achieve their aim was as traditional as the aim itself: the enfranchisement of those 'worthy of the franchise'. Usually this type of phrase had meant helots or *perioeci*; but in the circumstances of the time, their support must have come from the ex-*adscripti* of Livy, who had been enfranchised by Nabis and sold or exiled by Philopoemen. This aspect of their claim also had its clear anti-Achaean origins, and it must have been on this especially that Areus and Alcibiades based their claim for senatorial support. For the sale and banishment of these new citizens had been one of the specific objections which they had originally raised against Philopoemen's settlement, in their first appearance at Rome the previous spring. The result had been the appointment of Pulcher to examine the Spartan question;[1] and Pulcher had made their complaints the basis of his own objections to the settlement when he spoke to the Achaean *syncletos* at Cleitor.[2] Clearly this reaction must have seemed to be a demonstration of the Senate's sympathy for their complaints. Their policy was now more precisely formulated, and on it and the slogan of traditionalism Areus and Alcibiades based their hopes of renewed senatorial support.

The third Spartan group was led by Serippus. He urged the preservation of the conditions which had existed at Sparta since the city had become a member of the League.[3] His statement of policy suggests that Serippus was the current representative of the

---

[1] Pol. xxii. 12. 2–4; Liv. xxxix. 33. 6–7. [2] Liv. xxxix. 36. 3–4.
[3] Pol. xxiii. 4. 4.

pro-Achaean group, which had originally included Timolaus, which had been established in power by Philopoemen in 192, had been expelled late in 191, and had been re-established in Sparta after Compasion. This was the only Spartan party which had ever shown any enthusiasm for Achaea, for its position within Sparta depended wholly on Achaean federal support: for these men Spartan independence meant exile, as they had discovered between 191 and 188. Therefore now, as Timolaus had earlier, Serippus recommended the continuation of Sparta's union with the League, which would give his group internal power at Sparta and Achaean support for it.

The fourth Spartan group was led by Chaeron. Polybius specifically describes them as representing 'those who had been condemned to death and those exiled by the Achaeans' decrees'.[1] This faction is clearly the remains of the tyrants' party, who must have gone into exile if they escaped massacre at Compasion. The purpose which Polybius attributes to Chaeron is simply the restoration of these 'new exiles', and the re-establishment of some specific constitution.[2] Their aim was anti-Achaean, as Polybius makes clear. Chaeron's hopes of achieving restoration must have centred on the fact that his party was likely to find some favour at Rome, for it was the party which Flamininus had consistently favoured against Timolaus' supporters of the union with Achaea in 192/1; and this support had clearly continued after he left Greece, for the Spartan hostages were restored on request from this group. In 189 again, they had offered *deditio* to Fulvius; and it had seemed to them that the Senate's ambiguous reply in spring 188 had favoured their continuation in power at Sparta.[3] On many occasions since Compasion, Philopoemen's treatment of their party had been specifically condemned by the Senate or its representatives. There was therefore every reason for Chaeron to consider that his group had a good chance of success on this, its first appeal to the Senate since 188/7.

These representatives of conflicting Spartan interests appeared

---

[1] Pol. xxiii. 4. 5: ἀπὸ δὲ τῶν τεθανατωμένων καὶ τῶν ἐκπεπτωκότων κατὰ τὰ τῶν Ἀχαιῶν δόγματα.

[2] Pol. xxiii. 4. 5. The text contains a *lacuna* at the point where the constitution is mentioned. But it seems clear that this group would want the 'free' constitution, such as had been in operation (with the Senate's tacit acceptance) between the Spartan revolt from Achaea in autumn 189 and the settlement after Compasion.

[3] Cf. chapter VIII, pp. 143–4.

before the Senate and argued among themselves and with the Achaeans until it became impossible for the senators *en masse* to understand, still less to form an opinion on, all the issues involved. A committee was therefore appointed, consisting of former *legati* to Greece, Flamininus, Metellus, and Pulcher, who were expected to be well-informed on the complicated issues involved. They were to attempt to gain agreement for a compromise solution.[1] This committee eventually secured agreement that Chaeron's exiles should be restored and that union with Achaea should continue—no doubt pressure was exerted by Flamininus on these matters—but discussion was more heated, and no agreement was reached, over the property issue. Nevertheless, a schedule of points of agreement was drawn up, and the Achaean representative Xenarchus—rather unwillingly, since he had taken no part in the negotiations—was constrained to put his name to it, together with the Spartan groups, and in this way to give it his seal of federal approval. The single point about which the Achaeans could feel satisfied was that Sparta would continue in the League. Pausanias adds that the walls of Sparta were rebuilt and that the traditional Greek method of settling violently disputed cases—reference to a foreign arbitration court—was to be employed in capital cases; all others were to be settled by federal judges.[2] The reason for this is easy to see, and it was equitable enough; it removed from the federal jurisdiction the possibility of a repetition of events such as the federal condemnation of the anti-Achaean group at Compasion, and of Areus and Alcibiades at the *synodos* of 184: significantly, both parties who had suffered were present at the negotiations. From the local Spartan jurisdiction it removed the risk of judgements on property—now expected to be the chief remaining cause of party dissension—being left in the hands of biased local officials. The fact that we hear no more about this issue probably indicates that the ruling worked well.[3]

The two groups of Spartans which had gained at least part of what they had hoped for from the Senate were Serippus' and Chaeron's. It is accordingly not surprising to find that these two

[1] Pol. xxiii. 4. 7. Pulcher's name must be added from Paus. vii. 9. 5.

[2] Paus. vii. 9. 5. Nothing suggests that the 'laws of Lycurgus'—whatever this might mean—were now restored (as Castellani, *Contributi*, 99).

[3] Cf. Niese, *GGMS* iii. 49–50; Niccolini, *La Conf. Ach.*, pp. 156–7; De Sanctis, *Storia* iv. 1. 241–2; Castellani, *Contributi*, 98–9.

groups, rather than the divided groups of 'old exiles' with their unrealistic policies, were able to be dominant in Sparta until at least 178. The Senate had managed to avoid admitting that it had no ready-made, purposeful policy towards Sparta and Achaea by appointing the committee of ex-*legati* to clear up the incomprehensible confusion. Its mild policy of expressing limited disapproval of Achaean action at Compasion had almost recoiled by the confusion it had caused. The Spartans had belatedly recognized that the struggle of words could be turned to factional advantage. Once this had happened, it became no longer sufficient merely to demand the acknowledgement of *clientela*, and the 'eastern experts' were appointed to resolve some of the confusion. In general, however, the ineffective vagueness, which had been characteristic of Roman policy towards Achaea since the defeat of Antiochus, continued. Yet another ambassador was appointed to visit the Peloponnese after dealing with developments in Macedon. This time Q. Marcius Philippus was the ambassador.[1] His task may have been more specific, perhaps to examine progress towards the establishment of the agreed compromise at Sparta. But he had little success; and his presence had little effect when he tried to assert Roman influence in connection with trouble at Messene, which also came to a head during his year in Greece.

At some time after the appointment of *legati*, during the winter 184/3, Deinocrates of Messene arrived in Rome. On his arrival he found that Flamininus had already been appointed *legatus* to Prusias of Bithynia, which meant that he would have to pass through Greece on his journey. Deinocrates seems to have been satisfied with this and, as far as we know, made no attempt to have a formal interview with the Senate. His plans were quite straightforward: to gain Messenian independence from Achaea. And he clearly hoped that his long-standing friendship with Flamininus would be sufficiently powerful to have his desire for secession imposed on the federal government with the full weight of Roman patronage.[2] But despite his strong hopes from Flamininus, he did not neglect preparations for meeting the contingency in which Messene might unilaterally declare independence from Achaea as the Spartans did before Compasion. Accordingly,

[1] For refs. cf. Broughton, *MRR* i. 379.
[2] On their earlier relationship, see chapter VII, pp. 124 ff.

he spent the greater part of the summer making arrangements—
no doubt with the help of Flamininus—for war materials to be
shipped to Messene from Italy. By the end of the summer all
preparations were complete, and Flamininus, who had delayed his
departure, was accompanied by Deinocrates when he left Rome.[1]

In Achaea Philopoemen was elected *strategos* for the eighth time
at the autumn *synodos* of 183, thus maintaining the ascendency
which his group had asserted since the eclipse of Aristaenus after
his *strategia* in 186/5.[2] He soon heard that Flamininus had arrived
in Greece; but since Xenarchus had been in Rome at the time of
his appointment, it must also have been known that Flamininus
had no specific instructions from the Senate to deal with Achaea.
Philopoemen must also have known that Messene was disaffected,
and that Deinocrates had left for Rome. Philopoemen's knowledge
of Flamininus' past relations with Deinocrates can only have
led to his suspecting that Deinocrates would try to enlist Flamininus' support for his Messenian cause. Philopoemen's own personal distrust of Flamininus must also have encouraged the
suspicion. Tactics, therefore, had to be considered before Flamininus arrived, in case these suspicions proved justified. Philopoemen was fortunate that he already knew Flamininus' instructions,
for it made it possible for him to refuse, with the full backing of
Achaean law, any dangerous request which he might make for
a *syncletos*. No preparations were therefore made for calling a *syncletos* to meet him. The same tactics were to be used as had been
successful with Metellus: the full importance of this had been
emphasized by Pulcher's success before the *syncletos* at Cleitor.

Flamininus did not, in the event, visit Achaea. When he
arrived at Naupactus, he wrote to the Achaean *strategos* and
damiourgoi as expected, telling them to call a *syncletos* for him.
They replied with a request for details, citing, as to Metellus, an
Achaean law—in this case the law about the prior publication
of matters for discussion at the *syncletos*.[3] Flamininus, who may
have been in a hurry to reach Bithynia before the winter set in,
did not press his request, and Deinocrates' hopes were disappointed.[4] It is clear that Flamininus did not want to become

[1] Pol. xxiii. 5. On the chronology, see appendix 2 A (i), pp. 244–5.
[2] On the chronology, see appendix 2 A (i), pp. 241 ff.
[3] Pol. xxiii. 5. 17; Liv. xxxi. 25. 9; cf. Aymard, *Assemblées*, pp. 321–2; Larsen,
Rep. Gov., pp. 94–5.
[4] Pol. xxiii. 5. 14–18.

involved in a battle with the entrenched Achaeans over Messene, when he had no formal instructions from the Senate—and little personal inclination for lost causes—despite his friendship for Deinocrates. He had encouraged Deinocrates so far for the sake of *clientela*, without senatorial guidance. But he could not afford to indulge in positive trouble-making, which might bring the Achaeans to heel, but which might equally backfire and leave the Senate to rescue its endangered prestige at the risk of making the Achaeans even less clear about their true status. This was to be left to the Messenians themselves. But even then the Senate could not, in the nature of the relationship which it was fumblingly trying to establish, openly interfere: Flamininus' own hands were tied, the more so because the Senate's policy had in the first place been his own.

Shortly after this Messene rebelled from Achaea. Philippus, the Roman *legatus* to Macedonia and Achaea in this year, was present at the Achaean *syncletos* which discussed the question of war with Messene. He attempted to assert Roman patronage by trying to prevent the declaration of war, but the Achaeans considered action to be immediately necessary, and the Roman's advice— as that of Flamininus over Sparta in 192, given for personal political reasons—was ignored by the Achaeans.[1] The Achaeans' disregard of Philippus' intervention was the more serious as he had specific instructions from the Senate to investigate Achaea. It could not fail to precipitate a further deterioration in Achaean relations with Rome. By this declaration of war, Philopoemen had again shown that he was unwilling to allow the Achaeans to comply with the requirements of the *clientela* relationship. The Senate's frustration at the Achaeans' apparently wilful disregard for their obligations as Roman clients, in connection with matters in which it had only become interested through force of circumstances, showed itself at the annual reception of foreign ambassadors in Rome.

Philippus' official report of his mission was highly unfavourable to the Achaeans. He stated bluntly that they showed no intention of referring decisions on any matter to the Senate, had ideas

[1] Pol. xxiv. 9. 12 (this *syncletos* should be added to Larsen's list of assemblies in *Rep. Gov.*, appendix); cf. Castellani, *Contributi*, 100. Lehmann, *Glaubwürdigkeit*, pp. 184 ff., accepts Hoffmann's erroneous date of 183 for Philopoemen's death (cf. appendix 2 A (i)), and is accordingly unable to provide a satisfactory account of the events connected with the Messenian rebellion.

discordant with their status, and intended to resolve everything themselves. But if the Senate paid no attention to them for the time being and expressed its dissatisfaction moderately, Sparta would quickly sympathize with Messene. When this happened the Achaeans would be glad enough to appeal to Rome.[1] After some intermediate business, the Achaean ambassadors of the year were introduced. They naïvely asked for help against Messene; if no positive Roman help should be forthcoming, they asked that the Senate should at least stop the Italian help for Messene which Deinocrates had arranged the previous year. The reply which they received showed the Senate's justifiable frustration, for Philippus had tried to prevent the war's being declared at all, and to reach a negotiated settlement: even if Sparta or Corinth or Argos should secede from the League, the Achaeans should not wonder if the Senate thought it was of no relevance to itself.[2] This reply flung back in Philopoemen's face his own ambiguous position: on the one hand he refused to countenance unsolicited Roman intervention, which might affect the formulation of Achaean policies, and therefore compromise Achaean independence; on the other hand, Rome was an ally, and as such was open to be called upon to provide aid in an emergency. He could scarcely expect the Senate to accept the implications of this tactless sophistry, and it came to a confrontation over Messene. Philippus' intervention at the *syncletos* had been specifically aimed at preventing further trouble in the Peloponnese. He had no doubt had hopes that Messene could secure a negotiated settlement, in the way Sparta had done the previous year. This possibility had been rejected outright by the Achaeans, who, following the first precept of Philopoemen's policy, did not relish the idea of another imposed solution to one of their internal problems. But the necessity of invoking Philopoemen's second precept—the appeal for Roman help—came immediately. There is no sign of Achaean embarrassment at their application of double standards. But the Senate was naturally angry at this insult to its efforts at negotiation, which had simply resulted in an unnecessary complication of Peloponnesian politics.

Polybius adds that the Senate's reply was given full publicity, and was virtually an invitation to any state to secede from the League with Roman blessing.[3] But despite this anti-senatorial

---

[1] Pol. xxiii. 9. 8–10.   [2] Pol. xxiii. 9. 12–13.   [3] Pol. xxiii. 9. 14.

interpretation—no doubt coming from Lycortas—this was not altogether true. The Senate did not wholly yield to its frustration. The envoys who had received this reply were not allowed to leave Rome and were thus prevented from broadcasting the news of the Senate's attitude—although knowledge of it may have become current unofficially. They were kept in Rome until news of the course of the war should reach Rome. The Senate, despite its annoyance, could not take the risk of seeming, even ambiguously, to support the wrong side. When it was learnt that the result of the war was favourable to Achaea, the envoys were again summoned before the Senate. This time they were told that supplies would now be prevented from reaching Messene, as they had requested earlier. The time had passed when this could alter the course of the war. Polybius interprets this second reply more realistically than the earlier *senatus consultum*: 'This made it clear to everyone that, so far from shuffling off and neglecting less important items of foreign affairs, they were, on the contrary, displeased if everything was not referred to them, and done in accordance with their decision.'[1] It was this point which the Senate had been trying to make since 188, with progressively less success, until frustration had driven them to anger. But Polybius is not altogether accurate when he says that it was now clear to all: not until 179/8, when Callicrates became powerful, does there seem to be any greater desire among the Achaeans to accept the general obligation of their *clientela*. It was clearly an advantage to understand the Senate's wishes; but the Achaeans did not immediately show that they were prepared to comply with them.

In the same winter, 183/2, two Spartan embassies were at Rome. The first represented the 'old exiles', who had again been driven out of the city, probably as a result of the restoration of Chaeron's party. They, as much as Deinocrates, had hoped that Flamininus' presence at Naupactus in autumn 183 would retrieve their position; but they also had been disappointed when he refused to press the Achaeans.[2] In the first place their embassy had been headed by Arcesilaus and Agesipolis, who had been king of Sparta 'when a young man'—perhaps after the death of Cleomenes—but they had been captured by pirates *en route* and

---

[1] Pol. xxiii. 17. 3–4.
[2] Pol. xxiii. 5. 18; 9. 1; cf. appendix 9.

killed.[1] We do not know which section of the 'old exiles' they represented: their connection with the old royal houses suggests that they might have been attached to the group of Areus and Alcibiades. But since neither Areus and Alcibiades nor Lysis, who had led the other section of the 'old exiles' at Rome in winter 184/3, are again mentioned in the sources, it is impossible to decide firmly. If Arcesilaus and Agesipolis were attached to Areus' and Alcibiades' group, their embassy may suggest that Areus and Alcibiades had themselves been eliminated at the time of their re-exile. The remainder of the members of the embassy managed to escape the pirates, and continued their journey to Rome. The Senate's reply is unknown, but it cannot have been particularly favourable to requests for positive action. They had probably been exiled as a direct result of the implementation of the settlement—favouring Chaeron and Serippus—which had been agreed the previous year in the presence of the senatorial committee of ex-*legati*.[2] Fresh interference by the Senate clearly would involve the admission that the negotiated settlement was unsatisfactory: the exiles would, unflatteringly, no doubt say that it had broken down completely. In the circumstances of the Senate's newly strained relations with Achaea over Messene, it was important that Roman policy towards the Peloponnese should maintain at least the appearance of consistency.

The other embassy, from those who held the city—a coalition of Serippus and Chaeron which was hostile to the exiles—was headed by Serippus.[3] It is not altogether clear what Serippus hoped to gain from this journey to Rome, for Polybius does not make this explicit. But it seems likely that he had at least two purposes. On the one hand, in his capacity as representative of the Spartan government, he had to present his government's reasons for the new expulsion of the 'old exiles'. On the other hand he also represented his own section of the coalition government, whose chief policy was the maintenance of Sparta's union with Achaea. Since he differed from Chaeron on this it must have been necessary, in the new circumstances created by the expulsion of the 'old exiles', to reaffirm his own sectional commitment to preserving the union with Achaea. The Senate was committed

---

[1] Pol. xxiii. 6. 1–3.   [2] See appendix 9.
[3] Pol. xxiii. 9. 1; 11; cf. appendix 9.

to this as a result of its approving the agreement of the previous year. But nevertheless Chaeron had powerful friends at Rome as a result of his association with Nabis' party. Serippus, therefore, must have felt it necessary to gain a renewed senatorial commitment to support Sparta's union with Achaea. This he failed to do. Peloponnesian politics were every year becoming more confused and the events of this year were particularly irritating to the Senate, which refused to increase its commitment at Sparta: 'They had done all they could, and for the moment did not think the matter concerned them.'[1] But as with the Achaean ambassadors, they did not allow Serippus to leave Rome until the summer.[2] The Senate was non-committal, but it did not want official knowledge of its non-committal attitude to reach the Peloponnese until some clear line of development in events at Messene could be seen. It could then with some safety adopt a more positive attitude. When news of the Achaean success at Messene reached Rome, Serippus was allowed to leave. He reached the Peloponnese when it was already summer to find his position at Sparta seriously weakened by Chaeron's having declared Spartan secession from the League.[3]

After the winter, Achaea's war with Messene, the declaration of which Philippus had failed to prevent in the autumn, started again. By about the middle of April, the Achaean levy had been assembled to raid Messenia. Philopoemen, who should have been leading it as *strategos*, was at Argos suffering from a fever. Lycortas, who was hipparch, therefore assumed the command of the army until Philopoemen recovered. The war was urgent, since Deinocrates was supported by supplies from Italy, and it could not wait for the *strategos*. Achaean failure to attack at the first convenient moment would be interpreted in Messene as federal acquiescence in the secession, and accordingly as a success for Deinocrates. In the event, Lycortas' expedition achieved little: no battle was fought, no important position was taken, no concession was gained from the Messenians. It seems clear that it was merely the usual type of border-raiding expedition, which

[1] Pol. xxiii. 9. 11.
[2] Pol. xxiii. 9. 14. Although Serippus is not explicitly mentioned as having been detained at Rome, this must be inferred from the fact that his return was in the high summer, around the time of the final Achaean settlement at Messene (Pol. xxiii. 17. 5).
[3] See appendix 9, pp. 288 ff.

served only to announce that the federal government considered itself to be seriously at war.[1] Before Lycortas returned, however, news reached Argos that Deinocrates was attacking Corone.[2] It seems clear that this news had by-passed Lycortas. Philopoemen, who was by this time convalescent, was the only man who could take any action to retain Corone for Achaea. He therefore left Argos, and rode to Megalopolis in a day, a distance of some 50–60 miles, through the mountains—no small achievement for a 70-year-old convalescent, which duly became a feature of the Philopoemen legend when related by Polybius. There he collected some Thracians and Cretans and 60 young Achaean horsemen—probably those too young to serve in the mass levy which Lycortas led—and set out for Corone.[3]

The direct route from Megalopolis to Corone passes close to Messene, and before Philopoemen reached Corone he was ambushed at 'Evander's hill' by Deinocrates at the head of 500 Messenians. In the mêlée which followed, Philopoemen was captured when his horse stumbled and fell on top of him. Livy, reflecting Polybian panegyric, suggests that he could even now have escaped with the help of the Thracians and Cretans, had he not wanted to occupy the Messenians until the young Megalopolitans

[1] Paus. iv. 29. 11; viii. 51. 5. These are the only mentions of Lycortas' expedition, but may nevertheless be accurate, as the other sources are wholly concerned with Philopoemen at this point. Philopoemen's alleged death-cell inquiry about the safety of Lycortas (Liv. xxxix. 50. 7; Plut. *Phil.* 20. 2) supports Pausanias on this point.

[2] Liv. xxxix. 49. 1; Plut. *Phil.* 18. 3 gives the name of the threatened town, in the accusative case, as Κολωνίδα = Colonides. The two towns are in the same direction from Megalopolis and about 30 km. apart. In the absence of Polybius' own account we cannot recover the truth of this detail. Corone was more important and nearer Messene: it is therefore accepted here. Seeliger, *Messenien*, pp. 21–2, misreads Plutarch and invents an otherwise unknown settlement, Colonis, which he places in northern Messenia. He envisages Philopoemen's capture in northern Messenia, and argues that Philopoemen's attempt on Corone would not be frustrated in the north of Messenia. This is more faulty than a simple misreading of Plutarch, for no source says or implies that Philopoemen was captured near the threatened town: only that Deinocrates laid his ambush in the mountains near Messene. The direct route from Megalopolis to Corone (and Colonides) passes close by Messene. There were clearly numerous opportunities for ambush. Cf. Niese, *GGMS* iii. 52, n. 6.

[3] Plut. *Phil.* 18. 3–4; Liv. xxxix. 49. 2. Plutarch does not mention the Cretans and Thracians, but Livy's statement is conclusive for their having been in one of Polybius' accounts. The presence of this solid professional support made Philopoemen's undertaking less hazardous than Plutarch's account, centred on Philopoemen, suggests, for it mentions only the young Achaean cavalrymen.

made their escape.[1] In the event, he failed to take advantage of his opportunity, and fell into the hands of Deinocrates. His capture was an unexpected triumph for the Messenians, but in the moment of success they were not sure how to take full advantage of it. To one section, who, according to Polybius, had large popular support, it seemed that an invaluable bargaining counter had been given them; Deinocrates—who did not have the advantage of Polybius' sympathy—had not made up his mind as to the most beneficial use of Philopoemen's capture.[2] But all factions agreed that no risk of escape should be taken while policy was being formulated, and they locked Philopoemen up in a cave-like prison, where he was soon found dead. Polybius' story is that Deinocrates had had poison brought to him, and in this way indulged his personal hatred of Philopoemen and his desire to strike a heavy blow at Achaea.[3] But this must be considered uncertain. Polybius' account in some form is the basis of all of our accounts; and all information he was able to acquire must have been subject to interpretation by his personal emotional and political bias. In addition, the growth of the Philopoemen legend cast an aura of greatness over the Achaean hero's death. In the accounts we have, it survives in the alleged death-cell conversation with the slave who brought his poison, according to which he expressed his altruistic patriotic anxiety for Lycortas and his countrymen—which Livy carefully introduces with *ferunt*, although Plutarch gives a straight narrative.[4]

The problem of the account of Philopoemen's death is therefore essentially a source problem. The Achaean legend needed its hero, and embroidery was inevitable. The death-cell conversation is clearly part of this growth. But accurate information about the real intentions and disposition of the various Messenian groups *vis-à-vis* Philopoemen can only have come, in the first instance, from a Messenian source. It is clear from the picture which emerges of Deinocrates' part in the events that his account was

---

[1] Liv. xxxix. 49. 2.

[2] Liv. xxxix. 49. 7–12; Plut. *Phil.* 19. 1–2.

[3] Recorded in all sources: Pol. xxiii. 12. 3; Liv. xxxix. 50. 7–8; Plut. *Phil.* 20; Paus. viii. 51. 7. Uniformly accepted by all modern writers with no expression of uncertainty: Neumeyer, *Philopoemen*, p. 54; Seeliger, *Messenien*, p. 22; Niese, *GGMS* iii. 53–4; Niccolini, *La Conf. Ach.*, p. 160; De Sanctis, *Storia* iv. 1. 243; Benecke, *CAH* viii. 298; Hoffmann, *RE* xx. 1. 92–3, 'Philopoimen'; Castellani, *Contributi*, 102; Lehmann, *Glaubwürdigkeit*, p. 192.

[4] Liv. xxxix. 50. 7–8; Plut. *Phil.* 20. 2–3.

not the origin: it would scarcely be accepted by the Achaeans or appear in Polybius' version. But there is a sharp contrast made in the accounts of Livy and Plutarch between the masses, who were on the whole kindly disposed towards Philopoemen, and who at the most wanted to use him to protect themselves from Achaean hostility, and the leaders of the rebellion, who agreed on his death.[1] This distinction strongly suggests a major effort at political apologetics after Messene had capitulated. It was then clearly in the interest of every Messenian who had not been too closely associated with Deinocrates to lay the blame for the secession—and for the resulting major offence to the Achaeans of the death of Philopoemen—firmly on his shoulders. We know that there was indeed such a split between the leaders of the revolt and those of a more moderate party, who were finally responsible for capitulating to Lycortas and for handing over Deinocrates' party to the Achaean authorities.[2] It must, therefore, have been from this group that the account of the disposition of the Messenian parties at the time of Philopoemen's death, which we find in our Polybian sources, ultimately came.

The fact that this account was accepted by, and incorporated in, the Achaean tradition sheds no light on its inherent reliability, for the position of this group after the Messenian capitulation made it necessary for them to present a tale of unwilling complicity in the revolt. Any disreputable statements about Deinocrates would be immediately accepted by the Achaeans, perhaps even be believed by the masses. The Achaean *strategos* had died in captivity; the Achaeans could not be expected to accept that his death was natural. A scapegoat had to be found; and Deinocrates was the obvious choice, made even easier by his suicide before Messene capitulated.[3] It had to be said that Philopoemen was murdered: popular heroes do not otherwise die sudden deaths in enemy hands. The heroic tradition added the necessary drama —perhaps, in the first instance, Polybius himself in his *Life of Philopoemen*.[4] But in the circumstances a natural death would not be unexpected. Philopoemen was seventy years old; he had been ill before leaving Argos; he must have been exhausted as a result of his journeys and the fighting; he may well have suffered internal injuries as a result of his horse's falling on top of him. In

[1] Liv. xxxix. 50. 5–6; cf. Plut. *Phil.* 19. 2.   [2] Pol. xxiii. 16. 2 f.
[3] Plut. *Phil.* 21. 2; Paus. viii. 51. 8.   [4] Cf. appendix 1, pp. 232 ff.

addition, the place where the Messenians locked him up—the state treasury—was under ground, therefore airless and cold and perhaps damp. In the circumstances, death, as a cumulative result of these factors, would not be at all surprising. As we have seen, the poison story seems very like the traditional explanation of sudden death in enemy hands. There is, therefore, serious ground for doubting the genuineness of the sources' elaborate Polybian account of the circumstances in which it occurred.

The first steps in the creation of the Philopoemen legend were taken by the organizers of the funeral—Lycortas and his group. When Messene fell to Lycortas' subsequent campaign, Philopoemen's body was recovered and burnt.[1] As if to demonstrate that theatrical shows of emotion were not the sole preserve of Flamininus, the urn containing his ashes was dressed with funeral ribbons and wreaths, and carried to Megalopolis by Polybius, escorted by the whole Achaean army in full armour. The procession, says Plutarch, was a mixture of triumph and funeral, for the captives taken in the Messenian war were paraded in it. Public mourning extended beyond Megalopolis itself into the surrounding countryside, and the procession was joined by people from the villages and towns it passed as it travelled from Messene to Megalopolis.

As a climax to the pageantry, Philopoemen's urn was buried in his native city, and in a primitive ceremony of retribution, captive Messenians were stoned to death at his tomb. The expiation was complete: Messene paid for her destruction of a hero by having a legend created from her defeat. Posthumous honours for Philopoemen were naturally widespread in Achaea: for the most part, they took the form of expensive statues and paintings, which by 146 had acquired such decorative significance in the cities of the Peloponnese that they excited the greed of the Roman legionaries: Polybius felt it his duty to intervene on their behalf, and made his defence of Philopoemen which saved the honours. The statues were allowed to remain.[2] Outside Achaea also, Philopoemen was honoured: at Delphi an equestrian statue was erected by the Achaeans, which Plutarch saw there, and which Pomtow has tried to reconstruct.[3] But the most fulsome

---

[1] Plut. *Phil.* 21. 2–4.   [2] Plut. *Phil.* 21. 5–6; Pol. xxxix. 3. 3–11.
[3] Plut. *Phil.* 2; Ditt. *Syll.* 625; Pomtow, *Klio* ix. 160; cf. Daux, *BCH* 1966, 283–9. Cf. Bousquet, *BCH* 1964, 607 (Corinth).

honours were naturally granted by his native city. Diodorus' account is fully supported by a fragmentary inscription: 'In addition to the decrees in his honour voted by the Achaeans jointly, his native city set up an altar, instituted an annual sacrifice to him, and appointed hymns and praises of his exploits to be sung by the young men of the city.'[1] It would not be the fault of Lycortas and the Megalopolitans if the carefully sown legend failed to take root.

[1] Diod. xxix. 18 (Loeb); Ditt. *Syll.* 624; cf. Liv. xxxix. 50. 9.

XI

POLICIES AND POLITICIANS

I. CALLICRATES

DEINOCRATES, as fact and expediency suggested, was held responsible in Achaea for Philopoemen's death. Temporarily Achaea had no *strategos*; but in accordance with the law, Philopoemen's predecessor took over the administration until the next *synodos*, which was rapidly proclaimed to be held at Megalopolis—a convenient meeting-place for the immediate pursuit of the war. The army was also present, ready to march at once against Messene as soon as the *synodos* had decided who should be the next *strategos*. There could be little doubt about the result of the election in the prevailing highly emotional atmosphere, and Lycortas was quickly chosen.[1] The Messenians were soon defeated in the war, once a serious Achaean campaign was launched against them; and by July they had been reduced to asking for terms. Deinocrates had rapidly lost support when it became clear to the Messenians that Philopoemen's death had committed the Achaeans more than ever to complete success in the war. He therefore committed suicide before he could fall into Achaean hands.[2] The remainder of his party, whom the Achaeans made scapegoats for the death of Philopoemen, were also ordered to commit suicide when the settlement and the re-incorporation of Messene within the League were arranged at the second *synodos* of the year, which again met at Megalopolis, 'by the generosity of Lycortas and the Achaeans'. This Achaean 'generosity' was also responsible for the dependent Messenian towns of Abia, Thuria, and Pharae being separated from Messene and given independent membership of the League.[3] Lycortas

[1] Plut. *Phil.* 21. 1. This explanation follows Larsen, *Rep. Gov.*, p. 178. The law about the assumption of office by his predecessor when the *strategos* died in office is only known from 146 (Pol. xxxviii. 15. 1); but in the absence of contrary evidence it is reasonable to assume that it was operative in 182.

[2] Plut. *Phil.* 21. 2; Paus. viii. 51. 8.

[3] Pol. xxiii. 16–17. 2; cf. Niese, *GGMS* iii. 54–5.

was fortunate that it was his son who interpreted his generosity for the world, for his solution to the Messenian defection had two essential features in common with Philopoemen's violent Spartan settlement after Compasion. The anti-Achaean party, which had led the defection, was physically eliminated in order to prevent its becoming another threatening exile group; as a corollary the party which had negotiated the settlement was presumably confirmed in power. But as with Sparta after Compasion, it was a newly weakened Messene which was restored to the League: Lycortas clearly did not wholly trust his new 'pro-Achaean' supporters in Messene.

When Serippus finally returned to Sparta in summer 182 from his embassy to Rome, he found that Chaeron had taken advantage of his absence to declare Sparta independent of the League. Since the sources mention no Achaean military activity against Sparta this year, the conclusion must be that Philopoemen and Lycortas had been too fully occupied with the Messenian revolt to take any action against Sparta. But Serippus' delayed return restored the political balance at Sparta in Achaea's favour. With or without formal Achaean support, he soon managed to gain enough influence in Sparta to feel able to approach Lycortas with proposals for re-uniting the city with the League.[1]

The *syncletos* which met for this new discussion about Sparta was held at Sicyon after the Messenian settlement. Lycortas unashamedly appealed to Achaean self-interest. He urged that, since the Senate had declared itself to be uninterested in Spartan problems, Sparta should be taken back into the League, in order to preserve faith with those who had been faithful to Achaea (clearly Serippus' group), and, on the other hand, to keep out the 'old exiles'—whom the Achaeans had not been responsible for driving out—to pay them back for their ingratitude (Areus' and Alcibiades' group).[2]

Philopoemen's death had robbed his party of the personal prestige which he had used to promote his policy. Whereas there had previously been no serious doubts expressed that Spartan participation in the League was wholly desirable, at this *syncletos* Diophanes spoke in opposition to Lycortas' continuation of the same policy. He clearly thought that Philopoemen's death

---

[1] Pol. xxiii. 17. 5 ff.; cf. appendix 9, p. 288 ff.
[2] Pol. xxiii. 17. 7–11.

removed the Achaean commitment to unconditional Spartan participation in the League, and that there was now room for a final settlement which would remove the disastrous petty disputes from Achaean politics and restore some security and stability to the Peloponnese. He found some support when he opposed Lycortas' openly partisan arguments, and suggested that any settlement reached with Sparta should include a provision for restoring the exiles.[1] The unexpressed implication was that if this provision were not fulfilled, the Spartan application should be rejected. It seems clear that this opposition must represent a continuation of the factional struggle in Achaea between Diophanes and the Philopoemenists. But by 182 Diophanes clearly had greater hopes of success. Now that Philopoemen was dead, his policy might perhaps be overthrown, with favourable consequences for Diophanes. In the first place, many had suffered from the loss of life and destruction of property which Philopoemen's policy entailed. The continual political chaos might be ended by a less partisan interpretation of Achaean obligations towards Sparta, which might achieve at the same time a substantial benefit in internal stability and a less pretentious relationship with Rome. As far as Diophanes' own position was concerned, he would clearly benefit from both these results. He had formed a close relationship with Flamininus in 191, and Flamininus had again shown interest in Sparta as recently as 183. Diophanes clearly had well-founded hopes for Roman support for himself in Achaea. In addition, many Achaeans may have supported Philopoemen's policy only because of his personal reputation. When this ceased with his death to be a political reality, these men would appreciate the benefits conferred by the renewed peace and stability in the Peloponnese. For these reasons Diophanes was willing openly to support the cause of the Spartan exiles, who had been illegally and immorally expelled from their city.

This was the policy which, in a more logical and developed form, Callicrates explained to the Senate in 179/8. For the moment Philopoemen's ghost still walked in Achaea, and Diophanes gained only a partial success. But even this indicated the crumbling control of the Philopoemenist group. Diophanes had reminded the *syncletos* that the Spartan exiles would continue to

[1] Pol. xxiii. 17. 12.

be a major problem for Achaea if no action were taken. A compromise was accordingly arranged whereby Sparta re-entered the League, and those 'old exiles' who had not offended the League by their ingratitude were to be restored. The Achaeans then sent Bippus of Argos to the Senate to report on the events of the year. At Sparta the compromise by no means satisfied all groups; but the restoration of some of the exiles, and the continued hostility of Serippus and Chaeron to the remainder, seem to have made the two newly conscious of their common interests. Their coalition must have been patched up, for Chaeron was sent to Rome as representative of the Spartan government. Those exiles who were not intended to be restored by the Achaeans—probably the 'royalist' group originally led by Areus and Alcibiades—could now only hope for their restoration as a solution imposed on Achaea by the Senate. In order to lobby for this they sent Cletis and Diactorius to Rome.[1]

By the time these groups of Peloponnesian envoys came before the Senate, the Roman frustration of the previous year, caused by the apparently uncontrollable confusion of Peloponnesian affairs, had disappeared with the emergence of a comprehensible power structure in the Peloponnese. As soon as the Senate had heard the news of the Achaean success against Messene, it had immediately altered its first reply. Now its non-committal, cautious attempt at affecting the course of Achaea's independent policy was resumed. The Spartans were first to come before the Senate. The exiles obtained the promise of a letter to the Achaeans about their restoration, but nothing was said to condemn the Spartan government's action in expelling them. Such a statement could not have altered the present state of affairs. The previous policy of ineffectively condemning Achaean action at Compasion had been exploited by the various factional interests in the Peloponnese to the point of severe disaffection in the Achaean League and civil war in the constituent states, neither of which the Senate was able to control. The Senate, now tacitly admitting that it had burned its fingers, was willing to learn from its failure.[2]

When the Achaeans were given audience some days later, the

---

[1] Pol. xxiii. 18. 1–2 (decision of *syncletos*); 18. 3–5 (embassies to Rome). Cf. appendix 9, on Spartan parties.

[2] Pol. xxiv. 1. 1; 1. 4–5; Liv. xl. 20. 2.

Senate expressed no dissatisfaction at their settlement of the Messenian war, and received them in a friendly manner.[1] The contrast with the previous year could not have been greater. In addition to the new, more comprehensible conditions in the Peloponnese, which in themselves produced a more tolerant attitude on the part of the Senate, the Fathers must have realized that the ineffectiveness of Roman policy in the past year had been fully exploited by the Achaeans for their own advantage. There could be no objection to the Achaean success in itself; but the fact that it had been achieved as a direct result of the failure of the Senate's attempt at controlling events in the Peloponnese had shattered the value of this kind of petulant non-intervention, which had briefly given form to senatorial policy the previous year. The purpose of Roman policy was now the same as ever: the establishment of peaceful conditions through conducting diplomatic relations with the client state in accordance with a general acceptance of the mutual obligations of *clientela*. The simple proud assertion of patronage had failed because it had been deliberately misinterpreted, and had resulted in confusion. It was now necessary to be more careful: in order to preserve its prestige, the Senate must invariably support the successful factions.

From the Achaean point of view nothing had changed. The significance of the Senate's improved attitude escaped them, in the same way as the real significance of the Senate's earlier attitude had escaped them. Under the Philopoemenists, Achaea was no more ready to comply with apparent generosity than with open dominance, if the recommended action did not suit Achaean policies. The Spartan exiles were first to return to the Peloponnese, and they immediately presented their letter from the Senate to the Achaeans, who decided to wait for the return of their own envoy, Bippus, before taking any decision. At the same time the final settlement with Messene was agreed, whereby three years' exemption from federal taxes was granted to compensate for the serious long-term damage to the Messenian countryside caused by the war.[2] When Bippus finally returned from Rome he displayed the customary Philopoemenist *insouciance*

---

[1] Pol. xxiv. 1. 6–7; Liv. xl. 20. 2.
[2] Pol. xxiv. 2. 1–2 (return of Spartans); 2–3 (Messenian settlement); cf. xxiii. 15 (damage to Messene).

to the new aspect of Roman policy. He reported that the Senate's letter had been written 'not because of the Senate's enthusiasm, but because of the exiles' importunity'. As a result the Achaeans decided to take no action.[1] Bippus must have misinterpreted the Senate over this in the light of his own friendly reception. Polybius himself gives no hint of exile importunity in his brief but adequate account of the reception of the Spartans, and he had every interest in doing so had it been possible. In 188/7 he implies clearly enough that the Spartans acquired their letter from Lepidus by their importunity.[2] There is nothing of this in 181 until he records the return of Bippus. This can only imply deliberate Achaean misinterpretation of the Senate's attitude, conditioned by the Philopoemenists' attitude to the 'ungrateful' exiles. The eagerness with which they decided they could safely ignore the letter strongly suggests this. They were, in fact, acting in exactly the same way as they had acted under the influence of Philopoemen since 188, willing to yield only where circumstances were manipulated in such a way as to compel them by demands in terms of pure power-politics. The trouble and confusion over the exiles was again perpetuated by the Senate's failure to react positively to the Achaean interpretation of *clientela*, and accordingly to indicate its policy clearly in terms of unambiguous orders rather than simple advice, which its own interpretation of *clientela* required, but which merely created controversy. As long as this state of affairs continued, the Peloponnese would remain under the illusion of complete independence—a hang-over from Flamininus' propaganda of the war period—and therefore in confusion.

The exiles probably appealed to Rome again the following winter, for in summer 180 the *strategos* Hyperbatus presided over a *synodos* which again discussed the Spartan exiles. Before this, Chaeron had shown signs of autocratic behaviour at Sparta and had been suppressed by the *strategos*. It must have seemed to the exiles that another Spartan secession was at hand; and this threat, coupled with the intransigent attitude of the Achaeans to the Senate's letter of 181, would no doubt be sufficient to send a delegation of the exiles to Rome again.[3] Hyperbatus' election to the *strategia* marks a break in the succession of Philopoemenist

---

[1] Pol xxiv. 2. 4–5.   [2] Pol. xxii. 3. 2.
[3] Pol. xxiv. 7. On the chronology, see appendix 2 B, p. 263.

strategiai from autumn 181 and, following on the compromise which Diophanes had gained for the Spartan exiles in 182, must indicate that the policy represented by Lycortas had suffered a considerable loss of support since Philopoemen's death. Lycortas wanted to continue Philopoemen's exploitation of *clientela*; the newly dominant party was content to operate within it. At this *synodos* discussion of action on the new Roman letter about the Spartan exiles was the occasion for a confrontation of the two policies.

Lycortas' view was that on which Philopoemenist policy had always been based : the active assertion of Achaea's right to follow an independent policy, with appeal to the Achaean *foedus* with Rome as a last resort. He stated his conviction that the Senate would respect Achaean law if the necessity of this were expressed forcibly enough. If it were pointed out that fulfilment of the Senate's written request would involve the wholesale contravention of Achaean law, Lycortas argued that the Senate would be reasonable and would not insist. Hyperbatus and Callicrates vigorously denied the right of the client state to allow its laws to block Roman policy. They argued that the Achaeans should act in complete accordance with the Roman request, 'and should consider no law, engraved regulation, or anything else more compelling than this'.[1] At last a party in Achaea felt powerful enough openly to challenge the Philopoemenists, and to give formulation to the relationship which the Senate had been unsuccessfully trying to establish. Lycortas could not command the *auctoritas* which had been Philopoemen's alone. He had been elected into the vacant *strategia* in 182 on the wave of emotion aroused by Philopoemen's death. But his position had been gradually eroded since then : first by the partial success of Diophanes in 182 over the Spartan exiles; secondly by the election of Hyperbatus in autumn 181. In these circumstances Callicrates was able to develop Diophanes' policy, to formulate it in his own way, and to introduce it to the Achaeans with the full support of the *strategos* in 180. Philopoemen's death marked the fatal weakening of his party. But Callicrates' introduction of his new policy at the *synodos* was nevertheless only the first stage of its fulfilment, for the Philopoemenists were still strong enough to cause violent

---

[1] Pol. xxiv. 8. 1–7 : καὶ μήτε νόμον μήτε στήλην μήτ' ἄλλο μηθὲν τούτου νομίζειν ἀναγκαιότερον (6).

dissension. The only decision taken was to send ambassadors to Rome.

Polybius had no sympathy for Callicrates. He was the political opponent of Polybius himself, of his father Lycortas, and of the policy of Achaean independence formulated by Philopoemen. For Polybius, Callicrates was a traitor pursuing a policy of sycophantic compliance with senatorial wishes, while the independence party followed the noble ideal of the free alliance, in which co-operation could legitimately be refused. As we possess only Polybius' account of Callicrates' first major success before the Senate, it is necessary to attempt to penetrate his hostile web of bias and innuendo in order to make an unprejudiced examination of Callicrates' activities and successes.[1]

The *synodos* before which the hostile parties expressed their fundamental differences decided to send to Rome Callicrates, Lydiadas of Megalopolis, and Aratus of Sicyon, 'to explain Lycortas' opinion'.[2] There is no mention in these terms of reference of the major difference of opinion, although Polybius states explicitly that it was this which caused the embassy to be sent.[3] The very presence of Callicrates suggests either that the Achaeans foolishly hoped that he would represent the view of Lycortas—in which case, why had Lycortas himself not been sent? he held no official position—or that Polybius is guilty of *suggestio falsi* in his detail of the terms of reference of the envoys. Given Polybius' general attitude to Callicrates, the latter seems by far the more likely. The significance of the presence of Lydiadas and Aratus, both shown by their names to be members of the old Achaean aristocracy, cannot be certainly discovered. Aratus had been appointed along with Lycortas and Polybius to visit Egypt in 180, but that embassy had not travelled when news of Epiphanes' death arrived.[4] The party significance of Aratus' presence even then is not clear, for he was sent 'because of

---

[1] Polybius' opinion of Callicrates has usually been accepted at its face value as the basis of modern interpretations: cf. Niese, *GGMS* iii. 59; De Sanctis, *Storia* iv. 1. 247–8. Niccolini, *La Conf. Ach.*, p. 167, made a brief objection to this uncritical trend, but did not expose Polybius' bias at length. Cary, *Greek World*, p. 198, again is critical of the tradition, but Badian, *For. Cl.*, pp. 90–3, represents the first major attempt to come to terms with Polybius' assessment. Castellani, *Contributi*, 107, reverts to the traditional picture, which is also argued (unconvincingly) at length by Lehmann, *Glaubwürdigkeit*, pp. 284 ff.

[2] Pol. xxiv. 8. 7–8.   [3] Pol. xxiv. 8. 7.

[4] Pol. xxiv. 6. 3.

his family relationship with that kingdom'.[1] Lydiadas is not mentioned elsewhere.

If these two aristocratic nonentities were the delegates chosen to represent Lycortas' opinion, they were a bad choice, for they were totally outmanœuvred by Callicrates. The envoys' audience with the Senate provides Polybius with a further opportunity for indulging his disapproval of Callicrates. He says that Callicrates not only exceeded his instructions but even dared to lecture the Senate. If Polybius took Callicrates' positive approach amiss, the Senate did not share his disapproval. He advised the Senate openly to take sides in order to make absolutely clear to the Greeks what it wanted in Greece, and to ignore the inevitable unpopularity which would result, in the interests of putting an end to the general uncertainty which currently was making *clientela* unworkable. The point of his advice was soon illustrated by the presence of yet another Spartan envoy representing the exiles.[2] The Senate's favourable reaction to Callicrates' speech was to write at once an open letter to the Achaeans about the Spartan exiles. This was also circulated to the Aetolians, Epirots, Athenians, Boeotians, and Acarnanians—any or all of whom may have been sheltering some of the exiles. These external states were thus involved, by virtue of their common status as Roman clients, in the necessity for the Spartan exiles' restoration. In the Senate's official reply to the Achaeans, praise was lavishly bestowed on Callicrates.[3] His success in itself sufficiently explains Polybius' subsequent tirade against the man who was patriot enough to recognize that stability in the Peloponnese depended less on Achaea's establishing a relationship of freedom and independence of Rome and an inefficient and partisan internal party dominance, than on making the true Achaean position in relation to Rome clear both to the Achaeans and to the Senate. It is not necessary to follow Polybius when he shows his emotional partisan bias in describing Callicrates as 'the inaugurator of great miseries . . . for all the Greeks, but especially for the Achaeans'.[4] His implication is that before Callicrates everything in Achaea had been stable and smooth-running. Only a highly partisan interpreter could ignore the whole series of recent

---

[1] Pol. xxiv. 6. 6. On the part of Aratus and Lydiadas, see Niese, *GGMS* iii. 59; Castellani, *Contributi*, 106.

[2] Pol. xxiv. 8. 9–10. 2.   [3] Pol. xxiv. 10. 3–7.   [4] Pol. xxiv. 10. 8.

troubles within Achaea over Sparta and Messene, and the con-
spicuous failure of the Philopoemenist party, with its emphasis
on independence of Rome, to find any solution.

The reappearance of an active Roman policy Polybius blames
squarely on Callicrates, but he again ignores all the unsatisfactory
aspects of the earlier ambiguous relationship. No doubt it had
been possible prior to Callicrates to appear to be able 'to some
extent to deal with Rome on equal terms'.[1] But this was achieved
only by Achaean exploitation of *clientela* which obscured the real
relationship between the two states, and by Roman unwillingness
or inability to react unambiguously to it. In a world ruled by
power-politics, Callicrates' perceptiveness exposed as the ludi-
crous pretence it was the Philopoemenist claim to be following
a free and independent policy. The Senate was as much to blame
as the Achaean politicians for this pretence, through its failure
to break out clearly from the terms of its war-time propaganda.
It knew the relationship it required, but was ham-strung by the
emotional legacy of the war. No single opportunity appeared,
until Callicrates' visit to Rome, of making clear the formulation
of the essential post-war relationship. By his clarification of
Achaean *clientela*, Callicrates gained for the Achaeans an increased measure of security and prosperity—both essential
objectives for any patriotic statesman. Polybius' traditions and
emotionalism wholly failed to consider the most unsatisfactory
aspect of the 'free and independent' policy of Philopoemen,
whereby the safety and prosperity of the individual were sacrificed
to the national dignity of the state—which in turn suffered from
the partisan bickering of political vested interests. The circle was
complete. Callicrates certainly precipitated the crisis which broke
this vicious circle; but a crisis was bound to come, and it was
clearly less painful for the Achaeans if it originated on their side.
But Callicrates was nothing if not a realist, and he forecast his own
unpopularity in precipitating it. The ultimate origin of Polybius'
criticism of Callicrates is the traditional political commitment of
Lycortas' family. Even Polybius' assessment of the Roman
character, upon which he bases his own judgement of Callicrates'
action, reflects Lycortas' partisan argument at the *synodos* in 180.[2]
At the *synodos* it was intended as an argument to oppose those of

---

[1] Pol. xxiv. 10. 9: κατὰ ποσὸν ἰσολογίαν ἔχειν πρὸς Ῥωμαίους.
[2] Pol. xxiv. 10. 11–12 (Polybius); 8. 2–4 (Lycortas).

Hyperbatus and Callicrates; in his own version Polybius has added little of his own. It was clearly as much the domestic political victory of Callicrates as the diplomatic which affected Polybius' emotions and judgement, for this effectively rendered the policy to which he was committed by his father both unrealistic and unworkable.

Callicrates used his success at Rome and the Senate's commendation to support his candidature for the *strategia* of 179/8, which he secured with ease. In the course of this he restored the remaining Spartan exiles and those Messenians who had been rejected by the last Achaean settlement—the remains of Deinocrates' group who had refused Lycortas' invitation to commit suicide.[1] There is no means of checking Polybius' allegations of bribery and other corruption—coming from an opponent they must *a priori* be suspect—but whatever their worth, the fact remains that Callicrates' restoration of the exiles was the final stage in solving the Spartan and Messenian problems which had now dragged on for more than a decade, during which the Philopoemenists had brought them little nearer to a final solution. The political stability which this final settlement secured—no doubt, as a result of general recognition that Callicrates had the full support of the Roman Senate for his action—must have been of great advantage to individual and commercial, as well as more strictly political, interests in the Peloponnese. It seems probable that the majority of the apolitical mass of the people would be far better satisfied with Callicrates' stability through dependence than with the former insecurity of their sham independence.[2] Callicrates could deservedly take general thanks for this success in improving living conditions, which Philopoemen's party, by its excessive participation in local quarrels and its indulgence of political vested interests, had signally failed to achieve. Callicrates' acceptance of the benefits of the embryo *pax Romana* showed him to be more far-sighted than any of his traditionalist contemporaries. Polybius' partisan account must not be allowed to obscure this fact.

II. LYCORTAS

Despite Callicrates' overwhelming prestige when he took his place in Achaean politics after his return from Rome, Lycortas'

---

[1] Pol. xxiv. 10. 14–15; cf. Ditt. *Syll.* 634.   [2] Cf. Badian, *For. Cl.*, p. 91.

group maintained its policy of insisting on the legalistic interpretation of Achaean relations with Rome, which had been the keystone of Philopoemen's most recent policy. With this policy they opposed Callicrates, and succeeded in gaining some *strategiai*. Xenarchus, the brother of Archon of Aegira, was elected *strategos* for 175/4. A staunch Philopoemenist, he had been the Achaean ambassador to Rome in 184/3.[1] Yet despite its possession of the *strategia* Lycortas' party was unable to have its policy accepted at the *synodoi* which are recorded for Xenarchus' year. The immediate issue was Achaean relations with Macedon: on some previous occasion the Achaeans had passed a law which prevented Macedonians from setting foot in Achaea.[2] Some Achaean slaves had now escaped to Macedon, and because of the existence of this law could not be recovered. Callicrates was fully conscious of the current Roman interest in Macedon, and urged that the Achaeans should not allow the recovery of a few slaves to prejudice their future relations with Rome. On this very principle Callicrates had made his stand at Rome in 180/79: he had founded his position in Achaea on fear of Roman intervention and on the necessity of complying with the spirit and requirement of the Senate's wishes to the finest detail. Lycortas' group had already been compelled to yield in some aspects of Philopoemen's doctrinaire non-compliance with Roman requests. It had been forced to accept that the will of Rome was always the most important factor in a situation, and its arguments now took the form that vital Roman interests would not be damaged by its proposed action. This argument was the metamorphosed remnant of

---

[1] Liv. xli. 23. 4; 24. 1 (*strategia*); Pol. xxiii. 4. 11 (in Rome); Castellani, *Contributi*, 109, fails to see the significance of Xenarchus' connection with the Philopoemenists, and sees him simply as 'un esponente . . . di un risorto partito filomacedone'.

[2] Liv. xli. 23. 2; 6–7: xlii. 6. 2. There is no indication when the law had been promulgated. De Sanctis, *Storia* iv. 1. 106, n. 217, suggests that it dated from the time of Aratus' struggle against Macedon and was resuscitated in 198. Aymard, *Premiers Rapports*, p. 112, n. 4, prefers to place it in 198, and he is followed in this by Castellani, *Contributi*, 71. Against this are the Macedonian troops which participated in Flamininus' war against Nabis in 195 (Liv. xxxiv. 26. 10). Dubois's suggestion (*Ligues étolienne et achaïenne*, pp. 82–3) that in 174 it had been passed recently is attractive and is not wholly ruled out by the reference to it in 172 as *vetus decretum* (Liv. xlii. 6. 2). It could easily have been carried by Callicrates' group, whose rise to power in Achaea coincided with the deterioration in relations between Rome and Macedon. Both the fact that it only became an issue in 174 and Callicrates' eager defence of it (Liv. xli. 23. 5–18) suggest that its enforcement, at least, was only recent, and that Callicrates had been involved.

Lycortas' earlier appeal to the essential reasonableness of the
Romans—itself a refinement of Philopoemen's extravagant misinterpretation of Achaean freedom. The group still considered
itself the party of independence, although it now seems to have
accepted that only spheres in which Rome could have little interest were legitimate for the exercise of Achaean independence;
in addition, the existence of these spheres was now argued about,
whereas Philopoemen had simply assumed it. The party's stand
had changed from right to reasonableness.

In 175/4 Lycortas' spokesman was Xenarchus' brother,
Archon.[1] His position was weak, but he was supported by the
vested interests of the slave-owners. He argued that the political
consequences of resuming a normal diplomatic and social relationship with Macedon were by no means as desperate as Callicrates claimed, and that this essentially reasonable step would
bring the added advantage of regaining the escaped slaves. It
did not mean that Achaea's loyalty to Rome was being betrayed,
that in case of conflict between Rome and Perseus the Achaeans
would have any doubts about which side to support. An attempt
at gaining this present advantage could not harm Achaean relations with Rome. Archon's argument, an application of the
independence party's policy after Philopoemen's death, carried
some weight with the members of the *synodos*, many of whom
may have been interested parties in the recovery of the slaves.
Callicrates had to emphasize the undignified manner of Perseus'
approach—he had sent a letter rather than ambassadors—before
the *synodos* agreed to shelve the issue.[2] This was a narrow escape
for Callicrates and his conception of Achaean interests. In 174
annulment of Achaea's anti-Macedonian law might easily be
interpreted by the Senate as a fundamental change of heart.
Past experience had shown clearly enough that a point of view
which appeared reasonable in Achaea might have an entirely
different appearance in Rome. Callicrates recognized this. His
method of maintaining good Achaean relations with Rome was
simply to avoid any potential conflict. The policy might involve
prejudicing other Achaean interests, but its supreme achievement
and claim for acceptance was its secure maintenance of Achaea's
friendly relationship with Rome.

Perseus had nevertheless been encouraged by the reception of

[1] Liv. xli. 24. 1–18.   [2] Liv. xli. 24. 19.

his initial proposal, and he followed it by sending envoys to Achaea. A *synodos* was conveniently in session at Megalopolis when they arrived. They therefore asked permission to present their proposals. This time Callicrates had no difficulty in carrying his policy: so complete was his dominance that he persuaded the *synodos* even to refuse the envoys a hearing.[1] On this occasion Livy does not detail his arguments; but since he describes Callicrates' group as *qui offensionem apud Romanos timebant*, it seems likely that Polybius had a fuller account in which the 'unpatriotic' aspect of Callicrates' policy was emphasized. Callicrates' whole position depended on openly admitting fear of senatorial recriminations. He felt no shame in upholding his view of the interests of his country in this way, and he had probably made ample use of the interval between the two *synodoi* to re-emphasize his point of view.

The next year, 173, M. Claudius Marcellus visited Achaea, and at a *syncletos* expressed his pleasure at the Achaeans' maintenance of their law against the Macedonians.[2] Callicrates' persistence in the Roman cause was thus acknowledged and rewarded. At the same time, Marcellus was clearly attempting to arouse sufficient support for Callicrates in Achaea, which would remove Roman fears of Achaean disloyalty in the event of a conflict with Perseus. In spring 172 Eumenes also drew the attention of the Senate to the potential threat from Achaea.[3] Callicrates' success in preserving the anti-Macedonian law and Marcellus' praise of him had not prevented Lycortas' party from maintaining its challenge. Archon gained the *strategia* for 172/1,[4] in which he tried to confirm in practice the precepts of his speech of 174. When P. and Ser. Cornelius Lentulus travelled through the

---

[1] Liv. xli. 24. 20. Castellani, *Contributi*, 113, considers both meetings *syncletoi*. But cf. Larsen, *Rep. Gov.*, pp. 181–2 (apparently unknown to Castellani).

[2] Liv. xlii. 6. 1–2; cf. Castellani, *Contributi*, 113. Broughton, *MRR* i. 410, n. 3, accepts Weissenborn's opinion that this M. Claudius Marcellus was the consul of 183.

[3] Liv. xlii. 12. 6.

[4] Pol. xxvii. 2. 11. It is also suggested, from a speech of Xenon of Patrae in 167 recorded by Pausanias (vii. 10. 9: ἐστρατήγησα μὲν Ἀχαιῶν καὶ ἐγώ), that Xenon, another member of Lycortas' party, also held a *strategia* at about this time. Aymard, *REA* 1928, 61–2, and Niccolini, *La Conf. Ach.*, p. 311, offer either 174/3 or 173/2. De Sanctis, *Storia* iv. 1. 406, with reservations prefers 173/2. In fact, nothing can be built on this evidence: the conclusion can only be that Xenon was *strategos* before 167.

Peloponnese and indiscriminately urged the cities of the League
to support Rome, the Achaeans—no doubt in the person of
Archon—protested that they should not all be treated as potential enemies equally with the Eleans and the Messenians, who had
supported Antiochus.[1] Archon clearly felt that the tacit accusation was as dangerous as it was unjust, and he tried to prove his
point later in the year. When A. Atilius Serranus and Q. Marcius
Philippus were received at a *syncletos* at Argos and asked for
1,000 Achaean troops to garrison Chalcis against Perseus, Archon
had no hesitation in complying.[2] No Achaean of either party,
as the Roman war with Perseus drew closer, could afford any
Roman suspicion that his group showed any favour to anti-
Roman elements in Greece.[3] This was particularly important for
the independence party. But Archon's action was not sufficient to
remove his party's traditional image, fostered in the Roman mind
by Philopoemen and more recently by continued opposition to
Callicrates. Despite the help offered to Rome, increased in 171
to 1,500 infantry,[4] Achaean loyalty was not considered to be
proven, and in winter 170/69 Mancinus sent C. Popillius Laenas
and Cn. Octavius to Achaea, in a further attempt at confirming
support against Perseus. An advance 'leakage' of information
told the Achaeans that Popillius' first intention had been to call
a *syncletos* at which he would have accused Lycortas, Archon, and
Polybius of being time-servers and in essentials opposed to Rome.
He had no evidence—a fact which Polybius naturally emphasizes
—but the Senate's obvious fear of the activities of Lycortas' group
was sufficient to make Popillius' 'leakage' fully effective. When
he and Octavius actually arrived, they made no mention of a
syncletos. The *boule* met at Aegium and was addressed in friendly
terms—as the circumstances in the north demanded—before the
ambassadors departed for Aetolia. In this way the Romans had
succeeded in curbing any potential threat from Achaea without

[1] Liv. xlii. 37. 7–9. The text at 8 is corrupt. As printed by Weissenborn–Müller,
it makes the Achaeans claim that Elis and Messene had supported Philip. If the
restored text is correct, the accusation is wrong.

[2] Pol. xxvii. 2. 11–12; Liv. xlii. 44. 7–8.

[3] At some time a Spartan, Leonidas, who was in touch with Perseus, was condemned by the Achaeans for his activities. He later led a contingent of troops for
Perseus (Liv. xlii. 51. 8). Since the date is unknown, and since it is easily explicable
whichever party was responsible, it provides no information about Achaean parties.
Cf. Castellani, *Contributi*, 114.

[4] Liv. xlii. 55. 10.

bringing any specific accusations against the independence party.[1]

The presence of Popillius and Octavius in the Peloponnese had the effect they had intended, and caused some rethinking by Lycortas' party. Soon afterwards, the party tried to decide on its policy for Achaea to follow in the struggle between Perseus and Rome.[2] Lycortas' own position was the most extreme view expressed, and he merely advocated neutrality. His view still maintained a fragment of the group's original ideas: help to either side was disadvantageous when the victor would become all-powerful, yet they could not oppose Rome because of their established reputation for opposition. Lycortas must have known that conditions had changed, yet he unrealistically put forward his traditional view, that a measure of independent action, even if only neutrality, was still possible. He found no support in his party, for even Philopoemen had not hesitated to support Rome vigorously in a major conflict. Archon carried the meeting with him when he suggested that the party should adapt its policies to the changed circumstances, and give its political enemies no chance of gaining an advantage. He was formulating a principle which had been the basis of his action in his last *strategia*. Full compliance with Roman requests by the independence party might fail to rescue its reputation with a biased Senate, but any other course of action could only be disastrous. Archon's virtue was in recognizing this. The party could not obliterate all memory of its embarrassing past; but it must do as much as possible to adapt its outdated policy to the needs of the present. Archon was in effect suggesting that they should try to beat Callicrates at his own game. Lycortas' traditional position was untenable, and Polybius was wise enough to disagree with his father and to support Archon. Lycortas had apparently forgotten that Philopoemen had co-operated with Rome on the major issue of the war against Antiochus, and was advocating the application of Philopoemen's local Peloponnesian policy to the new major issue. His party would not follow him. This speech of Lycortas' is the last Achaean expression of belief in the

---

[1] Pol. xxviii. 3. 3–10; Liv. xliii. 17. 2–4; cf. Badian, *For. Cl.*, p. 96; Castellani, *Contributi*, 117–18. A decree of Argos in honour of Octavius has been found: Charneux, *BCH* 1957, 181 f.

[2] Pol. xxviii. 6; cf. Castellani, *Contributi*, 118–19; Briscoe, *JRS* 1964, 70.

possibility of an independent Achaean policy until the Achaean War. Lycortas' defeat by Archon marks the end of an era. The party continued to oppose Callicrates and to try to combine its opposition with obedience to Rome. But the show of independence was tempered by its essential unreality.

The party nevertheless retained sufficient support in Achaea to secure it the magistracies of 170/69: Archon was elected *strategos* and Polybius hipparch.[1] Towards Rome, Archon's policy was compliant, as he realized was necessary. He carried a vote in a *synodos* which offered the whole Achaean levy to Marcius Philippus in Thessaly. This unsolicited offer—stealing the thunder of Callicrates—was not accepted by the consul; but, Polybius adds, he was glad that it had been made. It meant that he could rest assured that there was no threat to the Roman cause from Achaea.[2] During the subsequent winter, however, when an embassy from Egypt asked Achaea for help against Antiochus IV Epiphanes, discussion was heated. Lycortas' party could see no vital Roman interests at stake, and wanted to send help. Callicrates knew that any military action in the eastern Mediterranean must arouse Roman interest, and therefore counselled caution. Further consideration was accordingly postponed to a *syncletos* at Sicyon. Again the discussion was heated and, according to Polybius, it showed extensive support for the Egyptian proposal. But before the *syncletos* had reached a final decision, Roman envoys arrived who urged the Achaeans to follow Roman policy and to help negotiate a settlement with Antiochus. At this show of Roman involvement Polybius, who had taken the lead in opposing Callicrates, withdrew his opposition, and ambassadors were appointed.[3]

This was the final defeat for Achaea's independence party. The present Roman intervention made it clear that any benefit which the party had achieved by adopting an ostentatiously pro-Roman policy had been undone by this further attempt at operating an independent policy. Callicrates knew that this was impossible.

[1] Pol. xxviii. 6. 9; 12–13; cf. Ditt. *Syll.*[2] 851; De Sanctis, *Storia* iv. 1. 406.

[2] Pol. xxviii. 12–13. The dispatch of the troops fits well enough with the declared policy of Archon for it to have been a serious offer: cf. Scullard, *Roman Politics*, p. 204; Briscoe, *JRS* 1964, 70. Against this view: De Sanctis, *Storia* iv. 1. 300; Meloni, *Perseo*, p. 313; Castellani, *Contributi*, 120–1.

[3] Pol. xxix. 23–5; cf. Niccolini, *La Conf. Ach.*, pp. 173–4; De Sanctis, *Storia* iv. 1. 347–8.

In the summer following these discussions in Achaea Aemilius Paullus defeated Perseus at Pydna. In the settlement which followed, some 1,000 Achaeans of Lycortas' party were removed to Rome, leaving Callicrates free operation in Achaea.[1] It was, no doubt, a violent solution which erred on the side of security; but the Senate was weary of having its policies deliberately misunderstood and exploited by a few influential Achaeans who possessed a large traditional support. Callicrates on the other hand was willing to adapt his policies to suit the Senate. Rome had supported him from the beginning for this reason, a fact which had forced the independence party to weaken its principles. But the existence of an opposition had remained possible until Pydna. During the Macedonian War it had been expedient for Rome to keep the Achaeans quiet: their troops were not required, but their peacefulness was. Yet possibilities of future conflict still existed. The Achaeans, if left to control their own foreign policies, could unwittingly affect issues in which Rome had an interest. This was clear from the support shown to Egypt in 169/8. The mass removal of this party, of which the Senate would never feel certain, was only the logical outcome of the Roman victory at Pydna and of the behaviour of the Achaeans over the past thirty years. Achaea was not the only Greek state to suffer mass deportations: the Senate took its victory to its logical extreme wherever it had met opposition. The relationship between Rome and the Greek states was at last openly based on power-politics.

In Achaea Callicrates remained supreme until his death in 149/8.[2] The strangest feature of the first phase of his predominance, between his *strategia* in 179/8 and Pydna, is that he exercised it without the sources mentioning another *strategia* for himself or for another member of his party. In this period only four *strategoi* are known, and all four were members of the independence party. Even if all the unknown *strategoi* were Callicrates' men, the surviving electoral strength of the Philopoemenists needs explaining. No *strategoi* at all are known between Pydna and 151/0, but the accident of the survival of information will account for this gap, in which Callicrates was supreme and in

---

[1] Paus. vii. 10. 7–10; cf. Liv. xlv. 31. 9–11; Pol. xxx. 13. 8–11. Cf. Niccolini, *La Conf. Ach.*, pp. 175–6; De Sanctis, *Storia* iv. 1. 348–9; Castellani, *Contributi*, 126–30.

[2] Paus. vii. 12. 8.

which his party must have held the *strategiai*. But in the early years the four known *strategoi* were all his opponents. Yet despite Callicrates' apparent failure to hold office, he had little difficulty in making his policy work, and this was the dominant feature of the period. It seems reasonably clear that in elections Callicrates could not rely on as much support as when a crisis of policy occurred, and that at the elections his opponents' traditional sources of power remained reasonably effective. But Callicrates' electoral failure cannot have been wholly accidental: he could have fought the elections by emphasizing the permanent crisis of the relationship between Rome and Achaea, and in this way have secured his party's election at the expense of the Philopoemenists. If the *synodos* was prepared to support his policy during the year, it would also have supported his party in the elections. It therefore seems that Callicrates may have been satisfied with simply controlling policy—which he certainly did— without caring excessively about holding office, and he may have been prepared to let the Philopoemenists have their fair share of *strategiai* in which they could demonstrate their internal differences over the attitude to be taken towards Rome. Their disagreements would eventually discredit them in Achaea: they were already discredited in Rome. Callicrates may have been happy to leave them in office, to share the responsibility for the policy which was his alone, and for which he alone would get credit from the Senate. In Achaea this method gave the Philopoemenists rope with which to hang themselves, while Callicrates avoided the double odium of both holding regular *strategiai* and following an 'unpatriotic' policy.

During the years after Pydna, the only activities of the remaining sympathizers with the independence party were concerned with the restoration of the deportees. Embassy after embassy travelled fruitlessly to Rome, until Polybius' influence with Scipio Aemilianus secured the release of the 300 survivors in 150.[1] The Senate considered that the hostages were now practically harmless. Yet the return of the hostages created a situation in which the Senate no longer held any important bargaining counter, and this may have contributed to the subsequent outbreak of the Achaean War. But for the most part it was a new

---

[1] Detail in Niccolini, *La Conf. Ach.*, pp. 179–82. On the date, see Astin, *Scipio Aemilianus*, p. 245, n. 6.

generation of independent Achaean politicians which was responsible for the final, inglorious phase of Achaean League history, although they may have found inspiration for their unrealistic attempt at a complete breakaway from Rome in the earlier policies of Philopoemen and his followers.[1]

Polybius was too realistic to have illusions about the potential success of the rebels, and roundly condemns the attitude shown by their desperate resistance to Rome. Neither he nor Stratius of Tritaea—both leading members of the old independence party, and both restored hostages—had any thoughts of supporting these latter-day patriots.[2] Whether or not others of the 300 restored hostages had learnt a similar lesson from their period in Rome is not clear. It may be more than coincidence that the events leading up to the final trouble began in 151/0, the year of the return of the hostages, but no connection between the rebels and any of the restored hostages can certainly be traced. No care was taken by the Senate to ensure the trouble-free reintegration of the hostages, and this may have caused dissatisfaction.[3] But the new generation of politicians seems to have been responsible. When Callicrates died in 149/8 while on an embassy to Rome, his restraining influence was removed from the control of Achaean policies. Callicrates had been so successful since Pydna that the peace which he assured had ceased to have an obvious purpose to a generation which could not remember the troubles during the period of Philopoemen's dominance. And it may be this attitude which led Polybius to moralize that 'man's natural love of novelty is sufficient cause for any change'.[4] This new generation, freed from restrictions on their actions by the restoration of the hostages and the death of Callicrates, defied Rome to fight. The war could have only one result.

The Achaeans had shown themselves finally incapable of undertaking their responsibilities and obligations as Roman clients: the difference in Rome's attitude after Pydna had been cushioned to a great extent by Callicrates' political adeptness in his long period of predominance. But in the long run it was not sufficient simply for the leading politicians to be willing to follow

[1] Pol. xxxvi. 13. 1.

[2] Pol. xxxviii. 10. 8–13 (Polybius); 17. 4 (Stratius).

[3] Pol. xxxv. 6. 3–4. Cf. Lehmann, *Glaubwürdigkeit*, pp. 322 ff.

[4] Pol. xxxvi. 13. 3: αὐτὸ τὸ φύσει φιλόκαινον τῶν ἀνθρώπων ἱκανόν ἐστι πρὸς πᾶσαν μεταβολήν.

a policy which suited the Senate, if their willingness was not wholly shared by the people they led. The popular support which the rebels attracted again demonstrates the unsatisfactory nature of Achaean *clientela*. In the settlement after the war, the Senate dissolved the League. The cities which had been most deeply involved in the fighting were united with the province of Macedonia; the remainder existed in various degrees of 'independence'. A measure of formal Roman supervision was at last reluctantly established; at last the Achaeans were forced to live within the relationship which the Senate had expected to come automatically into existence at the beginning.[1]

[1] Cf. Accame, *Dom. rom.*, pp. 124–62 (details of settlement); Larsen, 'Roman Greece', in Frank, *Economic Survey* iv. 301 ff.; Badian, *For. Cl.*, pp. 113–15.

XII

'THE LAST OF THE GREEKS'

PLUTARCH records the opinion of a certain unidentified Roman, that Philopoemen was 'the last of the Greeks', and he interprets this phrase as meaning, quite generally, that 'Greece produced no great man after him nor one worthy of her'.[1] The real point of the description Plutarch clearly found difficulty in understanding. Therefore he preferred to interpret it in the reflected light of his emotions about 'the glory that was Greece'. Modern writers have equally found difficulty in understanding the *mot*. Benecke,[2] for instance, sees it as a purely military description: '. . . with him ended the line of Hellenic generals who added a touch of genius to their virtuosity in the art of war.' De Sanctis denies him the right to the description at all, on grounds which are clearly influenced by modern ideals of national unification: Philopoemen had no sense of supreme 'national' Greek interests, but was tied too narrowly to his Achaean and Megalopolitan loyalties. He therefore failed to build a nation which could realistically resist Rome.[3]

Benecke's interpretation can be ruled out on grounds of inadequacy: no Roman would be likely to take notice of Philopoemen's military activities—the man who appeared to Flamininus as the 'Arcadian fellow, a general merely in unimportant border wars'.[4] De Sanctis's attitude is equally unrealistic, and takes no account of what 'Greece' could mean as a 'national' idea after 150 years of Macedonian domination. Isocrates' fourth-century panhellenism had found little encouragement in the minds of his contemporary free Greeks, but was adopted and forced upon the independent states by a Macedon whose imperialism found the panhellenic idea both convenient and congenial. More than a

---

[1] Plut. *Phil.* 1. 4; cf. *Aratus* 24. 2. Paus. viii. 52. 1 has a variant of the phrase which seems to be simply his own interpretation: Philopoemen was the last εὐεργέτης of Greece, as Miltiades was the first.

[2] *CAH* viii. 299.　　　　　　　　　[3] De Sanctis, *Storia* iv. 1. 243–4.

[4] Plut. *Flam.* 13. 2.

century later the key to the foreign policy of the individual Greek states lay in achieving sufficient local independence to be able to control local affairs without interference from the dominant power. One stage further than this—only rarely achieved—was to become sufficiently independent to be able to choose the protector. Because these two degrees of independence were briefly achieved by Aratus and Philopoemen for Achaea they were exceptionally honoured by their fellow-citizens; and because Philopoemen's achievement of local independence was the last such achievement by one of the states of Greece, he was called—on *one* occasion, according to Plutarch's *Philopoemen*: this was apparently not a general familiar term[1]—'the last of the Greeks'.

In this narrow political sense, the description is realistic; for despite De Sanctis's nationalistic longing for the creation of a Greek nation, this was a concept which had never played a major part in the politics of the 'free Greeks' of any period. Greek politics had always been local, had always aimed, in the first instance at the local independence of each city-state, in the second at the control of others. Nationalism in Greece had always meant local nationalism. This point must be made emphatically, for De Sanctis's interpretation of Philopoemen's career obscures the real issue. In fact, Philopoemen fits well into the ranks of conventional Greek politicians, the men who always put their view of the interests of their home area first, who claimed for it the right of forming its own independent policies. In Philopoemen's case, his original local loyalty to Megalopolis was confused—or broadened, depending on the point of view—by the incorporation of Megalopolis in the Achaean League in 235. But the federal movement was not a movement which developed any consciousness of a wider 'Greek' nationalism: it was simply the extension of the local political unit, which remained as conscious of its desire for local independence as any city-state. If allowance is made for the Hellenistic conditions in which Philopoemen was forced to operate, his local patriotism—in the sense of his willingness to seek personal advantage through the advancement of the general interests of his home area—was wholly Greek. And since

[1] Plut. *Phil.* 1. 4. In *Aratus* 24. 2, Plutarch does present the phrase as a common appellation in Rome. But since his primary interest in this passage is in Aratus, his item here about Philopoemen cannot be preferred to the more precise statement in his *Philopoemen*. But cf. Hoffmann, *RE* xx. 1.95, 'Philopoimen'; Stier, *Roms Aufstieg*, pp. 172 f.

Philopoemen was the last Greek politician with this kind of policy who achieved any kind of success, there is some justification for his appellation by a cynical Roman, 'the last of the Greeks'.

If it is misleading to judge a politician of Hellenistic Greece by the ideals of modern Europe, it is nevertheless historically informative. This is not perhaps so true of the 'psychological' interpretation conveniently formulated by Hoffmann: 'Seine Politik ist zu verstehen vom Soldatischen her . . .'[1] His soldierly disposition is used by Hoffmann as a key to explain Philopoemen's violent actions and his apparent lack of consideration of the effects of his actions, but it is uninformative as a historical explanation, for it does not explain the formation of his policies in their historical setting. The blame for this interpretation of Philopoemen's activities may be laid firmly at the door of the interpreters of the judgements of Polybius and Plutarch, both of whom assess Philopoemen by the comparative method. Plutarch's comparison of Philopoemen with Flamininus is concerned with only two aspects of their careers: their military life and the benefits which they conferred on the Greeks.[2] From Plutarch's point of view, these were easy issues on which to collect information and on which to write a discussion—he did not understand and was not interested in the political judgements which directed his protagonists' actions—and on which he could achieve a neatly balanced, if superficial, conclusion. He allows, rather surprisingly, to Philopoemen the crown of military experience and generalship, to Flamininus that of justice and honesty.[3] From Plutarch's point of view this was a satisfactory conclusion. He had pointed his moral and achieved a satisfying compositional balance. But from the point of view of the modern historian, the emphasis which he lays on the military aspect of Philopoemen's career may prove misleading.

In the case of Polybius' comparison of Philopoemen with Aristaenus,[4] misunderstanding and consequent misinterpretation are both more likely and more influential: more likely because the text requires close examination, more influential because Polybius' reputation can lead to uncritical acceptance of what he seems to say. A careful examination of the text shows that Polybius does

---

[1] Hoffmann, *RE* xx. 1. 94, 'Philopoimen'.
[2] Plut. *Comp. Phil. et Flam.*, *passim*.
[3] Plut. *Comp. Phil. et Flam.* 3. 3.
[4] Pol. xxiv. 11–13.

not attribute Philopoemen's policy to his militaristic attitude. The fragment which contains the comparison begins with a distinction between two aspects of the two men: '. . . it happened that they had neither the same natural disposition nor the same political principles.'[1] Their natural dispositions and political principles are clearly distinguished and are accordingly treated separately in the subsequent discussion. Polybius makes them two distinct and separate issues, and they should not be confused. Polybius first treats his subjects' natural dispositions: 'Philopoemen was by nature inclined towards the requirements of war, both physically and mentally, whereas Aristaenus' inclination was towards debate and diplomacy.'[2] So much for their natural dispositions. Polybius nowhere suggests that this difference was the reason for differences in their policies. He simply states facts: Philopoemen liked fighting and put his heart and soul into it; Aristaenus was more the stay-at-home politician, with neither the inclination nor the constitution for an active military life. These were the facts of their natures, and Polybius describes the point of contrast objectively, as Plutarch describes his points of contrast with Flamininus.

Polybius continues by discussing the political disagreements as another objective difference between the two men. It clearly interested him that there was more than one difference between them, but he does not link his contrasts causally. He therefore introduces his contrast of policies with a simple statement that their policies differed,[3] an introduction which he follows with a detailed description of his view of the salient points of their policies. In this part of his comparison, Polybius makes no mention of Philopoemen's military career. The conclusion to be drawn is clearly that he thought it simply irrelevant that the policies which each man followed were based on his own analysis of the situations with which he was faced, and that these analyses were expressed in political terms. Polybius does not say or imply that Philopoemen was more a soldier than a statesman: he says he was more a soldier than Aristaenus—clearly a completely different matter. We cannot therefore accept as either Polybian or meaningful the elegantly facile formulation by Benecke of the

---

[1] Pol. xxiv. 11. 1.   [2] Pol. xxiv. 11. 2.

[3] Pol. xxiv. 11. 3: τῇ δ' αἱρέσει κατὰ τὴν πολιτείαν τοῦτο διέφερον ἀλλήλων. A causal connection would require a much stronger conjunction than δέ.

'military hypothesis': 'He was more of a soldier than a statesman, at a time when Achaea needed a statesman rather than a soldier.'[1]

The only way in which Philopoemen's policies can be understood, and therefore become historically informative, is by examining their relationship to the problems they were intended to solve. It has already been shown that the phrase 'the last of the Greeks' should be understood as a reference to Philopoemen's political aim of Achaean local independence, an aim which gave him room for personal political advancement through local patriotism. It is this aspect of his policy which Plutarch describes when he says that Philopoemen made the Achaeans strong enough to be able to stop relying on foreign protectors.[2] But the issue could only be expressed in these simple terms before the alliance with Rome, and it will be convenient to distinguish three phases of Philopoemen's policy. The first is apparent between his two visits to Crete. In this period Plutarch's claim for Philopoemen is most easily seen to have some truth, for Achaean politics were not yet complicated by the problem of friendly relations with Rome. When Philopoemen returned from Crete in 211 and was at first supported by Philip's prestige in Achaean politics his position was very similar to that of Aratus after Doson's repossession of Corinth in 225/4. The Achaean army was too feeble to protect Achaea: there was no alternative to Macedonian domination. Only when Philip found Achaea's problems greater than he could conveniently cope with did he encourage Philopoemen to prepare Achaea to stand alone against Sparta. The Achaean achievement of the ideal of local independence was in this way facilitated by Macedonian co-operation.

Philopoemen's success against Machanidas in 207 may have been greater than Philip had anticipated, but it elicited little renewed interest in Achaea during the years between Macedon's wars with Rome. Philopoemen's army reforms had allowed Achaea to break free from Macedon, to reach the point of being able to choose her protector. Aratus had reached this point of achievement in 243 when his capture of Corinth expelled Macedonian interest from the Peloponnese, which Aratus replaced by nominal Ptolemaic hegemony. But since 225 Macedonian

---

[1] *CAH* viii. 299; cf. Stier, *Roms Aufstieg*, p. 172; Gelzer, *Kleine Schriften* iii. 149.
[2] Plut. *Phil.* 8. 3.

domination had been complete. The choice facing Philopoemen in 200, when the Roman mission first tried to wean Achaea from her traditional relationship with Macedon, was an innovation. Yet a choice was necessary. Achaea was again sufficiently independent to be able to choose between the protagonists, but was not strong enough to be able to remain neutral. Philopoemen chose Rome, and was initially defeated by Cycliadas' traditionalists. It seemed to him that he had little alternative to serving Achaean interests in Crete, in the parallel war against Sparta's Cretan possessions.[1]

The second phase of Philopoemen's policy is that of the time of the wars with Philip and Antiochus, the period between his return from Crete in 194 and the expulsion of Antiochus from Greece in 191.[2] Philopoemen's crucial problem in this period, given that the chief aim of his policy was to assert local independence as a free ally of Rome, was to achieve a satisfactory compromise, as a result of which the policy of co-operation with Rome on the major issue—currently the war with Antiochus—which had been followed by Aristaenus since 198, could be made consistent with his policy of local independence. As far as Philopoemen was concerned, his refusal to accept Roman interference in the Peloponnese did not alter his general willingness to co-operate in the major war. But the issue became confused as a result of the clash of personalities between Philopoemen and Flamininus in 192. The first sign that Flamininus wished to interfere in the Peloponnese against Philopoemen's view of Achaean interest came in the spring of 192, when he recommended the Achaeans to delay action against Sparta. Philopoemen's action was immediate, and aimed at denying all Roman right of interference in the Peloponnese. The clash of personalities and policies resulted in the political battle over Sparta, in which Philopoemen was initially successful. The city joined Achaea; Philopoemen gained the glory. But Flamininus could soothe his wounds by destroying Philopoemen's settlement at Sparta and his reputation at Rome. The chief result of Philopoemen's local policy in this phase of his career was to build, in his hostility to Flamininus, his reputation of being hostile to Rome.

Yet Philopoemen's reputation, on his own interpretation, was

---

[1] On this in detail, cf. chapters IV and V, *passim*.
[2] On this in detail, cf. chapters VI and VII, *passim*.

not solidly based. Denial of Rome's right of intervention in the Peloponnese was one thing, denial of Achaean co-operation in the war against Antiochus was another and a wholly different thing. By the end of the Achaean War in 146 Philopoemen's reputation at Rome for being anti-Roman had crystallized and threatened the safety of his statues and honours. Polybius felt compelled to protest. His defence consisted of a demonstration that Philopoemen's true attitude to Rome was to be found in his activities 'at the time of the wars with Philip and Antiochus'. For then he had played a major part in securing the Achaean declaration of war against Antiochus and the Aetolians four months before the Romans crossed to Greece.[1] This argument apparently convinced the Roman commissioners—although Polybius' personal presentation of his arguments was no doubt the compelling factor. But as far as Philopoemen's policy is concerned, the issue is clear: support of Rome on major issues was in the interests of Achaea; denial of Roman right of intervention in Achaea—which meant, in effect, the whole of the Peloponnese —was equally in the Achaean interest. And after the *foedus* was granted in winter 192/1, there appeared to be legal justification for this attitude. Polybius' defence was the truth, but it was only part of the truth. The real justification for the continuance of Philopoemen's reputation as anti-Roman comes in the third and final phase of his career, between the final defeat of Antiochus and Philopoemen's death—a period which Polybius' defence did not mention.

This third phase is crucial. For the first time since Rome became a major consideration for Achaea Philopoemen's policy of local independence was virtually the sole major issue in Achaean politics. The broader issues on which he admitted the legitimacy of Roman interest had temporarily passed away. The opportunity for Achaea to achieve total independence of action seemed to be present, offered by the Roman wartime propaganda of liberation, the permanence of which seemed guaranteed by the *foedus*. The policy was begun by genuinely misunderstanding *clientela* as expressed by Roman propaganda and by the *foedus*, and was continued by exploiting its ambiguity. The Senate simply required peaceful *clientela*. It had no general desire to interfere in Achaean internal affairs until interference was made necessary

[1] Pol. xxxix. 3. 3 = Plut. *Phil.* 21. 5–6; Pol. xxxix. 3. 4–8.

by the appeals of the Spartan exiles. Philopoemen seized the opportunity offered by the Senate's protestations of lack of interest: the massacre at Compasion led to his party's becoming politically entrenched behind the lines of the settlement which followed it. Deliberate refusal to accept that the Senate's messages meant more than their face-value indicated involved a complete exploitation of *clientela*, and was firmly based on doctrinaire claims of local independence.

This deliberate misinterpretation of *clientela*, which had developed from an original genuine misunderstanding at the time when Philopoemen was willing to co-operate with Rome against the Kings, destroyed Philopoemen's reputation at Rome. Polybius seems to have realized this, for his defence of Philopoemen in 146 dealt only with the time of the wars. He admits the source of the rumour which he was trying to scotch only in the most general terms, and then he adds extenuating circumstances: 'He often disagreed with the Romans over their instructions, but disagreed only so far as to advise and persuade them on the disputed matters; and even this he did not do lightly.'[1] Similarly in his comparison with Aristaenus Polybius makes no mention of specific issues on which Philopoemen yielded under protest, although he states that, as a matter of principle, Philopoemen objected to Roman requests which were not in accordance with Achaean laws or the terms of the alliance, but would give way under protest when argument failed. Aristaenus, on the other hand, was at times even prepared to anticipate Roman orders.[2] Again the time chosen for the contrast is 'the time of the wars with Philip and Antiochus'.[3] For only at this time of crisis was it true that Aristaenus was prepared to yield to, and even anticipate, the Roman orders; to appear to keep the Achaean laws while complying with Roman orders, but willing to break the laws if necessary.[4] Polybius makes this a point of contrast with Philopoemen. But conditions were different for Philopoemen: the only occasion on which he himself was faced with a major decision, such as faced Aristaenus in the years after 198, was in 192 when he encouraged the Achaean declaration of war on Antiochus and the Aetolians before Roman forces had even

---

[1] Pol. xxxix. 3. 5.   [2] Pol. xxiv. 11. 4–8.
[3] Pol. xxiv. 11. 3: κατά τε τοὺς Φιλιππικοὺς καὶ τοὺς Ἀντιοχικοὺς καιρούς. Cf. 13. 9.   [4] Pol. xxiv. 11. 5.

arrived in Greece: in short, he acted in exactly the same way as Aristaenus had earlier in similar circumstances. As far as actually breaking Achaean laws is concerned, Aristaenus can only be accused of this at the Sicyon *syncletos* in 198, when he failed to have the law maintaining the alliance with Philip annulled before he proposed the alliance with Rome.[1] This single instance cannot legitimately be developed into a general principle. It seems clear that in this respect Polybius was stretching the facts in order to make a contrast which did not, in reality, exist.

The aspect of Philopoemen's policy in which he was prepared to oppose the Romans as far as possible was the issue of Achaea's local independence and Roman interference with it. Throughout his later years Philopoemen insisted on this, and the citation of Achaean laws in order to prevent Roman interference was a regular method. There is only one example of his party's actually giving way under protest: in 184 at the *syncletos* at Cleitor Lycortas' appeal to the legality of Achaean action ended with the capitulation of the *syncletos* to Pulcher. But in the same way as Philopoemen did not differ from Aristaenus on the major war issues, so Aristaenus seems not to have differed essentially from Philopoemen on the issue of local independence after the wars. The only instance of Aristaenus' activity in this field is his treatment of Metellus at Argos in 185: there he insisted, as much as the other magistrates, on the sanctity of Achaean law and the undesirability of illegitimate Roman interference in internal Achaean affairs. The contrast which Polybius makes between the essential policies of the two men is therefore largely illusory, for it takes no account of changes in the direction of their policies or of the differing circumstances in which they were operative.

If there is a real contrast to be made, it should not be so much between the actual working of the policies as in the philosophies which directed them. This appears clearly from a discussion between Philopoemen and Aristaenus which Polybius records in some detail. From references in Plutarch and Pausanias it seems clear that it took place at the autumn *synodos* of 191, the *synodos* at which Philopoemen refused to allow Flamininus and Glabrio to interfere on behalf of the Spartan exiles.[2] This context gives

---

[1] Liv. xxxii. 22. 3 f.

[2] Plut. *Phil.* 17. 3; Paus. viii. 51. 4. But cf. Aymard, *Premiers Rapports*, p. 362, n. 23. Discussion also in Lehmann, *Glaubwürdigkeit*, pp. 242 ff.

a precise point to the arguments of Aristaenus: 'He said it was impossible to maintain friendship with Rome while extending at the same time both the spear and the herald's staff.'[1] This first formulation of the difference between Aristaenus and Philopoemen clearly has a precise reference to the events of the two previous years: Philopoemen had opposed Flamininus over the Spartan war (the spear), on the other hand he had also supported the Achaean declaration of war on Antiochus and the Aetolians in the Roman interest (the herald's staff). Now again, at this *synodos*, he was opposing Flamininus over the Spartan exiles, as he had opposed him at Sparta earlier in the year. The point of Aristaenus' complaint is that Philopoemen was not consistent. Aristaenus seems to admit—although the text is corrupt—that Achaea should stand up for her rights if this was possible; if not (and Philopoemen would agree that in the last resort resistance was impossible),[2] 'why, reaching for the impossible, should we neglect the possible?' He expands this by explaining that he sees two goals for a state's policy, the good and the expedient:[3] when the good (independence on Philopoemen's principles) cannot be achieved, it is foolish to neglect the expedient (friendly relations with Rome, which Philopoemen's ambiguous policy was prejudicing). Therefore, unless resistance was proved to be practicable, all orders should be obeyed.[4] Some Thucydidean influence is clearly traceable in this speech, but it may not be correct to attribute it to Polybius himself: the stock political cliché of the good and the expedient was not out of place in this kind of debate at an Achaean *synodos*, and Aristaenus would certainly have been familiar with it.

Philopoemen's reply was expressed in emotional terms. He recognized the difference in power between Rome and Achaea, but based his policy on appeals to equity and justice: by pointing out any illegalities in Roman conduct, he would make the burden of Roman domination lighter. So far the Romans had shown due regard for legality; the Achaeans should make use of this. It is understandable that in making this kind of reply he should misrepresent Aristaenus' policy: 'Aristaenus was eager to see the inevitable come as soon as possible, and was working forcefully

---

[1] Pol. xxiv. 12. 1.   [2] Pol. xxiv. 11. 8.
[3] Pol. xxiv. 12. 2: τό τε καλὸν καὶ τὸ συμφέρον.
[4] Pol. xxiv. 12. 2–4.

towards that end; but Philopoemen himself was struggling and thrusting against it as hard as he could.'[1] From Philopoemen's point of view, in 191 Aristaenus may have seemed to be resisting Rome too little. In fact, Aristaenus had simply taken a more serious view of Rome's commitment against Antiochus, a view in which Peloponnesian affairs were seen as part of the main war— and a view which was shared by Flamininus. Philopoemen's refusal to allow this had led to his clashes with Flamininus and Aristaenus. But in these circumstances it could not equitably be maintained that Aristaenus was *eager* to see complete Roman domination of Achaea: this was simply Philopoemen's own highly partisan and controversial viewpoint.

Aristaenus' misfortune was that Philopoemen's party was successful in gaining *strategiai* until 189/8, in which time they were able to establish their policy. By 186/5, the year of the meeting of the Achaean magistrates at Argos, Aristaenus' reputation which he had gained at the time of the wars—when Philopoemen too would have found it necessary to co-operate with Flamininus— was maintained and developed by his opponents, despite the fact that Aristaenus was as 'patriotic' on that occasion as any contemporary politician. For this reason he disappears from Achaean politics after 185, leaving the Philopoemenists in control.[2] Polybius nowhere assesses Philopoemen's and Aristaenus' policies during the post-war period. The wartime was noteworthy for two reasons: it was a critical time for Achaea on any judgement, and Philopoemen's policy at that time was defensible to the Romans. Therefore he can conclude his comparison with this judgement, to which he adds the partisan rumour that Aristaenus was more favourable to Rome than Philopoemen: 'It must be clear from these speeches that Philopoemen's policy was honourable, Aristaenus' respectable, and both safe. Therefore when the greatest crises faced the Romans and the Greeks at the time of the wars with Philip and with Antiochus, both men still maintained the rights of Achaea in her relationship with Rome undiminished.'[3] The point which Polybius' silence admits must be made: Philopoemen's activities in the post-war period were justly responsible for his anti-Roman reputation.

[1] Pol. xxiv. 13. 1–7 (7 cited).
[2] Cf. chapter IX, pp. 169 ff.
[3] Pol. xxiv. 13. 8–10.

Polybius regarded Philopoemen's aim as a noble ideal, Philopoemen as a patriot. His view was shared widely by those who supported Philopoemen, who honoured him, and who continued to support Lycortas after his death. But the essential inadequacy of his policy was sufficiently demonstrated when it was first seriously and successfully challenged after his death by Diophanes and Callicrates. It had been maintained by the personal prestige of Philopoemen, gained through years of successful military action and image-building, and could not stand without him. Achaean independence was temporarily feasible under Philip; but as soon as Rome seriously intervened in Greece, it was a mistake to insist on it so staunchly. Philopoemen's initial misunderstanding of *clientela* developed, when he recognized the Senate's inability to act because of its code of conduct, into wholesale exploitation. This drove him further than necessary in his treatment of Sparta. In 192 he had committed himself to keeping Sparta in the League. The resultant decade of political chaos and of destruction of lives and property was the responsibility of Philopoemen and his noble ideal. His commitment to Spartan participation in the League was immovable: it was achieved despite Flamininus' opposition and became the key issue in the Achaean relationship with Rome. Capitulation to Sparta meant loss of face before the Senate, Flamininus, and the Achaeans. Philopoemen failed to find an acceptable solution, and the instability and suffering of Sparta and Messene were the price of his stubbornness in the cause of a doctrinaire patriotism.

APPENDIX 1

SOURCES

THE ultimate source of almost all our information about Philopoemen and Achaean political activity during his lifetime is Polybius. Polybius was born at an uncertain date towards the end of the third century.[1] He was a Megalopolitan and, in addition to being a fellow citizen of Philopoemen, was the son of his closest friend and supporter, Lycortas.[2] The main part of Polybius' extant work, his *Histories*, covers the period from 220 to 146 B.C., and has as its theme the demonstration of 'how the Romans conquered the world in less than fifty-three years'.[3] His original intention was to end in 167, and he only later decided to continue to 146. The work, in its original form, included a detailed account of Roman relations with Greece; but as the books dealing with this survive only as fragments, we do not possess his full account of the policies and activities of Philopoemen during his period of political maturity.[4]

Polybius himself is eager that his readers should know his historical methods, and he describes them in some detail. The historian must first of all have had active political experience, without which he cannot expect to understand political history; similarly military experience is necessary if he is to write with understanding about military history. With this necessary preparation he can proceed to 'the study and collation of written sources, and acquaintance with relevant sites'. But in Polybius' opinion the most important source of information to the writer of contemporary history is the result of questioning as many

---

[1] For discussion of date, cf. Walbank, *Comm.* i. 1, n. 1; cf. also Pédech, *LEC* 1961 (supporting 208).

[2] Hiller von Gaertringen (*ad* Ditt. *Syll.* 626) suggested that Polybius was related to Philopoemen. Walbank, *Comm.* i. 228, objects that Polybius would have been sure to mention it. Cf. Ziegler, *RE* xxi. 2. 1445, 'Polybios' (i).

[3] Pol. i. 1. 5; 3. 1. Since the Achaean sections of the *Histories* appear to be outside this declared purpose, Gelzer has developed the view that these were either written separately and included when the main work was begun ('Die hellenische Προκατασκευή im zweiten Buche des Polybios' = *Kl. Schr.* iii. 111 ff.), or included separately from the main purpose as an attempt to open the eyes of the Achaeans to the fact that the glorious development of the League had been betrayed by Callicrates ('Die Achaica im Geschichtswerk des Polybios' = *Kl. Schr.* iii. 123 ff.). Cf. also 'Über die Arbeitsweise des Polybios' = *Kl. Schr.* iii. 161 ff.

[4] Philopoemen first appears (in the main part of the *Histories*) in x. 21; his death is recorded in xxiii. 12, and his policies and achievements are summarized in xxiv. 11–13.

as possible of those who participated in the actual events. It was partly for this reason that Polybius did not start the main part of his *Histories* until 220, for there were few survivors whom he could consult about earlier events. In addition to these materials, official archives were available for consultation, and also inscriptions.[1]

How do these methods affect the way in which Polybius wrote about Greek affairs during the period of Philopoemen's lifetime? Earlier written historical sources were strictly limited. For the earlier history of Greece which he wrote as part of the introduction to his main *Histories*—books i and ii—he used the *Memoirs* of Aratus and the *Histories* of Phylarchus.[2] But these could not be used for the later period, which involved Philopoemen more deeply, as they had both already ended. There may have been some contemporary local histories, on specific local topics, though if so they have vanished without trace. For the most part Polybius must have constructed the parts of his *Histories* which dealt with these years as a result of information gained from questioning contemporaries and by personal experience. As an Achaean statesman he would have ready access to federal records and archives; similarly as a Megalopolitan and a member of the family of a close associate of Philopoemen he would either know well or be able to discover easily the more personal and local aspects of Philopoemen's activities. This personal information was probably used in the first place for the composition of his *Life of Philopoemen*, and quarried from there when he came to need it for his *Histories*.[3] But it also required a broader interpretation in the *Histories* if it was to appear relevant to its context. The *Histories* were to 'distribute praise and blame impartially', an undertaking which implied the inclusion in detail of unpleasant but relevant facts which might have been glossed over or simply omitted in the *Life*.[4]

His wider conception of the *Histories* did not mean that Polybius was able to break clear completely from his own personal and political standpoint. Despite the fact that Philopoemen had been dead for some thirty years when Polybius was writing his *Histories*, he seems to have

[1] Pol. xii. 25e; iv. 2. 2–3. From xvi. 15. 8 it is clear that he made use of Rhodian documentary sources, but whether directly or through Zeno is not clear; from iii. 26. 1 it is clear that he used Roman. Cf. Walbank, *Comm.* i. 337. There is no explicit mention of his use of Achaean records, but it is unreasonable to assume that they were not consulted. For his use of epigraphic material, cf. iii. 33. 17–18; 56. 4 (the Lacinian bronze). For full discussion of Polybius' sources, cf. Walbank, *Comm.* i. 26 ff. On Polybius' 'pragmatic' history, cf. Gelzer, 'Die pragmatische Geschichtsschreibung des Polybios' = *Kl. Schr.* iii. 155 ff.

[2] Pol. ii. 56. 2; cf. Walbank, *Comm.* i, ad loc. and p. 27. On Phylarchus, cf. Africa, *Phylarchus, passim*.

[3] Cf. Treu, *Historia* 1954/5, 222.

[4] Pol. x. 21. 8: κοινὸς . . . ἐπαίνου καὶ ψόγου.

reacted to the original situations in retrospect in much the same way as he had at the time when they were wholly fresh. For instance, Polybius' treatment of Aristaenus is wholly responsible for his being accused of having been a traitor to his country: Polybius does not actually say as much, but it is at times all too clearly implied. The same type of bias is much more obvious later in his treatment of Callicrates. Here Polybius appears even less the impartial and dispassionate purveyor of facts: impartiality could apparently be broadly interpreted. A more general, but perhaps equally effective, bias is traceable in the whole of Polybius' treatment of the Aetolian League. This was patriotism and personal loyalty in action. His bias did not seriously affect the treatment of his general theme of the expansion of Rome. But since the present study is concerned with the same local issues with which Polybius explicitly admitted that it was legitimate to take liberties in interpretation, we must bear in mind that his bias can lead to distortion in interpretation—although probably not in matters of fact. There is no reason to dispute Polybius' claim to relate the facts accurately.[1]

The reason for this bias in favour of Philopoemen and his policies is clear enough. Polybius' father Lycortas was Philopoemen's successor as party leader; and Polybius—though not above disagreement with Lycortas in practice[2]—could not be expected to write otherwise than favourably of the policy which they both represented. He was personally too deeply concerned with Philopoemen, myth and man, to fail to support him with his writing. And this personal concern did not stop at simply writing about him favourably. After the Achaean War Polybius prevented the destruction by the Romans of Philopoemen's statues in the Peloponnese, and he had a personal interest in doing so. He could not accept the presentation of his father's friend Philopoemen as the enemy of Rome—though he could not deny that there was some basis for the tradition—and he set out to correct this. His defence was tendentious and ignored the part of Philopoemen's career which had caused his anti-Roman reputation. This tendentiousness also had the side-effect of misinterpreting the policy of Philopoemen's and his own opponents.[3]

---

[1] Pol. xvi. 14. 6 (patriotic bias); ii. 46. 3; iv. 3. 1; ix. 38. 6 (Aetolia). On Aristaenus and Callicrates, cf. chapters IX and XI, pp. 169 ff. and pp. 202 ff. Generally, cf. Walbank, *Comm.* i. 12 f.; chapter on Polybius in Dorey, *Latin Historians*. Lehmann, *Glaubwürdigkeit*, pp. 51 ff., in a detailed discussion, provides some support for the legitimacy of Polybius' hostility towards the Aetolians. His later attempt, however (ibid., pp. 156 ff.), to show that Polybius' account of the Achaean League is without bias, is much less successful and cannot be accepted.

[2] Pol. xxviii. 6; cf. chapter XI, p. 210.

[3] Pol. xxxix. 3; xxiv. 11–13; cf. chapter XII, pp. 223 ff.

This is not the place to discuss in detail the date of composition of the *Histories*. A full account up to 1956 of the attempts to fix a date with any precision is given by Walbank, and a summary of his conclusions will be sufficient here. It seems probable that publication was extended over many years, beginning about 150 and continuing until Polybius' death some time after 118. Although certainty is not possible, the books which contain Polybius' account of Philopoemen's collision-course with Rome seem likely to have been published after the destruction of Corinth in 146.[1]

Much material from Polybius' *Histories* which has not survived in the extant fragments is preserved in the form in which it was incorporated in the *Ab Urbe Condita* of Livy. In the books which cover the period of Philopoemen's political activity, Livy devotes considerable space to descriptions of Greek affairs.[2] Nissen has shown conclusively that these Greek parts of Livy have as their source Polybius' *Histories*.[3] Livy however does not simply translate Polybius. He was only interested in Greece in as far as it affected Rome, and the purely internal affairs of Greece were of little concern to him. He therefore had to be selective and to abbreviate Polybius to suit his own scheme. However, the parts which do depend on Polybius are usually faithful to their source and record Polybius' information with tolerable accuracy.[4]

The occasions when Livy leaves his source are when he takes his Roman readers into account and omits explanations of features of Roman life which Polybius, writing for a Greek audience, had felt it necessary to include.[5] Similarly, although it was unnecessary for Polybius to explain to his Greek readers familiar aspects and institutions of the Greek world Livy had to add an explanation for his Roman readers. In the process he sometimes misinterprets Polybius in his attempts to expand and explain him. Further slight changes in Polybius' emphasis or simple imprecisions Nissen explains as concessions to Roman patriotism on Livy's part. These may in fact be better explained as results of Livy's Rome-centred point of view and absorption in the affairs of Rome, rather than as conscious patriotic alterations.[6] The speeches are the most unreliable part of his work. His penchant for rhetoric led him to expand the speeches he found in Polybius, which

---

[1] Walbank, *Comm.* i. 292 f.; but cf. McDonald, review of Walbank in *JRS* 1958, 180; Erbse, *RhM* 1951, 157 ff. (the whole composed after 144 from earlier notes).

[2] From book xxiv onwards, Livy's interest in Greek affairs increases in proportion to the Roman involvement. He records the death of Philopoemen in xxxix. 50.

[3] Nissen, *Krit. Unt.*, *passim*.

[4] Cf. xxxv. 40. 1; xxxix. 48. 6; xli. 25. 8. Cf. Nissen, *Krit. Unt.*, pp. 81–2.

[5] e.g. Liv. xxxvii. 33; Pol. xxi. 13. 10–12 (the Salii); cf. Nissen, *Krit. Unt.*, p. 27.

[6] Nissen, *Krit. Unt.*, pp. 28–30; Walsh, *Livy*, pp. 143 ff.; 151 ff.

may themselves have borne little relationship to the originals they were supposed to represent—although Polybius did claim to be attempting speeches of a Thucydidean character, representing as accurately as possible the speaker's words.[1] Livy however is not so much interested in accuracy in his speeches as in rhetoric for sheer display and for the contribution it makes to dramatizing a situation. We must therefore always suspect the content of Livy's speeches, even when they are based on Polybian originals. Factual detail incorporated in them may be accurate, but the nuances and forms of expression are likely to be Livy's own contribution.[2]

Important historical *cruces* are also created by Livy when he fails to combine his sources correctly. This most seriously affects his chronology, for Livy's generally reliable list of Roman magistrates, taken from Roman annalists, is the most valuable general guide to the chronology of the period. On occasion he fails to relate the Greek events, dated by Olympiads by Polybius, under the correct consuls, and, since the later books of Polybius' *Histories* are fragmentary, Polybius provides little help in correcting Livy's mistakes. Occasionally Livy realizes that his account is muddled and adds further explanation of his own—which can have the effect of simply adding to the confusion.[3] On the whole, however, these places are obvious enough; and apart from these lapses Livy can be accepted as providing, in the main, trustworthy information for the history of Greece during the greater part of Philopoemen's career.

A second work of Polybius of importance for the study of the lifetime of Philopoemen was his *Life of Philopoemen*. The work itself is wholly lost, but we know of its existence from Polybius' own mention of it in an extant part of the *Histories*.[4] Plutarch and Pausanias may have used it as a source for their writings about Philopoemen. Polybius' own description of his work has been analysed by Pédech in an attempt to discover its content more precisely. His arguments must be examined in detail.[5]

He starts from Polybius' statement that the *Life* was written in three books, and attempts to fit Polybius' description to this *schema*. This procedure seems to be immediately rendered fruitless, for Polybius promptly proceeds to divide his material into only two parts, after

---

[1] Cf. Walbank, *Comm.* i. 13–14; see also in *Miscellanea di studi alessandrini in memoria di Augusto Rostagni*, pp. 211–13.

[2] Cf. Nissen, *Krit. Unt.*, pp. 23–7; Walsh, *Livy*, pp. 219–44. The rhetorical alterations do not occur only in the speeches, but it is here that they are most obvious.

[3] e.g. Liv. xxxix. 49–50 (death of Philopoemen in 182 related under 183: cf. appendix 2 A (i), pp. 241 ff.); xxxviii. 30–4: on the confusion here cf. Holleaux, *Études* v. 263 ff.

[4] Pol. x. 21. 5.   [5] *REG* 1951, 82 ff.

his initial mention of the three books: these are the παιδικὴ ἀγωγή and the ἐπιφανέσταται πράξεις.[1] The clear and obvious meanings of these two phrases are the activities of his youth and training on the one hand and the famous deeds of his maturity on the other. Polybius continues by saying that, as far as the *Histories* are concerned, it is best to omit any account τῆς μὲν νεωτερικῆς ἀγωγῆς καὶ τῶν νεωτερικῶν ζήλων— that is, in expanded form, the παιδικὴ ἀγωγή. He explains that he does this in order τοῖς δὲ κατὰ τὴν ἀκμὴν αὐτοῦ κεφαλαιωδῶς ἐκεῖ δεδηλωμένοις ἔργοις προσθεῖναι καὶ κατὰ μέρος.[2] By this he clearly means that the account which he gave in his *Life* of the ἐπιφανέσταται πράξεις (here called τὰ κατὰ τὴν ἀκμήν) was κεφαλαιώδης. As this word is used as a term which is compatible with αὔξησις τῶν πράξεων, it must indicate that the relevant background material was omitted in order to make Philopoemen's achievements appear exaggerated—μετ᾽ αὐξήσεως. The essential difference between the κεφαλαιώδης ἀπολογισμός of the *Life* and the treatment in the *Histories* is that the *Life* was ἐγκωμιαστικός, the *Histories* κοινὸς ἐπαίνου καὶ ψόγου; the *Life* he describes as κεφαλαιώδη καὶ μετ᾽ αὐξήσεως, the *Histories* ἀληθῆ καὶ . . . μετ᾽ ἀποδείξεως. This means, in fact, that in the *Life* Polybius was simply writing the whole work from the point of view of the hero, as was natural in an ἐγκώμιον. This analysis shows clearly that Polybius made no attempt to give a 'table of contents' here of the three books of the *Life*. His division is essentially bipartite. Since in the *Histories* he summarizes only very briefly Philopoemen's background before his hipparchy, we can conclude that he considered this background to be part of the παιδικὴ ἀγωγή. His fuller circumstantial account of the ἐπιφανέσταται πράξεις starts with the hipparchy, where Polybius himself specifically places Philopoemen's ἀρχή τῶν πράξεων.[3]

Pédech's treatment of this material is unconvincing. He finds, easily enough and with some *a priori* likelihood, material for the first of the *Life*'s three books in the παιδικὴ ἀγωγή and in Polybius' own definition of this—τίς ἦν καὶ τίνων καὶ τίσιν ἀγωγαῖς ἐχρήσατο νέος ὤν (though he badly misunderstands τίνων)—which Polybius describes again later as νεωτερικὴ ἀγωγή and νεωτερικοὶ ζῆλοι. This is reasonable, and some confirmation comes from Plutarch's similar treatment.[4] But serious difficulty occurs in Pédech's attempt to define the scope of the second and third books.[5] He associates rightly enough the νεωτερικὴ ἀγωγή with the παιδικὴ ἀγωγή, but ignores Polybius' indication that the νεωτερικοὶ ζῆλοι are equally considered to be part of the παιδικὴ

[1] Pol. x. 21. 6; Pédech, REG 1951, 83.
[2] Pol. x. 21. 7–8.   [3] Pol. x. 21. 1.
[4] Pol. x. 21. 5; Pédech, REG 1951, 84—ἀγωγαῖς must not be taken with τίνων. Cf. Treu, *Historia* 1954/5, 220 ff.
[5] REG 1951, 86–7.

ἀγωγή. He accordingly confuses them with the ἐπιφανέσταται πράξεις. In each case he wishes to make the double phrase a correspondence, and suggests that Polybius was using the phrases as synonyms. Although Pédech almost seems to realize that Polybius was not using the phrases in this way he prefers to ignore the difficulty: 'l'expression τὰς ἐπιφανεστάτας πράξεις paraît plus éloignée de τῶν νεωτερικῶν ζήλων, forme sur laquelle elle est reprise. En réalité ces deux titres pouvaient convenir à ce deuxième livre. L'auteur y étudiait les goûts de son héros et racontait ses exploits jusqu'au moment où il devînt hipparque.' No further discussion follows. A reference to Plutarch, who treats of Philopoemen's reading material and career up to the hipparchy in this order, is irrelevant, for we know from Polybius' own description that he did not describe these essentially minor events as ἐπιφανέσταται πράξεις. For him Philopoemen's hipparchy is the ἀρχὴ τῶν πράξεων. Polybius gives no basis for Pédech's assumption of a correspondence between ἐπιφανέσταται πράξεις and νεωτερικοὶ ζῆλοι, nor for forcing them together to form the second book of the *Life*. The facts do not fit his analysis.[1]

It is equally impossible to say exactly what Polybius included in his third book. Pédech has already disposed of the ἐπιφανέσταται πράξεις in the second book and must look for something else. This must accordingly be an account of Philopoemen's later life—the most significant historically, as Pédech willingly admits. We also have Polybius' word that he did treat this period, even if κεφαλαιωδῶς (in the sense already described). Pédech correctly understands that Polybius' phrase τὰ κατὰ τὴν ἀκμὴν αὐτοῦ refers to the period of Philopoemen's maturity; but he fails to see that a thought-connection exists in Polybius' text with ἐπιφανέσταται πράξεις: for Polybius they are essentially the same thing. It would be *a priori* likely that they would be treated in the third book; but it is not possible to prove that they were treated in the third book alone, as Pédech desires.

Pédech's analysis has added nothing to what was already known about the *Life* from Polybius himself. Philopoemen's education and youth, as well as his character and family background (τίς ἦν καὶ τίνων καὶ τίσιν ἀγωγαῖς), were recorded at greater length than in the *Histories*, to which they were not strictly relevant. His political career was treated in a personalized way, unrelated to the background of the time, therefore perhaps at shorter length than in the *Histories*. This technique was suitable to the biographical genre but not to the *Histories*: in the *Histories* Polybius promises to relate the man to his time. The

---

[1] In this connection, it is worth pointing out that μεταχειρίσασθαι πόλεμον (Plut. *Phil.* 7) does not indicate 'réformes dans l'armée crétoise' (Pédech, *REG* 1951, 88).

three books clearly suggest three parts, but on what system Polybius divided his material among the books there is no means of telling. The date at which the lost biography was written is also disputed. Polybius' own indications are that it was written before book ten of the *Histories*, in which he mentions it, therefore before 146.[1] It is possible that the reference to the *Life* in book ten may be a later addition, but there are no good grounds for believing this. The reference seems to rule out the suggestion of Lucas that the *Life* was written after 146 as part of Polybius' scheme to rehabilitate Philopoemen's memory, in the same spirit as his defence of him before the Roman commissioners.[2] Other dates suggested for the composition of the *Life* are soon after 182 (the death of Philopoemen must clearly be the *terminus post quem*), supported by Walbank and Ziegler,[3] and soon after 160, originally suggested by Wunderer and more recently argued by Pédech.[4] The arguments in favour of both of these dates are inconclusive. Soon after 182 is argued by Ziegler thus: 'Alle Wahrscheinlichkeit spricht dafür, daß diese enkomiastische Biographie Philopoimens der literarische Erstling P.'s gewesen ist, ins Auge gefaßt von ihm als Jüngling, vielleicht noch zu Lebzeiten des bewunderten Helden, dessen Urne er von Messene nach Megalopolis trug, fertig gestellt etwa um 180 oder wenig später.' This is hypothesis rather than argument; Walbank, who accepts the date, adds no new reasoning. This statement provides nothing to urge ready acceptance; but at the same time little objection can be brought against it: Polybius' emphasis on Philopoemen's early years seems to require explanation, which it does not satisfactorily receive if the Ziegler/Walbank date of soon after 182 is accepted. But this cannot be pressed.

The same is true of Wunderer's and Pédech's date. The purpose of the *Life*, it is suggested, was to provide reading material for the education of Scipio Aemilianus, on the lines of Xenophon's *Cyropaedia*. None of their arguments proves this, though the suggestion does have the virtue that it explains without difficulty the emphasis which Polybius laid in the *Life* on Philopoemen's early years. It can withstand with little difficulty such criticism as has been brought against it. It can be argued that Philopoemen, the anti-Roman (of the Roman tradition), would not be chosen as the hero of a work written to educate Aemilianus. The answer to this surely lies in the author: Polybius was not heir to the Roman tradition, and in his

---

[1] Pol. x. 21. 6. At xv. 30. 10, Polybius mentions Carthage as still existing, and therefore had written up to this point before 146. Cf. Walbank, *Comm.* i. 292 f.

[2] Lucas, *Ueber des Polybios Darstellung des ätolischen Bundes*, p. 35.

[3] Walbank, *Comm.* i. 2 and n. 2; Ziegler, *RE* xxi. 2. 1472, 'Polybios'; cf. Nissen, *Krit. Unt.*, p. 280.

[4] Wunderer, *Pol.-Forsch.* i. 87; Pédech, *REG* 1951, 88 ff.

opinion Philopoemen's policies were not in the strict sense anti-Roman. The whole point of choosing Philopoemen as a hero was that he was a patriot, and as far as educative value was concerned it made no difference whether Polybius wrote about a Roman, an Achaean, or a Persian, as long as the point of the exercise was made clear to his reader. If he had this purpose in mind, there need be nothing strange in his choosing Philopoemen.

The other objection is based on the fact that Cicero twice states that Scipio Aemilianus could scarcely keep his hands off Xenophon's *Cyropaedia*. Ziegler argues that it would have been ungrateful of him to prefer this work had his friend Polybius written a *Life of Philopoemen* especially for him.[1] It is idle to speculate on the reason for Aemilianus' preference for the *Cyropaedia*. Whether Polybius wrote his *Life* for Aemilianus or not, we can scarcely be expected to understand from Cicero's light-hearted remarks that Aemilianus read nothing but the *Cyropaedia*. It hardly needs saying that the *Cyropaedia* could be his favourite reading matter—which is all Cicero means—while he still paid due attention to other works including, if necessary, Polybius' *Life of Philopoemen*. There is therefore no reason for rejecting out of hand this later date for the composition and publication of Polybius' *Life*. At the same time, convenient though it is, no solid arguments are offered which make it more likely than the date preferred by Ziegler and Walbank.

It has been suggested by Nissen, who is followed by Hoffmann, that Polybius' *Life of Philopoemen* was used by Plutarch as the main source for his own extant *Life of Philopoemen*.[2] The basis of this argument is that since Plutarch gives details from Philopoemen's early life which can only have come from Polybius' *Life*, he must have used it as a chief source for the whole. It should accordingly be considered the source of everything which could come from it. On the other hand Ziegler can find no reason for assuming that Plutarch has used Polybius' *Life* as a general basis for his own work.[3] He explains the appearance of personal details—clearly taken from Polybius' *Life*—in the early chapters of Plutarch's work by assuming that Plutarch only glanced at the early chapters of the monograph, after which he consistently used the *Histories*. In favour of Ziegler's view is the fact that Plutarch certainly knew Polybius' *Histories*, since he includes in his *Life* Polybius' own defence of Philopoemen's reputation before the Roman commissioners in 146/5—an event which occurred long after the date at which Polybius wrote his *Life*.[4] The Greek sections of Plutarch's

[1] Cic. *Tusc.* ii. 62; *ad Q.fr.* i. 1. 23; Ziegler, *RE* xxi. 2. 1473, n. 1, 'Polybios'.
[2] Nissen, *Krit. Unt.*, pp. 280–7; Hoffmann, *RE* xx. 1. 77, 'Philopoimen'.
[3] *RE* xxi. 2. 1472, 'Polybios'.
[4] Plut. *Phil.* 21; Pol. xxxix. 3.

Flamininus also depend on Polybius' *Histories*. Another fact which lends strength to Ziegler's suggestion is that Plutarch gives no information about Philopoemen's activities in Crete: these were irrelevant to Polybius' *Histories*, but the *Life* cannot have ignored fifteen of Philopoemen's most active years. Ziegler's arguments therefore suggest that Nissen's conclusion about Plutarch's general use of Polybius' *Life* is likely to be incorrect, although a final decision on which of two irrecoverable Polybian accounts Plutarch used cannot be made.

In addition to his Polybian material Plutarch seems to have made use of at least two other sources. The first is Aristocrates of Sparta. Plutarch names him specifically when he quotes his higher alternative figure to Polybius' for those killed at Compasion. He seems to have known his work well, as he cites him also in the *Lycurgus*. But the Compasion incident seems to be the only certain attribution to Aristocrates in the *Philopoemen*. Aristocrates wrote *Laconica* at an uncertain date—although there are some grounds for thinking that he was later than Polybius. In any case it seems clear that he was used directly by Plutarch.[1] The remaining sources are uncertain. To them must be attributed all parts which cannot be assigned to named sources. They may be, as Nissen prefers, a collection of anecdotes; they may be simply 'tradition' or recollection of Plutarch's own from his extensive reading. It is impossible to name them specifically, but it is clear that Polybius and Aristocrates of Sparta do not adequately account for the whole of Plutarch's source material.[2]

Plutarch's *Flamininus* also contains information directly relevant to the history of Philopoemen's Achaea. Nissen's analysis of the sources has here survived fundamentally as it left his pen.[3] The main source for Greek affairs is Polybius' *Histories*: 'Hauptquelle ist Polybios, in zweiter Linie ein Annalist, dann eine Reihe von Bemerkungen und Anekdoten aus seinem umfassenden Excerptenschatz.' Klotz made an attempt to show that the annalist in question was Valerius Antias, but his arguments have been shown to be inadequate by Smith,[4] and the position is now much as Nissen left it. In any case, this disagreement does not affect the Greek sections of the work, for which Nissen indisputably established Polybius as main source.

Two other sources which have some quantity of information about Philopoemen remain. The article in the *Suda* presents no problems—

[1] Cf. Schwartz, *RE* ii. 1, 'Aristocrates' no. 25; Jacoby, *FGH* iii B, no. 591. We scarcely need to attribute the whole of Plut. *Phil.* 16 to Aristocrates, with Nissen, *Krit. Unt.*, p. 284, simply because it deals with Sparta: it is written essentially from an Achaean viewpoint.
[2] Nissen, *Krit. Unt.*, p. 281.
[3] *Krit. Unt.*, pp. 290-2.
[4] Klotz, *RhM* 1935, 46 ff.; Smith, *CQ* 1944, 89 ff.

and no independent information—as it consists merely of two transcripts, one from Polybius' *Histories*, the other from Pausanias' treatment of Philopoemen in his *Arcadica*.[1] Pausanias' account however is of more interest, and presents more source problems.[2] He has treated his sources unhistorically—for which he should not altogether be blamed: he was not writing history—but not unintelligently, and the relevant chapters contain scraps of information which seem to come directly from Pausanias' own fund of general knowledge. The problem is to discover how far this type of individualistic treatment is responsible for the variations which his account shows in comparison with the other extant sources. Nissen believed that he has simply made use of Plutarch, to whose information he has added some other scraps of information from an unidentified source, and concluded: '. . . ist diese ganze Übersicht des Pausanias vom Leben Philopoimens für die Kenntnis der Thatsachen wertlos.' In this judgement Hoffmann and Ziegler are prepared to follow him.[3] On the other hand, Rühl has argued that Pausanias' source was Polybius' *Life of Philopoemen*, and that similarities between his and Plutarch's account result from the fact that they were both using the same source.[4] Neither case is without its weakness, but at the same time there are important factors which support either. The conclusion to which we are inevitably led—if we do not *a priori* postulate *Einquellenprinzip* for Pausanias—is that Pausanias must have used both Plutarch's *Life* and one of Polybius' works. In addition there are phrases the origin of which cannot be traced: they may be additions or embroideries of Pausanias himself or simply his mistakes. There is little point in re-examining all the inconclusive evidence which has been cited in favour of either view. The present examination will therefore be confined to citing the strongest evidence, which shows with some certainty the use of both Polybius and Plutarch.

Nissen had the mass of probability on his side when he decided in favour of Plutarch. Pausanias follows his order of arrangement, even where this is not chronological. This could conceivably be explained by a common source, but it is unlikely that both Plutarch and Pausanias would abbreviate the (probably) much longer Polybian narrative in exactly the same details. It is nevertheless difficult to decide exactly what must come from Plutarch because it was not in Polybius. Choice is finally restricted to the accounts of Compasion. Both are confused,

---

[1] The *Suda*, s.v. Φιλοποίμην = Pol. x. 22; Paus. viii. 49 (with minor differences and omissions).

[2] Paus. viii. 49–52.

[3] Nissen, *Krit. Unt.*, pp. 287–91; Hoffmann, *RE* xx. 1. 77, 'Philopoimen'; Ziegler, *RhM* 1934, 229, n. 1.

[4] *Jahrb. für class. Phil.* 1883, 33–46.

and Nissen refused to use them to support his argument. It is clear however that Pausanias' figure for the dead, three hundred, is not Polybian, since Polybius gave eighty. Plutarch records Aristocrates' variant of three hundred and fifty without actually expressing his own opinion, and Pausanias' figure is clearly closer to this than to Polybius'.[1] It is possible that Pausanias had looked at Aristocrates' own account and miscopied or adapted it in some confused way, perhaps in the light of Polybius' figure. But on the whole it seems more likely that he has misused Plutarch's information in this way: there is no other evidence that he knew Aristocrates' work. This is as much as can certainly be said in favour of Pausanias' use of Plutarch: Nissen's other arguments are all inconclusive. But a reading of both texts leaves the firm impression that the general correspondence in the form of the material in the two accounts is too great to be entirely accidental; and although this cannot be irrefutably demonstrated, it seems likely that it represents Pausanias' use of Plutarch.

It is much easier to show that Pausanias knew and used Polybius. The clearest, and for the present purpose the most important, addition in Pausanias is in viii. 51. 5–6, where he details the part which Lycortas played in the Messenian War before Philopoemen's death: 'Now at this time the Achaeans had a grievance against the Messenians, and Philopoemen, dispatching Lycortas with the army to lay waste the land of the Messenians, was very anxious two or three days later, in spite of his seventy years and a severe attack of fever, to share in the expedition of Lycortas. He led about sixty horsemen and targeteers. Lycortas, however, and his army were already on their way back home, having neither suffered great harm nor inflicted it on the Messenians.' Plutarch has none of this information about Lycortas. Yet it is not possible that Pausanias simply made it up: it seems wholly Polybian, and is repeated by Pausanias in (or from) iv. 29. 12. Nissen does not attempt to identify Pausanias' source here, although he must have suspected that the writer supremely interested in the activities of Lycortas was Polybius. There is also clear confirmation of his use of Polybius in Pausanias' account of Philopoemen's force on his last expedition. Plutarch states simply that Philopoemen took cavalry with him; Pausanias knows—clearly from Polybius—that he had light-armed with him also (though he muddles the numbers).[2] The remainder of Rühl's arguments are not so strong. He may be right that Pausanias' different account of the evacuation of Megalopolis in 223, three times repeated, comes from Polybius' *Life of Philopoemen*:

---

[1] Plut. *Phil.* 16; Paus. viii. 51. 3. I cannot understand how Rühl (p. 43) can claim that the figure 300 comes from Polybius.

[2] Plut. *Phil.* 18. 7; Paus. viii. 51. 5; cf. Liv. xxxix. 49. 2.

Plutarch states simply, 'he stole the citizens in some way out of the city', whereas Pausanias specifies that more than two-thirds of the population, with women and children, were led to Messene by Philopoemen—a fact which finds confirmation in Plutarch's *Cleomenes*.[1] The ultimate authority for this detail may have been Philopoemen himself, who must have provided many details which Polybius used both in his *Life* and in the *Histories*. However, this argument rests on too many uncertainties for it to count as proof that Pausanias must have used Polybius.

Two other points which Rühl does not make have a bearing on this question. The statements of Pausanias and Plutarch regarding Philopoemen's appearance conflict. Plutarch counters an opinion which he has met—ὡς ἔνιοι νομίζουσιν—that Philopoemen was ugly by referring to his statue at Delphi which he himself had seen. Pausanias takes no account of this, but simply repeats the opinion.[2] This opinion can probably be defined as Polybius', who had, after all, seen the man in the flesh. Pausanias may therefore have been using Polybius for this detail—and choosing his source well. He was not misled by Plutarch's easy acceptance of the sculptor's heroic vision. The second additional point is the very close resemblance between Polybius' description of Cleander's having ξενία πατρική with the house of Craugis, and Pausanias' similar statement. Plutarch does not mention this.[3] Both of these items strongly suggest that Pausanias knew and used Polybius independently of Plutarch.

None of the other passages cited in the debate certainly adds anything to this. Final conclusions therefore about the total of Pausanias' sources must remain uncertain. It can however be regarded as proved that at least in his account of Philopoemen's last campaign he made use of a Polybian source; and there is evidence which strongly suggests that he may have used this for other parts of his narrative. On the other hand, the general character of his chapters on Philopoemen and his possible citation of information from Aristocrates suggest almost as strongly that Plutarch's *Philopoemen* was used as a general scheme.

Apart from these main sources for the life of Philopoemen, there is little other source material. Occasional passages of Appian, Diodorus, Justin, and Strabo usually add little to the picture gained from the other sources, and inscriptional material is only present in sufficient quantity to be an important aid in elucidating events in Crete.[4] The content of these minor sources is discussed more conveniently at the points where they are used.

[1] Paus. viii. 49. 4; 27. 15; iv. 29. 8; Plut. *Cleomenes*, 24; cf. Plut. *Phil.* 5.
[2] Plut. *Phil.* 2; Paus. viii. 49. 3.
[3] Pol. x. 22. 1; Paus. viii. 49. 2; cf. Plut. *Phil.* 1.
[4] Cf. chapter III, *passim*.

APPENDIX 2 A (i)

THE DATE OF PHILOPOEMEN'S DEATH

ATTEMPTS at establishing an acceptable, agreed date for Philopoemen's death have been unsuccessful. Opinion is divided into two groups, one favouring 183 and the other 182, depending on whether or not it is considered that Livy in xxxix. 49–50 has predated his account by one year. The two most recent attempts at the problem each suggest a new approach, but reach the same diversity of result. Aymard favours 182 and Hoffmann criticizes Aymard's method and supports 183.[1] Aymard's arguments certainly have not yet firmly established the case for 182. His weakness, as Hoffmann points out, is his excessive reliance on the order of the Polybian fragments in the excerpts in order to fix Archon's *strategia* in 184/3, to force the acceptance of Philopoemen's last *strategia* for 183/2, and as a result to establish that his death occurred in May or June 182 (to agree with Pausanias' περὶ ἀκμὴν σίτου).[2]

Hoffmann's arguments depend on a different approach to the problem and shed much new light; and, although his conclusion is unacceptable, his approach provides the possibility of a new argument for 182. Much labour has been expended on explaining the synchronism of the deaths of Hannibal, Scipio Africanus, and Philopoemen. Did Polybius here mean Roman consular year, Olympiad year, or Achaean *strategos*-year? Hoffmann's conclusion on this seems sensible, that Polybius simply meant a twelve-month period, and that it is not possible to press the synchronism further. The scheme proposed here will not resolve this controversy. It will fit an Olympiad year (and *a fortiori* Hoffmann's twelve-month period). But its validity does not depend on this.[3]

Hoffmann bases his argument for 183 on the chronological relationship between the embassy of Q. Marcius Philippus to Macedon and the Peloponnese, and the Messenian War during which Philopoemen died. This is suggested by Livy xxxix. 48. 5 ff. Hoffmann's other evidence is a reference in Callicrates' speech to the Senate—certainly accurate: neither Callicrates nor Polybius had reason to falsify the facts. 'For only recently during the Messenian troubles Q. Marcius

---

[1] Aymard, *REA* 1928, 43–53; Hoffmann, *Hermes* 1938, 244–8.

[2] Paus. iv. 29. 11. On the time of year see Olck, *RE* s.v. 'Ernte'.

[3] *Hermes* 1938, 245–6. The Olympiad year has found a new champion in Pédech, *La Méthode historique*, pp. 432 ff.

Philippus did everything in his power to prevent the Achaeans from deliberating about the Messenians without first consulting the Senate, but they did not listen to him, and voted for war . . .'[1] The obvious conclusion is that war had not been declared when Philippus met the Achaeans, but was shortly afterwards; also, that a situation existed in which war might be necessary at any time. Furthermore, Philippus' report to the Senate in winter 183/2 stated that the Achaeans wanted no Roman consultation, but would become tractable when Sparta joined the Messenians. This implies that when he made his report he knew that the Achaeans had declared war.[2]

From this evidence, from Livy xxxix. 48. 5 f., and from Plutarch's account which suggests that Philopoemen's expedition was unexpected,[3] Hoffmann concludes thus: Philopoemen died on the outbreak of war early in 183 (περὶ ἀκμὴν σίτου),[4] which was the war of Deinocrates, before the formal Achaean declaration of war which Philippus failed to prevent when he arrived in Achaea. The war then dragged on until early 182. It must have continued into 182 since two separate Achaean embassies went to Rome, one in winter 183/2, which asked the Senate to prevent strategic materials from reaching Messene from Italy. The second was sent after the peace, when Bippus of Argos reported the Achaean accomplishment to the Senate. This must have been the next winter, 182/1, as the settlement with Messene was not arranged until the second *synodos* (perhaps July).[5]

Considerable objections exist to telescoping in this way all the known events into 183, and then extending the war after Philopoemen's death for another whole year. First the declaration of war. Hoffmann claims the support of the second sentence of Livy xxxix. 48. 5

---

[1] Liv. xxxix. 48. 5: *legatus in Macedoniam Q. Marcius est missus, iussus idem in Peloponneso sociorum res aspicere. nam ibi quoque et ex veteribus discordiis residui motus erant, et Messene desciverat a concilio Achaico.* Pol. xxiv. 9. 12–13: πρώην μὲν γὰρ ἐν τοῖς Μεσσηνιακοῖς πολλὰ ποιήσαντος Κοίντου Μαρκίου πρὸς τὸ μηδὲν τοὺς Ἀχαιοὺς βουλεύσασθαι περὶ Μεσσηνίων ἄνευ τῆς Ῥωμαίων προαιρέσεως, παρακούσαντας καὶ ψηφισαμένους αὐτοὺς τὸν πόλεμον . . .

[2] Pol. xxiii. 9. 8–10: περὶ δὲ τῶν κατὰ Πελοπόννησον ὁ Μάρκιος τοιαύτην ἐπεποίητο τὴν ἀπαγγελίαν διότι, τῶν Ἀχαιῶν οὐ βουλομένων ἀναφέρειν οὐδὲν ἐπὶ τὴν σύγκλητον, ἀλλὰ φρονηματιζομένων καὶ πάντα δι᾽ ἑαυτῶν πράττειν ἐπιβαλλομένων, ἐὰν παρακούσωσι μόνον αὐτῶν κατὰ τὸ παρὸν καὶ βραχεῖαν ἔμφασιν ποιήσωσιν δυσαρεστήσεως, ταχέως ἡ Λακεδαίμων τῇ Μεσσήνῃ συμφρονήσει. τούτου δὲ γενομένου μετὰ μεγάλης χάριτος ἥξειν τοὺς Ἀχαιοὺς ἔφη καταπεφευγότας ἐπὶ Ῥωμαίους.

[3] Plut. *Phil.* 18. 3: ὁ δὲ Φιλοποίμην ἔτυχε μὲν ἐν Ἄργει πυρέσσων, πυθόμενος δὲ ταῦτα συνέτεινεν εἰς Μεγάλην πόλιν ἡμέρᾳ μιᾷ σταδίους πλείονας ἢ τετρακοσίους. κἀκεῖθεν εὐθὺς ἐβοήθει τοὺς ἱππεῖς ἀναλαβών . . . Cf. Liv. xxxix. 49. 1 f.; Paus. viii. 51. 5.

[4] Paus. iv. 29. 11.

[5] Pol. xxiii. 9. 12 (first embassy); 18. 3 (second embassy); cf. Aymard, *Assemblées*, p. 275 (second *synodos* in July).

for his dating the existence of the war in summer 183 : *nam ibi quoque et ex veteribus discordiis residui motus erant, et Messene desciverat a concilio Achaico.* But he has not analysed the passage adequately. If any reliance is to be placed on this sentence, it must be understood in its context with the first sentence of 48. 5, which records the appointment of Philippus. The implication, marked by *nam*, is that he was appointed because of the Messenian secession. This means that the trouble must have broken out in 184 for news to have reached Rome in time for consideration. It is therefore not possible to press Plutarch's statement that Philopoemen expected an easy year, as Hoffmann does, in favour of his last *strategia* having been in 184/3 rather than in 183/2.[1] For Philopoemen must have known about the impending war at the time of the election, even if Messene had not actually seceded. Thus Hoffmann explains the evidence no better with 184/3 than with 183/2.

If the war existed during the spring and summer of 183, and if Philopoemen had been killed before Philippus' arrival, it would be improbable to find the declaration of war postponed to the autumn, with the result that Philippus—whose main task was with Macedonia —could still participate in the discussions. Hoffmann argues that Philopoemen's expedition was an 'improvisiertes Unternehmen'. But he ignores Pausanias' evidence that Lycortas had already been dispatched with the army when Philopoemen ἠπείγετο μετασχεῖν Λυκόρτᾳ τοῦ ἔργου. Philopoemen's action is not explained, but if the background is supplied from Plutarch and Livy—Deinocrates' sudden attack on Corone—a sound reason appears for Philopoemen's expedition.[2] The war, in fact, seems to have been on a comparatively large scale, involving a large Achaean army and clearly necessitating a prior declaration of war. If Philippus tried to prevent the declaration, it must have been before this expedition and therefore before Philopoemen's death. This is possible, though it necessarily places Philippus' visit to the Peloponnese early in the year.

There is however further objection. To suit the records of Achaean ambassadors to Rome, Hoffmann makes the war drag on for a further year. This is not the impression which the sources give : Plutarch, Livy, and Pausanias are agreed (all take their accounts in some way from Polybius) that Lycortas' retributive expedition was soon after the death of Philopoemen ; and Polybius himself implies unequivocally that the war was over by the second *synodos* (perhaps July).[3] No source

---

[1] *Hermes* 1938, 247–8. Cf. Liv. xxxix. 48. 5 (quoted above, p. 242, n. 1) ; Plut. *Phil.* 18. 1 : ἤλπιζεν οὐ μόνον ἐκείνην τὴν ἀρχὴν ἀπολέμως διάξειν, ἀλλὰ καὶ τοῦ βίου τὸ λοιπὸν αὐτῷ μεθ' ἡσυχίας καταβιῶναι τὰ πράγματα παρέξειν.

[2] Hoffmann, *Hermes* 1938, 247; Paus. viii. 51. 5; Plut. *Phil.* 18; Liv. xxxix. 49. 1.

[3] Plut. *Phil.* 21. 1 : οὐδ' ἡντινοῦν ἀναβολὴν ἐποιήσαντο τῆς τιμωρίας . . . Liv. xxxix. 50. 9 : *non diuturnum mortis eius gaudium auctoribus crudelitatis fuit.* Paus. viii. 51. 8 :

allows the suspicion that this should be the second *synodos* of the year *after* Philopoemen's death. If Hoffmann insists on 183 for Philopoemen's death, the end of the war must also be in 183. This leaves us with the insoluble problem of the Achaean embassies to Rome. If 183 is the year of Philopoemen's death and of the end of the war, the two embassies must have appeared at Rome in the same winter. Clearly they did not: the first would be rendered futile by the second, and Polybius records that the Senate replied to both. 183 therefore cannot be accepted.

One last objection to 183 concerns the mission of Deinocrates to Rome and his relationship with Flamininus. Early in 183 Deinocrates appeared at Rome. Flamininus had already been appointed *legatus* to Prusias, and Deinocrates does not seem to have been officially received by the Senate. The passage of the *Suda* included by Büttner-Wobst as Pol. xxiii. 5. 4–13, even after making due allowance for Polybius' tendentiousness where an enemy is concerned, suggests that Deinocrates spent a considerable time in Rome. No doubt his junketting was combined with making arrangements for shipping to Messene the supplies which worried the Achaeans later in the year.[1] In fact, it seems quite possible that he stayed in Rome at least until the Peloponnesian harvest time—the time of year of Philopoemen's death. This means that if Deinocrates was in Rome in spring 183 he cannot at the same time have been in Messene fomenting revolution. Polybius says that he hoped, until Flamininus' request to the Achaeans for a *syncletos* was refused, that his influence with Flamininus would achieve his aims for Messene. Only when this failed can he have put his secondary plan of open war into operation—which must even then have taken some time.[2] There was not enough time for all this before the Peloponnesian harvest time of 183. Therefore another scheme for the chronology which accounts for all the evidence must be preferred to Hoffmann's.

It is first necessary to reject the implications of Livy xxxix. 48. 5, that the war started in 184—as would Hoffmann—as a confusion of the usual junction-passage type. At the same time Livy has pre-dated by one year his Polybian chapters 49 and 50, which are nevertheless internally reliable. The reconstruction can now be attempted. In spring 183, some time after senatorial appointments had been made,

---

Λυκόρτας δὲ μετ' οὐ πολὺ ἀθροίσας ἔκ τε Ἀρκαδίας καὶ παρ' Ἀχαιῶν δύναμιν ἐστράτευσεν ἐπὶ Μεσσήνην. Pol. xxiii. 16. 12–13: τῆς μὲν οὖν ὑπὲρ τῶν ὅλων διαλήψεως τὴν ἀναφορὰν ἐπὶ τὸ ἔθνος ἐποιήσατο—καὶ γὰρ ὥσπερ ἐπίτηδες συνέβαινε τότε πάλιν συνάγεσθαι τοὺς Ἀχαιοὺς εἰς Μεγάλην πόλιν ἐπὶ τὴν δευτέραν σύνοδον . . . Cf. Aymard, *Assemblées*, p. 275 (second *synodos*).

[1] Pol. xxiii. 5; cf. 9. 12.

[2] Pol. xxiii. 5. 18: αἱ μὲν τοῦ Δεινοκράτους ἐλπίδες . . . καὶ συλλήβδην ἡ τοῦ Τίτου παρουσία καὶ προσδοκία τοῦτον τὸν τρόπον διέπεσεν.

Deinocrates arrived in Rome, made contact with Flamininus and other influential persons who helped him to acquire and to ship war material to Messene. This took most of the summer, and when Deinocrates, travelling with Flamininus, arrived in Greece, autumn had come and Philopoemen had taken office as *strategos*. Placing Flamininus' departure so late in the year causes no difficulty, as he was not in Rome again until 181.[1] Philopoemen refused to call a *syncletos* for Flamininus. It must have been already well-known in Achaea that Deinocrates was close to secession when his hopes from Flamininus' intervention were dashed. A discussion on the matter of war with Messene must therefore have followed soon after Deinocrates' return. Philippus, returning from Macedonia, ineffectively attempted to have the matter referred to Rome, but the Achaeans only sent an embassy asking the Senate to prevent supplies from reaching Messene. During winter 183/2 Philippus reported to the Senate, and the Achaean embassy received an unsatisfactory reply. In the spring Achaea renewed the war with Messene, and Philopoemen was killed in May or June. After his death Lycortas took about two months to finish the war before the second *synodos*. In the autumn Bippus of Argos was sent to Rome to inform the Senate of the result of the war.

This scheme for the events of 183/2 explains all the source problems. Livy's mistake is common enough to arouse no serious objection. Polybius' synchronism is easily explained either by Olympiads or by Hoffmann's twelve-month periods. Scipio's death can be as late as August 183[2] (though the present argument does not require it to be placed at its chronological limit) ; Hannibal's, as Hoffmann says, can be spring or summer 182—while Flamininus was in the east, to account for his traditional association with Hannibal's death ;[3] Philopoemen's will have been at harvest time—May or June—182.

[1] Cf. Gundel, *RE* xxiv. 1. 1093, 'T. Quinctius Flamininus'.
[2] Mommsen, *Röm. Forsch.* ii. 488 ff.
[3] Cf. Plut. *Flam.* 20; App. *Syr.* 11; Liv. xxxix. 51. 1.

APPENDIX 2 A (ii)

THE DATE OF PHILOPOEMEN'S BIRTH

THE date of Philopoemen's birth cannot be ascertained with absolute certainty. The only reference to it in Polybius' own words is in connection with his death: εἶχε γὰρ ἑβδομηκοστὸν ἔτος.[1] It has been demonstrated above that his death occurred in May or June 182. If Polybius knew what he was talking about and expressed himself clearly, he implies here that Philopoemen had completed sixty-nine years, but not yet seventy, by his death in the early summer of 182. Therefore his date of birth must have as *terminus post quem* the early summer of 252.[2]

It may not be possible to approach closer than this date. Plutarch provides the only other separate reference to Philopoemen's age.[3] In the autumn before the battle of Sellasia—now generally agreed to have been fought in 224[4]—Cleomenes attacked and captured Megalopolis. At this time Plutarch says that Philopoemen had lived for thirty years: ἤδη δὲ αὐτοῦ τριάκοντα ἔτη γεγονότος. His form of expression cannot be checked against Polybius—from whom his information must ultimately have come—as Polybius in his *Histories* does not give Philopoemen's age at that time. It is therefore quite possible that Plutarch has slightly altered the form of Polybius' expression: for his statement as it stands implies that Philopoemen had lived for thirty but not thirty-one years, and provides a range of autumn 254 to autumn 253 for his birth date, which is incompatible with Polybius' figure which gives a *terminus post quem* of summer 252.

The solution may lie in the possibility already mentioned, that Plutarch has understood thirty completed years where Polybius meant only to indicate twenty-nine completed years—as Livy and Pausanias have done in the case of the other number, where Plutarch is more accurate in reproducing Polybius.[5] If this has happened, Plutarch's Polybian date would become compatible with the calculation from the date of Philopoemen's death, as it would give a range of autumn

[1] Pol. xxiii. 12. 1.
[2] Hoffmann, *RE* xx. 1. 76 f., 'Philopoimen', bases his calculations wrongly on a death date of June 183, and accordingly reaches 253 for Philopoemen's birth.
[3] Plut. *Phil.* 5. 1.
[4] Cf. literature and discussion in Walbank, *Comm.* i. 272. The death of Ptolemy Euergetes, who received Cleomenes after the battle, has now been fixed by Samuel, *Ptolemaic Chronology*, pp. 106–7, to between 18 October and 31 December 222, thus adding further support to the date 222 for Sellasia.
[5] Liv. xxxix. 49. 4; Paus. viii. 51. 5; cf. Plut. *Phil.* 18. 1.

253 to autumn 252, into which Polybius' *terminus post quem* of May/ June 252 would fit satisfactorily. The result would be that the date of birth can be narrowed down to between *c*. May and *c*. October 252. This precision cannot be insisted upon, as it depends upon the hypothesis of Plutarch's imprecision. But it has the virtue of making Plutarch's date fit with the *terminus post quem* of summer 252 which is calculated from Polybius' own words.

APPENDIX 2 B

ACHAEAN *STRATEGOI*, 211/10–179/8

THE establishment of the list of *strategoi* is essential for a detailed historical study of Achaea. It is made difficult by the fragmentary nature of the material, and when all is done some gaps inevitably remain unfilled. Nevertheless, the results which are achieved are fundamental to the political reconstruction. The *strategoi* of the early years of the League have been discussed in detail by Walbank, and little of relevance to the present study will be gained from repeating his arguments.[1] Those of the whole period of Philopoemen's political activity have been discussed in detail by Niccolini; from 202/1 onwards by Aymard, with always illuminating if not always acceptable results; from 201/0 onwards by De Sanctis.[2] A parallel table of these lists, together with earlier treatments, is included at the end of this book for comparison with the results of the present study. In addition to these comprehensive studies, the contributions to the *Realencyclopädie* on individual *strategoi* occasionally offer new discussion, and will be cited where relevant.

The first years after 211/10 offer little scope for disagreement. The *strategos* in 211/10 was Euryleon. Polybius mentions him at the beginning of his formal introduction of Philopoemen into his *Histories*, a fact which suggests that Euryleon was *strategos* at the time of Philopoemen's return from Crete. Since Philopoemen was hipparch under Cycliadas, who will be shown to have been *strategos* in 210/09, and since he was elected to that office immediately after his return from Crete, Polybius' mention of Euryleon is only relevant if he was *strategos* in 211/10.[3] Cycliadas is shown to have been *strategos* in 210/09—Livy says: *penes eum summa imperii erat*—by the date of the battle at the river Larisus. Plutarch says that Philopoemen was hipparch then, and the

---

[1] Walbank, *Aratos*, pp. 167–75; cf. also *Comm.* ad locc., on individual problems and bibliography.

[2] Niccolini, *La Conf. Ach.*, pp. 285–313; Aymard, *REA* 1928, 1–62; De Sanctis, *Storia* iv. 1. 402–6. Older treatments include: Nissen, *RhM* 1871 (210/09–180/79) and Büttner-Wobst, *Beiträge zu Polybios*, 1901. Further reference will not be made in every case to these studies. They represent the basic groundwork on Achaean chronology, and their results may be consulted most conveniently in the comparative table, pp. 300–1.

[3] Pol. x. 21. 1: ὅτι Εὐρυλέων ὁ τῶν Ἀχαιῶν στρατηγὸς ἄτολμος ἦν καὶ πολεμικῆς χρείας ἀλλότριος. τοῦ δὲ καιροῦ τοῦ κατὰ τὴν διήγησιν ἐφεστακότος ἡμᾶς ἐπὶ τὴν ἀρχὴν τῶν Φιλοποίμενος πράξεων ... Cf. Niese, *GGMS* ii. 483, n. 5.

battle is dated by Livy's mention of the Nemea which took place in 'odd' years, therefore in 209. Livy causes some confusion by recording these events under the consuls of 208, M. Claudius Marcellus and T. Quinctius Crispinus. This must simply be a mistake in collating his sources, Polybius for the Greek events and an annalist for the Roman. It does not indicate any unreliability in the Greek information he provides, which is soundly Polybian.[1] Livy also provides the name of Cycliadas' successor, Nicias. He is securely dated by the Olympic festival of 208, Elean preparations for which were disturbed by Machanidas shortly before Nicias' expedition to Aetolia with Philip. Nicias was therefore *strategos* in 209/8.[2]

In 208/7, following Nicias, Philopoemen held his first *strategia*. The evidence for the date comes from the position in Polybius' text of the fragment in which he describes the battle of Mantinea, and from the fact that Philopoemen was *strategos* for the second time at the Nemea of 205. He must therefore have held his first *strategia* in 208/7 if we are to avoid attributing to him the illegality of successive *strategiai*.[3] The date of the battle of Mantinea also makes it clear that by this time the entry-time to office of the Achaean *strategoi* must have been in the autumn. Before the battle Philopoemen had trained the Achaean army οὐδ' ὅλους ὀκτὼ μῆνας (Pol. xi. 10. 9). This means that if the *strategos* at this time entered office at the beginning of May, as earlier (περὶ τὴν τῆς Πλειάδος ἐπιτολήν (Pol. iv. 37. 2)), the battle would have occurred in the latter part of December. This time of year would be so unusual for major military activity that we would expect Polybius, in the detailed account which he gives of the battle (xi. 11–18), to have given some indication that the season was abnormal. Also Plutarch (*Phil.* 11) says that at the Nemea after Mantinea Philopoemen was *strategos* for the second time and was applauded for his victory. The Nemea was held biennially about July in 'odd' years, therefore a Nemea must have been held in 207.[4] If Philopoemen had fought Mantinea before this (i.e. in December 208, had he entered office in May 208) his reception must surely have been at this Nemea. It was not; therefore his battle must have been after July 207. The calculation of Polybius' 'nearly eight months' will therefore have been from the spring *synodos*, which could be held about February. The battle will accordingly have been about September, a time of year which suits Polybius' mention of the dust clouds raised by the armies (Pol. xi. 13. 2), but which is incompatible with an official year running from May to

[1] Liv. xxvii. 31. 10 (Cycliadas); Plut. *Phil.* 7 (Larisus); Liv. xxvii. 30. 17–31. 9 (Nemea). Cf. Walbank, *Philip*, appendix III, p. 304.
[2] Liv. xxviii. 8. 10 (Nicias); 7. 14 (Olympiad).
[3] Pol. xi. 9–18; Plut. *Phil.* 10 (Mantinea); Plut. *Phil.* 11. 1 (Nemea).
[4] Cf. Boethius, *Der argivische Kalender*, p. 51.

May. It seems clear therefore that at some time between Aratus' *strategia* of 217/16 (Pol. v. 30. 7: θερείας ἐναρχομένης) and the present *strategia* of Philopoemen (208/7) the time of entry of the *strategos* into office had been altered, and that the official year now started in the autumn. Larsen argues that the change occurred in 217, for which date he claims the support of Pol. v. 106. 1. It is possible that the change occurred at this time, but no weight can be attached to Pol. v. 106. 1, which merely records in general terms a return to peacetime activities: neither the election of Timoxenus nor his entry into office are here precisely dated to autumn 217. Aymard is rightly more cautious when he leaves the date imprecise, and Walbank commends his caution.[1] A further possibility, not hitherto considered, is that the change was put into effect when Aratus died in office in his *strategia* of 214/13. It must have then been necessary to elect a replacement. If the idea was current at the time that a change in the entry-date of the *strategos* would be beneficial, use might have been made of the accidental necessity of electing a *strategos* in the autumn to have the entry-date of the *strategos* permanently changed to that time of year.

The *strategos* of 207/6 is unknown. In 206/5 Philopoemen was again in office. This second *strategia* is dated by the Nemea after Mantinea, which must be that of 205.[2] His successor we do not know; but it seems very likely that in one of the years 204/3 or 203/2 Philopoemen again held the *strategia*. He was in his eighth *strategia* when he died,[3] and we shall see that it is very unlikely that he was *strategos* in 187/6. The only years which are then vacant in order to complete his eight *strategiai* are 204/3 and 203/2, the *strategoi* of which are unknown, but either of which Philopoemen may have occupied. If a choice has to be made, 203/2 seems slightly preferable, as Nabis had by that time fully revealed himself to be as great a threat to Achaean security as Machanidas had been. This cannot have been quite so obvious in 204.

The *strategos* of 202/1 was Lysippus. His *strategia* is dated by Nabis' attack on Messene, which Polybius places at about the time of Philip's battle off Chios. This latter Walbank rightly dates to 201, which accordingly places Lysippus' *strategia* in 202/1.[4] In his account of

---

[1] Pol. v. 106. 1: Ἀχαιοὶ μὲν οὖν ὡς θᾶττον ἀπέθεντο τὸν πόλεμον, στρατηγὸν αὑτῶν ἑλόμενοι Τιμόξενον, ἀναχωρήσαντες εἰς τὰ σφέτερα νόμιμα καὶ τὰς διαγωγάς ... Cf. Larsen, *Rep. Gov.*, p. 93; Aymard, *Assemblées*, pp. 238–47; Walbank, *Philip*, p. 300, n. 2.

[2] Plut. *Phil.* 11. 1 (wrongly dated by Boethius, *Der argivische Kalender*, p. 43, to 207).

[3] Plut. *Phil.* 18. 1; Paus. viii. 51. 5.

[4] Pol. xvi. 13–14. 1 (Messene and battle off Chios); Plut. *Phil.* 12. 4 (Lysippus); cf. Walbank, *Philip*, pp. 121–2.

events of 200—*autumno fere exacto*—Livy mentions that the *strategia* had passed from Philopoemen to Cycliadas. The implication is that Philopoemen must have succeeded Lysippus, and therefore must have been *strategos* in 201/0, and that Cycliadas was *strategos* in 200/199.[1] He was followed in office by Aristaenus (199/8), who in turn was followed by Nicostratus (198/7).[2] The next known *strategos* is again Aristaenus who led the Achaean section of the allied army during Flamininus' war against Nabis in 195: therefore Aristaenus was again *strategos* in 196/5.[3] A gap of two years for which there is no information is followed by Philopoemen's fifth *strategia* (193/2) after his second return from Crete: this is firmly dated by the Roman magistrates for 192, *coss*. L. Quinctius Flamininus and Cn. Domitius Ahenobarbus, during whose year the propaganda commission to Greece, headed by T. Quinctius Flamininus, was operating.[4] Philopoemen was followed by Diophanes (192/1), dated by the consul M'. Acilius Glabrio and the continued presence of Flamininus in Greece.[5]

The identification of the *strategos* of 191/0 is disputed. Before Aymard published his discussion of the Achaean *strategoi*[6] it had been commonly accepted that Philopoemen was *strategos* illegally in two successive years, 190/89 and 189/8. The evidence for this seemed to be cut and dried in the statement of Livy, referring to events of spring 188, *Philopoemeni continuatur magistratus*.[7] Aymard's attempt to argue Philopoemen into a legal succession of *strategiai*, 191/0 followed by 189/8, met little favour; but he reaffirmed his belief in the correctness of his earlier conclusions, without adding any further discussion, in *Les Premiers Rapports*.[8] There matters have rested. Aymard's presentation of his arguments is inadequate. He does not deal with the Livy passage, which is the crux of the whole problem, until after presenting his other arguments—none of which is in itself decisive—and then only in a perfunctory manner. This has inevitably led to the rejection of his theory. But, despite some faults in argument and presentation, his date for this sixth[9] *strategia* of Philopoemen deserves serious consideration.

---

[1] Liv. xxxi. 22. 4; 25. 3. Cf. Ditt. *Syll*. 600; cf. below, p. 253.

[2] Liv. xxxii. 19. 2; 20. 3; 21. 1 (Aristaenus); 39. 7 (Nicostratus).

[3] Liv. xxxiv. 24. 1; 25. 3; 30. 7.

[4] Liv. xxxv. 25. 7; 26. 3 f.; for Roman magistrates, see Broughton, *MRR* i, *ad* 192.

[5] Liv. xxxvi. 31; 32. 1–2.

[6] *REA* 1928, 1 ff.

[7] Liv. xxxviii. 33. 1.

[8] p. 365, n. 26 (cites criticism of earlier work, to which add: Hoffmann, *RE* xx. 1. 87, 'Philopoimen').

[9] By Aymard's reckoning (cf. table II), this is Philopoemen's *fifth strategia*, and is discussed as such in his article.

In discussing the Livy passage Aymard fails to dispose of it with a sufficiently decisive explanation.[1] Since the publication of his article, Holleaux has re-examined the chronology of the whole Polybian section of Livy in which this passage occurs, and has shown conclusively that Livy himself was very confused about the chronology of 189/8.[2] At one point Aymard suggests that Livy was here adding one of his own explanations for his Roman readers of Polybian material which he thought they might find confusing: Philopoemen was undoubtedly *strategos* both in autumn 189 and in spring 188; Livy's *Philopoemeni continuatur magistratus* is intended to explain this phenomenon. Aymard implies here that Livy was using *continuatur magistratus* without any reference to iteration. But the phrase is a regular technical Latin term which seems always to imply iteration. It is therefore impossible to accept that Livy is here using it in a confusing non-technical way.[3] But Aymard's basic point, that Livy's *Philopoemeni continuatur magistratus* is not Polybian in origin, is useful. Holleaux's demonstration has shown that Livy himself did not understand the exact chronological relationship between the beginning of the siege of Same, the outbreak of hostilities in the Peloponnese, the election of Philopoemen, and the visit of Fulvius to Rome to conduct the Roman elections. These two considerations bring us closer to understanding the confusion which led Livy to write *Philopoemeni continuatur magistratus*.

The phrase seems, in fact, to be another case of Livy's interpreting what he failed to understand.[4] It may be regarded as certain that he meant iteration and intended iteration to be understood by the phrase: he would not clarify for his Roman readers details of a situation which was perfectly clear to him by torturing Roman official language. He was rather trying to rationalize the results of his own misunderstanding and confused abbreviation. He may well have thought that the Achaean year began at the same time as the Roman. If so 'logic' demanded iteration as an explanation of Philopoemen's exercise of the *strategia* both in autumn 189 and in spring 188. But whatever the true explanation of its origin, the fundamental point must be emphasized, that the confusion, as in the whole of the passage in which this phrase occurs, is Livy's own. Aymard has shown conclusively that no extraordinary conditions which required illegal iteration on military grounds existed at the time of the Achaean elections.[5] Together with

[1] *REA* 1928, 19–23.

[2] *BCH* 1930, 1–41 = *Études* v. 249–94, esp. 263 ff. (cited in this form). For a summary of Holleaux's chronology, cf. ch. VIII, pp. 137 f.

[3] Aymard gives no examples of this suggested non-technical usage, and none is cited in *TLL*, s.v. 'continuare'.

[4] Cf. examples in Nissen, *Krit. Unt.*, pp. 31 f.

[5] *REA* 1928, 14 ff. (some of which requires alteration in the light of Holleaux's article).

Livy's general chronological confusion regarding the order of events in the Peloponnese which Holleaux has demonstrated, this consideration seems to allow the rejection of Livy's apparently certain evidence. As yet no positive evidence with regard to the identity of the *strategos* of 191/0 has been assembled. Aymard dismisses unreasonably, without evidence or argument, the possibility of a fourth *strategia* for Philopoemen before his second visit to Crete. An inscription from Mantinea records a dedication by some Achaean soldiers, including Cretans, in Philopoemen's fourth *strategia*. It is otherwise undated. On the available evidence, this could as easily be placed in 201/0 as in 193/2, in both of which years Philopoemen was certainly *strategos* and in both of which he led Achaean armies which included Cretans. The earlier dating is preferred here, as it will be seen that Philopoemen is unlikely to have been *strategos* in 187/6. This means that, since he was in his eighth *strategia* when he died in 183/2, he must have held an unattested *strategia* either in 204/3 or in 203/2. Thus the known *strategia* of 201/0 will have been his fourth.[1] Plutarch, after explaining Philopoemen's objection to Flamininus' and Glabrio's attempt to have the Spartan exiles restored at the *synodos* of autumn 191, writes: στρατηγῶν εἰς τοὐπιὸν αὐτὸς κατήγαγε τοὺς φυγάδας. The restoration was, in fact, after Compasion in 188. In the circumstances, στρατηγῶν εἰς τοὐπιόν— 'when *strategos* in the next year' (Aymard)—prima facie suggests that Plutarch has simply made a mistake or has misunderstood his source. Aymard's dissection of this sentence, whereby he uses στρατηγῶν εἰς τοὐπιόν to refer to a *strategia* in 191/0, while at the same time he accepts that the remainder of Plutarch's sentence must refer to 189/8, is an abuse of language which can find no acceptance.[2]

If στρατηγῶν εἰς τοὐπιόν is to be legitimately pressed for chronological information, it must be with reference to Polybius' mixture of *strategos*-years and Olympiad years which Plutarch may have telescoped in this section.[3] For the purpose of this argument, the autumn *synodos* of 191

---

[1] Ditt. *Syll.* 600 (dated by Dittenberger to 193/2): ἐπὶ στραταγοῦ τῶν Ἀχαιῶν Φιλοποίμενος τὸ τέτα[ρ]τον. Cretans at lines 26 ff. For Cretans in 200, cf. Pol. xvi. 37. 3 (Didascalondas and probably others).

[2] Plut. *Phil.* 17. 4. The meeting with Glabrio was at the autumn *synodos* of 191: Liv. xxxvi. 35. 7. For Compasion, cf. Liv. xxxviii. 33–4; cf. Aymard, *REA* 1928, 8 ff. For the purpose of the argument Aymard's translation of εἰς τοὐπιόν ('in the next year') is used. However, it seems probable that the phrase should bear a much vaguer meaning, simply 'in the future' (distance unspecified). This usage is found from Thucydides (iv. 61. 5; v. 9. 8) to Lucian (*Hist. Conscr.* 13; *VH* ii. 27), and seems better fitted to the imprecise and anecdotal character of chapters 16 and 17. The usage cannot be proved however for this instance, and it seems best to meet Aymard's arguments as they are presented. But if the looser interpretation is accepted, the arguments used in the text are unnecessary.

[3] I am grateful to Dr. A. H. McDonald for this suggestion.

must be considered to be in the *strategos*-year 191/0 (i.e. the *synodos* marks the beginning of the year). The following equivalents result:

strategos-year 191/0 = Ol. 147. 2/3;
strategos-year 190/89 = Ol. 147. 3/4;
strategos-year 189/8 = Ol. 147. 4/148. 1.

In this way it is possible to regard εἰς τοὖπιόν in Ol. 147. 3 (191/0) as referring to Ol. 147. 4 (189/8). Plutarch's accuracy in taking his evidence from Polybius is thus to some extent (but tortuously) vindicated. The system is ingenious, but argument must be brought against it on the following grounds. It seems doubtful that εἰς τοὖπιόν, even meaning 'in the next year', in such a heterogeneous section of Plutarch can be pressed to give this type of logical chronological consistency of detail. In fact, it is unlikely that Plutarch knew or cared about the dates of the events which he is allegedly defining so accurately. The phrase seems to be no more than another of Plutarch's attempts to pay lip-service to chronology, using it in the main to provide vividness through chronological relativity for the events he describes. The system implies that he has consciously or unconsciously preserved the accuracy of his Polybian original, despite the fact that he has himself grossly telescoped the events. This seems unlikely. Furthermore, it misrepresents Plutarch's method and use of sources. It is clear that he did not sit down to write with all his sources in front of him, and simply extract portions which were relevant to the scheme which he had drawn up for his work. The continuity of his narrative depended to a large extent upon Plutarch's memory of his reading of his sources to fill out the framework of the chapters which he had drawn up. Constant checking of detail, where accuracy in minutiae was unnecessary for his purpose, was not his method. In these circumstances the possibility of relying with security on εἰς τοὖπιόν for argument about the detail of chronology seems remote.[1]

In addition, and of more immediate relevance to the present purpose, this system provides no information about the *strategos* of 191/0. One piece of evidence, which is virtually ignored by Aymard, suggests that Philopoemen was nevertheless *strategos* in 191/0. Plutarch's account of the autumn *synodos* and of the part played by Philopoemen in leading the objections to Glabrio and Flamininus, gives the impression that Philopoemen was in a leading position. He wanted the exiles to be restored 'through himself and the Achaeans'. This in itself is no proof that he was *strategos* at the time of the *synodos*; but if the motivation, taken from Polybius, is correct, his statement must imply that it was generally known that Philopoemen was able, if not in the event willing,

[1] For a sympathetic description of Plutarch's method see Gomme, *Commentary on Thucydides*, i. 78.

to carry out the restoration which the Senate's representatives were beginning to insist upon. Clearly this must have been by virtue of an official position. For this reason he was leader of the opposition at the *synodos*. This suggests that, if he was not actually *strategos* at the time of the *synodos*, he must at least have been already elected : the assembly which was prepared to elect him would naturally support his opposition to Glabrio and Flamininus. The argument is not absolutely decisive for a *strategia* of Philopoemen in 191/0, for it could be argued that Plutarch's Polybian motivation is simply apologetic—in which case no conclusion can be drawn at all. Such an extreme view, however, seems unlikely to be correct, and the balance is weighted in favour of a *strategia* of Philopoemen in 191/0.

The *strategos* of 190/89 is not known. It is possible that it was Archon of Aegira. Polybius records an undated conversation between Philopoemen and the *strategos* Archon at which he himself had been present. He would have been very young in 190/89, and his age is an objection to the date for Archon's *strategia*. However, although *a priori* a later date would be preferable, Archon cannot be ruled out as *strategos* for 190/89 for this reason alone, as our knowledge of Polybius' date of birth is so imperfect.[1] The order of the fragments in the Vatican palimpsest (Vaticanus Gr. 73 : Büttner-Wobst's M) is also against this, although again this need not be decisive : the passage may not have been included in the *Histories* at the point at which the conversation occurred, or its position may have suffered alteration at the hands of the excerptor. Although no certainty is possible, it seems likely that if Archon was not *strategos* in this year, the post would be occupied by another of Philopoemen's supporters : he had remained in the forefront of Achaean politics since his return from Crete; he had himself twice been *strategos*, and Diophanes had been elected as his supporter; he was again *strategos* himself in 189/8. It seems inconceivable that this pattern should have been broken in 190/89.

After general agreement about Philopoemen's *strategia* of 189/8, the year of Compasion and the Spartan settlement, which is dated by Livy,[2] disagreement starts again. Aymard, with De Sanctis, leaves the *strategia* of 188/7 with no name, suggests Philopoemen for 187/6 and Aristaenus for 186/5. Niccolini, following Büttner-Wobst, places Aristaenus in 188/7, followed by Lycortas in 187/6; but to do this he ignores the date of the successive embassies to Achaea of Q. Caecilius Metellus (185), Ap. Claudius Pulcher (184), and Q. Marcius Philippus (183).[3] The details of these embassies recorded by Livy, though

---

[1] Pol. xxii. 19. On Polybius' date of birth, cf. Walbank, *Comm.* i. 1.
[2] Liv. xxxviii. 30–4.
[3] Cf. table II. On the Roman embassies, cf. Broughton, *MRR* i, ad locc.

dependent on the accuracy of the recording techniques of the annalists, must go back to senatorial records, and must be accepted as the most accurate chronological indication extant. Aymard's system preserves the necessary relationship between the Roman embassies and the Achaean *strategoi* who dealt with them, but it does not account adequately for the reason which caused Niccolini to ignore Livy's chronology altogether. This is the passage of Polybius in which is recorded an embassy sent to Rome by δυσαρεστήσαντές τινες τῶν ἐν τῇ Λακεδαίμονι τοῖς γεγονόσι, and he dates this μετὰ τὴν ἐν τῷ Κομπασίῳ τῶν ἀνθρώπων ἐπαναίρεσιν. After spending some time in Rome these envoys managed to extract a letter from the consul of 187, M. Aemilius Lepidus, in which he said that he disapproved of the Achaean treatment of Sparta. Philopoemen countered this embassy ὧν πρεσβευόντων, εὐθέως . . . πρεσβευτὰς καταστήσας τοὺς περὶ Νικόδημον τὸν Ἠλεῖον ἐξέπεμψεν εἰς τὴν Ῥώμην.[1] To be able to do this, it is clear that Philopoemen must have been *strategos*. On Nicodemus' return he made his report to a *synodos* when Aristaenus was *strategos*.[2] It is generally agreed that Nicodemus could not have taken two years over his urgent mission:[3] hence Aristaenus appears to have been *strategos* in 188/7. These considerations form the reason why Büttner-Wobst and Niccolini preferred to ignore Livy's dates for the Roman embassies, in order to preserve faith in Polybius. Aymard recognized that it is illegitimate to abandon Livy's chronology, and accordingly accepted the secure dates offered by Livy, with consequent difficulties over explaining Polybius' information. He then set out to resolve the dilemma raised by the date of the embassy of Nicodemus. His arguments must be examined in detail.

The main part of his proof is his attempt to show that Pol. xxii. 3 can be used to prove that the embassy of Nicodemus set out in the (hypothetical) seventh *strategia* of Philopoemen (187/6), and arrived back in Achaea after a suitable interval so that this would fit in with the *strategia* of Aristaenus in which Metellus was entertained at Argos in 185 (Pol. xxii. 7–10). It will become clear that his arguments about this passage are highly tendentious and that it is impossible to accept them. The fragment of Polybius xxii. 3 gives a perfectly clear and consistent picture of what actually happened, and although there are obvious difficulties, they cannot be resolved by dismembering Polybius' clear statement.

In order to support his case, Aymard has to argue that the Spartan ambassadors went secretly to Rome, unknown to Philopoemen, and

---

[1] Pol. xxii. 3.
[2] Pol. xxii. 7. 2 (*strategia* of Aristaenus); 5–7 (report of Nicodemus).
[3] Aymard seems to accept this too, *REA* 1928, 32–3, though his own system, as he admits, necessitates an eighteen-month absence for Nicodemus.

stayed there for several months without his even finding out that they
had gone. He argues that they must have acquired their letter from
Lepidus only a short time before he left for his province, and then have
returned to the Peloponnese and presented it to the Achaeans. When
Philopoemen was elected in autumn 187—several months after the
return of the Spartans—he sent Nicodemus. Polybius describes the
same series of events much more comprehensibly: Philopoemen sent
Nicodemus ὧν πρεσβευόντων εὐθέως. Later he describes the time of the
embassy of Nicodemus as ἔτι Φιλοποίμενος στρατηγοῦντος (xxii. 7. 1),
showing clearly that it left *late* in the *strategia* of Philopoemen, not
early, as Aymard's argument for 187/6 requires. This last phrase
Aymard does not discuss; the first he virtually ignores. He claims to
be interpreting the phrase, whereas he is in fact making nonsense of
Polybius' language. According to him ὧν πρεσβευόντων εὐθέως (ob-
serve the present tense) must mean 'some months after the Spartan
envoys had completed their embassy and brought back a letter from
Lepidus'. This he claims is 'nullement en contradiction avec les textes'.[1]

Aymard also provides various supporting arguments for his central
thesis, and they must also be examined: 'Si . . . tous les événements
racontés par Polybe dans les fragments 22. 3 et 4, montrent Philopoemen exerçant sa sixième, et non sa septième stratégie [by his reckoning
this would be 187/6: cf. table II], s'ils doivent par conséquent se
placer avant l'automne 188, Polybe n'en parlerait très probablement
pas dans la 148ᵉ olympiade, comme il le fait.'[2] The reason for this
argument is that Polybius tends to protract his Olympiad years in such
a way that they coincide with the Achaean *strategos*-year. In this case
the excerptor's introduction to the previous fragment in the *Excerpta
de Legationibus Gentium ad Romanos* dates it to the 148th Olympiad.[3] If
the order of the fragments is to be preserved, Aymard argues, xxii. 3
must also have been dated to the 148th Olympiad by Polybius. Therefore the Spartan embassy was sent to Rome after the end of Philopoemen's *strategia*.

Another factor in dating the fragments of Polybius, which may
be used to supplement and emend the order of the fragments in the
Constantinian collections—which must have been liable to accidental
alteration—is the internal evidence provided by each individual fragment. This was not subject to displacement by the excerptors; and
where such internal evidence exists it is a much sounder basis for
calculation than the order of the fragments in the excerpts, since it
certainly goes back to Polybius himself. In this case Polybius' own
words specify that the Spartan embassy was dispatched μετὰ τὴν ἐν τῷ

---

[1] Pol. xxii. 7. 1; Aymard, *REA* 1928, 30–4.   [2] *REA* 1928, 35.
[3] Pol. xxii. 1. 1.

Κομπασίῳ τῶν ἀνθρώπων ἐπαναίρεσιν, and ὧν πρεσβευόντων εὐθέως (not πρεσβευσάντων, which Aymard's interpretation would require) dates the action of Philopoemen in dispatching Nicodemus. Clearly the whole point in Polybius' dating the Spartan embassy by referring to Compasion is that it was closely subsequent to it. As the massacre at Compasion took place in June 188 at the latest, and was quickly followed by the ratification of Philopoemen's settlement by the *syncletos* at Tegea, this discontent could easily have come to a head by August, and have caused the Spartan embassy to be sent to Rome. There is no need with Aymard to assume that every detail of the settlement had to be completely put into operation before discontent could take this physical form.

The internal evidence of xxii. 3 decisively confirms that the actions recorded in it took place in the same *strategos*-year as the Compasion massacre, and therefore (by Aymard's system of reckoning) in the sixth, rather than in the seventh *strategia* of Philopoemen. There remains, however, the difficulty of the order of the fragments. The principle that certain internal evidence should take precedence over the Constantinian order of the fragments in case of conflict will be readily agreed. In this case there is more reason than usual for rejecting Aymard's reliance on the apparent evidence from xxii. 1. For xxii. 1 and xxii. 2 are simply a table of contents for book xxii, which contains the bulk of the 148th Olympiad. In this table, the events actually detailed in the crucial xxii. 3 are not even summarized; and although Aymard tries to make light of this, it could clearly only be if they were certainly attributed to Ol. 148 by the excerptors in the fragment of introduction xxii. 1, that we could be sure that this was so, and therefore be prepared to seek an alternative explanation of the obvious date of events mentioned in xxii. 3. It is clear that the attribution of events actually mentioned in xxii. 1-2 to Ol. 148—which there is no reason to dispute in itself—does not affect in any way the dating of events recorded in xxii. 3, which is an independently collected fragment, containing events not mentioned in xxii. 1-2, and offering sufficient internal chronological evidence to refute Aymard's objection.

Aymard's second objection has already been dealt with: that all the terms of the settlement would have to be fulfilled before the Spartans thought it worth while appealing to Rome. He says—without showing why—that the embassy could not have arrived in Rome before November.[1] It has already been suggested that as early as August matters at Sparta would be quite clear enough in outline to justify an embassy from the humiliated party, and Aymard raises no issue which would cast doubt on this.

[1] *REA* 1928, 36–7.

His third objection to the reasonable interpretation of xxii. 3 is that 'très probablement, Philopoimen n'envoie Nikodémos à Rome qu'après avoir connu la lettre de Lepidus'.[1] In this objection he simply ignores the present tense of Polybius' ὧν πρεσβευόντων εὐθέως: 'On pense en effet qu'il constitue cette ambassade dès qu'il apprend le départ des Lacédaimoniens. C'est supposer que ce départ n'est pas tenu secret; mais rien ne le prouve.' The reason why we conclude that Philopoemen sent his embassy when he heard of the Spartans' is because Polybius says he did, and not as a result of any a priori reasoning such as Aymard tries to use to discredit Polybius' statement. There is no need to follow him further through the intricacies of his fundamentally faulty argument, or to show disagreements at each stage: once the keystone is removed, the whole edifice falls.

After disposing in this way of Aymard's attempt to postdate the embassy of Nicodemus, we are reduced to the original dilemma which made Aymard set out on his precarious course, of fitting together the return of Nicodemus in the strategia of Aristaenus and the reception of Q. Caecilius Metellus by the Achaeans, also in the strategia of Aristaenus. The embassy of Metellus is dated by Livy to 185, making Aristaenus certainly strategos in 186/5. Aymard's arguments for a strategia of Philopoemen in 187/6 depend on his dating the embassy of Nicodemus to that year; since this is not possible, the identity of the strategos must remain in doubt. The dilemma arises from the admitted impossibility of allowing more than two years for the embassy of Nicodemus, on which all writers are agreed.

It seems that the resolution of the difficulty must lie in an examination of the fragment of Polybius in which the return of the embassy of Nicodemus is reported, as well as the return of Lycortas from Egypt, who had also been sent by Philopoemen the previous year. Two meetings are recorded in the fragment: the first a synodos when Aristaenus was strategos, the meeting which heard the reports of the embassies of Nicodemus and Lycortas, and received those from Eumenes and Seleucus IV. The second is the meeting of the magistrates (ἀρχαί) at Argos τῆς πανηγύρεως ἀκμαζούσης to receive Metellus, also summoned by the strategos Aristaenus. This meeting is dated by Polybius quite vaguely as μετὰ δὲ ταῦτα.[2] All previous writers have assumed, as the apparently homogeneous character of the fragment suggests, that both of these meetings were in the same year, and that there is therefore conflict between Livy's date for the mission of Metellus and the return of the Achaean embassies from Rome and Egypt. Yet the difficulty is resolvable if the possibility of a break is allowed in what prima facie appears to be the middle of the fragment.

[1] REA 1928, 37–40.   [2] Pol. xxii. 7–9 (synodos); 10 (magistrates).

If one may suggest that a copyist has accidentally conflated accounts taken from two separate fragments, the suggested break would occur between xxii. 9. 14 and xxii. 10. 1 (in the text of Büttner-Wobst), the point at which the account of the first meeting ends and that of the second begins. As the text stands, a difficulty exists in xxii. 10. 1, which begins μετὰ δὲ ταῦτα, τῆς πανηγύρεως ἀκμαζούσης . . . No prior mention of what this πανήγυρις was occurs in Polybius' text as it stands: it is left to be concluded from the fact that the ἀρχαί were summoned to Argos and that 185 was a Nemea year, that it is the Nemea which is in question. Now the Nemea was held in the early part of July:[1] it will be shown below that the *synodos* at which the embassies reported must (if in 187, as all other considerations suggest) have been around September. Polybius' τῆς πανηγύρεως ἀκμαζούσης cannot therefore refer back to a previous mention, in an intervening lost portion of the text, of the Nemea of 187, as the meeting described in xxii. 9. 14 ends after the Nemea of 187. It must accordingly refer to the Nemea of 185 (the next celebration) and this fits satisfactorily with Livy's date for the embassy of Metellus. Aristaenus was therefore *strategos* in 186/5. This fact, at least, must be accepted as established, and Aymard was right to emphasize it.

The dispute comes over the first meeting. Aymard simply assumes that it was earlier in 185, and his arguments, as we have seen, become very involved in his attempt to prove this. But if we accept the postulated contamination of the fragment, there is no reason why the *synodos* should not have been in 187—the natural date at which the Achaean embassies would be expected to return. Aymard argues against 187, since he thinks that this involves pre-dating the embassy of Metellus, and most of his arguments derive from this assumption. But one further objection which he raises against 187 might be raised against it still, despite the recognition that Metellus' embassy probably need not be in the same year as the *synodos*. This objection concerns the presence of ambassadors from Seleucus IV at the *synodos* in order to renew the existing alliance.[2] Antiochus III did not die until 3 or 4 June 187: therefore Seleucus could not send out ambassadors until this date. This precision for the date of Antiochus' death, which creates a *terminus post quem* for Seleucus' dispatch of the envoys, depends on evidence which was not available when Aymard was writing.[3] Nevertheless, he would have found it sufficiently conclusive for his

---

[1] 18 Panemos = early July, cf. Boethius, *Der argivische Kalender*, p. 51.

[2] *REA* 1928, 41–2.

[3] New Babylonian evidence published by Sachs and Wiseman, *Iraq* 1954, 202 ff., who deduce a date of 3 or 4 July 187. However Aymard, *REA* 1955, 108, has shown conclusively from the same evidence that this is one month late, and that the true date is 3 or 4 June 187.

purpose, since he thought the *synodos* must be earlier in the year than the Nemea (July), which, it is here suggested, was actually nearly two years later. Without this objection, the *synodos* can easily have been in the late summer of 187. If the embassy to Achaea was sent out quickly, it could without difficulty be in Achaea by September, in sufficient time to be received by the *strategos* Aristaenus before the end of his year. Thus the appearance of Seleucus' ambassadors at the *synodos* need be no objection to a *strategia* of Aristaenus in 188/7 as well as in 186/5.[1]

Reasonably secure dates can now be given to the events recorded in these fragments of Polybius, which Aymard has called into question. xxii. 3 can refer, as seems obvious, to 188; xxii. 7–9 deals with the *synodos* of late summer 187, in the third *strategia* of Aristaenus (188/7); xxii. 10, if the suggested division of the fragment xxii. 7–10 is accepted, can refer, in agreement with Livy xxxix. 24. 13, to 185, accordingly to the fourth *strategia* of Aristaenus (186/5). The apparent conflict between Livy and Polybius can thus be resolved, and in the process another *strategia* for Aristaenus has been found.

With Aristaenus fixed with reasonable security in 188/7 and in 186/5, the *strategos* of 187/6 must be considered. Aymard, as a result of his scheme for the dates of the two meetings and his consequent post-dating the embassy of Nicodemus, fills in the gap with the seventh *strategia* of Philopoemen. The evidence for this disappears with the collapse of his system for the *strategiai* of Aristaenus. Büttner-Wobst and Niccolini, who do not attempt to reconcile the evidence of Polybius and Livy, are of no help in completing the list at 187/6. In fact, there is no evidence pointing to the name of the *strategos* for this year, and it is accordingly impossible to fix it. The argument in favour

---

[1] Some doubt is possible as to the likelihood of such a rapid announcement in Greece of the accession of Seleucus IV, but in fact two considerations strongly suggest that it would be in the interest of the king to have the announcement made as rapidly as possible. (i) Seleucus was bound to be reminded at his accession of the situation at the beginning of the reign of Antiochus III, when Antiochus was faced with the potential opposition of Achaeus (Pol. iv. 48. 10). Seleucus cannot have wanted to encourage in his own case a repetition of Antiochus' initial insecurity, and would broadcast the news of his accession as soon as possible. (ii) Achaea would be particularly likely to be high on the list for the dispatch of envoys by a new Seleucid, as a result of the friendly relations Achaea was reputed to have with Rome (cf. Liv. xxxviii. 32. 9), and the importance for the Seleucids after Magnesia of maintaining good relations with the friends of Rome. It is fairly clear therefore that a general announcement of Seleucus' accession could be expected very soon after the death of Antiochus, and that, as a result, the envoys from Seleucus to Achaea to renew the treaty could be in Achaea before the end of Aristaenus' *strategos*-year, 188/7. The same considerations argue against this *synodos*' having been in 185, since this would mean that Seleucus would have been king for nearly two years before his friendly relations with Achaea were formally established.

of Philopoemen is that he was in his eighth *strategia* when he died,[1] and we have so far only accounted with certainty for six others. In fact, it is quite possible—indeed, likely—that he had held another unknown *strategia* before his second visit to Crete, a possibility which has already been considered.[2] On the other hand, as Aymard prefers, he may have been re-elected in 187. Heavily against this is the gross incompetence which he had been shown to have exercised over the renewal of the treaty with Ptolemy. This, as has been shown, was in the late summer 187, therefore only a short time before the elections. It was a major triumph for Aristaenus, and it makes it extremely doubtful whether Philopoemen would have been elected so soon after this demonstration of his incompetence.

Another possibility for 187/6 is Archon. The evidence for this is the same as that used to suggest the possibility that he might have been *strategos* in 190/89.[3] The date Büttner-Wobst and Niccolini fix for Archon is 185/4; Aymard prefers 184/3, as he rightly has Lycortas in 185/4 at the time of the embassy of Ap. Claudius Pulcher. Aymard's date for Archon depends on the position in Polybius' text of the fragment from the Vatican palimpsest which Büttner-Wobst arranges as xxii. 19. In the case of this fragment, there is no precise internal evidence regarding the date of the conversation between the *strategos* Archon and Philopoemen which it records. The previous fragment from this manuscript is specifically attributed to book xxii, but this is the only indication: it places the fragment, but it does not necessarily date the conversation. It is therefore possible that Archon was *strategos* in 187/6. There is not, to the same extent, the objection which was raised against 190/89 about the age of Polybius. But in neither case is it possible to be sure. In the circumstances, it is perhaps best to leave 187/6 without a name, while acknowledging the possibilities.

For 186/5 Aristaenus is secure. 185/4 is equally securely fixed for Lycortas by the embassy of Ap. Claudius Pulcher, who was appointed on the return of Metellus, in spring 184.[4] Since it has already been established (Appendix 2 A (i) above) that Philopoemen met his death in 182 in his eighth *strategia*, he must have been *strategos* for 183/2. This again leaves a gap unfilled, 184/3. Aymard argues from the order of the fragments in the Vatican palimpsest that Archon was *strategos* in 184/3. But we have seen that Archon's *strategia* cannot be fixed exactly by this method. 184/3 is clearly a possibility for Archon, but only in the same way as 187/6 is a possibility. The *a priori* argument from Polybius' age which was used against 190/89 cannot be applied

---

[1] Plut. *Phil.* 18. 1; Paus. viii. 51. 5.   [2] Cf. above, p. 253.
[3] Pol. xxii. 19.   [4] Liv. xxxix. 33. 3–5.

at all against 184/3, but this is no positive argument. However, we can conclude with some likelihood that the *strategos* of 184/3, if not Archon, must have been some other supporter of Philopoemen, who thus maintained unbroken the succession of Philopoemenist *strategoi*.

After Philopoemen's death Lycortas, with the intermediacy of Philopoemen's predecessor, was elected to the vacant office for the remainder of the year.[1] The *strategos* for 182/1 is again extremely uncertain. Büttner-Wobst, Niccolini, and Aymard all suggest that it was Lycortas; and De Sanctis accepts this with an expression of doubt. Reasons are not very compelling. As Aymard points out, it is not possible to show that the *syncletos* at Sicyon, at which the re-incorporation of Sparta within the League was discussed, was after the beginning of the *strategos*-year 182/1. His own argument, which stems from the proposed embassy of Lycortas, Polybius, and Aratus to Ptolemy Epiphanes (which never actually set out, as Ptolemy died in the meanwhile), is suggested by the order of the fragments of Polybius and cannot be regarded as conclusive.[2] His *a priori* rejection of a possible ratification of the Achaean treaty with Ptolemy during Lycortas' *strategia* of 185/4, which he bolsters up with his faulty dating of the Megalopolis *synodos* of 187, equally cannot serve as proof. There is no reason why the ratification should not have occurred in 185/4.[3] This admission destroys Aymard's arguments for a more certain *strategia* of Lycortas in 182/1, but it does not affect the *a priori* likelihood of this. Lycortas was now head of Philopoemen's party and his stop-gap *strategia* in 182 was conspicuously successful. It is easy to conceive the possibility of his being re-elected in the autumn—there was probably no room for the application of the non-iteration rule here, as the stop-gap *strategia* was irregular (though the application of the rule to this case is actually unknown). The Achaeans' unwillingness to act on the letter supplied by the Senate to the Spartan exiles, and their eagerness to shelve the matter as soon as Bippus made his report also suggest Philopoemenist control, but add nothing to make Lycortas more certainly *strategos*.

The *strategos* of 181/0 was Hyperbatus. During his *strategia* the abortive embassy to Ptolemy Epiphanes was planned, and a meeting was held at which the Spartan question was discussed.[4] The order of the fragments—in this case, the only chronological indication—suggests that the mission to Ptolemy was planned and frustrated before the meeting which discussed the exiles and which sent the embassy of Callicrates, Lydiadas, and Aratus to Rome. Since Aratus was a member

1 Plut. *Phil.* 21. 1; cf. Larsen, *Rep. Gov.*, p. 178.
2 Pol. xxiv. 6 (Egyptian embassy); Aymard, *REA* 1928, 53 ff.
3 Argued above, chapter IX, pp. 164–5; cf. De Sanctis, *Storia* iv. 1. 246, n. 20.
4 Pol. xxiv. 6 (Egyptian embassy); 8. 1–8 (meeting).

both of the abortive mission to Epiphanes and of the mission to Rome, the embassies cannot have been contemplated at the same time. Since the order of the fragments suggests that the mission to Rome was second, the date of the abandonment of the Egyptian mission must be defined as clearly as possible. Since the news that Epiphanes had died prevented the mission from setting out, it cannot have been planned long before his death. The last known document from the reign of Epiphanes is dated 16 Pharmouthi year 25 = 20 May 180.[1] The Achaean embassy cannot therefore have been abandoned before this date, and was in fact probably somewhat later.

Given this date for the abandonment of the Egyptian mission, the meeting at which the Spartan exiles were discussed must be placed after this. The date allows the possibility that the matter was perhaps raised by the return of another (otherwise unknown) letter from the Senate brought by the Spartan exiles, rather than raised spontaneously by Hyperbatus, as Aymard suggests. If Aymard were correct, the discussion might be expected to have taken place as soon as Hyperbatus gained office, in autumn 181, but the date of the Egyptian mission shows clearly that this was not so. There was plenty of time before the date of the *synodos* (after 20 May) for a Spartan embassy to have returned from Rome with a more forthright letter.[2] The Achaean embassy would only then have been sent, and it is unlikely that they would be received by the Senate before the winter 180/79, as they could scarcely at the earliest have arrived before the autumn. This means that Callicrates could not have been elected *strategos* in autumn 180, as he was then engaged in this mission to Rome. He cannot therefore have directly succeeded Hyperbatus, as Aymard, De Sanctis, and Niccolini agree he did, and have been *strategos* in 180/79. The return of the embassy, if received by the Senate at the usual time, would be in spring 179. As Polybius is at pains to point out that Callicrates used the prestige and influence which he had gained on the embassy to secure the *strategia* for the next year,[3] he must have been

---

[1] Skeat, *Reigns of the Ptolemies*, p. 32; but cf. Samuel, *Ptolemaic Chronology*, p. 139: 'The ostrakon is from Hermonthis, and since this is quite a distance up river, it is entirely possible that Epiphanes was dead before 20 May 180. To be safe, we should allow three months for the news of his death to reach Hermonthis, and that would mean we might say that Epiphanes was alive on 20 February 180, but possibly also he was still alive when the ostrakon was written. At any rate, it is hardly likely that he was dead before 20 February 180, and so it is between that date and 6 October 180, the end of the 25th year, that we place his death.'

[2] Cf. Aymard, *REA* 1928, 58 ff.; Larsen, *Rep. Gov.*, pp. 180–1, considers this meeting a *syncletos*: 'Since there seems to have been no *synodos* in the autumn after the elections, the meeting must have been a *syncletos*.' With the necessary dating of this meeting to summer 180, it is no longer necessary to consider it a *syncletos*.

[3] Pol. xxiv. 10. 14–15.

strategos in 179/8. This leaves a gap for 180/79 which it is not possible to fill. It is just possible that the mission to Rome had been quickly accomplished in the summer, and that Callicrates was elected for 180/79; but this involves leaving little time between each stage of the course of known events during the year, and making the Senate meet in high summer to receive the Achaean embassy—which by this time must have been regarded as an annual occurrence and of little importance—and allowing little or no time for news of Callicrates' success in Rome to become sufficiently widespread in Achaea to influence the elections. It seems altogether more likely that the embassy was received at the usual time under the new consuls of 179.

APPENDIX 2 C

EARLY ACHAEAN CHRONOLOGY

POLYBIUS describes the re-formation and early development of the Achaean League in book ii.[1] As with other series of events in books i and ii, he gives synchronisms for the dates of the beginning and end of the series, but denotes the intermediate dates only by numerical references from one of the terminal points. There has accordingly been some divergence of opinion among scholars as to whether Polybius counted inclusively or exclusively, both methods having been argued to provide a satisfactory account of the series. The most recent exponents of a theory of exclusive counting are P. Pédech and R. Werner.[2] I have shown elsewhere in detail that their theories are untenable, and in the course of that examination provided evidence for Polybius' inclination to use inclusive counting when his source material allowed him to do it himself.[3] The clearest demonstration of this inclination is the opening sentence of book iii, where he writes: 'In my first book, the third from this counting backwards . . .'[4] Here Polybius' method cannot be doubted; the solidity of the *termini* is indisputably established; and there is no reason to believe that Polybius would have counted otherwise in chronological matters. Other evidence which supports this view is assembled in the article cited below, and leaves no doubt that Pédech's and Werner's attempts to distinguish between cardinal and ordinal numbers on the basis of exclusive counting are untenable. Walbank, writing of the series in which Polybius deals with the Gallic Wars, seems certainly right on the issue of cardinal and ordinal numbers when he says that Polybius made no distinction between them.[5]

Inclusive counting is therefore attested as the type of counting which Polybius used. It is accordingly the method which provides the most satisfactory explanation of the Achaean series. Polybius was inevitably limited for information in books i and ii by what his sources could provide, whether or not this was accurate. His chronology has inevitably been affected by this condition, as have other aspects of his work. For his accounts of the Gallic Wars and for the first Punic War

---

[1] Pol. ii. 41 ff.
[2] Pédech, *CRAI* 1955, 367 ff.; *La Méthode historique*, pp. 488 ff.; Werner, *Der Beginn der römischen Republik*, pp. 96–7.
[3] In *JRS* 1967, 96 ff.   [4] Pol. iii. 1. 1.   [5] *Comm.* i. 186.

Polybius was able to exert very little control over the factual material of his sources (apart from some rare rationalizing attempts), and none at all over their chronology.[1] The situation was different in the case of the Achaean League, for an accurate list of *strategoi* from the re-foundation of the League was certainly preserved and has clearly been used by Polybius. For his account of Achaean political history, of course, he was compelled to rely extensively on Aratus' *Memoirs*. But Aratus did not become an active participant in the League until 250/49, and since his *Memoirs* were little more than a personal apologia, it is unlikely that they dealt in detail with events which occurred before his political career began. The fact that these years are not mentioned at all in Plutarch's *Aratus* and the lack of political detail in Polybius' account combine to support the view that Aratus regarded a treatment of the early years of the reconstituted League as irrelevant to his purpose. It therefore seems entirely reasonable to work on the assumption that Polybius made his own examination of the Achaean *strategos*-list and made his own calculations from it in terms of *strategos*-years.[2]

It will be most convenient to examine the series in reverse order, as the precise date of the commencement needs to be argued. Polybius provides a suitable terminal point for this examination by giving a synchronism with the battle of the Aegates Islands in the first Punic War. Eutropius dates this battle *vi Idus Martias*[3] = 10 March 241—a date which may actually have been earlier in terms of the solar year, since the Roman calendar is usually considered to have been about one month ahead of the solar year at this time.[4] But whenever this battle actually occurred in terms of the solar year, if Polybius took his date from a Roman calendar, he would find it recorded as March. Since March is before the beginning of the Achaean *strategos*-year, which at this time began in May, at the rising of the Pleiades,[5] the year of the battle must have been correlated with the Achaean *strategos*-year 242/1. On the other hand, if Polybius took his date from a Greek source, and found it recorded in a Greek form—in Olympiads, or in Philinus' almost co-terminous 'years of the war'[6]—March (or earlier) 241 came in Ol. year 134. 3 = 242/1. Since at least nine months of the Achaean *strategos*-year 242/1 coincide with Ol. year 242/1, it seems incredible that they would not have been correlated

---

[1] Cf. Errington, *JRS* 1967, 96 ff.   [2] Cf. Walbank, *Comm.* i. 233.

[3] Eutrop. ii. 27. 2.

[4] Cf. Holzapfel, *Römische Chronologie*, pp. 291–2, on the basis of Pol. i. 40-1 (40. 2: ἀκμαζούσης τῆς συγκομιδῆς). Cf. Varro, *RR* i. 32; Plin. *HN* xviii. 264 ff.

[5] Pol. v. 1. 1.

[6] On the impossibility of distinguishing Olympiad years and Philinus' years, cf. Errington, *JRS* 1967, p. 103.

by Polybius. By both counts, therefore, the Roman and the Greek, Polybius must have placed the battle, in Achaean terms, in the *strategos*-year in which it actually occurred, 242/1.

Polybius dates the capture of Corinth by Aratus (in his second *strategia*) to the year before the Aegates battle: therefore to *strategos*-year 243/2.[1] Corinth was captured in the eighth year after the liberation of Sicyon, which by inclusive reckoning was thus 250/49.[2] The liberation of Sicyon was carried out in the fourth year after an administrative change, whereby the Achaeans substituted one annual *strategos* for the previous annual administration of two *strategoi* and one *grammateus*: the change was therefore in 253/2.[3]

The next interval is made clear by Polybius' description of the administrative change: εἴκοσι μὲν οὖν ἔτη τὰ πρῶτα καὶ πέντε συνεπολιτεύσαντο μεθ' ἑαυτῶν αἱ προειρημέναι πόλεις . . .[4] Αἱ προειρημέναι πόλεις must refer to all the cities of Achaea whose union Polybius has mentioned earlier. The interval of 25 years must therefore take us back to the point at which *all* the cities previously mentioned were first (τὰ πρῶτα) united: this must therefore have been 277/6. The last accessions mentioned before this date are Bura and Cerynea, which both joined shortly after Aegium—almost certainly in the same year.[5] Aegium itself, the chief city of the original Achaean League, was not one of the first negotiators of the revival, but only joined 'in

---

[1] Pol. ii. 43. 6; cf. Walbank, *Comm.* i. 236.

[2] Pol. ii. 43. 4. Plutarch, *Aratus*, 53. 5, adds that the Sicyonians celebrated a festival on 5th Daisios honouring the anniversary of Aratus' success. This month, he says, 'the Athenians call Anthesterion', an approximate equation which gives a date of February/March 249 for the liberation. Walbank (*Comm.* i. 235; *Aratos*, p. 176) and Porter (*Plutarch's Aratus*, p. 85) make the time May by assuming the month to be the Macedonian Daisios, which Plutarch elsewhere equates with the Athenian Thargelion (*Camillus*, 19; *Alexander*, 16). But Bischoff (*RE* x. 2. 1594 and 1598, 'Kalender') and Skalet (*Ancient Sicyon*, p. 85) reasonably assume that Plutarch's equation refers to a Sicyonian month called Daisios: he is describing a Sicyonian festival and there is no reason why he should have dated it by the Macedonian calendar. Professor A. E. Samuel (in a private letter) agrees that Plutarch probably means the Sicyonian Daisios, but warns against *a priori* acceptance of Plutarch's correlation with Anthesterion, which may be correct only for his own time. However, the information from the Achaean *strategos*-year seems to confirm that February/March 249 would be the most suitable time for Aratus' exploit.

[3] Pol. ii. 43. 1–3. The first of the new-style annual *strategoi* was Margus of Cerynea (Pol. ii. 43. 2), presumably in the year immediately after the reorganization had been accepted, 252/1. This makes possible the lapse of the legal interval of a year (Plut. *Aratus*, 24. 4: a provision perhaps instituted at the same time as the single annual *strategia*) before his holding the *strategia* again in 250/49, the year of Aratus' liberation of Sicyon (Pol. ii. 43. 3; cf. chapter I, p. 2, n. 3).

[4] Pol. ii. 43. 1–2.

[5] Pol. ii. 41. 13–15. Bura joined ἑξῆς δὲ τούτοις (the Aegienses), Cerynea ἅμα δὲ τούτοις (the Burians).

about the fifth year'.[1] This information means that the first *strategos*-year of the federation must have been 281/0.

The revival of the League—obviously an important event for Polybius—is further dated by a synchronism: 'It was in the 124th Olympiad that Patrae and Dyme took the initiative by entering into a League just about the date of the deaths of Ptolemy son of Lagus, Lysimachus, Seleucus, and Ptolemy Ceraunus, which all occurred in this same Olympiad.'[2] He continues with a brief résumé of previous Achaean history before returning to the foundation: 'But, as I said above, about the 124th Olympiad they changed their minds and began to form a fresh League. This was about the time of Pyrrhus' crossing to Italy. The first cities in the federation were Dyme, Patrae, Tritaea, and Pharae.'[3] The 124th Olympiad runs from summer 284 to summer 280, into which the date calculated above for the revived federation (281/0) fits comfortably. Pyrrhus' crossing was in spring 280, and since Polybius knew the Olympiad date he will have correlated it with the Achaean official year of which nine months coincided, i.e. the first year of the revival, 281/0.[4] For convenience of reference a table of these dates is appended at this point. Dates are in Achaean *strategos*-years.

281/0	First *strategos*-year of League.
277/6	Accession of Aegium, Bura, and Cerynea.
253/2	Administrative change.
252/1	*Strategia* of Margus?
250/49	Liberation of Sicyon. *Strategia* of Margus?
243/2	Liberation of Corinth.
242/1	Battle of Aegates Islands.

[1] Pol. ii. 41. 13: μάλιστά πως ἔτει πέμπτῳ.
[2] Pol. ii. 41. 1–2.   [3] Pol. ii. 41. 11–12.
[4] Lévêque, *Pyrrhos*, pp. 286–8; Walbank, *Comm.* i. 49 f. (Pyrrhus' crossing). Walbank, *Comm.* i. 241 ff., takes 280/79 as the first *strategos*-year. Polybius continues after the last quoted phrase: διόπερ οὐδὲ στήλην ὑπάρχειν συμβαίνει τῶν πόλεων τούτων περὶ τῆς συμπολιτείας. This phrase has generally been understood to mean that no *stele* was necessary because these were the first cities (Busolt–Swoboda, *Griechische Staatskunde* ii. 1537, n. 1); or that, since Aegium was not one of the founding cities, the old federal sanctuary, the Homarion, was not yet in federal possession for setting up a *stele* (Aymard, *Mélanges Cumont*, p. 12. Cf. Walbank, *Comm.* i. 233, accepting both views). Neither explanation is satisfactory: a *stele* was clearly necessary for prestige as well as constitutional reasons from the beginning of the new League; the Homarion in the territory of Aegium can certainly not have been the only place in Achaea where a federal *stele* could be erected at a time when it was unclear whether Aegium would *ever* join the new League. Polybius, in fact, seems to be referring to his own time, when no *stele* of the early federation was extant: it is entirely comprehensible that the terms engraved on the first *stele* expressing *sympoliteia* between four cities would be considered inadequate and be replaced when the League became a much larger federation.

This explanation of the chronology of the early development of the Achaean League was first suggested by Mommsen without argument.[1] Its validity has generally been denied by successive scholars, but on no very certain grounds.[2] It would be tedious and valueless to examine every slight variation in every account: the basis for the present explanation has already been stated. One objection, however, consistently recurs and must be dealt with. The crux is the 25-year period between the union of αἱ προειρημέναι πόλεις and the institution of the sole *strategia*. It seems clear that the only natural explanation of αἱ προειρημέναι πόλεις is that it refers to all the cities which Polybius has mentioned earlier in chapter 41, including the last named: Aegium, Bura, and Cerynea. It is difficult to see how it can legitimately be understood to exclude them. This is the interpretation implicit in Mommsen's scheme and is explained above. The objection runs as follows. Strabo, in his description of the Peloponnese, says that the time which elapsed before the administrative change was 20 years.[3] Aymard explained this[4] by assuming that Strabo was calculating from the accession of Aegium, because he proceeds to mention the federal sanctuary, the Homarion, which was in the territory of Aegium. If Polybius' 25 years is calculated from the foundation, Strabo's 20 years, so Aymard argues, represents an adaptation of Polybius' figure to suit his calculation from the accession of Aegium: Polybius conveniently states that Aegium joined 'in about the fifth year'. In this way Aymard defends Strabo's accuracy.

This explanation seems to depend upon a lapse of critical method. Strabo clearly based his account on Polybius—as Aymard would agree—to which he added some information, mainly ethnographical, from an unknown source. We ought therefore to regard it as certain that Strabo relied on Polybius for the historical details, and that he did not consult the Achaean archives and make his own calculation. Strabo cannot therefore be used to 'correct' Polybius. Since Polybius' own extant text gives a clear calculation of the 25 years from the accession of Aegium, Bura, and Cerynea, it is necessary to conclude that Strabo's text, as it stands, is simply wrong. Whether the mistake is Strabo's own—from failing to appreciate Polybius' precision—or a copyist's, will never be known; but it seems clear that five years have been lost in the course of the transmission.

Another possible objection to the present explanation is shown by

---

[1] *Römische Forschungen* ii (Berlin, 1879), 360.

[2] Niese, *Hermes* 1900, 53 ff.; Leuze, *Die römische Jahrzählung*, p. 137, n. 168; Niccolini, *La Conf. Ach.*, pp. 267 ff.; Beloch, *GG* iv. 2. 226–7; Walbank, *Aratos*, p. 203; *Comm.* i. 229 ff.; Pédech, *CRAI* 1955, 367 ff.; *La Méthode historique*, pp. 448 ff.; Werner, *Der Beginn*, pp. 96–7.

[3] Strabo viii. 385.   [4] *Mélanges Cumont*, pp. 19–20.

Walbank's account. He makes the first year of the League 280/79 on
the assumption that Polybius would equate the *strategos*-year with the
Olympiad year in which it began: Pyrrhus' crossing was in spring
280 (Ol. 124. 4), therefore the first Achaean year must have been
280/79 (starting in May 280).[1] But the method of correlation seems
extremely doubtful. It makes it necessary to assume that Polybius
knew exactly when, in terms of the Achaean official year, Pyrrhus
crossed to Italy—an external event which can have found no record
in the Achaean archives. Unless such accurate knowledge were available to him—which seems very unlikely—it seems quite incredible
that Polybius would adopt this method of correlation, according to
which only three months of every twelve coincided. Unless the method
can be firmly established, it seems much more satisfactory to allow
Polybius' natural correlation to be with the nine months' actual
coincidence of the years in the two systems. It has already been shown
that Polybius' calculations, consistently applied, bring us to 281/0 for
the first *strategos*-year, a date which provides a perfectly satisfactory
explanation of Polybius' two attempts at precision: 'in the 124th
Olympiad' and 'at about the time of Pyrrhus' crossing to Italy'.[2]
Walbank's method of correlation seems to be inadequately established
(and *a priori* highly unlikely) to allow it to upset this conclusion.

[1] *Comm.* i. 234–5.   [2] Pol. ii. 41. 1; 41. 11.

APPENDIX 3

SOME ACHAEAN COINS

COINAGE of the Achaean League is notoriously difficult to date or even to assign to its cities of origin. These are the tasks of the professional numismatist and no attempt is made here to offer a comprehensive examination of the extant coins. One silver series, however, seems to offer evidence for the active continuation of the Arcadian League after Arcadia had been incorporated in the Achaean League. This issue has occurred regularly in every hoard. The coins are: obverse, head of Zeus (the regular obverse of both the Arcadian and Achaean Leagues); reverse, naked seated Pan with the monogram either *MEΓ* or *AP* (instead of the regular Achaean wreathed monogram).[1] The condition of these coins in two hoards probably buried in the second century has led the scholars publishing them to suggest that they must have been struck comparatively soon before they were buried, therefore certainly during the period of Achaean League dominance in Arcadia.[2] The question arises why the city or cities striking these coins were allowed to perpetuate this vestige of Arcadian separatism instead of participating fully in the federal coinage.

It seems clear that the coins with *MEΓ* represent Megalopolis, those with *AP* Arcadia—though it is possible that some of the *AP* coins also originated in Megalopolis.[3] Miss Grace, in publishing her hoard, tentatively attributes the coins to Megalopolis or Mantinea, and suggests that they were 'a manifestation of "national consciousness"'. This may, she suggests, have taken the form of a brief revival early in the second century of the Arcadian League under the leadership of one or other of the two cities to which she attributes the coins. The real objection to this—which she herself recognizes—is that there is no shred of evidence for such a movement; and general political conditions are strongly against the hypothesis. The one known case of

---

[1] On League coinage in general, see Clerk, *A catalogue of the coins of the Achaean League*; Weil, *ZN* 1882; Gardner, *BMC* Peloponnesus, Achaia; Löbbecke, *ZN* 1908; Crosby and Grace, *Numismatic Notes and Monographs* 1936; Thompson, *Hesperia* 1939; Head, *Historia Numorum*[2], p. 417.

[2] Crosby and Grace, op. cit.; Thompson, op. cit.

[3] Thompson, op. cit., 142, is firmer: 'That Megalopolis minted these issues of the seated Pan with the Zeus obverse seems beyond question. The identical type with the letters *MEΓ*, significant of the city name, is well known, and there is no reason for supposing that the League coins originated from anywhere else but the same city.'

disenchantment in Arcadia which led to a secession is the case of the small towns which Philopoemen caused to secede from Megalopolis in 193. But although these towns seceded from the Megalopolitan *koinon*, they were not lost to the Achaean League, for they were enrolled as independent states.[1] Miss Thompson, in publishing her hoard, suggests that the coins of this type were struck by Megalopolis purely as local issues intended for local circulation only, and for this reason did not come into conflict with federal coinage policy. If this were the case, we should not expect these coins to have survived to the quantity of approximately 11 per cent in these hoards of mainly federal silver. In any case, it seems unlikely that coins intended for purely local circulation would be struck in silver.

However, the basis of Miss Thompson's suggestion, that the continuance of apparently independent Arcadian coinage need not indicate a nationalistic conflict or secessionist movement among the Arcadian members of the Achaean League, may provide the way to a solution of the problem. The Arcadian League might be politically defunct by the end of the third century, as the other evidence suggests,[2] but it certainly would not be religiously defunct. In the religious sense, it might be possible to speak of a 'national consciousness'—without any of the political overtones which the phrase seems to imply; for there is no evidence of mass dissatisfaction among the Arcadian cities at their membership of the Achaean League.

Continuance of the Arcadian League on a religious basis after 234—the date of Megalopolis' entry into the Achaean League and therefore critical for our purpose—is suggested by two inscriptions in addition to the coins. The first,[3] from Magnesia on Maeander, records a decree, probably of Megalopolis, in favour of recognizing *asylia* for the cult of Artemis Leucophryene. It concludes ἀκολούθως δὲ ἔδοξεν ψηφίσασθαι καὶ τοῖς ἄλλοις Ἀρκάσιν, followed by a list of eighteen cities, which include the non-Arcadian cities of Pellene, Tritaea, and Cerynea. A reasonable explanation of the presence of these cities in the list is that the Magnesian mason or official responsible for the terminology simply did not distinguish the Arcadians from the non-Arcadians: to him it was convenient to describe all relatively obscure Peloponnesians as Arcadians. The date of the inscription is not known exactly. It is one of a series of *asylia* decrees for Artemis Leucophryene at Magnesia which Dittenberger, following Kern, places in 207/6.[4]

---

[1] Plut. *Phil.* 13. 5.

[2] Cf. Tarn, *CR* 1925 (though his criterion of the use of the ethnic Ἀρκάς to indicate the continuance of the Arcadian League as a political entity must be rendered doubtful by the suggestion advanced here).

[3] Ditt. *Syll.* 559.

[4] Ditt. *Syll.* 557–62; Kern, *Die Inschriften von Magnesia*, 16–87.

For the present purpose the exact date is unimportant, as it is agreed that the inscription is certainly after 234. The inscription affords no grounds for believing that this list of Arcadians—which includes three Achaean cities—represents a secessionist movement from the Achaean League. As they are involved in a purely religious function, the natural interpretation is that they retained their 'national consciousness' for this religious purpose.

The other inscription yields the same result.[1] It is a mutilated decree recording the posthumous heroic honours to be paid to Philopoemen. Again the purpose is essentially religious, and although the relevant section is too fragmentary to provide more than a general outline of the sense, the words Ἀρκάσι ἀξίαν are clearly preserved in line 34. The context of the decree makes it abundantly clear that the emphasis is laid on the religious aspect of Arcadia, and that the heroic honours for Philopoemen recall the traditional religious and nationalistic background of Arcadia and do not express any sentiments as to its present political orientation.

J. A. Dengate, in discussing the Megalopolitan coinage in general,[2] notes among it 'so-called Arcadian League issues' (which he classifies as group I, period I), which are noticeably heavier by an average of c. 0·25 grammes than any of his other Megalopolitan series, which seem to have all been of the lower League standard. He remarks on this difference in standard;[3] yet when he fixes the dates of the coins[4] he pays little attention to it, and attributes all the coins uniformly to the period of Megalopolis' membership of the League. Yet this heavier coinage offends against Polybius' statement that the cities of the League used the same coinage[5]—even though we have to interpret this as meaning in practice the same standard. We are thus confronted with both a real difference in standard in a well-defined group of coins and an explicit statement of Polybius concerning League uniformity in coinage, weights, and measures, which implies that the cities joining the League must have changed their standard, if it was different. The most reasonable explanation is surely to connect the two phenomena by attributing the heavier coins to the period before Megalopolis entered the League (the traditional view), and interpreting the change in standard as having taken place at the time of the accession.

The demonstrable continuation of an Arcadian 'national consciousness' in religious matters offers an acceptable explanation of the *AP* and *MEΓ* coins of the League period. There was no secessionist

---

[1] Ditt. *Syll.* 624.
[2] 'The Triobols of Megalopolis', *ANSMusN* xiii, 1967, 57 ff.
[3] Ibid., p. 99.   [4] Ibid., pp. 107 ff.   [5] Pol. ii. 37. 10.

implication in their issue. There is little difficulty in envisaging a special Achaean concession to Megalopolis in 234 which allowed her to continue minting coins in something very like the old style, as long as she used the League standard: Megalopolis was an imporant acquisition for the League, quite important enough for the influential Lydiadas to be able to extract this type of concession in the early stages of her membership. If the demonstrable change in standard is correctly dated above to 234, this serves as a confirmation that the concession about coin types was given to Megalopolis as a *quid pro quo* for her adopting the League standard, and emphasizes Megalopolis' importance to the League from the beginning—an importance which is more noticeable at a later time. On this interpretation, therefore, these coins offer an illustration of the importance of Arcadia, and particularly Megalopolis, within the Achaean League, but add little to our detailed knowledge about political movements.

APPENDIX 4

ARISTAENUS

THE identification of Aristaenus' place of origin is important for identifying all the references which the sources provide. Yet it poses such problems that no more than a probable conclusion can ultimately be reached, for the evidence is conflicting. It will be most convenient first to summarize it.

(i) An inscription from Delphi of about this time records a dedication by the Achaeans of a statue to Ἀρίσταινον Τιμοκάδεος Δυμαῖον ἀρετᾶς ἕνεκεν καὶ εὐνοίας τᾶς εἰς τὸ ἔθνος καὶ τοὺς συμμάχους καὶ τοὺς ἄλλους Ἕλλανας.[1]

(ii) Plutarch calls Aristaenus a Megalopolitan.[2]

(iii) An inscription from Aptera records a proxeny decree for Ἀρίσταινος Δαμοκάδης Ἀχαιός.[3]

(iv) Polybius, in his account of the battle of Mantinea in 207, calls the Achaean hipparch Ἀρισταίνετος Δυμαῖος.[4]

If this evidence is all taken at its face value, there seem to be references to four distinct and separate men, of whom three are named Aristaenus, and all of whom are Achaeans and contemporaries. Aristaenus is a comparatively rare name: the indexes to *IG* iv and v yield only three examples: the father of an Epidaurian *proxenos* from Heraea and (probably) a father and son from Hermione, none of whom are otherwise known.[5] It would therefore seem improbable that we should know of three separate distinguished Achaean contemporaries of this name, two of whom clearly played an important political role (the Megalopolitan and the son of Timokades). Although the evidence is not strong and is ultimately inconclusive, it is worth exploring the possibilities of identifying one or more of these men as the same person.

Niccolini has already produced the basic arguments on this question, and his results have been accepted by most subsequent writers.[6]

---

[1] *FD* iii. 3, no. 122. Text and discussion also in Ditt. *ad Syll.* 702.

[2] *Phil.* 17. 3.

[3] *Inscr. Cret.* ii. III. 6F.

[4] Pol. xi. 11. 7.

[5] *IG* iv. 925, line 27; ibid. 722. The whole of *SEG* yields only one more instance: on the handle of a Cnidian amphora found at Athens (*SEG* xxi, no. 824).

[6] *SSAC* 1913, 194 ff. Cf. De Sanctis, *Storia* iv. 1. 57, n. 113; Aymard, *Premiers Rapports*, p. 68, n. 93; Holleaux, *Études* v. 353 = *CAH* viii. 168.

First, he has shown clearly enough that the occurrence of the name
Ἀρισταίνετος in the manuscripts of Polybius at xi. 11. 7 is likely to be
an error. In three of the places where Aristaenus' name occurs in
Polybius, in two passages of Plutarch, and in one of Pausanias, some
manuscripts read Ἀρισταίνετος.[1] Where such confusion is demonstrably prone to occur on a wide scale, it seems at least unwise to insist
on the correctness of the manuscripts' reading Ἀρισταίνετος at Pol.
xi. 11. 7. Clearly the possibility should be seriously considered that
this reading is another error of the manuscripts, and that we ought
to have here a reference to an Aristaenus from Dyme. If this is accepted, there is no difficulty in identifying him with the son of Timokades from Dyme of the Delphic inscription. We then have this
Aristaenus of Dyme, federal hipparch in 208/7, and honoured by the
Achaeans for his services to themselves, their allies, and the other
Greeks at some subsequent time.

The next stage of the identification procedure is more difficult. By
it we identify Aristaenus son of Timokades of Dyme with the famous
Aristaenus, whose place of origin was, according to Plutarch, Megalopolis. Polybius, in the surviving fragments—which contain a substantial amount of information about Aristaenus—nowhere mentions
Aristaenus' place of origin, unless we accept Niccolini's very reasonable
conjecture Ἀρίσταινος at Pol. xi. 11. 7. In this case, a simple reading
through the remains of Polybius would produce the natural conclusion that this Aristaenus, whose birthplace was Dyme, is the same
man as the Aristaenus who occurs regularly throughout the following
books. Yet this assumption produces a direct clash with Plutarch. If
Polybius' transmitted text at xi. 11. 7 were certainly incorrect,
Plutarch's variant for the place of origin could be easily explained
as a simple error.

It is this aspect of Niccolini's case which has recently been attacked
by J. Deininger.[2] He refuses to accept that Plutarch's variant is a
mistake, and argues: that Plutarch must have had good evidence for
calling Aristaenus a Megalopolitan, as he used Polybius in some form
as a source (Deininger prefers Polybius' *Life of Philopoemen*; but cf.
appendix 1, pp. 236–7), and Polybius must have known exactly Aristaenus' place of origin. Concerning the Delphic inscription, Deininger
argues against Niccolini that it is not really peculiar to find an inscription of this kind set up to an otherwise unknown man. Further,
Deininger allows that the mention of Aristaenetus of Dyme at Pol.
xi. 11. 7 may be a manuscript error for Aristaenus of Dyme, in which

---

[1] Pol. xviii. 1. 4; 13. 8; xxiv. 11. 4 (from the *Suda*); Plut. *Phil.* 13. 4; 17. 3; Paus.
viii. 51. 4. Cf. Niccolini, *SSAC* 1913, 196; Deininger, *Historia* 1966, 379, n. 21.

[2] *Historia* 1966, 376 f. Cf. the brief remarks, in disagreement with Deininger,
of Lehmann, *Glaubwürdigkeit*, pp. 391–2.

case he would allow Niccolini's identification of him with the son of Timokades. As far as the Aptera inscription is concerned, Deininger allows that the patronymic Δαμοκάδηος may be a corruption of Τιμοκάδεος (as Guarducci), and says that because of the rarity of the name Aristaenus, this inscription may refer to either of the known Aristaeni, but probably not to another different man.

It must be admitted that a final irrefutable proof of identification is impossible. But there seems to be, despite Deininger's objections, more claim to validity in Niccolini's arrangement of the evidence than he allows. Firstly, it is entirely possible that Plutarch has made a mistake, and it is faulty method to argue (in a case such as this, where a comparatively unimportant error of fact is concerned), that because Plutarch wrote 'Megalopolis', Polybius must also have written 'Megalopolis'. Plutarch was no slavish copyist of his sources, and a mistake of this kind—perhaps simply a slip of memory—is entirely possible. Also, since Deininger allows the possibility of a corruption in the manuscripts at Pol. xi. 11. 7, he thereby allows the possibility that Polybius is no longer silent on the place of origin of Aristaenus, but gives it explicitly as Dyme. There is then no reason whatsoever for supposing, solely on the basis of Plutarch's variant information, that there were two influential contemporaries with the same rare name Aristaenus. For when there is a direct contradiction between Plutarch and his source, Polybius is clearly to be preferred. If Deininger wished to insist so strongly on Plutarch's accuracy, he should not have allowed the possibility of a mistake in the manuscripts at Pol. xi. 11. 7.

The issue resolves itself to this. If it is allowable to read Ἀρίσταινος at Pol. xi. 11. 7, there is little difficulty in explaining the evidence: the hipparch of 208/7, the son of Timokades honoured at Delphi, and the famous Aristaenus will be the same man, since Plutarch's information cannot be preferred to that of Polybius on such a domestic Achaean matter. There can be no doubt that this information fits together well enough: the Delphic inscription can be viewed as having been raised to the man who prevented Achaea from being destroyed along with Philip by his well-timed alliance with Rome. Another factor—though based on the *argumentum ex silentio*—is that it might have been expected that if both Aristaenus and Philopoemen came from Polybius' own home city, he would have said so, particularly since he does in fact spend some effort on comparing the policies and careers of the two men.

If, on the other hand, Ἀρισταίνετος is defended as the true reading at Pol. xi. 11. 7, there is more support for Deininger's insistence on the correctness of Plutarch's information, for the direct clash with

Polybius disappears. But Deininger perhaps places less weight than he should on Niccolini's argument that it is unlikely that an Achaean (with a rare name), honoured at Delphi by the League for services of a more than usually wide extent, would not be otherwise known in the fairly full information which we have of leading Achaean politicians. Polybius' silence, too, about the origin of his distinguished fellow-citizen seems to require an explanation. Other information is even more inconclusive. The Aptera inscription adds nothing, although it is tempting to identify Aristaenus son of Damokades with Aristaenus son of Timokades: but this cannot be certain. Similarly, a recently discovered statue-base from Delphi adds nothing.[1] It records honours to Τίτον (probably Flamininus) by an Ἀρίσταιν[ος? But the stone is broken in such a way that no patronymic or place of origin survives and the length of the line is unknown.

On the basis of the evidence we have, therefore, probability in various degrees points to:

(i) reading Ἀρίσταινος for Ἀρισταίνετος for the hipparch of 208/7 at Pol. xi. 11. 7;

(ii) identifying this man with the son of Timokades from Dyme of the Delphic inscription;

(iii) rejecting Plutarch's Megalopolis as Aristaenus' place of origin, and identifying the famous politician with the son of Timokades from Dyme;

(iv) accepting the customary identification of the son of Damokades of the Aptera inscription with the son of Timokades of the Delphic;

(v) accepting that the Aristaenus on the Flamininus base from Delphi is the same man.

[1] *BCH* 1964, 607 ff. Cf. Deininger, *Historia* 1966, 511.

APPENDIX 5

EUMENES AND ACHAEA

T H E view adopted in the text,[1] that an alliance with Pergamum was first formed with Attalus in 198, and in 190 was confirmed by the Achaeans who then sent help to Eumenes, is based on that of Aymard.[2] There is, however, a difficulty: it was already seven years after the death of Attalus when Eumenes appeared to apply for a renewal of the alliance.[3] For this reason it seems preferable not to consider the request in 190 as an application for a formal renewal, which ought to have been carried out soon after the death of Attalus, but as a strictly unnecessary (but tactful) inquiry as to whether the Achaeans were prepared to stand by the terms of the alliance and send help. This would help to explain Polybius' use of ἐπικυροῦν instead of ἀνανεοῦσθαι, which puzzled Aymard. But there is a textual problem connected with the original alliance. At Liv. xxxii. 23. 1 Weissenborn–Müller print: *societatem cum Attalo ac Rhodiis praesenti decreto confirmarunt*. *Attalo* is in fact a conjecture by *editores veteres*, who often emend from context. The manuscripts, however, read: *cum Romanis ac Rhodiis (B)*, or simply *cum Rhodiis*. The reading of *B* can be defended only by assuming a temporary treaty with Rome for the duration of the war; otherwise it is contradicted by the following sentence, which deals with relations with Rome. Attalus is nowhere mentioned in the manuscripts.[4]

There is therefore no manuscript authority for an alliance with Attalus in 198; and Pol. xxi. 3b, as has been suggested, need not refer to a renewal (prima facie it does not). The later application of the alliance now becomes relevant. In 187 Eumenes sent ambassadors to Achaea who τὴν συμμαχίαν τὴν πατρικὴν ἀνενεώσαντο.[5] Two points here tend to support the present interpretation of Pol. xxi. 3b. First, the use of πατρική to describe the alliance. It could be argued that the word is simply used emotively to describe an alliance which was, in fact, only formed as recently as 190; but it is far simpler to allow the word its full meaning, and assume an alliance with Attalus. Secondly, ten years had already passed since the death of Attalus (and

---

[1] Chapter VIII, p. 136.
[2] *Premiers Rapports*, p. 374 and n. 9.
[3] Pol. xxi. 3b.
[4] This is more clearly indicated in McDonald's O.C.T. edition.
[5] Pol. xxii. 7. 8.

since Eumenes' renewal of the alliance, if he did this immediately), only three since 190. The evidence is by no means conclusive, but an alliance for ten years would seem more probable than one for four. On the whole, therefore, the evidence supports the conjecture of the *editores veteres* at Liv. xxxii. 23. 1, who added *Attalo* to our text.

APPENDIX 6

AN ACHAEAN LAW

In 191 Cato visited Corinth, Patrae, and Aegium as representative of the new consul Glabrio.[1] The legality of these visits in Achaean law has been questioned by Aymard, who concludes that they were, if not formally illegal, at least contrary to the spirit of an Achaean law which regulated embassies to external powers from the independent cities of the League.[2] The example usually cited to illustrate this law is that of the Megalopolitans to Macedon in 229/8.[3] But in this case it is not made clear by Polybius that the Megalopolitans were legally obliged to consult the Achaeans. The whole point of this consultation with the federal government was that Aratus had organized the willing Megalopolitans to open negotiations with Doson *on behalf of the League*. Clearly this required federal endorsement. But it is not relevant to a discussion of the legal obligations of the member states which wished to negotiate on their own behalf.

In fact, the only restriction of this kind for which there is evidence is on sending embassies to the Senate. Evidence for this comes from Pausanias, and is based on Polybius: 'Appius and his colleagues jeered at Lycortas' speech and absolved Areus and Alcibiades of any offence against the Achaeans. They allowed the Spartans to send an embassy to Rome, a procedure which was contrary to the agreement between Rome and Achaea: for this made provision for the Achaean League to send ambassadors to the Roman Senate, but forbade any constituent city of the League to send ambassadors independently.'[4] Pausanias shows that this provision had been the subject of a convention agreed between Rome and Achaea—clearly included as one of the terms of the *foedus*. It is obvious that it was as much to the advantage of the Senate as it was to that of the Achaean federal government that all Achaean matters arising on any one occasion should be presented by one set of ambassadors. That this convention was often broken or ignored, especially by the Spartans—who were in many cases encouraged by the Senate's agreeing to receive them—is not in dispute. But it is clear that the convention was essentially a matter of mutual convenience, which the Senate could set aside if it suited it,

---

[1] Plut. *Cat. Ma.* 12.
[2] Aymard, *Premiers Rapports*, p. 330; cf. *Assemblées*, p. 166, n. 3.
[3] Pol. ii. 48. 6–7.
[4] Paus. vii. 9. 4; cf. 12. 5.

and which the federal government found difficult to enforce. Such an agreement clearly was not concerned with regulating the reception of Roman missions in Achaea, whether by the federal government or by the constituent states. There is therefore no evidence which suggests that Cato's action in 191 was in any way illegal or irregular, either in contravention of an Achaean law or of the convention between Rome and Achaea.

APPENDIX 7

POLYBIUS XXI. 32c. 3-4

THIS fragment of Polybius (from Vaticanus gr. 73), which ought to be most informative for understanding the nature of and the reasons for Philopoemen's settlement of Sparta after the massacre at Compasion, is desperately corrupt in the most crucial passage. For the lacunae in lines 1-4 of page 69 of Büttner-Wobst's text, Büttner-Wobst prints on the whole satisfactory supplements. However, in line 1, the lacuna followed by an alpha was estimated by Boissevain to contain nine letter-spaces. Büttner-Wobst prints ⟨καταφονεύσαντ⟩α, which involves supplying thirteen letters. The meaning here is also less than satisfactory, for since the word to be supplied governs the (legible) τοὺς δεδορυφορηκότας, we must conclude that Polybius is thus describing the Spartan leaders who were killed at and after Compasion. These are described by Livy[1] as *auctores defectionis* who were specifically named by Philopoemen as ringleaders, and *alii illustres viri, et advocati privatis, et quia pertinere causam eorum ad rem publicam censebant.* The sense of δεδορυφορηκότες is rather to indicate soldiers than leaders;[2] and there is no indication in Livy that mercenaries were killed in the course of the settlement (though, despite Livy's silence, they may have been). A suggestion by Pédech[3] seems to avoid the difficulties of Büttner-Wobst's supplement: ⟨ἐξηλάσαντ⟩α has the required nine letters, if the space which Boissevain indicated was available is to be most satisfactorily used. It also has the clear merit of finding confirmation in Livy. For he records[4] that *omnes externi auxiliares, qui mercede apud tyrannos militassent, terra Laconica excederent. Externi auxiliares* is clearly a much more satisfactory translation of δεδορυφορηκότες than any other group indicated in Livy's account. Pédech's emendation has accordingly been accepted as the basis of the interpretation in the text.[5]

The remainder of Büttner-Wobst's suggestions are acceptable. However, he makes no attempt to fill the lacuna in line 5, which Boissevain assessed at seventeen letter-spaces. All the supplements which he records in his *apparatus* (none of which, in fact, reach Boissevain's seventeen letter-spaces) are in general agreement on the sense of the

---

[1] Liv. xxxviii. 33. 2-4.
[2] Cf. Mauersberger, *Polybios-Lexikon*, s.v. δορυφορέω.
[3] *La Méthode historique*, p. 329, n. 151.
[4] Liv. xxxviii. 34. 1.   [5] Ch. VIII, pp. 144 ff.

lost words, although variations occur in detail. Clearly, however, certainty is not possible. In an attempt to illuminate the problem, Professor E. Badian was kind enough to examine the manuscript in the Vatican on my behalf, but was unable to read anything in the crucial place, even with the aid of ultra-violet rays. It is therefore necessary to continue to rely wholly on what earlier scholars read— or claimed to read: a glance at Büttner-Wobst's *apparatus* will show that there is not even total agreement on this. However, since philological scholars have at least been able to agree on the general sense, it seems legitimate to use this as the basis for political interpretation. Accordingly, the emendation of Hultsch has been accepted as the basis of the interpretation in the text.[1] This makes the passage read:

θεωρῶν δ' ὅτι πάσης βασιλείας ἐπανορθ⟨ώσεως αἴτια⟩ τὰ χρήματα ⟨γέγονεν, ἅ⟩τε φύσει νουνεχὴς ὢν καὶ στρατηγικός, περιέβ⟨λεπεν ἵνα μή ποτε |⟩ γένοιτο κομιδὴ τῶν ἔξω ⟨πορι⟩ζομένων χρημάτων.

[1] Ch. VIII, p. 147.

APPENDIX 8

THE DATE OF THE SPARTAN EMBASSY IN POLYBIUS xxi. 1

THE embassy in question is that in which some Spartans asked the Senate for the restoration of their hostages and the coastal towns, but were met with the question, why had they not restored the 'old exiles' now that Sparta was free? The usual date for this embassy is winter 191/0, where Büttner-Wobst places the fragment in his text. There are good reasons for this date. It has been shown[1] that the idea of using the restoration of exiles both to gain patronage from correcting an injustice and to harass Achaea was essentially Flamininus', and was first put into practice in summer 191 (after Thermopylae) at Messene.[2] The first hint that it was also to be applied at Sparta came at the Achaean autumn *synodos* of 191, where the proposal of Flamininus and Glabrio was thwarted by Philopoemen.[3] The relevance of this to dating the embassy of Pol. xxi. 1 is obvious: the policy of Flamininus, formulated in the course of 191, is most unlikely to have been adopted by the Senate until Flamininus had himself persuaded the Fathers of its validity. Therefore, the Senate's reply about the 'old exiles' cannot have preceded Flamininus' return to Rome, which did not occur until the late autumn or early winter 191/0.

Aymard, however, wishes to place this embassy in summer 191.[4] His chief reason is his assertion that Philopoemen would not have authorized the embassy after the Achaean autumn *synodos*, at which he had refused to capitulate to Flamininus and Glabrio on the question of the Spartan exiles. But his arguments are inadequate to change the date of the embassy. When Philopoemen's attitude to Sparta became clear in the course of the year, and more particularly when he was again elected *strategos* for 191/0, there was every reason for the Spartans, after overthrowing the pro-Achaean regime,[5] to look for support in Rome regardless of whether they received Achaean permission. There is clearly no difficulty in this. Aymard also dismisses too lightly the usual senatorial custom of receiving foreign embassies under the new consuls. Although it is true that this was not a rule incapable of relaxation, the present instance offers no exceptional circumstances

---

[1] Ch. VII, pp. 123 ff. [2] Liv. xxxvi. 31. 9.
[3] Liv. xxxvi. 35. 7; cf. ch. VII, pp. 130 f.
[4] *Premiers Rapports*, pp. 356 ff., n. 1. [5] Cf. ch. VIII, pp. 133 ff.

which would argue for a change in the customary procedure.[1] Accordingly, there seems to be no reason for altering Büttner-Wobst's perfectly satisfactory and explicable dating to winter 191/0.

[1] Examples of such exceptions are comparatively rare: Liv. xxxiv. 57. 3; xxxvii. 46. 9; Diod. xxxi. 5. 1; cf. Pol. xxx. 4; Ditt. *Syll.* 612.

APPENDIX 9

SPARTAN PARTIES, 183–178 B.C.

CLOSE attention to the chronology of the various references to Spartan political groupings during this period can make a comprehensible picture of the apparently contradictory evidence. It is convenient to take as starting-point Polybius' description of the Spartan parties at Rome in winter 184/3. Four groups were present, of which two represented factions composed of 'old exiles' who had been restored by Philopoemen after Compasion, one represented the pro-Achaean party (led by Serippus), and one the former tyrants' party, essentially anti-Achaean (led by Chaeron). The agreement which was reached with the Roman senatorial committee, and which Xenarchus, representing the Achaeans, was induced to endorse, contained two points relevant to the present discussion: it was agreed that Chaeron's group, in exile since Compasion, should be restored; and that Sparta should continue to belong to the Achaean League.[1]

By autumn 183,[2] when Flamininus unsuccessfully asked the Achaeans for a *syncletos*, the 'old exiles' were again in exile; and their hopes, along with Deinocrates', were disappointed by Flamininus' failure.[3] Although Polybius is not explicit, the exiles' hopes were clearly for their restoration. But since there had been no problem about their restoration to be discussed at Rome the previous winter, they must have been exiled in the period between the return of the embassies and the appearance of Flamininus at Naupactus in the autumn.

The next evidence is from the following winter. This year two Spartan embassies were present at Rome, one representing the exiles (originally led by Arcesilaus and Agesipolis), the other led by Serippus.[4] The exiles clearly wanted their restoration; Serippus' demand is not made clear, but it is unlikely that he had changed from his previous support of Sparta's union with Achaea. The Senate's answer to him was non-committal: βουλόμενοι μετέωρον ἐᾶσαι τὴν πόλιν, διότι πάντα πεποιήκασιν αὐτοῖς τὰ δυνατά, κατὰ δὲ τὸ παρὸν οὐ νομίζουσιν εἶναι τοῦτο τὸ πρᾶγμα πρὸς αὐτούς.[5] The Senate's reply to Serippus became known in Achaea in the late summer of 182, after the death of

---

[1] Pol. xxiii. 4; Paus. vii. 9. 5. Cf. ch. X, pp. 178 ff.
[2] On the date, see appendix 2 A (i), pp. 244 f.
[3] Pol. xxiii. 5. 18.
[4] Pol. xxiii. 6 (Arcesilaus and Agesipolis); 9. 1 (both embassies).
[5] Pol. xxiii. 9. 11. Cf. ch. X, pp. 188 f.

Philopoemen and the settlement of Messene. Lycortas called a *syncletos* at Sicyon to consider its implications: ⟨ἀν⟩εδίδου διαβούλιον ὑπὲρ τοῦ προσλαβέσθαι ⟨τὴν Σπάρτην⟩ εἰς τὴν συμπολιτείαν, φάσκων 'Ρωμαίους μὲν ἀποτρίβεσθαι τὴν πρότερον αὐτοῖς δοθεῖσαν ἐπιτροπὴν ὑπὲρ τῆς πόλεως ταύτης· ἀποκεκρίσθαι γὰρ αὐτοὺς νῦν μηθὲν εἶναι τῶν κατὰ Λακεδαίμονα πραγμάτων πρὸς αὐτούς· τοὺς δὲ κυριεύοντας τῆς Σπάρτης κατὰ τὸ παρὸν βούλεσθαι σφίσιν μετέχειν τῆς συμπολιτείας. διὸ παρεκάλει προσδέχεσθαι τὴν πόλιν.[1] This makes it clear that by late summer 182, the time of the *syncletos*, Sparta was no longer a member of the League. Yet the passage also states that the party in power at the time was in favour of reunion. Lycortas continues by describing this party as τοὺς διατετηρηκότας τὴν πρὸς τὸ ἔθνος πίστιν, and contrasts them with the 'old exiles' who had failed to show due gratitude for their original restoration (by Philopoemen after Compasion). Lycortas implies that their present exile is nothing more than they deserve.[2]

The gaps in the information which Polybius gives are considerable; yet they do not present wholly unsurmountable difficulties. The *terminus ante quem* for the expulsion of the 'old exiles' is autumn 183 (Flamininus at Naupactus); that for the Spartan secession from the League summer 182 (Achaean *syncletos* at Sicyon). The expulsion of the 'old exiles' so soon after the return of the embassies from Rome in spring 183 seems likely to have been closely associated with the restoration of Chaeron's party—the party which, in its various earlier guises, had created the original 'old exiles'. In this new expulsion, there is no reason to deny the complicity of Serippus' group, or even of the Achaean federal government. For Philopoemen had not really wanted to restore the 'old exiles' in 188; and the ingratitude of Areus and Alcibiades since then must have made him and his associates regret his earlier decision. It therefore seems possible that this expulsion in 183 was carried out by a coalition of all elements hostile to the 'old exiles'. This means that in Sparta Chaeron and Serippus must have co-operated. They were clearly united in their hostility to the 'old exiles'. Yet there was a major difference between them: Serippus' main policy for Sparta was co-operation with Achaea and participation in the League; Chaeron, whose group was formed of those exiled by Philopoemen and the Achaeans in 188, must have been fundamentally opposed to the League. At the conference in Rome he only accepted Sparta's continued participation in the League as part of a compromise which also involved his group's restoration. The coalition was therefore fundamentally unstable.

Polybius does not specify the purpose of Serippus' visit to Rome in winter 183/2, and the Senate's reply gives no more information than

---

[1] Pol. xxiii. 17. 6–9.　　　　[2] Pol. xxiii. 17. 9 ff.

that it was concerned with the status of the city—on which the Senate suspended judgement. Serippus cannot have been urging the restoration of the city to Achaea, for the secession had not yet taken place: the *Senatus Consultum* of the same winter which contains the Senate's reply to the Achaeans clearly implies this: ἀπεκρίθησαν δὲ διότι οὐδ᾽ ἂν ὁ Λακεδαιμονίων ἢ Κορινθίων ἢ ⟨τῶν⟩ Ἀργείων ἀφίστηται δῆμος, οὐ δεήσει τοὺς Ἀχαιοὺς θαυμάζειν ἐὰν μὴ πρὸς αὐτοὺς ἡγῶνται.[1] If Sparta had already seceded, it was not known at Rome; therefore Serippus cannot have been contending for its restoration to Achaea. On the other hand, the Senate's settlement of Sparta the previous winter had already been upset by the rapid expulsion of the 'old exiles'. The Spartans might easily think that the Senate would insist on negotiating the whole settlement afresh. In this case, Serippus would need to justify to the Senate the treatment of the 'old exiles' on behalf of the Spartan government as a whole. In addition, on behalf of his own group, he had to make his sectional position clear: he would attempt to obtain a *Senatus Consultum* confirming that, even in the new conditions, the Senate would ensure that Sparta remained Achaean. This was the more important to Serippus as his partners in the coalition had the opposite intention.

Serippus cannot have been responsible for the secession; and it is unlikely that Chaeron himself would be able to command sufficient support to declare Spartan secession once Serippus had returned from Rome. This rules out action in accordance with the *Senatus Consultum* which announced the Senate's lack of interest, for Serippus brought it with him.[2] If Chaeron was eager to secede the best time was while his coalition partners, who were certain to oppose the secession, were away from Sparta, while their influence could not be brought to bear, and while the winter prevented Achaean military activity. Yet, although the secession had taken place by the summer of 182, after the return of Serippus it was possible for Lycortas, in recommending the acceptance of Sparta into the League, to say that those in power at Sparta κατὰ τὸ παρόν wanted to rejoin the League, and that these were the people who had preserved faith with Achaea. In the circumstances the only possible meaning this can have is that Serippus in his turn had carried out a coup on his return, and was, κατὰ τὸ παρόν at least, in power and strong enough to be able to enforce his policy. There is no question of either of the groups of 'old exiles' having changed sides *vis-à-vis* Achaea, for they were only selectively restored after Sparta was re-united with the League.[3]

There was no further question of Spartan secession. But despite the restoration of the less offensive 'old exiles'—those who had not

[1] Pol. xxiii. 9. 13.   [2] Pol. xxiii. 17. 5.   [3] Pol. xxiii. 18. 2.

abused Achaean friendship—the problem of the die-hard loyalists of the 'old exiles' remained. In winter 182/1 Chaeron was in Rome and disputed before the Senate with envoys sent by the remaining 'old exiles', Cletis and Diactorius. It seems clear that Chaeron was acting on behalf of the Spartan government—Polybius says: Λακεδαιμόνιοι τοὺς περὶ Χαίρωνα κατέστησαν[1]—and it must be assumed that the coalition had been patched up after Serippus' coup and the reunion with Achaea had brought the unwanted restoration of part of the 'old exiles'. They must also have remained united in opposition to the activist 'old exiles'. In the circumstances, Chaeron could clearly be a useful representative for the Spartan government, with his old connections with the Senate resulting from his association with Nabis' party. Serippus clearly would not dare to leave Sparta again himself and take the risk of a repetition of the events of the previous year.

The result of the embassies of 182/1 was that the Senate sent a letter to the Achaeans, which was duly ignored.[2] Probably the next winter, 181/0, the exiles were again represented at Rome, and the Senate sent another letter to the Achaeans.[3] In 180 Chaeron had, by some means, managed to gain a dominant position in Sparta. Polybius says nothing about the political aspect of this, but mentions only the personal; but the threat was considered serious enough for Chaeron to be suppressed by federal intervention.[4] Federal interference must mean that Chaeron was thought to be planning another secession; and Hyperbatus, learning from the last period of Chaeron's dominance in 182, stepped in before the threatened secession became a fact. Achaean ambassadors were again sent to Rome—Callicrates, Lydiadas, and Aratus—during winter 180/79: the result was Callicrates' triumph, which included, in its working out, the final restoration of the remaining Spartan 'old exiles', and the ending of another phase of Spartan confusion.[5]

---

[1] Pol. xxiii. 18. 4.   [2] Pol. xxiv. 1. 5; 2. 4.

[3] The Achaeans discussed a letter from the Senate in summer 180 (Pol. xxiv. 8. 1 f. On the date cf. appendix 2 B, pp. 263–4) and it seems likely that this would only result from a request by the representatives of the Spartan exiles.

[4] Pol. xxiv. 7.

[5] Pol. xxiv. 8. 9–9. 15 (Callicrates in Rome); 10. 15 (*strategia* and restoration of the exiles).

BIBLIOGRAPHY

THIS bibliography collects works cited in the notes, except for some reference works, for which the list of abbreviations should be consulted. A few relevant works which have been used but are not actually cited in the notes are also included.

ACCAME, S., *Il dominio romano in Grecia dalla guerra acaica ad Augusto*, Roma, 1946.

—— 'Elatea e la nuova epigrafe di Stinfalo', *RFIC* NS xxvii, 1949, 217 ff.

AFRICA, T., *Phylarchus and the Spartan revolution*, Berkeley–Los Angeles, 1961.

ANDERSON, J. K., 'Philopoemen's reform of the Achaean army', *CPh* lxii, 1967, 104 ff.

AYMARD, A., 'Les stratèges de la confédération achaïenne de 202 à 172 av. J.-C.', *REA* xxx, 1928, 1 ff.

—— *Les Assemblées de la confédération achaïenne*, Bordeaux, 1938.

—— *Les Premiers Rapports de Rome et de la confédération achaïenne*, Bordeaux, 1938.

—— 'De nouveau sur la chronologie des Séleucides', *REA* lvii, 1955, 102 ff.

BADIAN, E., 'The treaty between Rome and the Achaean League', *JRS* xlii, 1952, 76 ff.

—— *Foreign clientelae (264–70 B.C.)*, Oxford, 1958.

—— 'Aetolica', *Latomus* xvii, 1958, 197 ff.

—— *Studies in Greek and Roman history*, Oxford, 1964.

—— and ERRINGTON, R. M., 'A meeting of the Achaean League (early 188 B.C.)', *Historia* xiv, 1965, 13 ff.

BALSDON, J. P. V. D., 'Rome and Macedon, 205–200 B.C.', *JRS* xliv, 1954, 30 ff.

BELOCH, K. J., *Griechische Geschichte*, edn. 2, 4 vols., Strassburg–Berlin and Leipzig, 1912–27.

BOETHIUS, C. A., 'Excavations at Mycenae', *ABSA* xxv, 1921–3, 408 ff.

—— *Der argivische Kalender*, Uppsala Universitets Årsskrift, Uppsala, 1922.

BRISCOE, J., 'Q. Marcius Philippus and *Nova Sapientia*', *JRS* liv, 1964, 66 ff.

—— 'Rome and the class struggle in the Greek states, 200–146 B.C.', *P & P* xxxvi, 1967, 3 ff.

BROUGHTON, T. R. S., *The magistrates of the Roman republic*, 2 vols. and suppl., New York, 1951–60.

BÜTTNER-WOBST, T., *Beiträge zu Polybios*, Beigabe zum Jahresbericht des Gymnasions zum heiligen Kreuz zu Dresden, Dresden, 1901.

CARDINALI, G., 'Creta e le grandi potenze ellenistiche sino alla guerra di Litto', *RSA* ix, 1904–5, 69 ff.

—— 'Creta nel tramonto dell'ellenismo', *RFIC* xxxv, 1907, 1 ff.

CARY, M., *A history of the Greek world, 323–146 B.C.*, edn. 2, London, 1951.

CASTELLANI, A. M., 'Le relazioni fra Roma e la confederazione achea da T. Quinzio Flaminino a L. Emilio Paolo', *Contributi dell'Instituto di filologia classica* (Milano, Univ. cattolica), i, 1963, 66 ff.

CHRIMES, K. M. T., *Ancient Sparta*, Manchester, 1949.

CLERK, M. J., *A catalogue of the coins of the Achaean League*, London, 1895.

COLIN, G., *Rome et la Grèce de 200 à 146 avant J.-C.*, Paris, 1905.

CROSBY, M. and GRACE, E., 'An Achaean League hoard', *Numismatic Notes and Monographs* lxxiv, 1936.

DAUX, G., 'La base de Philopœmen à Delphes', *BCH* xc, 1966, 283 ff.

DEININGER, J., 'Aristainos von Megalopolis und Aristainos von Dyme', *Historia* xv, 1966, 376 ff.

DELBRÜCK, H., *Geschichte der Kriegskunst im Rahmen der politischen Geschichte*, 4 vols., Berlin, 1900–20.

DE SANCTIS, G., *Storia dei Romani*, 4 vols., Torino, etc., 1907–64.

DUBOIS, M., *Les Ligues étolienne et achaïenne*, Paris, 1885.

ERBSE, H., 'Zur Entstehung des Polybianischen Geschichtswerkes', *RhM* xciv, 1951, 157 ff,

ERRINGTON, R. M., 'Philip V, Aratus, and the "Conspiracy of Apelles" ', *Historia* xvi, 1967, 19 ff.

—— 'The chronology of Polybius' Histories, books i and ii', *JRS* lvii, 1967, 96 ff.

—— and BADIAN, E., see BADIAN, E., and ERRINGTON, R. M.

FEYEL, M., 'T. Quinctius Flamininus, Philippe, et les Achéens', *REG* lvi, 1943, 235 ff.

FINE, J. V. A., 'The background of the Social War of 220–17 B.C.', *AJPh* lxi, 1940, 129 ff.

FLACELIÈRE, R., *Les Aitoliens à Delphes: contribution à l'histoire de la Grèce centrale au IIIᵉ siècle av. J.-C.*, Paris, 1937.

FORBES, C. A., *Neoi: A contribution to the study of Greek associations*, Middletown, Connecticut, 1933.

FREEMAN, E. A., *A history of federal government in Greece and Italy*, edn. 2, London, 1893.

GARDNER, P., *A catalogue of the Greek coins in the British Museum (Peloponnesus)*, London, 1887.

GELZER, M., *Kleine Schriften*, 3 vols., Wiesbaden, 1962–4.

GRACE, E., see CROSBY, M., and GRACE, E.

GRIFFITH, G. T., *The mercenaries of the Hellenistic world*, Cambridge, 1935.

GUARDUCCI, M., 'Intorno all'epigramma cnosio di Tharsymachos', *RFIC* xxii, 1934, 71 ff.

—— *Inscriptiones Creticae*, 4 vols., Roma, 1935–50.

—— 'Osservazioni intorno al trattato fra Hierapytna e Priansos', *Epigraphica* ii, 1940, 149 ff.

—— 'Note sul *koinon* cretese', *RFIC* xxviii, 1950, 142 ff.

HEAD, B. V., *Historia Numorum*, edn. 2, Oxford, 1911.

294 BIBLIOGRAPHY

HERZOG, M., "Κρητικὸς πόλεμος", *Klio* ii, 1902, 316 ff.

HEUSS, A., *Die völkerrechtlichen Grundlagen der römischen Außenpolitik in republi-kanischer Zeit, Klio*, Beiheft xxxi, Leipzig, 1933.

HOFFMANN, W., 'Das Todesjahr des Philopoimen', *Hermes* lxxiii, 1938, 244 ff.

HOLLEAUX, M., *Rome, la Grèce et les monarchies hellénistiques au IIIe siècle av. J.-C.* (273–205), Paris, 1921.

—— *Études d'épigraphie et d'histoire grecques*, 5 vols., Paris, 1938–57.

HOMOLLE, T., 'Le roi Nabis', *BCH* xx, 1896, 502 ff.

KLAFFENBACH, G., 'Der römisch-ätolische Bündnisvertrag vom Jahre 212 v. Chr.', *SDAW* 1954, no. 1.

KLOTZ, A., 'Die Quellen Plutarchs in der Lebensbeschreibung des Titus Quinctius Flamininus', *RhM* lxxxiv, 1935, 46 ff.

KROMAYER, J., and VEITH, G., *Antike Schlachtfelder*, 4 vols., Berlin, 1903–31.

—— —— *Heerwesen und Kriegführung der Griechen und Römer*, München, 1928.

LARSEN, J. A. O., 'Roman Greece', in T. Frank, *An economic survey of Rome*, vol. iv, Baltimore, 1933–40.

—— 'Was Greece free between 196 and 146?' *CPh* xxx, 1935, 193 ff.

—— 'The Assembly of the Aetolian League', *TAPhA* lxxxiii, 1952, 1 ff.

—— *Representative government in Greek and Roman history*, Berkeley and Los Angeles, 1955.

LEHMANN, G. A., *Untersuchungen zur historischen Glaubwürdigkeit des Polybios*, Münster, 1967.

LÖBBECKE, A., 'Ein Fund achäischer Bundesmünzen', *ZN* xxvi, 1908, 275 ff.

LORING, W., 'Some ancient routes in the Peloponnese', *JHS* xv, 1895, 25 ff.

McDONALD, A. H., and WALBANK, F. W., 'The origins of the second Mace-donian War', *JRS* xxvii, 1937, 180 ff.

McSHANE, R. B., *The foreign policy of the Attalids of Pergamum*, Urbana, 1964.

MEISCHKE, K., *Symbolae ad Eumenis II Pergamenorum Regis Historiam*, Diss. Leipzig, 1892.

MELONI, P., *Perseo e la fine della monarchia macedone*, Roma, 1953.

MITSOS, M., 'Inscription de Stymphale', *REG* lix–lx, 1946–7, 150 ff.

MOMMSEN, T., *Römische Forschungen*, 2 vols., Berlin, 1864–79.

MUNDT, J., *Nabis, König von Sparta (206–192 v. Chr.)*, Diss. Münster, 1903.

NEUMEYER, A., *Philopoemen, der Letzte der Hellenen*, Prog. Amberg, 1879.

NICCOLINI, G., 'Aristeno e Aristeneto', *SSAC* vi, 1913, 194 ff.

—— *La Confederazione Achea*, Pavia, 1914.

NIESE, B., *Geschichte der griechischen und makedonischen Staaten seit der Schlacht bei Chaeronea*, 3 vols., Gotha, 1893–1903.

NISSEN, H., *Kritische Untersuchungen über die Quellen der vierten und fünften Dekade des Livius*, Berlin, 1863.

—— 'Die Ökonomie der Geschichte des Polybios', *RhM* xxvi, 1871, 241 ff.

OOST, S. I., *Roman policy in Epirus and Acarnania in the age of the Roman conquest of Greece*, Dallas, 1954.

PASSERINI, A., 'I moti politico-sociali della Grecia e i Romani', *Athenaeum* xi, 1933, 309 ff.

—— 'La condizione della città di Elatea dopo la seconda guerra macedonica in una nuova iscrizione', *Athenaeum* xxvi, 1948, 83 ff.

PÉDECH, P., 'Polybe et l'éloge de Philopoimen', *REG* lxiv, 1951, 82 ff.

—— 'La méthode chronologique de Polybe d'après son récit des invasions gauloises', *CRAI* 1955, 367 ff.

—— 'Notes sur la biographie de Polybe', *LEC* xxix, 1961, 145 ff.

—— *La Méthode historique de Polybe*, Paris, 1963.

PORTER, W. H., *Plutarch's Life of Aratus*, Cork, 1937.

PRITCHETT, W. K., *Studies in ancient Greek topography*, Berkeley and Los Angeles, 1965.

ROEBUCK, C. A., *A history of Messenia from 369 to 146 B.C.*, Chicago, 1941.

ROLOFF, G., *Probleme aus der griechischen Kriegsgeschichte*, Berlin, 1903.

RÜHL, F., 'Der letzte Kampf der Achäer gegen Nabis', *Neue Jahrb. für Philologie und Pädagogik* cxxvii, 1883, 33 ff.

SACHS, A. J., and WISEMAN, D. J., 'A Babylonian king list of the Hellenistic period', *Iraq* xvi, 1954, 202 ff.

SAMUEL, A. E., *Ptolemaic chronology*, München, 1962.

SCHMITT, H. H., *Rom und Rhodos*, München, 1957.

SCHORN, W., *Geschichte Griechenlands von der Entstehung des ätolischen und achäischen Bundes bis auf die Zerstörung Corinths*, Bonn, 1833.

SCULLARD, H. H., *Roman politics, 220–150 B.C.*, Oxford, 1951.

SEELIGER, K., *Messenien und der achäische Bund*, Prog. Zittau, 1897.

SEGRÉ, M., "Κρητικὸς πόλεμος", *RFIC* lxi, 1933, 365 ff.

SKEAT, T. C., *The reigns of the Ptolemies*, München, 1954.

SMITH, R. E., 'The sources of Plutarch's Life of Titus Flamininus', *CQ* xxxviii, 1944, 89 ff.

STIER, H. E., *Roms Aufstieg zur Weltmacht und die griechische Welt*, Köln und Opladen, 1957.

TARN, W. W., 'The Arcadian league and Aristodemus', *CR* xxxix, 1925, 104 ff.

THOMPSON, M., 'A hoard of Greek federal silver', *Hesperia* viii, 1939, 116 ff.

TREU, M., 'Biographie und Historie bei Polybios', *Historia* iii, 1954–5, 219 ff.

VAN EFFENTERRE, H., *La Crète et le monde grec de Platon à Polybe*, Paris, 1948.

VEITH, G., see KROMAYER, J., and VEITH, G.

WALBANK, F. W., *Aratos of Sicyon*, Cambridge, 1933.

—— 'Aratos' attack on Cynaetha', *JHS* lvi, 1936, 64 ff.

—— *Philip V of Macedon*, Cambridge, 1940.

—— 'Alcaeus of Messene, Philip V, and Rome', *CQ* xxxvii, 1943, 1 ff.

—— *A historical commentary on Polybius*, vol. i, Oxford, 1957.

—— 'Three notes on Polybius XII', *Miscellanea di studi alessandrini in memoria di Augusto Rostagni* (Torino, 1963), pp. 203 ff.

—— see McDONALD, A. H., and WALBANK, F. W.

WALSH, P. G., *Livy: his historical aims and methods*, Cambridge, 1963.

WEIL, R., 'Das Münzwesen des achäischen Bundes', *ZN* ix, 1882, 199 ff.

WELLES, C. B., 'New texts from the chancery of Philip V of Macedonia and the problem of the *diagramma*', *AJA* xliii, 1938, 245 ff.

WERNER, R., *Der Beginn der römischen Republik*, München–Wien, 1963.

WILL, E., *Histoire politique du monde hellénistique*, vol. i, Nancy, 1966.

WILLETTS, R. F., *Aristocratic society in ancient Crete*, London, 1955.

WISEMAN, D. J., see SACHS, A. J., and WISEMAN, D. J.

WOOD, F. M., 'The tradition of Flamininus' selfish ambition in Polybius and later historians', *TAPhA* lxx, 1939, 93 ff.

—— 'The military and diplomatic campaign of Flamininus in 198 B.C.', *AJPh* lxii, 1941, 277 ff.

WUNDERER, C., *Polybios-Forschungen*, 3 vols., Leipzig, 1898–1901.

ZIEGLER, K., 'Plutarchstudien XVI: zu Philopoimen–Titus', *RhM* lxxxiii, 1934, 211 ff.

TABLE I

EVENTS AT SPARTA, 192–178 B.C.

Autumn 192	Sparta united with Achaean League by Philopoemen; Timolaus' group installed in power; tyrants' party not exiled.
Spring 191	Factional trouble at Sparta: tyrants' party gains supremacy and secedes from the League. Philopoemen intervenes: restores Timolaus to power and Sparta to the League; prevents Flamininus and Diophanes from helping the tyrants' party to power.
Spring onwards 191	Flamininus continues to support the tyrants' party.
Autumn 191	Achaean *synodos*: Glabrio and Flamininus begin Roman policy to restore Spartan exiles. Philopoemen refuses to allow Roman interference and does nothing himself.
Later autumn	Timolaus' group expelled from Sparta by tyrants' party.
Winter 191/0	New Spartan government (tyrants' party) asks Senate for restoration of hostages given by Nabis in 195. *S.C.* reiterates Flamininus' and Glabrio's policy about restoring the exiles, and describes the exiles from the earlier tyrants as 'old exiles' for the first time.
Spring/summer 190	Spartan hostages, except for Nabis' son Armenas, restored to Sparta. No action on the exiles.
Autumn 189	Spartan government (tyrants' party) attacks exiles —perhaps Timolaus' group—at Las; exiles appeal to Achaea. Sparta secedes from League; first stages of war; Spartans appeal to consul Fulvius at Same.
Winter 189/8	Ambiguous *S.C.* in reply to embassies from Achaea and Sparta.
Spring 188	Achaean war with Sparta: Compasion; judicial murder by Achaeans under Philopoemen of 80 of tyrants' party. Restoration of 'captive exiles'—perhaps Timolaus' group—and 'old exiles' by Philopoemen. Survivors of tyrants' party exiled; Sparta restored to League after brutal settlement.
Winter 188/7	Some discontented Spartans at Rome complain about Compasion and Philopoemen's settlement of

Sparta—probably sympathizers with the tyrants' party. Receive letter from consul Lepidus to Achaeans deploring Compasion, but not recommending any action.

July 185

Metellus complains to Achaean magistrates about Compasion: departs dissatisfied. No Achaean action.

Winter 185/4

Areus and Alcibiades ('royalist' 'old exiles') dispute before the Senate with the Achaean representative, Apollonidas, about the merits of Philopoemen's settlement after Compasion.

Spring/summer 184

Areus and Alcibiades condemned to death *in absentia* by an Achaean *synodos* for their activities at Rome.

Summer 184

Ap. Claudius Pulcher at Achaean *syncletos* at Cleitor accompanied by Areus and Alcibiades: death sentence on Areus and Alcibiades annulled; Pulcher gives general permission to the Spartans to send envoys to the Senate.

Winter 184/3

Four Spartan embassies in Rome: Serippus, Areus and Alcibiades, Lysis, Chaeron. Roman commission of Greek experts arbitrates on the conflicting demands.

Before autumn 183

Coalition of Serippus and Chaeron expels 'old exiles' from Sparta.

Winter 183/2

Serippus in Rome. In his absence Chaeron leads Spartan secession from League.

Summer 182

Serippus returns and regains control in Sparta.

About August 182

Achaean *syncletos* at Sicyon discusses Sparta: reunion negotiated.

Later 182

Selective restoration of 'old exiles' (those who had not offended the Achaeans). Spartan coalition between Serippus and Chaeron patched up.

Winter 182/1

Chaeron, on behalf of the Spartan government, and Cletis and Diactorius, on behalf of the exiles, dispute before the Senate.

Spring 181

Letter from Senate about exiles reaches Achaea: no action taken.

Winter 181/0

Envoys from remaining exiles again in Rome.

Spring 180

Chaeron's newly acquired dominance crushed by Achaean federal intervention under the *strategos* Hyperbatus. Another letter from the Senate to the Achaeans about Spartan exiles arrives in Achaea.

Winter 180/79	Callicrates, Lydiadas, and Aratus in Rome; envoys from Spartan exiles again present ther case to the Senate.
Autumn 179–autumn 178	*Strategia* of Callicrates: restoration of all remaining Spartan exiles.

TABLE II

ACHAEAN *STRATEGOI*, 211/10–179/8

	ERRINGTON	AYMARD[1]	DE SANCTIS[2]	NICCOLINI[3]	BÜTTNER-WOBST[4]	NISSEN[5]
211/10	Euryleon	..	..	Euryleon	..	See note 6
210/09	Cycliadas	..	..	Cycliadas	..	Cycliadas
209/8	Nicias	..	..	Nicias	..	Nicias
208/7	Philopoemen I	..	..	Philopoemen I	..	Philopoemen I
207/6	..	..	..	..	..	..
206/5	Philopoemen II	..	..	Philopoemen II	..	Philopoemen II
205/4	..	..	..	..	..	..
204/3	Philopoemen III?[7]	..	..	..	..	..
203/2	Philopoemen III?[7]	..	..	..	..	..
202/1	Lysippus	Lysippus	..	Lysippus	..	Lysippus
201/0	Philopoemen IV (III)[8]	Philopoemen III	Philopoemen III	Philopoemen III	..	Philopoemen III
200/199	Cycliadas II	Cycliadas	Cycliadas	Cycliadas	..	Cycliadas
199/8	Aristaenus I	Aristaenus	Aristaenus I	Aristaenus I	..	Aristaenus
198/7	Nicostratus	Nicostratus	Nicostratus	Nicostratus	..	Nicostratus
197/6	..	..	..	..	..	..
196/5	Aristaenus II	Aristaenus	Aristaenus II	Aristaenus II	..	Aristaenus
195/4	..	..	..	..	..	..
194/3	..	..	..	..	..	..
193/2	Philopoemen V (IV)[8]	Philopoemen IV	Philopoemen IV	Philopoemen IV	..	Philopoemen IV
192/1	Diophanes	Diophanes	Diophanes	Diophanes	..	Diophanes
191/0	Philopoemen VI (V)[8]	Philopoemen V	..	..	..	..
190/89	Archon?[9]	..	Philopoemen V	Philopoemen V	..	Philopoemen V
189/8	Philopoemen VII (VI)[8]	Philopoemen VI	Philopoemen VI	Philopoemen VI	Philopoemen VI	Philopoemen VI
188/7	Aristaenus III	..	..	Aristaenus III[10]	Aristaenus[10]	Archon

187/6	Archon?[9] (or Philopoemen VII??)[8]	Philopoemen VII	Philopoemen VII	Lycortas I	Lycortas	Philopoemen VII
186/5	Aristaenus IV	Aristaenus	Aristaenus	Philopoemen VII	Philopoemen VII?	Aristaenus
185/4	Lycortas I	Lycortas	Lycortas I	Archon	Archon	Lycortas
184/3	Archon?[9]	Archon	Archon I	Lycortas II[11]	Lycortas II[11]	Philopoemen VIII
183/2	Philopoemen VIII (after his death, his predecessor (Archon?) until the next *synodos*: then Lycortas II)	Philopoemen VIII / Lycortas	Philopoemen VIII	Philopoemen VIII / Lycortas	Philopoemen VIII / Lycortas	Lycortas
182/1	Lycortas III??	Lycortas	Lycortas II?	Lycortas	Lycortas	..
181/0	Hyperbatus	Hyperbatus	Hyperbatus	Hyperbatus	Hyperbatus	..
180/79	..	Callicrates	Callicrates	Callicrates	..	Hyperbatus
179/8	Callicrates	..	..	..	..	..

[1] *REA* 1928, 1–62.
[2] *Storia* iv. 1. 402–6.
[3] *La Conf. Ach.*, pp. 267–311.
[4] *Beiträge zu Polybios.*
[5] *RhM* 1871, 241 ff.
[6] In n. 1, p. 248, Nissen recognizes that Euryleon may have been *strategos* in 211/10, but he does not include him in his printed list.
[7] Philopoemen was most likely *strategos* III in 204/3 *or* 203/2.
[8] The bracketed number indicates the number of Philopoemen's *strategia* otherwise unaccounted for was 187/6.
[9] Archon was *strategos* for *one* of the years 190/89, 187/6, 184/3.
[10] Büttner-Wobst makes no attempt to use Livy's lists of Roman magistrates as a chronological guide; hence his error in placing the Aristaenus/Lycortas series in 188/7 and 187/6. Niccolini follows him in this mistake.
[11] Büttner-Wobst and Niccolini have Lycortas here in order to comply with the Achaean law regarding the succession to a dead *strategos*. This is not necessary.

INDEX

This index is intended to be a reasonably full collection of proper names, but is to some extent selective. Romans are cited by *nomen*, with cross-references for the most important *cognomina*; men of consular rank are designated by the date of their first consulship only. References to countries (or cities) and inhabitants will be found under the name of the state. Institutions and offices without geographical description are those of the Achaean League.

Cretan *prostasia*, 30, 33, 35, 39, 41, 47; war with Rhodes, 39 f.; relations with Achaea, 40, 49, 52 ff., 76, 220; relations with Sparta, 40, 41; first war with Rome, 25, 50 ff.; supports Philopoemen, 51 ff., 58, 62 f., 73, 220; and Aristaenus, 73; negotiates with Rome, 55 f., 60 f.; repels Romans from Corinthia, 57; at Heraea in 209, 55; at the Nemea in 209, 56 f., 76; Elean expedition in 209, 57 f.; repels Dardanians, 58; castles in Achaea, 25, 57, 61, 83, 86; threat of Machanidas, 60 f.; encourages Achaean self-defence, 51 ff., 58, 61 f.; proposes to evacuate castles, 62, 66, 76; changes mind, 67, 70, 75, 77; actually withdraws, 67, 83, 88; peace with Aetolia, 68 f.; attempted assassination of Philopoemen, 70 f., 83; peace with Rome, 69; interests in Aegean, 71, 80; reputation for assassinations, 71; gives Argos to Nabis, 87; defeated by Rome, 88; receives Aetolian embassy, 92.

Philippides, 107.

Philippus, *see* Marcius.

Philocles, 43.

Philopoemen: background, 7, 13 ff., 139; appearance, 240; courage, 23; date of birth, 246 f.; at Ladoceia?, 14; rescues Megalopolitans from Cleomenes, 14 ff.; at Sellasia, 20 ff.; relations with Antigonus Doson, 22 f., 28, 33 f., 46; hipparch in 210/09, 23, 28, 33, 49, 51, 52 ff., 62, 75, 86, 248; in Crete, 27 ff.; reasons for, 28, 32, 46; return from, 49, 51 ff.; relations with Philip V, 23, 28, 33, 46 f., 49 ff., 53, 59, 62 f., 73, 86, 98, 220 f.; relations with Gortyn, 27, 33, 37, 44, 46 f., 85; second visit to Crete, 34 f., 38, 40, 41, 43, 44, 47, 72, 73 f., 81, 84, 87; attitude to Rome at first, 43, 70, 72 f., 75, 83 ff., 93, 158, 221; friendly relations with Aristaenus, 43, 72 f., 74, 81, 86; reorganizes cavalry, 51, 54; Elean expedition, 57 f.; *strategos* in 208/7, 62, 86, 249; reorganizes infantry, 63 ff.; battle of Mantinea, 65, 66, 220, 249; ravages Laconia, 65; aims at Achaean independence of

Macedon, 70 f., 82, 83, 86, 98, 220 f.; attempted murder by Philip V, 70 f., 83; attitude of Megalopolitans to Cretan absence, 72 f., 90 f.; *strategos* in 206/5, 75 f., 249 f.; honoured at the Nemea, 76, 83, 106; *strategos* in 204/3 or 203/2, 78 f., 250, 253; defends Messene, 79 ff.; *strategos* in 201/0, 34, 41, 74, 80 f., 251; receives Roman *legati* in 200, 82 f., 86; loses support in Achaea in 200, 84 ff., 87; returns to Achaea, 90; causes secessions from Megalopolis, 90 f., 273; *strategos* in 193/2, 44, 91, 93, 158, 251; sends Achaean garrison to Gytheum, 93; sends embassy to Rome, 93, 97; sends to Flamininus, 95 ff., 97; relations with Flamininus, 97 ff., 106, 113, 122, 129 f., 142, 184, 221; aims at Achaean independence of Rome, 98 ff.; attacks Nabis, 44, 49, 102 ff.; honours, 106 ff., 217, 230; brings Sparta into League, 109 ff., 134, 227; refuses Nabis' property, 111 f.; friendly to Diophanes, 112 f., 114; loyal to Rome on major issues, 113, 132, 210, 221, 224; attitude to Achaean troops in 191, 114; at Sparta in 191, 118 ff., 135; opposes Diophanes, 122, 128 f.; opposes Aristaenus, 122, 158 ff., 169 ff., 218 ff., 224 ff.; *strategos* in 191/0, 129, 251 ff.; attitude to Spartan exiles, 130 f., 140 ff., 224 ff., 254 f., 286; ravages Aetolia, 132; *strategos* in 189/8, 137 ff., 157, 251 ff.; changes place of *synodos*, 137 ff.; Spartan settlement, 140 ff., 148 f., 157, 180, 223, 253; reason for unsatisfactory character, 147; sends Nicodemus to Rome in 188/7, 149; attitude to *clientela*, 100, 151, 185 f., 222 f., 225 ff., 227; restoration of Zeuxippus, 153 f., 157; emends Flamininus' Messenian *diagramma*, 154 ff.; hostility to Deinocrates, 156 f.; interpretation of *foedus*, 158; sends embassy to Egypt, 163; discredited by Aristaenus, 163 ff.; probably not *strategos* in 187/6, 165, 250, 255 ff., 262; speaks against Metellus, 168, 170; attacked by Metellus in Rome, 173; *strategos* in

PRINTED IN GREAT BRITAIN
AT THE UNIVERSITY PRESS, OXFORD
BY VIVIAN RIDLER
PRINTER TO THE UNIVERSITY